ANTONY CUMMINS is the founder of the Historical Ninjutsu Research Team, which has previously published the first two manuals in its ninja series – *The Book of Ninja* being the last in the trilogy. Antony also works as a consultant and co-presenter of Urban Canyon Films to produce high-end documentaries on Japan that are distributed by National Geographic. He has been recognised by peers as a leading expert in the discovery of military arts of medieval Japan. Other books by this author include *True Path of the Ninja*, *The Secret Traditions of the Shinobi*, *Iga and Koka Ninja Skills*, *In Search of the Ninja* and *Samurai War Stories*.

YOSHIE MINAMI was born in Tokyo and currently lives in Saitama, Japan. She has a BA degree in Linguistics from the International Christian University. As a translator, she has published *True Path of the Ninja*, *Secret Traditions of the Shinobi*, *Iga and Koka Ninja Skills*, *Samurai War Stories* and has worked with Antony on various projects including the Japanese book *True English*.

BY THE SAME AUTHOR

Ninja Skills: The Authentic Ninja Training Manual

Fundamental Samurai Teachings (The Book of Samurai Series, Book I)

Samurai Arms, Armour & the Tactics of Warfare (The Book of Samurai Series, Book II)

Iga and Koka Ninja Skills: The Secret Shinobi Scrolls of Chikamatsu Shigenori

In Search of the Ninja: The Historical Truth of Ninjutsu

Old Japan: Secrets from the Shores of the Samurai

Samurai and Ninja: The Real Story Behind the Japanese Warrior Myth that Shatters the Bushido Mystique

Samurai War Stories: Teachings and Tales of Samurai Warfare

Secrets of the Ninja: The Shinobi Teachings of Hattori Hanzo

The Dark Side of Japan: Ancient Black Magic, Folklore, Ritual

The Illustrated Guide to Viking Martial Arts

The Lost Samurai School: Secrets of Mubyoshi Ryu

The Lost Warfare of India: An Illustrated Guide

The Secret Traditions of the Shinobi: Hattori Hanzo's Shinobi Hiden and other Ninja Scrolls

True Path of the Ninja: The Definitive Translation of the Shoninki

THE BOOK OF

NINJA

The First Complete Translation of

THE BANSENSHUKAI

JAPAN'S PREMIER NINJA MANUAL

ANTONY CUMMINS & YOSHIE MINAMI

WATKINS
Sharing Wisdom Since 1893

This edition first published in the UK and USA 2013 by
Watkins, an imprint of Watkins Media Limited
19 Cecil Court
London WC2N 4EZ

enquiries@watkinspublishing.com

Design and typography copyright © Watkins Media Limited 2013
Text copyright © Antony Cummins 2013

5 7 9 10 8 6 4

Designed and typeset by Jerry Goldie Graphic Design

Printed and bound in the United Kingdom

A CIP record for this book is available from the British Library

ISBN: 978-1-78028-493-4

Watkins is supporting the Woodland Trust, the UK's leading woodland
conservation charity, by funding tree-planting initiatives and woodland maintenance.

www.watkinspublishing.com

READER WARNING

The *Bansenshukai* is a Japanese military manual based on *samurai* guerrilla tactics, espionage, assassination and destruction, which contains dangerous and deadly information. Instructions include: theft, explosives, poisonous gases, toxins, clandestine and underhanded action and arson, among many other military topics. This translation has been made available in English for the purpose of history and for education and is a deep and academic look into the misunderstood arts of the Japanese *shinobi no mono*, or *ninja* as they are more commonly known. Therefore, the information contained within is for research purposes only and should not be recreated nor re-enacted in any way.

DEDICATION

We should remember that within these pages is the combined knowledge of genera-tions of men who fought in forgotten wars and confrontations, who were unknown, faceless and who died, not on the front lines, but way beyond its borders. We must also remember that while the shinobi *have become iconic in our world, they were once real people who were caught up in the horrible reality that is war, a practice humans still cling to even in our 'enlightened society'. These men of Iga and Koka should be collectively remembered, as while they were part of that world, they pushed the conventional limits and went beyond the required norm and perfected themselves on the darker path of clandestine warfare. Thus, we should take their teachings and forge them into positive ways for future generations, taking their seed of perfection and detailed thinking, making the* shinobi *of tomorrow individuals who can fathom the logical outcomes of today's decisions and who can help make those decisions count, for the benefit of everyone.*

SPECIAL THANKS

A special thank you must go to members who have helped with the pursuit of and the interpretation of this manual. Firstly and most importantly to Steven Nojiri, who has become a corner stone of the Historical Ninjutsu Research Team and whose knowledge on Japanese locks, history, politics and subtleties is profound. Secondly, to Dr Nakashima Atsumi, whose avid research into the lives of the people of Koka and Iga is helping to rediscover and respect the ways of the untold numbers of faceless combatants from the past and to all the family members and friends who have understood our *need* to drag ancient writings into this modern age. Lastly, a thank you to our editor, James Hodgson, for his phenomenal effort in bringing this script to life and to Rebecca and Deborah at Watkins for all their hard work.

Contents

The *Bansenshukai*

The *Bansenshukai Gunyo-hiki*

Foreword

by
Dr Nakashima Atsumi

First of all I would like to express my sincere admiration to Mr Antony Cummins and Ms Yoshie Minami, who have translated the *Bansenshukai* and introduced it to the English-speaking world. Therefore, to appreciate their devoted work, I am going to comment on how this publication has been realized and also on the outline of the *Bansenshukai* manual itself.

Antony came here to Japan, from the other side of the world, from the distant land of England, and has travelled around this country of Japan with Ms Minami conducting thorough research. Through these travels, we came to be known to each other due to the fact that I have previously published a commentary on the *Shoninki ninja* manual and other books on the subject of *ninjutsu*. The first time we met, I realized that they were amazingly passionate and strongly determined to publish the English translation of my *Shoninki* and then to follow up with the *Bansenshukai* too, which moved me so deeply and in truth left me feeling a little envious.

Of the numerous *ninjutsu* scrolls, the *Bansenshukai* is profound, and is the largest compiled volume of information from the *ninjutsu* schools of both Iga and Koka, which were considered the lands of the *ninja*. Fortunately, compared to the *Shoninki* – which I believe is a real masterpiece – the text of the *Bansenshukai* is straightforward and self-explanatory. In addition, it is also fortunate that the transcription kept in the National Archives is written in a style comparatively close to modern Japanese and can be read and understood by those who are not so familiar with old writings, which is a great advantage. Therefore, it is possible to convey to people what is written within without making many serious mistakes. However, in order to achieve a complete interpretation of the text, as there are so many places in its pages which have deeper connotations and are difficult to understand in a profound way, even a discourse of three thousand pages would not be enough to make a perfect explanation of all the meanings within and it would take many years of study to truly explain every detail. This is because hidden within the meaning of the text is the masses of knowledge that was made up of *kuden* or oral tradition, which now, unfortunately, has been lost.

Generally, when defined in short, *ninjutsu* is a set of arts, including: life skills, espionage, sabotage, murder, military science, divination, astrology, astronomy, magic, various kinds of observation skills, and any other skills people needed to survive and achieve their aims. These might also include the martial arts, for a *ninja* would have to train himself in arts such as *jujutsu* grappling, *kenjutsu* swordsmanship, archery and horse riding etc. Also, there are many other skills required by the *ninja*, but they are too extensive and various to mention here. Manuscripts on *ninjutsu* have only the simplest mention of general skills of living or astrological skills and the arts of astronomy, and assume that the reader should well understand these things. In particular, they have no mention of swordsmanship, horse-riding skills or other combat skills, because it was taken for granted that people would naturally train themselves in those areas. Other general skills that the *ninja* learned are left not in *ninjutsu* manuals but in other forms. For example, in the Umasugi clan of Koka, they have passed down a *menkyo* certificate for the horse-riding skills of the *otsubo ryu* in their family, meaning that simply looking at just the *ninja* scrolls limits our understanding of the full range of skills in which *shinobi* would have been proficient.

Most writings on *ninjutsu* have only simplified information, and where it needs detailed explanations, they would not write down everything but simply say '*kuden*', which means 'passed down in oral traditions'. Therefore, to interpret those manuscripts, you need a great deal of capability. In other words, it depends on your level of comprehension as to whether you feel that the *Bansenshukai* is marvellous or it is not.

Even with the titanic work of the *Bansenshukai*, if you were a *ninja*, you would not be able to fully understand everything at once. Therefore, please take your time and try to read between the lines and with patience.

A number of transcriptions of the *Bansenshukai* have been left and, as they were all transcribed by hand and not mechanically, no two transcriptions are completely identical. I myself have interpreted four versions of the manual, which are different from each other, some having missing parts, some adding supplementary sections, or even omitting that which the transcriber thought was unnecessary, etc.

Of the multiple transcriptions that exist today, this English translation is based on the text kept in the Cabinet Library in the National Archives and the Ohara version, which are considered to be standard versions, and has straightforward and reasonable interpretations. It clearly indicates what is unknown, so I believe it makes a great introduction to the *Bansenshukai*, and gives an objective understanding of *shinobi no jutsu* to foreign people of different cultures.

Like most *ninjutsu* manuscripts, the *Bansenshukai* was written in the Edo period, in 1676, which was a long tranquil time without war, leaving many *ninja* – including the Koka *ninja* – unemployed. As a result, some Koka *ninja* travelled the distance to Edo to appeal to the shogunate against their difficult situation in the hope of recovering their status by offering them the *Bansenshukai* manual in 1789. To their disappointment, however, their appeal was not accepted. Through this deposit in Edo, this secret information was revealed and later used in cartoons and stories, which even today is supplying Japanese children with future dreams. The *Bansenshukai* is full of very interesting stories, as it is a compilation of skills from various schools from Iga and Koka and therefore documents the histories of various people.

The definition of *ninja*, however, is not so clear. In my opinion, *ninja* were those who met the following two conditions:

1. They should have knowledge of the skills and arts of the *ninja*
2. They should work for a clan, have a clear aim, and measures that enable them to fulfil their mutual aim successfully without delay and with the greatest result possible.

The above is exactly what Iga *mono* and Koka *mono* were, and the *Bansenshukai* was born in such an environment. If the *Bansenshukai* could be of any help to an individual person, it would be only thieves, robbers or bandits. That is exactly why it preaches the need for a correct mind and at great length. The *ninja* had to lead a life as in-betweens, who were *samurai* and not *samurai* at the same time. Most lived as farmers who carried their skills as their side business through the pre-modern era of the Edo period, as those *bushi* of the early Warring States period gradually faded into the mists of time.

It is fun for us to find the traces of *ninja* in the skills and tools of the *shinobi*. A recent master whose name was Fujita Seiko, who acclaimed himself as the last Koka *ninja*, founded the *Bujutsu* Research Institute and was involved actively as the first chairman of the organization, an organization to which I once belonged. Mr Fujita was the penultimate teacher of mine and he also taught at the Nakano war school of the Japanese imperial army, which was a facility for the training of spies during World War II. This teaching was on the subject of *ninjutsu*. My beginnings and now this link with Antony and Yoshie make me feel that fate has brought me to write this foreword.

Lastly, I am sincerely hoping that the *Bansenshukai* will be read by myriad people from various fields and with interest, and furthermore that it will give you inspiration to improve your life.

Dr Nakashima Atsumi

Chairman, the Federation of Japanese *Koryu Bujutsu*
(an organization for the traditional schools of the martial arts in Japan)

Author's Notes

In all my years of training, there was no way on earth that I would have believed that one day the three greatest *ninja* manuals ever written would be in the laps of other people, written in English and passing their knowledge on to a new audience. Only in a dream did those books have my name upon them and it was only in fantasy that it was I who caused them to exist. Then, Yoshie Minami stepped into the breach, a new friend and a new partner, year by year she has helped me pass through the issues of the Japanese language and its complexities and has allowed me to creep deeper into *ninja* territory. One after the other, the combined forces of her language ability and my historical training pushed us forward, etching out a new path in the historical record, a way to the true history of the *ninja*, through the writings of the *shinobi* themselves. Tearing away the media image, the real and very professional *ninja* came into view and reconstructing their world started to look achievable. Then, the sheer wall that is the *Bansenshukai* confronted us, the gleaming black ramparts of a fortress that we could look into but yet whose vastness was incomprehensible. Yet, hour after hour, day after day and even month after month, and eventually into years, together we chipped away at those black foundations of the ancient text and have found ourselves at the heart of the keep, no longer on the outside but now a central part of the story of the *Bansenshukai*, the greatest of all *ninja* texts.

With this volume now in English, the hidden world of the *shinobi* is no longer in the darkness nor is it covered by the whisper, 'it is secret', but it is here and fully in the light for all to enjoy. So powerful is this manual that it breaks open a window to a forgotten and misunderstood world and for the first time in the English-speaking world, the most comprehensive set of instructions on *ninjutsu* (*shinobi no jutsu*) can be studied. It is simply a joy to be even a small part of that history and to have enabled the arts of the *shinobi* to penetrate the West for the first time in full.

Without the aid of Yoshie and without the support of my team, family and friends this would have been an impossible task, yet here we all stand at the goal's end and here you stand about to embark on one of the greatest journeys into history you will ever take part in. Therefore, enjoy the practical and appreciate the archaic but overall remember the people who lived this art for real, those who are now long gone.

Antony Cummins
Saitama, Japan, 2013

Introduction

A brief introduction to the Japanese *shinobi*

The Japanese *ninja*, or *shinobi no mono*, as they were originally known, were military units or single agents utilized by the medieval *samurai* clans and families of Japan. These were specialists in clandestine and guerrilla warfare, espionage and infiltration, arson and explosives and thievery – areas that all come under the term *shinobi no jutsu*[1] or the *arts of the ninja*. The *ninja* themselves were taken from any social class but tended to come from the lower *samurai* ranks and worked as retainers for a clan lord. This relationship was either a continued and loyal service or was temporary and mercenary in nature. While still a part of the *samurai* culture, the *shinobi* were specialized and few in number when seen in army listings; approximately one for every four hundred men in an army, and should be considered as extremely far-reaching scouts, men who partook in what are colloquially known as 'black operations' and undercover agents who infiltrated the enemy lines and acted in espionage.

The *shinobi* themselves do deserve the popularity and respect that is attributed to them, as they represent some of the most well trained military units that history has seen, with the premier groups coming from the provinces of Iga and Koka, which to this day cling to their *ninja* fame. While their physical martial arts and fighting skills were no different from the rest of their *samurai* 'brothers' they were trained in other elements, such as infiltration and burglary and, whether the target be a mountain-top castle or a fortified manor house, the image of the *shinobi* creeping in the black of night is historically correct. However, in tandem with this, the *ninja* were the street peddlers, the merchants and entertainers, swordsmen for hire, and they even took the guise of priests. No one knew who the *ninja* were; a *samurai* lord might realize that *ninja* had infiltrated his army or province, but the problem was how to find out who they were and how to get rid of them. Recorded as early as the late fourteenth century and finally in the turmoil of the nineteenth century restoration, the *ninja* enjoyed an extended

---

1   *Shinobi no jutsu* is commonly known as *ninjutsu*. However, while both versions are correct, phonetic markers on historical documents show *shinobi no jutsu* was used whereas there are no records of the word being spoken as *ninjutsu*.

period of military use before they were superseded by the modern spy and army Special Forces unit. From here on out the spy would take up espionage and the Special Forces unit would take on the role of forward shock troops, sharing between them the two main functions of the *ninja*.

When the Tokugawa family took control of Japan in 1603, the country entered a period of relative peace and totalitarian control, which led to the decline of the *shinobi* as a force on the battlefield and prompted them to concentrate more on the espionage aspect of their skill set. This decline prompted an increase in the compiling of *ninja* records, with the aim of preserving the ways of the *ninja*, and in 1676 one *shinobi* named Fujibayashi Yasutake, who was probably of Iga and from a former *samurai* family, finished working on his masterpiece, a collection of *shinobi* information that he had obtained over an unknown amount of time and through personal experience. This work was known as the *Bansenshukai* 萬川集海, which translates as 'A Myriad of Rivers Merging into One Ocean'.

A brief history of the *Bansenshukai*

In the dark recesses of *ninja* popularity, the name *Bansenshukai* has been bandied around with a limited understanding of the work's contents and details and until now it has never been published outside of the Japanese language (even then only in small sections). It has always been spoken of next to the *Shinobi Hiden* (*Ninpiden*) and the *Shoninki ninja* manuals, and together they form the triumvirate of *ninja* information. The *Shinobi Hiden* is a collection of skills attributed to the sixteenth-century *ninja* master Hattori Hanzo, the *Shoninki* is a record of the Natori family's secret tactics, and the *Bansenshukai* is the universal collection of *ninja* skills from Iga and possibly also from Koka. Written by Fujibayashi in 1676, the *Bansenshukai* is a document that was written to preserve the disappearing skills of the *shinobi* and to retain the complexities of the detailed art known as *shinobi no jutsu*. Written in Japanese, in bound form it consisted of ten books, which were divided into twenty-two volumes,[2] with a later additional volume titled *Bansenshukai Gunyo-hiki*, which is a collection of military strategies. This complete collection of books appears to have been put together by the author after extensive research and information-collecting from other families and clans in the region who also held the arts of *shinobi no jutsu*. From here multiple transcriptions appear, with slight variations, including examples of reduced 'pocket versions'.

---

2 It is possible that other sections did exist as there are slight variations between versions. However, the differences tend to be in organization rather in the text itself. The original *Bansenshukai* is now missing from the historical record.

Bansenshukai or *Mansenshukai*?

The ideogram 萬 can be read as 'ban' or 'man', which means that this title can be read as either *Bansenshukai* or *Mansenshukai*. Without a direct lineage from the Fujibayashi school or any school that can directly trace itself back to the manual, the correct reading is impossible to gauge. A phonetic marker or *kana* would allow us to know the correct reading, but sadly none exists in connection with this title. The only option left is to take into account the opinions of families who still own copies of the manual, which have been passed down as family heirlooms. The descendants of the Ohara family, who have given permission for their version to be published as a collector's piece, have allowed the manual to be presented as the *Bansenshukai* as did other researchers and enthusiasts who worked with the manual in the twentieth century. However, according to the researcher Mr Ikeda of Iga, there are Iga families who claim that the correct name is the *Mansenshukai*. It is impossible to establish if this is a regional difference – being *Mansenshukai* for the Iga and *Bansenshukai* for the Koka – or if it is because of contamination from modern research and communications networks between enthusiasts, who may have swayed the opinions of the families on the naming of the manual. It would take a gathering or conference with all the families who own this manual to establish if they had adopted one pronunciation over another or if they could testify that their pronunciation was a direct teaching or not. Therefore, despite the possibility that the manual may have been named *Mansenshukai* by some or all of the families, we have decided to continue with the name *Bansenshukai* because of its popularity and the possibility that it also was an original pronunciation.

Versions of the *Bansenshukai*

Only a relatively small number of versions of the *Bansenshukai* are left to us, and of those only a select number are actually 'complete' versions of the original text, and even then the texts differ slightly – not in content *per se*, but in terms of extra snippets found here and there in the body, or extra volumes (currently unavailable). While it is known that other versions of the manual exist in private collections in Iga and have not yet been identified and catalogued, the most complete list at present of the known translations (predominantly of Koka descent) is as follows:

1. A full transcription of the Ohara Kazuma version – National Archives of Japan
2. The Fujita Seiko version – Iga Ueno Museum
3. The Okimori version – Iga Ueno Museum

4. The Osawa version – private collection
5. The Yamaga extract – Tokyo University
6. The Taki version – private collection
7. The Sawamura version – private collection

The Ohara (Katsui) of Kyoto family private collection – entrusted to the Koka Ninja Village
1. The Ohara (Katsui) full version (on which the modern reproduction is based)
2. *Otsu*³-*bon* – volumes thirteen and twenty-one
3. *Hei-bon* – volumes thirteen and twenty-two
4. *Tei-bon* – volumes twenty-one and twenty-two
5. *Ju-bon* – a two-page extract dealing with tools

Also, the Ohara family of Koka:
1. The Ohara Kazuma version

The book that represented the *shinobi*

As the age of peace accelerated and the age of the *shinobi* declined, more and more families who were trained in the arts of *shinobi no jutsu* began to fail in their military education and the *shinobi*, while not extinct, in many respects became less functional as agents. This turbulent shift into an age where the *ninja* were no longer required, and their subsequent 'fall', was well documented during the Edo Period (1603–1868) and must be viewed alongside the decline of Iga and Koka, which were independent and self-sustaining regions, where the social elite were considered as independent families, who then dramatically fell into the category of 'lower people' and were without land income and who now came under the heavy hand of taxation and servitude. These issues, alongside a lack of demand for their military services, pushed *shinobi* 'families' to their limits financially and poverty started to take its toll. As a result of this there were various attempts by the families of Koka to gain government employment and sponsorship to help continue the military training of the *ninja*. In 1667 Akutagawa Gingobei attempted to gain employment for the families of Koka warriors, which is recorded in a document similar to, or connected to, the Koka Ninshi Yuishogaki of 1815 – a transcription of a 1789 document discussing the background and activities of warriors of Koka. It lists the Koka *samurai*,

---

3   *Otsu, Hei, Tei* and *Ju* mean A, B, C, D in this context.

Figure 1. Antony Cummins and Yoshie Minami (out of shot) in the National Archives of Japan, viewing the document presented to a Japanese government magistrate in 1789 by three Koka *shinobi* with the aim of gaining employment.

Figure 2. Antony Cummins and *ninjutsu* researcher, author and *ninja* theme park owner Mr Shun'ichiro Yunoki, who currently publishes the only available reproduction of the *Bansenshukai*, which is an exact copy of the Ohara Katsui version.

what they did and their ancestry and in this record, they insisted that the Koka warriors first served Tokugawa Ieyasu in 1560 (this should most likely be 1562), and at the battles of Mikawa, Udono and Taiji. It also includes their service at Komaki Nagakute which was in 1584 and the defence of Fushimi castle just before the battle of Sekigahara (1600). And also the hiring of a band of one hundred Koka warriors by the shogun, and finally the service of Koka warriors at the Shimabara Christian rebellion, where ten warriors of Koka fought under warrior Matsudaira Izu-no-Kami Nobutsuna (he himself was not a *shinobi*). The next major attempt at employment by the warriors of Koka was made in 1789 when Ohara Kazuma, Ueno Hachizaemon and Oki Moriichiro visited the capital of Edo with a copy of the *Bansenshukai* and presented it, along with a sake cup, to the magistrate, Matsudaira Ukyonosuke. Their aim was to display their heritage and professionalism and the dire status of the families in Koka, some of which they claim no longer taught their ancient family arts of the *ninja*. After accepting the *Bansenshukai*, the magistrate offered them a small donation of silver coins (much less than they actually needed and more of a parting gift) and another token amount of silver to give to the other families in Koka. The copy of the *Bansenshukai* that they presented is the primary version used for this translation and is still kept in National Archives of Japan.

Is it an Iga or a Koka manual?

Both Iga and Koka are fiercely proud of their *shinobi* ancestry and clearly display their connection to the *ninja* with pride. At the centre of that pride is the *Bansenshukai*, the greatest *ninja* record in history. However, the origin and authorship are claimed by both parties. The most common version of the *Bansenshukai* is the Ohara family version, which has been on the market in its original Japanese for a long time and clearly states at the beginning that it is a manual of Koka. However, alongside this there is version held at the Ueno Iga Museum, but unavailable for viewing. This latter version has twenty-six volumes compared with twenty-four in the Koka edition. The *Bansenshukai* is commonly thought of as a collection of both Iga and Koka material. However, on closer inspection it appears that the document is primarily one of Iga, and the word 'Koka' is found *only* on the title page as an indication of origin but does not appear in the text in reference to it being a manual of Koka[4] – meaning that it is possible that this transcription had the word Koka added by those of Koka. In fact, all references to any origin firmly place this as an Iga document and the researcher Ishida Yoshihito claims to have seen a version transcribed as 'Iga' and

---

4 The term 'Koka' appears when discussing history, but always second to 'Iga'.

also states that the change of text to Koka was made for the presentation to the government by the Koka families. Throughout the manual, hints at Fujibayashi's homeland can be found; he states that the eleven best infiltration *shinobi* are from Iga and uses the term *Iga no mono* (men of Iga) yet fails to mention *Koka no mono*. He also gives anecdotes to explain sections of *shinobi no jutsu*, all of which involve people from Iga and any of the families mentioned in the manual in connection with *shinobi no jutsu* are Iga-based. Alternatively, upon a visit to Mr Shun'ichiro Yunoki of the Koka Ninja Village, he put forward the theory that the two versions of the manual were compiled by two members of the Fujibayashi family, Fujibayashi of Iga and Fujibayashi of Koka. While plausible, this theory does not account for the lack of Koka references within the Koka version, which points to it being a copy of the Iga edition. Therefore, it is logical to conclude that the *Bansenshukai* is an Iga manual, which was happily shared with Koka in an attempt to stop the arts of the *shinobi* from slipping out of history.

The importance of the text

The text itself has clearly been of paramount importance to the *shinobi* community from its first incarnation and has been held as the highest form of *shinobi no jutsu* documentation from that day until this. The mere concept of it being given to the shogunate as an official application and its use among the collective families of Iga and Koka prove beyond doubt that these families, famous for their *shinobi* arts, held this text with reverence and trust. It has also been claimed but not substantiated that the *Bansenshukai* was also not available for public viewing until the mid-twentieth century owing to its dangerous nature. If true, this is another factor to support the power and the respect accorded to the manual. Also, it is recorded that Yamanaka Tonai swore an oath of secrecy to Ohara Kazuma and Ueno Tamaki in order to obtain an extract of the first few books of the *Bansenshukai*.

Upon reading the manual it is clear to see that the elements within the text clearly match other more 'respected' documents, such as the *Gunpo Jiyoshu* or the *Gunpo Gokuhi-densho*, where the authors discuss the *ninja* from an outside perspective. But here, with the *Bansenshukai*, we get the full internal view. Where other authors may simply say, 'be careful of gaps in your defence and of the *shinobi*', the *Bansenshukai* tells us how to find and infiltrate those gaps, giving the world the most comprehensive view of the workings of the *ninja* infiltration arts.

With the explosion of the *shinobi* in the West, the *Bansenshukai*, along with the *Shoninki* and the *Shinobi Hiden*, is a defence against the false. For years 'ninja masters' have claimed *ninjutsu* lineage and hidden behind the shield of the *Bansenshukai* and other manuals to supply and drip feed information on *ninjutsu*. With the full publication of these three texts, people will have a clear understanding of the truth of historical *shinobi* arts and are no longer left in the dark about them. Here for the first time the world may see the deadly and complex ways of the *shinobi* and appreciate the subtleties of Japanese spying and operations in enemy territory.

The future of the *Bansenshukai* rests along two lines. Firstly, as a survival and guerrilla warfare manual, it allows a single human to train diligently to become a clandestine operative with knowledge that rivals modern Special Forces, and the skills it teaches, if adapted, can have relevance for modern espionage and clandestine warfare even today. Secondly, the *Bansenshukai* makes an immense contribution to Japanese and military history; with this manual, historians can gain access to countless areas of research, from army marching orders to the art of hanging a decapitated head on a horse saddle, from architecture to lock production, from social interactions to attitudes to women, the list goes on. This is not only a manual for *shinobi* and *samurai* enthusiasts but also required reading for anyone involved with military history, Japanese architecture, the influence of Chinese religion on Japan and much more.

A word on the Chinese influence

Initially, some researchers have stated that the *Bansenshukai* is a manual based on Chinese thought and is highly influenced by the Chinese classics; however, upon inspection, this is simply not the case. There is undoubtedly a Chinese influence on the *Bansenshukai* but it has never been investigated to any depth nor analysed with a critical eye. The absolute first step in understanding the Chinese connection to the Japanese text is to understand that Japanese society across most of its medieval history viewed China as a centre of culture and civilization, and it must be remembered that Japanese culture itself is based on imported ideas, architecture, philosophy and warfare, all of which stemmed from mainland Asia. At the time of Fujibayashi, Chinese thought and writings were the realm of the educated, the military elite and aristocracy, and to read in Chinese, to understand Chinese and to educate others in Chinese was a sign of quality and status. It is no surprise, then, that Fujibayashi should quote and teach Chinese military tactics within the *Bansenshukai*.

With this understanding, the next step is not to fall into the trap of believing that the manual was written in Chinese or that the information is simply a collection of stolen Chinese ideas. Firstly, it is a misconception that the *Bansenshukai* is written entirely in the Chinese style of *kanbun*; it is not. It is in fact written mainly in Japanese with the addition of quotes from Chinese classics in their original Chinese form, which is *kanbun*, making the manual a Japanese text. Secondly, the Chinese elements in the text are not evenly distributed throughout nor are they integral to the text; the use of Chinese is purposeful and deliberate. Primarily, Fujibayashi uses anecdotes from the Chinese classics to add support and credence to *his* ideas, and to establish the content of the text as valid in the eyes of the contemporary audience. The earlier chapters of the book, for this reason, are quite full of references to Chinese episodes, all of which are there simply to highlight the truth of what he is saying and to reinforce his ideas in the minds of the educated reader. However, interestingly, the quotations begin to thin out as he gets closer to the core skills of *shinobi no jutsu*. By the middle chapters, which focus on the 'hands on' skills of the *ninja* such as burglary, infiltration and espionage, one notices that Chinese thought has been almost entirely replaced by a very practical and purely Japanese collection of arts. These are conveyed in a 'matter of fact' way and apparently without any support, as readers would presumably have recognized them as *ninjutsu* without needing to be convinced. Then, in stark contrast, come volumes sixteen and seventeen, which are written with a heavy Chinese slant. Here Fujibayashi is recording the Chinese arts of divination, the methods of establishing if a direction, day or time is auspicious or not. If this section did not include Chinese influence, then it would indeed be strange. Fujibayashi himself states that these skills are dubious and not to be trusted. The skills themselves were forms of divination that were standard among Japanese generals and well understood to be Chinese teachings. Therefore, the two major Chinese sections are openly acknowledged as such and are loaded with the warning that these practices are not to be trusted, but that the knowledge of them is useful when conducting warfare against a general who does believe in their supernatural power. This is echoed in the *Shoninki* manual, where the head of the Natori school of secret tactics also quotes from Chinese literature on the arts of physiognomy and divination. The *Bansenshukai* continues after these Chinese teachings with follow-up volumes on tools and explosives. Fujibayashi comments on the newness of some of the tools, indicating that they are purely Japanese inventions. He appears to be unaware of, or fails to state, the probable Chinese origins of other tools that had been in existence in Japan for a long time.

Therefore, on the whole, it can be concluded that Fujibayashi was not 'stealing' from Chinese texts, but simply utilizing them to support his theories, to give the art of *shinobi no jutsu* a history and to underline for the reader the importance of keeping the art alive. Now, with his target audience in mind, it is possible that Fujibayashi may have had an egotistical need for such Chinese inclusions, to

THE BOOK OF NINJA

ensure that his social inferiors would respect his level of education and that his social superiors would be impressed by his understanding of matters that they would have assumed to be beyond his station. Remembering that the *shinobi* were drawn mainly from the lower end of the *samurai* class, such erudition may have seemed beyond the so called 'farmer-*samurai*' of Iga, yet it is clearly apparent in the works of Fujibayashi that Iga was not such a backward and isolated region, but a place of contemporary culture.

The Chinese calendar

One of the most difficult concepts to grasp when trying to imagine the life of a *shinobi* is the dating system used and the recording of the passage of time. Based on the lunisolar system, a complex equation of the cycle of the moon and the adjustments required to align it with a solar year, the whole system is alien to a Western understanding. This makes Fujibayashi's commentary on times, dates and celestial points far more difficult to understand than it would have been for a contemporary and expressions like 'hour of the Monkey', 'day of the Rat', 'count five steps from the time of the Boar', cause havoc and can become a nightmare for any student of *shinobi no jutsu* who has not had a chance to investigate the topic. Therefore, beyond the borders of this work it is recommended that a good understanding of the Chinese calendar is undertaken and knowledge of the Ten Celestial Stems and the Twelve Earthly Branches is acquired, for without an appreciation of these main issues an understanding of some sections of the *Bansenshukai* will not follow. For example, the text may state: do 'such and such' an action on a day of Kinoe (one of the Ten Celestial Stems) or even when the day of Kinoe and the day of the Boar meet (one of the Twelve Earthly Branches). Fujibayashi often adds a direction, which also has a connection and connotation in the above system, which only compounds the confusion of the uninitiated. Therefore, a basic understanding is required to fully appreciate and interact with the teachings. However, for ease, the following illustration will guide the reader through most of the instructions found, particularly in volumes sixteen and seventeen, the most esoteric of the manual.

In *figure 3*, you will be able to find any time expression the text states, such as the day, hour or direction of the Tiger, Boar, Hare etc., and in most cases simply count in a clockwise or anticlockwise direction. It is very important to note that in this manual Fujibayashi classes the animal he names as the first in the count. For example, counting four places in a clockwise direction from the Rat will include the Rat and finish at the Hare.

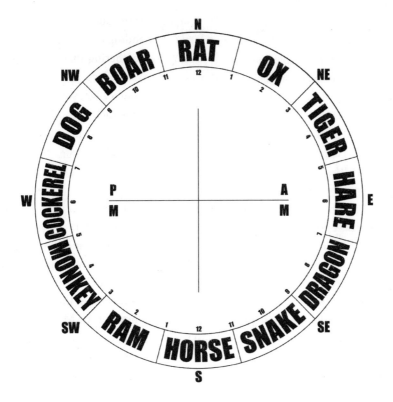

Figure 3. The Chinese calendar

Counting four places in a clockwise direction from the Rat as seen in the image above:

1. Rat
2. Ox
3. Tiger
4. Hare

This is different from the standard Western way of starting to count on the position adjacent to the starting point. Also, it is beneficial to notice that in the above diagram the animals have associated directions: Rat – north; Hare – east; Horse – south; Cockerel – west, etc.

The Japanese within the text

Deciding how much Japanese to leave in the text is always difficult: too much and the lay-reader becomes confused, too little and the avid practitioner feels frustrated. Therefore, in this book you will find snippets of Japanese to help any student and researcher to get to grips with the connotations of specific words and phrases. Also, Chinese ideograms have been inserted where relevant for anyone who is researching and who wants to know which ideogram was used in the original. The translation aims to retain the flavour of the original document and to capture the spirit of the times in which it was written, in order to bring the world of the *shinobi* vividly to life.

Lastly, there is the issue of the ubiquitous Japanese term *kuden*, which translates as 'passing on information by word of mouth alone'. An actual student of *ninjutsu* may have been given a manual, but this would have been accompanied by oral explanations, giving more information than could be written down – sometimes to shed light on deeper meanings or to provide mundane explanations that would have weighed down the written text. For example, an explanation of how to make a form of waterproof torch may have had the basic instructions, but a final piece of information may have been required to perfect this, or the instructions on binding may have been judged to be too long. In these situations, the ideogram *kuden* 口傳 has been placed at the end of the text in question. This placement does not come with a grammatical link and was simply added on at the end of a section of information. Translating *kuden* into English causes many problems and it gets truly repetitious to continually state 'oral tradition' at the end of sections or even in the middle of paragraphs. However, it is too much to translate *kuden* as 'secret', as the term does not always represent the concept of secret – indeed, everything in the manual was a secret. Therefore, to avoid confusion, we have opted simply to translate every occurrence of *kuden* in the original manual as 'oral tradition' or 'to be passed on by oral tradition', even though it is repetitious.

Ninja or *shinobi* and *ninjutsu* or *shinobi no jutsu*?

The term *shinobi* dates back to the fourteenth century and without a doubt predates the word *ninja*. However, the reading of *shinobi* 忍 instead of *nin* 忍 is only guaranteed when it is found in certain grammatical positions and when found in these positions within the text, we have translated it simply as *shinobi*. There is an ongoing debate, both public and within the Historical Ninjutsu Research Team, as to which reading is correct for the ideograms 忍者. First it must be established that this term can be read either as *shinobi no mono* or *ninja*. The question is actually, which reading did Japanese people of the medieval period use and in which way should it be translated? There is a strong case for *shinobi no mono*, as whenever there are phonetic markers to help the reading of the ideograms, they always and without fail indicate *shinobi no mono*. However, when there are no phonetic markers the reading could be either. Also, in all cases where a different ideogram is used, the reading is always *shinobi*, when there are no ideograms but only phonetics in use, then it is always and without fail, *shinobi*, so in all likelihood *shinobi no mono* is the correct reading. But, from a native English speaker's point of view, constantly reading out *shinobi no mono* is not comfortable and *ninja* flows better and also has more educated connotations than the sometimes derogatory term *shinobi*. Therefore, it is debatable when and where the change from *shinobi no mono* to *ninja* came about, and whether our author, Fujibayashi, meant *ninja* or *shinobi no mono*.

Similarly contentious are the ideograms 忍術, which can be read as *ninjutsu* or *shinobi no jutsu*, and mean the arts of the *ninja/shinobi*. Only one example of a phonetic marker has been found to date and that marker gives *shinobi no jutsu* as the reading; nevertheless, the same argument applies. Because of this, as a team we have opted to divide our translation between both. Therefore, where the ideograms 忍者 and 忍術 appear in the text, we shift between *ninja* and *shinobi no mono*, and *ninjutsu* and *shinobi no jutsu*, yet the connotations are the same for both versions.

Measurements and numbers

Throughout the original text, there are numerous names, tools, recipes and skills involving a myriad of Japanese measurements, which have been translated in the text in their original form to avoid confusion. Measurements in the English-speaking world differ from region to region and between age groups; some people measure weight in stones while others use pounds or kilograms and some measure distance in feet while others use metres. Therefore, to avoid misunderstandings or even mathematical errors in the text, we have left all the measurements as they appear in the original, so words such as *shaku*, *ryo*, *bu* etc. will become all too familiar as you progress through the text. To aid understanding, the following table has been produced so that the reader can calculate the measurement using the conversion they are most comfortable with.

Measurement	Ideogram	Metric	Imperial
Lengths			
rin	厘	0.3mm	0.01in
bu	分	3.03mm	0.11in
sun	寸	3.03cm	1.19in
shaku	尺	30.3cm	11.93in
ken	間	1.81m	5.96ft
cho	町	109.1m	357.9ft
ri	里	3.92km	2.435 miles
Mass or Weight			
bu/fun	分	0.37g	0.013oz
momme	匁	3.75g	0.132oz
ryo	両	37.5g	1.32oz
kin	斤	600g	21.16oz
Volume or Capacity			
shaku	勺	18.04ml	0.63fl oz
go	合	180.4ml	6.34fl oz
sho	升	1.8l	3.17pt
to	斗	18.4l	31.74pt
koku	石	180.4l	317.4pt

Furthermore, numbers within the text will be given in their written form – one, two, three, etc. – to allow for titles of skills and chapters to begin with a word and not a numerical. However, numbers given in recipes or dates will be given in their numerical format of 1, 2 3, etc. Finally, some of the articles and sub-articles will be titled with Roman numerals (I, II, III, etc.) where appropriate. This has been done to fit with previously published works to maintain a theme.

A Short Introduction to Japanese Locks and the Art of Lock-picking

by
Steven Nojiri

Japanese lock bypassing is both simpler than its modern-day equivalent but yet, in some regards, paradoxically, can be more complicated. To understand the world of the *shinobi* and the lock bypassing sections of the *Bansenshukai*, the reader must comprehend – to some extent – the old Japanese practice of 'stealing in'. While this topic is certainly complex and takes time to appreciate fully, it can be explained rather succinctly and without too much confusion.

To begin, the reader should know that Japanese locks of this period were not based on the same mechanics of those of today. The majority of modern-day locks rely on revolving cylinders whose movements are allowed or disallowed by a series of spring-loaded pins. 'Picking' them entails a combination of pin manipulation and proper torque to the cylinder. In comparison, old Japanese locks were designed centuries before such intricacies could be machined, and therefore contain larger and less complex parts. The Japanese locks of the time of the *Bansenshukai* relied on prongs, latches and natural forces of gravity and tension. The designs of the locks were not complicated, but they were nonetheless effective at barring entry and a *shinobi* would have had to be very familiar with lock typology and, as Fujibayashi states, efficiency and knowledge only comes with hands-on practice.

Lock picking and lock bypassing

Before I briefly summarize the locks and their standard picking methods, I must explain the difference between *picking* and *bypassing*. The act of picking a lock is the act of manipulating the internal components in such a way that your picking tools and your actions with them replace the key. Thus, you are able to operate the lock, which in turn, allows you actually to unlock the door. Alternatively, *bypassing* is literally a disregard for the lock internals and even the idea of lock picking. Instead, it is a manipulation of the door and/or lock itself in a way that is not a simulation of the key. It is of paramount importance to understand the difference between the two, as lock picking and lock bypassing both have different methods and different results. For example, breaking a lock is a form of bypassing. However, breaking a lock can never be a form of picking. The *Bansenshukai* touches on both aspects and shows the picking of locks and the bypassing of bars, locks, latches and hooks.

The *Bansenshukai* is not only a critically important piece of *shinobi* history, but an intriguing window into Japanese culture as well. The final chapters of the *in-nin* segment contain historical Japanese lock-picking and bypassing methods, which are almost impossible to find recorded in any other document. This document allows us a view of the workings of a *samurai* household, its make up, and the measures it took to remain secure.

Fujibayashi first explains the main types of locks, such as bars, hooks-and-rings, latches and padlocks. He then follows this up with brief teachings on the methods for picking and bypassing most lock typologies. Further, Fujibayashi explains and even provides pictures of the handful of special tools utilized in the *ninja*'s breaking-and-entering arts – tools that have too often been misunderstood and misinterpreted in modern times. While some of these tools make appearances in other *ninjutsu* documents, the *Bansenshukai* seems to provide a particularly large and cohesive assembly of these implements, giving the reader a larger view of *shinobi no jutsu* lock-picking and bypassing skills. This allows the reader to 'creep in' to history and view a darkened secured *samurai* house from a *ninja*'s viewpoint.

Lock typology

The locking mechanisms vary in design dramatically. However, this does not mean that one lock is better than another. Historically, most locations would be locked with a combination of lock types and at various points. For example, a single door may have been both latched on the internal face and secured externally with a padlock. In this case, a *shinobi* had to break through and manipulate the door latch and also pick the padlock, making his task doubly complex. There were numerous padlock styles, but all of them relied on the same 'winged prong' design.

In this design, a selection of prongs, when the two halves of a lock are pushed together, snap into place, securing the lock. This was only opened when a key was slid along the prongs to force them together, allowing the lock to open and disengage back into two sections ... or when a skilled *shinobi* simulated the same effect.

Figure 4. The internal wings, or 'prongs' as they have been translated in this edition

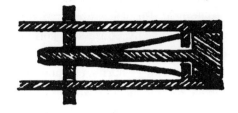

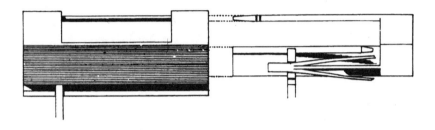

Figure 5. An example of a typical two-part Japanese lock showing the 'prongs' method of entry

In the case of a ring-and-hook latch, the *shinobi* had to find a way to knock the hook out of the ringlet from the external side of the door, which usually involved inserting an L-shaped probing device in a crack in the door or a hole – the hole usually having been made by the *shinobi*. Once through, this probe was used to manipulate the hook and spring open the latch.

Numerous approaches to the locks were taken by the *shinobi*, each requiring finesse, skill and the correct tool and these fundamentals still apply today in modern-day locksmithing. It is because of the timelessness of the principles that the lock-picking teachings of the *Bansenshukai* are still applicable to this day. As a trained locksmith myself, I can assure the reader that many of the techniques and principles found in the *Bansenshukai* are used to pick and bypass modern-day locks, which creates a three-fold value for this document: its historical *ninjutsu* value, the Japanese cultural value, and the modern-day relevance of the principles.

Overall, the lock-picking section can appear too technical to some. As you read this section, try to imagine the scenario – a *ninja* carrying lock-picking tools, entering bamboo thickets, using auspicious times, contemplating the position of the moon and waiting for the correct volume of wind – to take your mind deeper into ancient Japan. As you make this journey, see the *shinobi* as he plans his route in and out of a location. Come to understand the reality of the *shinobi*'s assignment. This will, without a doubt, help you to erase the myth of a *ninja* carrying multiple weapons while storming a location and it will reveal to you the true picture of the lightly armed spy creeping through a house, listening to all he can, possibly even burning the location down eventually.

In the end, we owe Fujibayashi for putting this reality into writing and preserving this information, so that here, many years later, the truth of *ninjutsu* lock picking can be known to us all.

THE
BANSENSHUKAI
萬川集海

BY

FUJIBAYASHI YASUTAKE

1676

TRANSLATED BY

ANTONY CUMMINS
& YOSHIE MINAMI

VOLUME ONE

Preface

The military is the final line concerning the safety of a country and the issue of state survival. It is of extreme importance because it is the basis of statecraft and the nation's safety and is by no means a minor issue. Military craft is incredibly deep and vast and it is not a matter to be taken lightly.

In any military situation you need to construct a detailed and precise plan beforehand, speculate clearly with the Five Constant Factors and the Seven Plans,[1] understand the feel of your people thoroughly and then, based on these factors, devise a stratagem and conduct your frontal and your surprise ways of attack. Also, if the five characteristics of wisdom, benevolence, trust, courage and strictness are achieved, and if advantages are derived from the three areas of Heaven, Earth and Man, then, even if you have only one thousand soldiers and have to fight an enemy of multitudes, you can be victorious one hundred times out of one hundred battles with absolute certainty. Even though it is the case that there are not so many lords of wisdom [at this time], you should remember the Chinese general Sun Tzu, who served King Helu,[2] or also the Duke of Pei, who unified the country by utilizing the strategist Zhang Liang. Alongside this, if a lord highly treasures the wisdom of his wise generals, governs the country well and disciplines his clan, then there is nothing to be afraid of, even if the borders of his country are vast. This is because a wise lord makes preparations for the whole country, which as a consequence, makes his generals all the more accomplished.

Since ancient times there have been numerous good generals in our country of Japan. However, they governed the country only through conquering it by sheer power. Is there any one of them who has ever achieved true benevolence? Kusunoki Masashige and some others coped with their [difficult] situation but their lords were not highly virtuous. Therefore, they ended up dying in battle, keeping their loyalty firm to the end. Since then has anyone else achieved this? In this age of decadence that we live in, people's minds are twisted and only words are loved but not practical

---

1   Sun Tzu's *Art of War* states that the Five Constant Factors are: Path, Heaven, Earth, General and Law. The Seven Plans are: which lord understands his people's mind more; which commander-in-chief is better; which side heaven and earth benefit; on which side the discipline is strictly followed; which army is stronger; which side has better-trained soldiers; which is the principle of 'work and you will be rewarded well'.

2   The King of Wu (544–496 BC)

deeds. Looking back to ancient China, the people of the Zhou Dynasty (1023–255 BC) were not as good as those of the Shang (1766–1122 BC), who were in turn not as good as the Xia Dynasty (c2070–c1600 BC), who were not so good as those of the period of Emperor Shun (who preceded the Xia Dynasty). Thus, will people in future days compete with those of this age? How many people are ready to keep righteousness and to carry forth their lord's orders if the time comes, or will they fight for loyalty and resourcefulness? If a great general excels in planning a strategy but none of his soldiers can act appropriately according to circumstances, then it is hard for him to gain victory. In warfare, you should catch the enemy in a state of unpreparedness, hit them quickly and by surprise and grasp the enemy intention correctly. If you have myriad strategies but do not have *ninjutsu* or the arts of the *ninja*, then in this case you will not be able to obtain details about the enemy's secret plan or their conspiracies.

Looking into the military manuscripts by Wu Qi 呉氏 and Sun Tzu 孫子, reading the secret books written by Zhang Liang 張良, Han Xin 韓信 and others, if you do not have spies, you can never know what is substantial or insubstantial concerning your enemy's intention, you cannot succeed in invading a massive wall of numerous miles, or lead an entire [enemy] army into a trap and achieve victory in every battle that you enter.

Is there anything else which enables a single person to ruin a force of countless people? You have every reason to study until you reach a mastery of the art of *ninjutsu* and by any means you can. Then, with the mastery of *ninjutsu*, even if the enemy has built up a strong siege or iron-like defences, there will be no way to prevent your force from infiltrating its keep.

The skills of *ninjutsu* are not occult or wondrous but are just like the strategy of swordplay; that is, it is about hitting the enemy through their gap, hitting by taking advantage of their responses or hitting by surprise. Therefore, with the main points taken from the *Kanrinseiyo*[3] 間林精要 manual, I here write more than twenty volumes on the subject of *ninjutsu* together with the Questions and Answers section, introductory notes and other subjects. I do this to record these secrets of the military arts.

Written in the fifth lunar month of Enpo Four, in the Year of the Dragon (1676) by a warrior of small renown,[4] Fujibayashi Yasutake of Koka[5] in Goshu[6]

---

3 A military manuscript that is most probably an Iga Gunpo manual.

4 Literally 'hidden warrior'; however, it is a statement of modesty to imply that he is not of great achievement or learning, or is a masterless Samurai.

5 The author lived on the borders of Iga in Yufune. It has been theorized that his home has been transcribed as Koka here because this translation is from the manual used by the Koka families mentioned in the Ohara document as discussed in the introduction. Fujibayashi's syntax usually places Koka second to Iga, making the title here most probably an addition by the Koka families.

6 Commonly known as Omi.

Introductory notes

This writing is hereafter titled the *Bansenshukai* and from its beginning to its end, it is in accord with important points found in the *Kanrinseiyo* manual. This *Bansenshukai* refers to *ninjutsu* and *ninja* tools, which have been kept secret by the eleven *ninja* of Iga and Koka. Alongside this, I have discarded the negative and included only the positive elements from various schools that are present to this day. Also, I have collected all the *ninjutsu* strategies constructed by excellent generals in both Japan and China and I dare to release what has not been made known before.

By revealing moral principles, pursuing righteousness and not concealing injustice, we come to the extreme secrets of *ninjutsu* and thus we express everything in a proper order. Thus *all rivers in the world flow into the ocean*, into something extremely deep and vast and that's why I titled this entire writing the *Bansenshukai*, 'A Myriad of Rivers Flowing into the Ocean'.

This collection of volumes [is the true way of the *ninja*] and is far removed from any lesser construction made by other *ninja*, who being from another place have only learned one or two things but claim themselves to be men from Iga.[7] Alongside this, there are numerous expert skills that should be mastered completely for every single plan or achievement and people in the world should not know how deep these skills go. That being said, here I chose to make the descriptions simplified but not so simple that they can be easily understood just from this writing alone. The intention behind this is to prevent lay people from talking about these skills without respect and treating them as an object of light entertainment. Only when a student makes effort to deepen his knowledge for a considerable length of time while being taught orally by his teacher, will he find out by himself how deep this art truly is. If you are not taught orally by a teacher and try to learn only with this writing alone, you will not be able to arrive at the deepest meaning of its secrets.

This manuscript consists of six parts: The Correct Mind; A Guideline for Commanders[8]; *Yo-nin*; *In-nin*[9]; Opportunities Bestowed by Heaven (astronomy and astrology); and *Ninja* Tools. Of these, the Correct Mind chapter is placed in

---

7   Fujibayashi is saying that while others may be *ninja* and know a small amount, their teachings are extremely limited compared to the teachings of Iga and the collective information he has gathered.

8   A closer translation would be 'Wisdom for Generals' but we feel that 'A Guideline for Commanders' better represents the text.

9   *Yo-nin* is the art of disguise, while *in-nin* is the art of infiltration.

a primary position because a correct mind should be the basis for everything and every deed. At first *ningei*[10] arts seem close to the arts of thievery, as within its tactics and strategy you need to climb a fence or stone wall or pick various kinds of padlocks, bolts, hooks and rings or locking sticks. Therefore, if a vile person who does not have a reverence for divine justice masters these skills and commits every evil within this writing, the end result will be that I have taught them the art of robbery. To avoid such a risk, I put the Correct Mind chapter first of all.[This chapter] will discuss the path of loyalty first of all, then the reason for your life and death, which will together help you acquire the correct mind. Although to dedicate yourself to sincerity and wisdom might bring ridicule upon yourself, doing something with the correct intention will aid you in the end. However, a mere novice should use this chapter as a lead, and keep its teachings close to heart all of the time, even when taking rest, sitting or sleeping, building a brave and fearless mind, with his eye firmly on loyalty, and with the aim to continue practising these skills for a long time to come. Having achieved this, he will be enlightened naturally and know what 'correct mind' means. If you know this skill in every way, a soft and weak person will become hard and strong, an evil-minded person will become loyal and a stupid person will become wise. With justice, courage and wisdom, there is no way you cannot 'steal in'. However, if you have an evil mind, deep tactics will not succeed. No matter if you try to carry out a conspiracy, your plot will be given away to the enemy at some time or another. No matter how courageous you are, you will not be able to achieve a hard mission. This is because a correct mind should come first.

A Guideline for Commanders should be placed as the second most important element. When a *ninja* has mastered every aspect of loyalty, courage, tactics and achievement, if his lord does not use him, any tactic will hardly be able to succeed. If tactics cannot be successfully accomplished, the said commander does not understand how useful *ninjutsu* truly is. If a lord does not have a good understanding of this art, suspicion [of the *ninja* arts] will form in his mind, which will prevent him from taking these arts into account and thus will prevent him from sending a *ninja* into the enemy's position. If he is not going to send *ninja*, he has no way to know the enemy's secret tactics.

Furthermore, if he cannot know the enemy's secret tactics, he will not be able to decide how to deploy his army or what tactics he should have. If he cannot decide on these things, it will invite dire consequences. Also, if he makes tactics or decides the deployment of his force by only speculating the status of the

10 *Ninja* skills 忍芸.

enemy, without using a *shinobi*, it will be akin to throwing a stone in the darkness at night that will not hit its target and therefore the strategy and deployment he decides upon will not play out well.

Therefore, it is often the case that if a commander is preparing in anticipation of attack from the east, the enemy will attack from the west and he will be overturned. If preparing for attack from the south, he will get attacked from the north and be thrown into confusion and defeat. Alongside this, in the case where a general does not know how to use a *shinobi* and even if that *shinobi* infiltrates the enemy's castle or position, the unknowing commander will fail to achieve a synchronized attack with the *ninja* who is inside the castle, while he, the commander, is on the outside and in this way he will not be able to realize his desired result. In this case he will not win the battle and/or the *ninja* may die an untimely death. This is why I have put the Guideline for Commanders in the rank and importance of second place.

In the second section of this volume, I mention the methods of preventing enemy *ninja* from getting into your position; this was placed here so that a lord will become familiar with these defence tactics. With these latter techniques, I also describe how to get your *ninja* into the enemy's position.

Yo-nin or 'open disguise' is placed before *in-nin*, which is 'hidden infiltration'. This is in accordance with the fact that *yo* (*yang*) means birth while *in* (*yin*) means death or the end. Even a resourceful person will not make a good *yo-nin* performer without training regularly, especially if he learns this skill by word alone. Anyone who wants to master this skill of disguise should always train himself with the utmost effort.

In the third section of *yo-nin*, I write on the skills of 'seeing', 'observing' and 'inferring', because there should be nothing that you do not see or hear concerning the enemy – this is the task of the *shinobi no mono*. Those studying this art should not think that these skills of observing and listening are not the skills of the *shinobi* and must remember not to neglect anything.

In the fifth section of *in-nin*, I write about *shinobi* night attacks, robbery, etc. You should not make light of these tasks either, as you may think they are not what a *shinobi* should do. Night attacking is a *shinobi*'s job in every respect. Therefore, night attacks without the knowledge of *ninjutsu* will not be effective. Also a *ninja* without the knowledge of how to attack at night cannot reach the true essence of *ninjutsu*.

To capture someone or to chase criminal targets was not originally the path of the *ninja*. However, it seems to be regarded as a *ninja*'s job these days, and therefore I write an outline of the techniques that have been done since ancient times. It originally would not be included in this, the path of the *ninja*, because it is not a *ninja*'s task but a task of lower-class people.[11]

The volumes on divination [the time of heaven] and astronomy and astrology are placed fifth in position and are based on the philosophy of the wise men of old. They say that the time of heaven is not as influential as the benefit of the earth, and in turn the benefit of the earth is not as important as [the harmony of man].[12] However, in these volumes, there are quite a few important things for *ninjutsu* and you should not neglect to learn them, but then be careful not to pay *too* much attention to them.[13]

The use of *ninja* tools is a measure needed to fulfil the art of *in-nin*, but the volumes on the tools teach how to use and produce them but they do not contain the principles of the *shinobi*. Therefore, these are placed in sixth and last position.

You should try to learn the use of these tools on your own to decide if they are good or not. Unless you prove their worth for yourself you should not use them. It is good for you to concentrate on creating as simple a tool as possible so that it can serve in various ways. The method of manufacturing each tool is mentioned in detail within the said volume.

---

11 Fujibayashi is harking back to a time when most *shinobi* came from the warrior class, but by the time of writing, the men of Iga had become *musokunin*, a lower form between the *samurai* and peasant classes but who were not given fief, a drop in status which can be tracked through the historical record.

12 This transcription missed this ideogram; however, the passage itself is a famous quote from the Chinese philosopher Mencius.

13 This is an important point to remember: the Chinese-based skills of weather forecasting and divination and calculating the position of the moon are common skills used in an agricultural society and their usage can be important to *ninjutsu*. Fujibayashi talks of the skills with reserve and caution owing to their possibly dubious nature.

Table of contents[14]

Volume One

Preface, Introductory notes, Table of contents, Questions and answers about *ninjutsu*

Volume Two

正心上
Seishin I
The Correct Mind I

Volume Three

正心下
Seishin II
The Correct Mind II

Volume Four

将知 一
Shochi I
A Guideline for Commanders I
About ninpo – *the* shinobi *treasure*

Volume Five

将知 二
Shochi II
A Guideline for Commanders II
About promises
Three points about the prohibitions within *shinobi no jutsu*
Two points on secret writing
Two points on *yabumi* secret letters, which are sent tied to an arrow

---

14 The table of contents does not always faithfully mirror the text. This may be as a result of transcription errors or it may be that the original was written this way. Where needed, we have added the major missing sections.

Four points on signals
Secret letters with occult power [text missing]
Six points on promises
Three points on cooperation with the general
Two points on the promise for the guarantee of the security of the *ninja*
Reasons as to why a *shinobi no mono* should be employed

Volume Six

将知三
Shochi III
[All the original text appears to have been omitted]

将知四
Shochi IV
A Guideline for Commanders IV
How to protect against the enemy's plans I
Six[15] points on how to avoid employing enemy *shinobi*
Seven[16] points on the discipline of the army

Volume Seven

将知五
Shochi V
A Guideline for Commanders V
How to protect against the enemy's plans II
Three points on watch fires
Five[17] points on passwords, identifying marks or signs or actions of identification
Six points on behaviour in the guardhouse
Three points on night patrols
Two points on *togiki* listening scouts
Two skills for defending against the enemy by using tools

---

15 The original manual says five.
16 The original manual says six.
17 The original manual says six.

---

18 This is in the wrong position in the original manual but has been moved into the correct place.

Volume Ten

Volume Eleven

---

19 The original table of contents states four.

---

20 The text only has twelve points but states thirteen in the original.
21 The original manual states three.
22 Not found in the original table of contents.
23 Not found in the original table of contents.

Volume Fourteen

陰忍四

In-nin IV

Hidden Infiltration IV

Gates and doors

Three points on the preparation for opening doors

Six points on discovering the position of *shirizashi* locking sticks by touch

Four points on how to unlock locking sticks

Five points on how to find the position of *kakegane* hooked latches by touch

Eight points on how to unhook latches

Two points on how to detect door bolts

Three points on how to unlock bolts

Two points on how to know if there is a *sen* wooden peg in the latch

Two points on how to release a *sen* wooden peg

Six[24] points on how to identify *joshi* padlocks [and their workings]

Eight points on how to open various padlocks

Two secret points on how to open various padlocks

Volume Fifteen

陰忍五

In-nin V

Hidden Infiltration V

Shinobi *night attacks*

Two points on *monomi* scouting

Four points on the outfit to be worn on night raids

Seven points on the instructions to be given during a night attack

Four points on the tactics to be used before a night attack

Four points on the appropriate time for a night attack

Eighteen points on the ways of *shinobi* night attacks

Twelve points on the *gando* burglar raid

Twenty[25] points on capturing people

---

24 The original table of contents states sixteen.
25 The original text says twenty-one.

Volume Sixteen[26]

天時上

Tenji I

Opportunities Bestowed by Heaven I

Tonko – *auspicious ways*

A general survey on how to choose a date or direction

The Five Precepts and the times of the day

Knowing a lucky day or direction by the generating and destructive cycles of the Five Elements

Volume Seventeen

天時下

Tenji II

Opportunities Bestowed by Heaven II

Astronomy and astrology

Fifteen points on forecasting the wind and rain

Three points on calculating the time of moonrise and moonset

Four points on how to know the ebb and flow of the tides

Two points on identifying the direction

Two points on knowing the time

Volume Eighteen

忍器一

Ninki I

Ninja Tools I

Climbing tools

Illustrations of tied ladders, flying ladders, cloud ladders, rolled ladders, spiked ladders, high ladders, *kunai*, probing irons, the long bag, grappling hooks, spider ladders, the dragon climbing tool and hooks

Volume Nineteen

忍器二

Ninki II

Ninja Tools II

---

26 Many titles are missing from the original table of contents.

Water tools

Illustrations floating bridges, sinking bridges, cattail rafts, jar rafts, wicker-basket rafts, water spider floating seats, flippers, the 'cormorant bird' tool,[27] marsh shoes[28] and collapsible boats

Volume Twenty

忍器三

Ninki III

Ninja Tools III

Opening tools

Illustrations of the *toihazushi* probing tool, *hamagari* angled saw, *nobekagi* extendable key, *irekokagi* retractable key, *hasami* snippers, *nomi* chisel, drills, the *shikoro* saw, *kama* folding sickle, *kuginuki* nail remover, padlock keys, the listening-iron[29] and silent sandals

Volume Twenty-One

忍器四

Ninki IV

Ninja Tools IV

Fire tools I

The spider [tool],[30] tinder, eight points on *tsutsunohi* fire cylinders, illustrations of *torinoko*, the fire box, the everlasting fire, the immortal torch, Yoshitsune's torch, *gando* lanterns and the *irekohi* adjustable torch

Recipes for signal fires, the waterproof *hinawa*, the toothpick fire,[31] the torch of appearance and disappearance, water torches, five ways of the wind and water torch, two alternatives for the water fire, *yakigusuri* ignition powders, *kumabi* bear fire [missing], the *kuruma* torch, sleeping medicine, keeping sleep at bay medicine, the powder of immediate death [missing], powder for travelling [missing], the basket torch, the camp fire in the cold, the attack torch, the watch fire, blinding powder, rolled fire [missing] and the water musket shot

---

27 This tool is missing from the text.
28 This tool is missing from the text.
29 This tool is missing from the text.
30 This tool is missing from the text.
31 This tool can be found in the author's book *Iga and Koka Ninja Skills*.

Volume Twenty-Two

忍器五
Ninki V
Ninja Tools V
Fire tools II

Supplementary Volume[32]

軍用秘記
The *Bansenshukai Gunyo-hiki*
Secrets on Essential Military Principles by Sasayama Kagenao of the Ohara Clan

---

32 This does not appear in the original table of contents as it was not written by Fujibayashi.

Questions and answers about *ninjutsu*

Question: *In which period did* ninjutsu *come into existence?*

Answer: Originally the art of war [including *ninjutsu*] appeared in the period of Emperor Fu Xi[33] and afterwards became more prosperous in the period of the Yellow Emperor.[34] Since then it has been passed down through the generations and there was no person of prudence and discretion who did not value it greatly. Thus, *ninjutsu* is the key to military affairs. Even though it existed in the periods of Fu Xi and the Yellow Emperor, there is no mention of *ninjutsu* directly in any written documents. Only its essence was there. In this sense you can find it in some ancient writings.

Question: *Why do you say* ninjutsu *is the key to military affairs?*

Answer: In the volume on the employment of spies, which is found in the thirteen volumes of the *Art of War* written by Sun Tzu, *ninjutsu* is mentioned. Other than this, almost all military manuscripts through all periods in China and in our country as well, have a reference to *ninjutsu* in their text. If *ninjutsu* were not the essential key to strategy, why did it happen that those wise sages in history wrote down this art for future generations, or have you not heard that? Some military manuscripts say, 'The military arts concern disciplining the inside and knowing the outside.' In short, you should know your enemy's secret tactics and obtain precise information about them.

In order to fully know the enemy's condition, the skills you would need to utilize are: [Normal] scouting warriors, these should scout quickly from a distance to get information such as topography, if the enemy is advancing or retreating, how large the enemy's forces are, how far away they are, etc. and report it back to the lord.

On the other hand, *ninjutsu* makes it possible for you to covertly get very close to the moat or fence of the enemy's castle or position, observe the situation, infiltrate the castle or position, gather every piece of information, such as what the inside is like, the enemy's stratagems, secrets, etc. by watching and listening closely and bringing this back to the lord so that he can decide what kind of

---

33 Mid-2800s BC.
34 A legendary Chinese sovereign; tradition holds that he reigned from 2697 BC to 2597 BC.

deployment has to be taken, and also whether regular or surprise strategies are to be employed in order to defeat the enemy. If it were not for this skill of *ninjutsu*, it would be difficult to know the enemy's tactics and secure a victory over the country. With this in mind, you should know that *ninjutsu* is the key to the military.

Question: *Is this art called* shinobi *in China as well?*

Answer: *Shinobi* is a name that was invented in our country. In the state of Wu[35] it was called *kan* 間; in the Spring and Autumn period, *cho* 諜; and in and after the [Chinese] Warring States period, *saisaku* 細作, *yutei* 遊偵, *kansai* 姦細 and so on. All these names refer to *ninjutsu*. Alongside this, in the *Six Secret Teachings*[36] it is referred to as *yushi* 遊士 ('playing warrior') and in the *Yin Jing* 陰経 manual written by Li Quan it is known as *kojin* 行人. As seen in these manuals, it has been called many different names according to the period, or the lord's intention. It is quite similar in our country, as we call it *shinobi, yato, suppa, nokizaru, mitsumono, kyoudan*, etc.

Question: *Is there any reason* ninjutsu *is named* kancho, yutei, saisaku, kansai, yushi, kojin *etc?*

Answer: In the chapter on the employment of spies in the *Art of War*, the character for *kan* is annotated and means 'gap' or 'opening' and is to have a person get into a gap within the enemy with the aim of getting information about their condition. Thus *kan* means 'gap'. It is sending a person to look for the enemy's gap to take advantage of it and to get into the enemy's castle or position so that he will gather information about the enemy's plot, or secret plans, in full and report them to you. Otherwise, it is to take advantage of an enemy's gap, infiltrate the castle or position, set fire or deliver a night attack.

The character for *kan* has the second meaning of 'estrange'. Similarly, *ninjutsu* includes a skill 'to estrange'. *Ninja* estrange the enemy's lord from his retainers by making false charges, by disturbing the agreements made between the enemy and the lord of their neighbouring province so that they cannot expect reinforcements, or by estranging the enemy's lord from his retainers so that they will be offended by each other. There have been lots of examples since ancient times both in China and Japan where victory was obtained by creating confusion among the enemy. A theory says as the character for *kan* 間 consists of the two

---

35 A state during the Spring and Autumn period (c585–473 BC) in China.

36 A treatise on military strategy in ancient China, which is believed to have been written by Jiang Ziya. He was the military advisor to King Wen and King Wu and helped them to establish the Zhou Dynasty. It is one of the Seven Military Classics.

parts 'gate' 門 and 'sun' 日, that, therefore, the essence of this art is to infiltrate the enemy's castle and position without delay, even through the smallest gap, which is the same as the sunlight immediately coming through an open gate. This principle is so deep and subtle that ordinary people can hardly understand it, and also the characters for *cho* 諜 and *tei* 偵 mean 'to detect'. Generally, the art of *shinobi* looks like playing[37] while the job of the spy is to look for a gap within the enemy, sneak in and observe their condition. This is why they were also called *yutei* or 'playing detectors'.

In Kusunoki Masashige's *ninjutsu*, there was a skill where he divided forty-eight *ninja* into three and always had one of the groups of sixteen people staying in Kyoto. They observed the situation there by utilizing various secret plans and kept Kusunoki informed. This is exactly what *yutei* means. Also, *saisaku*[38] means that *ninja* go over to the enemy, observe their condition fully and report to their lord so the lord can make his strategy with precision. [*Ninjutsu*] is also called *kansai* because *kan* means 'wicked' as it is used in *kankyoku* ('evil-minded') or *mokan* ('falsehood'). Hence, even though *ninjutsu* looks normal on its surface, it always has an extremely distorted and a deeply plotted tactic beneath the surface. Even though [a *shinobi*] is on the righteous path of loyalty, his methods have injustice within them and are crooked inside, thus the negative word *kansai* was also used.

Yushi originates in the way of looking like one is 'playing', but in reality a deep plot is in mind. It is also called *kojin*[39] because [*shinobi*] go between the enemy and the allies. *Ko* also has the other meaning of 'to convey' or 'to suppress'; this is the reason they were named *kojin*.

Question: Why was it called such various names in China?

Answer: In the *Art of War* it was named *kan* and since then those in this job are called *kanja* and upon hearing the word *kan* people would clearly have an idea as to what they do. Originally, as the deepest way of this art says, you are not allowed to let your name, skill or art be known to people, this is so that you will be able to fulfil your purpose without being discovered by others. Thus it is essential to keep this art a deep secret.

For this reason, it seems that in China they changed the names for this skill from generation to generation so that they could keep the fact that they were involved in *ninjutsu* a secret.

---

37 The character for *yu* in *yutei* means 'to play'.
38 The character for *sai* means 'in detail' or 'closely', and the one for *saku* means 'to make'.
39 The characters for *kojin* are: *ko* ('to go') and *jin* ('person').

Question: While it has changed names in China, it is called shinobi *in our country. Why is this?*

Answer: All the names in China, such as *kancho, yutei, saisaku, kansai, yushi, kojin* etc., as mentioned above, were designated because their job is to detect a gap within the enemy, or estrange the lord of the enemy from his retainers or the enemy from their neighbouring countries. That is, the names have originated because of the consequences of the objective for the *ninjutsu* used.

On the other hand, in our country, we call it *shinobi* 忍 because the character means 'blade' 刃 and 'heart' 心. It is named this way because it refers to the essence that is fundamental to all sections of *ninjutsu*. Without considering this meaning, you can hardly know the real origin of this art.

Question: If possible, I would like to know the details of the above statement.
Answer: The essence [of their character] which enables [*ninja* to perform such deeds] and to detect gaps within the enemy, and even to 'creep in' while under-taking all the risks which are involved in such actions, displays that they [the *ninja*] have a heart which is hard and virtuous, just like a blade which is hard and sharp. If the heart is not so sharp or hard but instead is blunt and soft, even a most skilful plan cannot be completed, as such an agent will be faint-hearted when getting close to the enemy. Even if they could manage to get close to the enemy, they will be nervous and grow flustered and talk so much that they will give the plot away and end up being captured, which will result in not only themselves being killed but obviously in damage being caused to their lord. Therefore, you can only sneak in through a gap within the enemy if you have a hard and loyal heart that is tempered like a blade. This is why we have changed the names from China and refer to this art using this character 忍, which means 'a heart like a blade'. For *shinobi* it is essential to get close to the enemy, there is a poem found in Ise no Saburo Yoshimori's one hundred poems:

忍ヒニハ習ヒノ道ハ多ケレド先ツ第一ハ敵ニ近ツケ

Though there are so many things a shinobi *should keep in mind, the first thing of all is how to get close to the enemy.*

Question: The name shinobi *as just mentioned has been changed in various ways like* yato, suppa, nokizaru, mitsumono, kyodan *etc. Suppa* and yato *have been commonly used for a long time in Iga and Koka, and they are obvious. But the name* nokizaru[40] *is used instead of* shinobi *just because it is their job to look*

---

40 Literally means 'a monkey in the eaves'.

at the inside of the enemy and their position. Then for what reason are shinobi *called* mitsumono *or* kyodan?

Answer: The *shugo* ('provincial lord') of Kai, called Takeda Shingen Harunobu, was an excellent warlord. He had a special unit called *mitsumono* consisting of thirty loyal brave people who were competent to carry out his tactics very skilfully. He would give them a good stipend, reward them enough, keep them by his side and utilize them as the key to the military. The unit was divided into three: Espionage, Strategy and Counterespionage, thus it was called *mitsumono* – 'men of three matters'.

Of Shingen's poems,[41] there are some that include the word *mitsumono*:

合戦に三者なくして大将の石を抱いて淵に入るなり

If it were not for mitsumono, *the lord would kill himself by jumping into deep water with a stone in his arms.*

戦いに日取方取さしのぞき三者をやりて兼ねて計らえ

For battle, set aside the divination for the date or the direction and send mitsumono *before you make any plan and consider everything.*

Lord Oda Nobunaga named *shinobi* as *kyodan* and utilized them. He achieved an amazing victory over the great force of the Imagawa clan and won scores of impregnable castles such as Inuyama castle of Bishu and Udono castle of Sanshu. Also he beat strong enemies in various provinces without any serious damage to his own forces, all because of the services of the *kyodan*.[42]

Uesugi Kenshin of Echigo province is said to have given great importance to them, thinking he achieved complete victory because of their work.

As in the above, great commanders employed *shinobi* under various names to serve them because they could bring very subtle advantages to the fray. For any lord, it is essential to make much of the *shinobi*.

Question:[43] *It is said in the above that the path of the* shinobi *came into being in the period of Fu Xi and became prosperous in the period of the Yellow Emperor. After the Yellow Emperor, how has it been passed down until now?*

---

41 This following section is not in the version of the text from the National Archives and is taken from the Iga Museum's modern translation. Therefore, the ideograms may have been changed by the Iga Museum to present a more modern slant.

42 The Iga version from the Iga museum ends at this point.

43 This question and its answer are not in the National Archives version, but are found in the transcriptions of the Iga Useno Museum.

Answer: As I am neither educated nor talented, and am ignorant about the details, all I can say is that as far as we know, generally that is, there have been only a few people who have known *ninjutsu* since the time of the Yellow Emperor. Though few people would use this path, as late as in the period of Yin, a person named Yi Yin mastered this way and served King Tang. He crept into the place of King Jie of the Xia Dynasty and killed him.

In ancient times, the rise of the Yin Dynasty was due to Yi Yin who had served under the Xia Dynasty. It was believed that the tyrant drove him away to the Sung Dynasty. He took the side of Jie five times and the side of Tang five times; however, people did not know that Yi was working as a spy. Afterwards the tradition was passed down to Jiang Ziya[44] and he wrote a treatise on *ninjutsu* that consisted of seventy-one chapters and introduced it to the world. The proof for this is in the Question and Answer between Tang Tai-zhong and Li Jing and states 'Li Jing says that with the seventy-one chapters of Tai Gong, troops cannot be exhausted.' According to the footnote [in this ancient manual], this saying means 'the art of spying', which means *shinobi* here.

This writing [by Jiang Ziya] has not been brought here to our country. However, according to the *Yiwen Zhi*,[45] 'the three elements of strategy, speech and battle are all recorded in the *Six Secret Strategic Teachings*.' Therefore, we must conclude that, as the *Six Secret Teachings* also talks about *shinobi*-related things, the seventy-one chapters about spying are contained in the writings of the *Six Secret Teachings*.

Alongside this, the *Art of War* mentions in its chapter on the use of spies that Jiang Ziya sneaked into the enemy ranks of King Jie and ruined him. According to the chapter, 'Zhou rose and Lu Ziya helped the enemy.' According to an annotation, Zhou was the name of the dynasty when King Wu conquered the country and Lu Ziya was in fact Jiang Ziya and his enemy was King Jie. People only know about the battle of Mu-ye but do not know that [Jiang Ziya] went to the enemy, offered them women and bribes, then freely carried out a conspiracy. This quote explains the reality of what went on behind this battle.

Afterwards, [these arts] were passed down to Sun Tzu and he thought out the five types of spies that are called *gokan* and wrote of them in the chapter on the use of spies. Since then there have been no great generals who have not used *ninjutsu*, all through the Spring and Autumn period, the [Chinese] Warring States period, the Three Kingdoms period, the Tang period, the Five Dynasties period, the Northern and Southern Sung periods and all to the present time.

---

44 A prime minister of King Wen of the Zhou state; also called Tai Gong.
45 The *Hanshu Yiwen Zhi* is the oldest surviving bibliography of ancient China.

However, it seems that the art of the *shinobi* of Jiang Ziya and Sun Tzu was passed down to Zhang Liang (?–1898 BC) of the Earlier Han Dynasty and also to Han Xin (?–196 BC). This fact has been supported by the *Dialogue of Tai-Zong*, in which Li Ting (571–649) says:

'Zhang Liang learned the Six Secret Strategic Teachings *and the* Three Strategies of Huang Shigong *written by Jiang Ziya. Also, Han Xin learned Sima Rangju*[46] *and Sun Tzu.*'

However, it was limited to the Three Focuses[47] and the Four Schools.[48] One of these three focuses is about *ninjutsu*.

Question: *When did this way come into use in our country?*

Answer: A brother of the thirty-eighth Emperor, Tenchi,[49] was Emperor Temmu.[50] In this period when Prince Seiko plotted treason against him and holed up in a castle that he had constructed in Atago of Yamashiro province, the Emperor Temmu had a *shinobi* named Takoya 多胡弥 and he infiltrated the fortress. Takoya got into the castle and set fire to it, and in unison with this the Emperor penetrated its defences from the outside and the castle fell without difficulty. This is the first time that *ninjutsu* was used in our country. This is written in the Chronicles of Japan. Since then no general has not used this skill. The generals who fully exploited *ninjutsu* are: Ise no Saburo Yoshimori; Kusunoki Masashige and his son; Takeda Shingen; Mori Motonari; Kenshin of Echigo; and Lord Oda Nobunaga. Of them Yoshimori made one hundred poems about the *shinobi* and they have been passed down to this day.

Kusunoki Masashige wrote down the secrets of military affairs and *shinobi no jutsu* in six sections and then integrated them into one volume. He kept it secret and when he was killed in a battle in Hyogo, it was handed to Onchi Sakon Taro to pass down to his son Masatsura, so it has been left to posterity. This writing is called Kusunoki's *Ikkan no Sho* ('one-volume writing').

Every one of the great generals in our country, such as Yoshimori, Kusunoki and his son, Shingen, Motonari, Lord Nobunaga and Lord Hideyoshi, achieved victory by utilizing *ninjutsu* and there are too many examples of this to count them all.

---

46 A famous Chinese military general during the Spring and Autumn period.

47 Strategy, troops and resources.

48 'Strategies and tactics', 'circumstances and developments', '*yin* and *yang*' and 'techniques and crafts'.

49 Lived 626–672 and reigned 668–672; also, the original text refers to him as the *thirty-ninth* Emperor.

50 The fortieth Emperor (631–686), who reigned 673–686.

Question: *I heard that this art was widely used all through the country. But what is the reason that Iga and Koka are the most renowned of all the various provinces for* shinobi?

Answer: In ancient times after the shogun Ashikaga Takauji ruled the country, his descendents inherited the shogunate successively but the court could not govern very well and the rank system became confused. Officials were already corrupt, and there was a constant state of war. On top of this, one after another lord or official came out to subjugate each other and there was no peace at that time in our country. This continued as late as the government of the thirteenth shogun after Lord Takauji, who was called Lord Kougen-in Yoshiteru, at which point the political relationships were becoming more and more confused, resulting in the complete devastation of [the three] ways of morals, [which are the paths of 'lord and vassal', 'father and son', and also 'husband and wife' ,] and also the devastation of virtue.

Throughout the whole country, as all were at war, all tribes[51] were in extreme confusion, all places were in dispute. However, apart from the people of Iga and Koka, every province had its *shugo* provincial military governor and the people there were ruled by them.

The people of Iga and Koka had never had a *shugo* governor and each clan was self-governing; they constructed small castles in each estate independently and had free rein. As having no *shugo* or a lord, there was not a governor to oversee them. There were numerous instances of them fighting with each other to take away the other's land. Therefore, their main concentration was set on battles, each morning and every evening, and their life revolved around armament and defence.[52] They would search for a gap within each other, send *shinobi* to infiltrate and to set fire on each other's castles, get inside information on the enemy, interfere with the enemy's plans of alliance by disinformation, carry out raids or night attacks, and conduct strategy with innumerable changes to catch the enemy off guard. Thus they would always keep their horses saddled, even those of lower rank would have their straw sandals put on the scabbards of their swords[53] and never let their guard down.

Therefore, the result was that they thought that, in order to defeat the enemy's greater forces by using only a small number of people and defeating the hard and strong, it is best to use the flexible and supple, and nothing is better than the

---

51 Fujibayashi uses a Chinese idiom to mean tribe here, but by definition it should be clan.

52 This is an important point as it shows the warlike nature of life in Iga, and dispels the image of unity and democracy, before the clans unified against Oda Nobunaga.

53 An idiomatic expression meaning 'to be in a constant state of preparedness for war'.

use of the *shinobi* to do this. Therefore, they[54] had every *samurai* hone himself with the skill of the *shinobi* and the lower people or *genin* 下人 learn *in-nin* or 'stealth' techniques.[55] Thus it turned out that eleven low-class people distinguished themselves as skilful performers of *in-nin*. For these people, in their own provinces or in others, sneaking into places to take others' possessions, capture a castle and achieve victory was as easy as 'rolling an object in the palms of their hands'.

Because of this, though there were several powerful *daimyo* with great forces in the neighbouring provinces, none of them could take possession of Iga. Even such a formidable[56] lord as Lord Nobunaga was once defeated in Iga. Thus it was even less likely that other lords would have the ambition to take this land. There was simply no opportunity to take this province. Even though [Iga] was a small domain with a small number of people, had no lord and was a jumble of small clans and did not look resolute in position, it had not succumbed to the great forces led by the powerful lords in the neighbouring provinces. Why was it possible? It can *only* be attributed to the achievements of *ninjutsu*. Thus Iga is made the homeland of the *shinobi*.

Question: I would like to know the names of the eleven masters of in-nin.

Answer:

1. Nomura no Odaki Magodayu 野村之大炊孫太夫
2. Shindo no Kotaro 新堂ノ小太郎
3. Tateoka no Dojun 楯岡ノ道順
4. Shimotsuge no Kizaru 下柘植ノ木猿
5. [Shimotsuge no] Kozaru 子猿
6. Ueno no Hidari 上野ノ左
7. Yamada no Hachiemon 山田ノ八右衛門
8. Kambe no Konan 神部ノ小南
9. Otowa no Kido 音羽城戸
10. Kabutoyama Taro Shiro 甲山太郎四郎
11. Kabutoyama Tarozaemon 甲山太郎左衛門

These people were of the utmost importance, but when it comes to modern[57]

---

54 This paragraph's subtext here relates to the people of Iga and Koka.

55 This sentence is of great importance, it appears that high-ranking people performed predominantly *yo-nin* as it required a high level of education; however, it is difficult to assess how much of each discipline the different classes learned.

56 In the text, it says 'weak general' and is thought to be a transcription error.

57 Seventeenth century.

shinobi, the teachings [*ryu*] of Dojun are divided into forty-eight separate schools, thus there are forty-nine[58] schools of *shinobi* in Iga and Koka.

Question: For what reason did Dojun's ryu produce a further forty-eight schools?

Answer: Sasaki Yoshikata's religious name was Bakkansai Jotei, and he was the *shugo* political governor of Omi domain. In his lower warriors there was a man whose name was Dodo. He rose in revolt and holed up in the castle of Sawayama within Omi domain. Jotei attacked him for several days but the castle had such an impenetrable terrain surrounding it, that it seemed hard to take it by assault. Then having thought out a plan to employ some master *shinobi* of Iga to get him in there, he called the skilled *ninja* named Dojun to him and asked him for help in his infiltration. Upon his request, Dojun assembled forty-four men from Iga and four from Koka, and went to Jotei's Moriyama castle with the forty-eight people. On the way they stopped at a temple named Heisenji in Yufune in Iga, and a diviner whose name was Miyasugi lived in the area. Dojun took audience with him and had him cast a fortune for their *shinobi* mission. The diviner said it would be a lucky mission. On top of that, he made and gave Dojun a poem to celebrate their departure.

沢山ニ百々トナル雷モイカサキ入レハ落ニケル哉

*The thunder roaring is Dodo and is above Sawayama mountain, but
it will fall when the lightning strikes.*

Lightning is a play on words here. It has the double meanings of lightning and the surname of Dojun, and thus Dojun[59] was very pleased with this poem and gave the diviner one hundred *hiki* coins.[60] Then he went to Jotei and prearranged the signs and promises needed for the infiltration. Soon after that he infiltrated Sawayama castle with the skill of disguise that is called *bakemono jutsu* and then set fire inside of the castle, while Jotei conducted a quick assault from the outside. Dodo's force, while trying to put out the fire, had to cope with the enemy intruding while also trying to defend against the enemy attacking from the outside; the fire was raging more and more furiously and they could not do anything and were ruined at last.

Afterwards the forty-eight men founded schools and named them independently. Thus it is said Dojun's school spawned forty-eight schools.

---

58 This move from forty-eight schools to forty-nine is because of the addition of the original school Dojun created.

59 The connotation here is that Dojun will win the battle.

60 *Hiki* was a unit of money at that time.

Question: *Can it be said that across the ages these eleven and forty-eight men of Iga and Koka are great* shinobi?

Answer: On other paths and in other skills, the names of those who are good at their own skills come to be known to people. However, this path of the *shinobi* is different from other arts; those who are known as good are only medium-grade *ninja* 中吉ノ忍者 and are not as accomplished as *shinobi no mono*. If people do not know how good they are and if they are skilful at the art, then they are considered to be *jo no shinobi* 上ノ忍, or high-level *ninja*. An ancient saying says that water makes sound when it is shallow, while deep water makes no sound. Just like a mountain stream makes sound as it is shallow. If you reflect on this concept, medium-grade *ninja* who do not have deep strategy tend to be famous for various reasons. This is because those excellent *ninja* who have a deep strategy usually will not give themselves away as *ninja* but hide it deeply and pretend to be an ordinary *samurai*, a hermit or a masterless *samurai*. They would not give the slightest indication that they know *ninjutsu* but look like ordinary people. When an opportunity comes, without letting even senior counsellors or principal retainers know, they would only make promises such as the required signals to the lord himself and in secret, then they would go to infiltrate the enemy's castle, and carry out deep and subtle strategies so that the enemy will be depressed and ruined.

Even after the enemy spoken of above had fallen into ruin, the *ninja* would not talk about what they did, about having sneaked in and laid their plot. For this reason, people do not know that the enemy was ruined because of his achievements but believe that he went to ruin as a matter of course, as if the enemy had run out of luck.

As in the above case, competent *ninja*, even if they have accomplished the extraordinary, make no sound, leave no smell and get no fame or honour for their bravery. The results they have brought about look as natural as if they were being created by nature itself. Universally, in spring it is beautiful and trees and plants grow and flowers bloom. In summer it is hot and trees and plants grow luxuriantly. In autumn it is cool and trees and plants turn their colours and the leaves fall. In winter it is cold, snowy and frosty. Trees lose dead leaves and plants return underground. As well as the four seasons, during one day, so many various [and natural] things take place, but nobody knows who is doing these things.

Similarly, the wisdom of a competent *ninja* 能キ忍者 is as vast as heaven, so that no human being can know it exactly. A *ninja* should look stupid while their strategies are as profound and deep as the earth or an abyss and beyond mere human knowledge.

In conclusion, the roots of *ninjutsu* are far beyond the above eleven skilled *shinobi* and the forty-eight men [who were under Dojun]. These fifty-nine people are famous because they are shallow. Even though not known to the world, their masters knew *ninjutsu* so deeply that they did not leave their names for us to give fame to.

Question: Our castle is firmly guarded, in a faultless defence taking a proper formation according to any of a number of well-known formulae and kept invulnerable. Passwords or identifying signs are prearranged, watch fires are made properly at night, the guardhouses and the gates are strictly guarded, night patrols are performed one after another, and any suspicious person is questioned carefully so that almost any ninjutsu performer will be shut out. How can he sneak in successfully under these circumstances?

Answer: No matter how firmly the lord fortifies his castle, no matter what formation he takes for defence, no matter how strictly he organizes his force and guards with the goal of keeping the enemy at bay, all these measures are insufficient and trivial. To start with, *ninjutsu* should be prepared in times of peace, they should observe the politics of the entire country, see how good or bad the lords are, if the retainers are right-minded or if the *samurai* down to lowest people respect their lord or not, and so on. When things are urgent, a *ninja* will already have an amazing and subtle strategy ready and will be easily able to get into position without any hint of their plan even before the enemy starts to prepare. Only after they do this, do they have such perfect control over all strategies without any breaks, just like a ring has no ends.

The *Art of War* says, 'Be subtle, be subtle and you can use spies anywhere.' The *Yin-jing* says:

'If you shoot at a falcon and it hides in a dense forest, if a fish is swimming around and gets into a deep abyss, there will be no trace for you to follow. Therefore, if Li Lou[61] could not see with his head bent down and Kuang[62] could not hear a subtle sound without listening to it, how can a general who is brave and thinks nothing of his life, so much so he would throw it away like dust, how could even someone as great as this possibly detect a *kojin* 行人 spy?'

Question: As was stated above, if it is difficult to block a ninja, is it certain that the enemy's shinobi will get into our castle or position, or is there any way to prevent them from infiltrating?

---

61 A legendary Chinese character who was said to have had amazingly good vision.
62 A legendary Chinese character who was said to have had an acute ear and a mastery of music.

Answer: The skill is extremely advanced. No matter how good a *ninja* is at defending against the enemy's *shinobi*, [his efforts] will be fruitless if the lord is not on the righteous path as a ruler. Therefore, the lord should teach justice to his retainers first and then love all of his people, which would make his soldiers even in a situation of certain death not disobey his orders in the slightest. This is possible because he teaches and loves them by the right path at all times. If the lord understands the righteous path as stated above, then, if an urgent situation takes place, the general will use large-scale tactics and will use *ninjutsu* to prevent enemy tactics and to fortify his castle or position, and in this way he may build up a perfect defence. On top of that, highly skilled *ninja* 上巧ノ 忍者 should also defend against lesser tactics used by the enemy *shinobi*, they should help establish military policy, question old and new soldiers, divide them into groups, deploy them, arrange for the password or identifying signs at each instance required, have watch fires kept properly during the night, assign those for the task of night patrols and the search of blind spots, make up fake walls, scatter caltrops or lay an ambush where the enemy should come on and keep strict guard at every gate. Then if this is done the enemy's *shinobi* will not be able to get in. In a case like this where the lord and *shinobi* are working on the right path together, it would be easy to get into the enemy's force but difficult for the enemy to find a gap within your own defences.

Question: *In times of peace as today, suppose that a ninja wants to serve a lord in some country and so the lord tells him: 'Here is a test. I will get my soldiers together in my castle, make them guard every gate firmly, and keep them on alert strictly just as if they were defending against the enemy's* shinobi *in a real battle, so that you cannot get in. Can you infiltrate our castle quickly, if it is guarded strictly like this? If you can do this, I will give you as much stipend as you like.' What should he do in such a situation?*

Answer: Originally *ninjutsu* is a strategy that should have its root in fidelity and honesty and there is no skill to deceive your lord. As is stated in the chapter The Correct Mind Part II, those who are on the path of *ninjutsu* should not use it for the benefit of their own desire under any circumstance. Nor should they deceive a lord who is against reason. However, it is not that there is no way to infiltrate your lord's castle during such a time of peace as described. As Jiang Ziya points out, you should be very attentive in making stratagems. In times of peace it is not appropriate at all to seek for the fame of the *ninja* by performing the subtle ways of *ninjutsu*. If what the lord wants is to know something about the inside of a castle of another province, he could send the *shinobi* for that purpose. However, why should [the *ninja*] deceive his allies, which will not achieve fame but lose the true benefits of *ninjutsu*? Even if you display to the lord your ability to infiltrate through your extreme understanding and demonstrate your skills with ease, it will be of no use, as the lord will only see the direct outcome of your actions but not realize what the true underlying principles are. Therefore, you should not serve a foolish lord who does not use the right path from the beginning. This is a principle for all *ninshi* 忍士 or *shinobi* [*no*] *samurai*.[63]

The *Art of War* says, 'If you are not a sage, you cannot use spies properly. If you have neither justice nor benevolence, again, you cannot manage spies properly. If you are not subtle, you cannot discover the truth from the information that spies bring to you.'

With these points in mind, you should think and be aware that *ninjutsu* should not be shown in times of peace, but if the true principles [of *ninjutsu*] are realized, it will enable you to help the lord to govern the country in a time of turbulence. Also, the *ninja* will without fail accomplish amazing achievements.

---

63 The two ideograms here are *ninja* and *samurai*, and the two ways listed are the two possible ways of pronouncing the word. Also, in this context, the warrior here is without question of *samurai* status.

Seishin I

The Correct Mind I

The basic principle of the *shinobi* is to have correct mind in all respects, even though the end results of this art are conspiracy and deception. Therefore, unless you can control your mind in a righteous way, you cannot carry out your tactics in a flexible manner. Confucius says that no man has ever governed himself while his own foundations are confused. What we call Correct Mind is about keeping benevolence, righteousness, loyalty and fidelity in check. Without these factors in mind, you cannot attain any great courageous achievement nor fulfil any tactics required for the circumstances at hand.

Therefore, the Great Learning[1] says, 'If your mind is not present in the "here", you cannot see even if you look, you cannot hear if you listen, or you cannot taste if you eat.' 'Here' means the principles of benevolence, righteousness, loyalty and fidelity. Those who take this path should not neglect their roots nor regard the branches too much.

Zheng Youxian said:
There have been no ancient people who achieved a righteous end, who did not follow the righteous way when going about a great affair. If you utilize power, not by taking advantage of power but by saving the righteous path, what could not be done? Wherever right principles are, there will be justice in the end.

Thus, power itself does not harm but is instead the virtue of a saint. In some military schools this art is called kan 間 *and by some sages it is called power* 権.

Without the help of Yi, King Tang could not have known every evil deed of King Xia. Also, if it were not for Yi in Xia, King Tang's righteous acts would not have

---

1 One of four books in Confucianism.

been fulfilled. *Without Lu, King Wu could not have exercised his virtuous rule.*

Without these two men mentioned above, the kings in question could not have followed heaven's will, and on earth they could not have sympathized with people according to the needs of each, nor have punished the guilty, nor have established a reign. What else could have brought back the way of justice in the end, if they had performed the spying required?

When you study the meaning of these passages, you should be aware that the skills of the *shinobi* should not be used for your own desire or for a lord who does not have a moral code. In the case that you use *ninjutsu* or devise stratagems for your self-interest or to help an unprincipled lord, no matter what schemes you are trying to carry out, they will end up failing, this is without doubt. Even if these deeds manage to escape being detected and benefit you for the time being, it will inevitably turn out to do harm to you in the end. Therefore you should behave carefully.

Here are some *ninja* poems to guide you:

忍トテ道ニ背キシ偸セハ　神ヤ仏ノイカデ守ラン

If a shinobi *steals for his own interest, which is against common morals, how can the gods or Buddha protect him?*

モノノ士ハ常ニ信心イタスヘシ　天ニ背ハイカテヨカラン

A mononofu[2] *should always be religious. How could he be protected if he is against heaven?*

偽モ何カ苦シキ武士ハ　忠アル道ヲセント思ハバ

How could you be ashamed of telling a lie, since you, as a mononofu, *think that faithfulness to your lord is the principal issue?*

Principles for the correct mind

Those who are following this path should appear most gentle and kind-hearted and act right with justice and reason from the bottom of their heart. One writing says that 'a gentle look is the start of a stratagem.' An ancient saying states:

---

2   *Samurai.*

Fan Kuai's anger is like Yang Guifei, who could successfully get through any gate with her smile.

Therefore, you should be able to distinguish the true from the false in other people's speech and tactics and you should never be deceived.

The *Analects* say:
I will not be concerned that others do not know me but will be afflicted if I do not know others.

You should only tell the truth and should not joke or lie or cheat even on a small matter at normal times. If you go against this and your words and deeds are inconsistent, then even when you say the truth, people will say 'he is a liar so we should not use him' and thus they will leave you unused.

One text says, 'Those who do not lie at any time say important things at the time of war.' Yangyou of Tang, who became a general of Jin,[3] once heard that the enemy's general Lu Sun became sick at the front line. As Lu Sun was his old friend, he sent him medicine. Then Lu Sun took it without a slightest doubt. Even though it was given by an old friend, he was the enemy's general, so by right it should have been regarded as a stratagem. However, Yangyou was always so trustful and faithful a person that Lu Sun took it without doubt. If even the enemy's general thought him truthful, imagine how much his own soldiers respected and admired his words and deeds.

Zi-lu[4] was always of deep trustfulness and sincerity. He would always keep a promise, even if it were a promise that was given on the spur of the moment. He did that without any hesitation and kept himself to truth and faith in everything, so that once he started to say something, people held it in high regard, even before he finished saying it.

Therefore, Confucius said, 'Of all my disciples, it seems only Zi-lu can settle a lawsuit with a few words and convince people.'

Once a man named She of Xiao Zhi was going to form an alliance with the Lu Dynasty. However, She said if Zi-lu gave his word, then he would call off the treaty on his advice. Normally, such an alliance would be held above the words of a single man; however, this was possible only because people thought Zi-lu was faithful and sincere without doubt and his word carried such weight. However, truth is not always positive, as in the case of Wei-sheng. Wei-sheng once waited

---

3 A dynasty of ancient China, having two separate periods: the Western Jin (265–316) and the Eastern Jin (317–420).

4 543-480 BC, one of the ten great philosophers of Confucianism.

to meet a woman under a bridge, and even when the tide was coming in he would not leave there and was drowned in the end. He thought he would break his promise if he were waiting on the bridge instead of below it.

Those engaged in this way, at the time of war, should carry out loyalty to the lord as far as they can, hoping only to succeed in great achievements, and know that all depends on if the lord is safe as to whether the dynasty can survive or not, and with this in mind know that you can only fulfil your duty as a vassal by working hard to attain success and then to retire from your position with full honours. If you get involved with unimportant trifles and ruin yourself for your own interest without bearing even the tiniest shame, it should be considered as fief stealing or just a simple man's valour. Therefore, those who get a stipend from their lord should always say the following points to people:

My life is not what I can spend or give as an end at my own will because I have offered it to my lord for the stipend I receive. For this, even if someone tramples or beats me, I will have to bear it like a Buddhist priestess.

I should not do anything against what I have always said in the past; also it is shameful for a samurai *to beat such a person just like when beating a priestess. Therefore you should always tell people not to trample or beat you and you should always tell people the above with an honest mind.*[5]

The *Shiji* manual says that those who are seized with an unimportant duty cannot attain fame and those who hate to bear even a tiny shame cannot achieve great results. Confucius also says that want of forbearance in small matters confounds great plans.

Han Xin was the Marquis of Huaiyin and he liked to wear a sword in his early years. Some boys talked about him and word spread that this boy Han Xin always wore a long sword but that in fact he was actually a coward. So it was decided to humiliate him in the market place and he was challenged to fight or to crawl between the challenger's legs in humiliation. The sword-carrying boy looked up to the sky and crawled between the challenger's legs. People saw him and laughed hard at this. However, Han Xin had high aspirations and he did not want to die because of such a street hoodlum. Later, it turned out that he served Emperor Gao of the Chinese Han Dynasty and became the general of a force of tens of thousands. He was never defeated even when fighting in a small force against a large one and he defeated Xiang Yu of the Great Chu and was appointed as a lord of Qi in the end.

---

5   In English this appears cowardly; however, in Japanese it implies bravery.

Du Mu⁶ wrote in one of his poems, which reflects the above:
'He who can hide disgrace or bear shame, that is a man.'

You should always strictly abstain from alcohol, lust and greed. Never indulge in any of them. These three vices are your enemies, which deprive you of yourself and your better nature. Since ancient times there have been countless people who have indulged in alcohol, sex or greed and ended up giving away a strategy or it having a serious influence on the outcome of things.

One manual says that you should not fail to read the truth behind something by looking only at the surface, nor should you neglect it once you have read it.

The *Analects* of Confucius say that:
If a man takes no thought about what is distant, he will find sorrow near at hand.

Tai Gong said:
For those who are greedy, you should give money to distract them and for those who are lusty, then give pretty women to delude them.

忍
Shinobi – the heart of an iron blade

This chapter is titled 忍 – *shinobi*. While in China, these sets of [espionage] skills are called *kan* 間, *cho* 諜, *saisaku* 細作 and *yutei* 游偵 or even *kansai* 姦細; however, in our country, the ideogram *shinobi* 忍 has been used as it has a deep meaning underlying it. Without realizing the meaning, it is difficult to even step onto this path. Therefore, this chapter is entitled 刃ノ心 *The Heart of an Iron Blade* and discusses the reason why the word *shinobi* 忍 is used.

First of all, the character for *shinobi* 忍 consists of 'blade' 刃 and 'heart' 心. Why was this name used for these skills? It is because the entire system of *ninjutsu* is aimed toward bravery and valour. Therefore, those who have set their mind on this path should single-mindedly try to achieve bravery. To achieve this way you should keep the following in mind: if you do not know the following points, your efforts will be of no use. That is, you should throw away brute courage or blind daring and totally commit to the way through courage of duty. Even though brute courage is, in essence, a form of courage, the courage a wise man should keep in mind is the type that arises from a sense of duty. Brute courage may make you strong or hard out of temporary rage, but it is difficult to keep

---

6 A poet (803–852) of the late Tang Dynasty.

your mind strong and hard deep at the bottom of your heart as the rage calms down. Even if that strength through force gets to the bottom of your mind and makes you work brave and hard, it is just based on hot blood and so in most cases it is no more than your blind rage acting and what you are trying to do is bring others to terms by force alone. As a result, you will not have foresight nor be ready to defend yourself fully, and you will only destroy yourself and will not ruin the enemy to any significant level. Think of ancient people. Has anyone who had brute courage ever been able to succeed in getting out of trouble and destroying an entire enemy?

That is why Zhong Ni (a pseudonym of Confucius) and Zi-lu both object to being impetuous. They say you should not align yourself with anyone who has no fear of dying as a result of doing something stupid, like attacking a tiger unarmed or crossing a river without a boat. You should take sides with those who have reasonable fear when on the verge of an emergency and those who prefer secret plans as a measure for success. Those who learn this path should know this in detail.

In contrast to the above raging and hot courage, the courage of duty is what you are compelled to have to complete your function and obligations. This kind of courage never gets weak, never, and since it is detached from motive, you can have control over your desire or greed, and make decisions in response to the situation. If you fight to the fullest with the knowledge that you will survive only if you are highly determined to die – through the courage required during your duty – then you will be able to escape death and kill the enemy. According to a military proverb, 'Softness overcomes hardness and weakness overcomes strength.'

To have courage of duty, there is a certain way you need to follow. Unless you fully want to know and follow with action, benevolence, righteousness, loyalty and fidelity, you will not be able to have such courage. As there is so much to learn on the issues of righteousness, loyalty and fidelity as well as benevolence, I would like to write only the outline to give a start for first-time learners on this path.

Benevolence is a principle for being gentle and affectionate. The mind is rich and warm, gentle, compassionate and charitable to everything. However, if you kill a criminal with the intention of saving thousands of people by cutting down one man, it can be considered benevolence. As benevolence is essential to mankind, it can be interpreted that a man without benevolence should not be regarded as a human being. It is benevolent as well to be graceful when receiving favours and to be filial to your parents.

Righteousness is the guiding principle for decisions, so it changes according to the situation and what you perform is dependent on the reason appropriate for the time and the place. Alongside this, righteousness is about a sense of shame. If a man is diligently serving his lord even when that lord has his back against the wall, or if a man is willing to fight to die for his lord when his life is in danger, it is all owing to righteousness. However, there are those deeds that resemble righteousness but are not in truth righteous. Righteousness changes according to reason and situation, but it is not righteous to indulge your desires or to find courage only for selfish reasons or an unprincipled cause. Righteousness should be carried out according to the reason of the situation, but it is not righteous, for example, to commit robbery when you are in poverty, and then to make the excuse that it makes sense in the situation. This looks like righteousness but it is not. Also, though righteousness has much to do with having a sense of shame, it is not righteous to be ashamed of what you do not have to be ashamed of. With a righteous mind, you should serve your lord single-mindedly and die in battle for the lord, but it is not righteous to serve an outrageous lord and to die for him. It is like in the case of Zi-lu, who served an outrageous lord who was the Duke Wen of Wei, and thus Zi-lu later died in battle because of this.

Originally, military tactics, swordsmanship and any kind of art to kill others were about defeating an unprincipled but powerful man. Think then, how can it be possible to take the side of an outrageous and unprincipled man and help him with skills if the skills in question were originally devised to defeat such men?

Question: *No matter how unreasonable your lord is, if you are serving that lord, and a life-or-death situation arises concerning him, people will call you a coward if you don't die for him then and there. What should you do in such a case?*

Answer: You should not serve such an unprincipled lord from the beginning. If you have come to serve him without knowing that he is immoral, you should quit immediately upon finding this fact out. Then how could it happen that you should die for an unreasonable lord?

Question: *What if the unprincipled lord interferes with your request to serve a new master?*

Answer: According to Confucius, an unprincipled lord will stay that way all his life and remain firm in his way. With this teaching in mind, you should look up to Bo-Yi or Shu Qi as your guide. Unless you are determined like this, you cannot follow the correct way of the *shinobi*. Further details are to be transmitted orally. Ancient people say life or death depends on your own destiny and hardships are opportunity driven. Those who resent heaven's will do not know their destiny and those who resent poverty do not know their position [and place appointed by heaven[7]].

Loyalty is to devote your mind entirely to your lord. For example, to serve your lord, you should give yourself into the hands of your lord, serve him whole-heartedly and not leave anything for yourself. Loyalty could be considered at its best when you have no fear of death or if you lose your family for your lord and pay no attention to your feelings or affections. The views of loyalty should be shared between parents and children, brothers, husband and wife and friends as well. However, as the ideogram for loyalty means a balanced mind, it cannot be considered loyalty if you devote yourself to anything without keeping these basic principles at the core of your thoughts.

Fidelity means having only truth but nothing false or wrong in the mind. If you pretend to be true-hearted but are wrong or have half-truths deep in your heart, it is not fidelity. Fidelity is a principle of earth, in terms of the Chinese doctrine of the Five Elements. As every season has a *doyo* period,[8] benevolence, righteousness or loyalty should have fidelity within them. Without fidelity inside, then these elements will not be as they should be.

These four principles listed above are not what you should seek for from the outside of oneself. People are naturally endowed with the principles of the Five Elements, thus they have them provided in their bodies and embedded in mind as it is nature and all is found within.

In heaven there are *principles* while in humans there is *nature*.

The above *natures* are given to the stupid as well as to the saintly and wise, in exactly the same way. However, while the wise and able are right-minded and are very familiar with principles, the stupid and those who are not right-minded know nothing about these principles. Why is this so? It is so because as the wise and able act according to what is righteous, which is given from heaven, they are right-minded and principled. Whereas the stupid act according to their self-interest and desire, which are encouraged by the six sense organs of the eyes, the ears, the nose, the tongue, the body and the mind; therefore, they are gloomy and not principled. Though a man's mind and heart[9] are simply his mind and heart, there are in fact two types of this central being: there is *jinshin* 人心, which is the mind of man, and there is *doshin* 道心, which is the mind of principles and

---

7 Literally 'time' but in context means 'their placement by heaven'.

8 With reference to the lunar calendar, this was the eighteen days before the first day of each of the four seasons and it was considered a period governed by the element of earth.

9 Here the ideogram is simply 心 which translates as 'heart', but it means a man's character, as in the English, 'in the heart of a man'. Therefore, it has been translated as 'mind and heart'.

is understood as having an affinity to what is right.

The mind of man is easily affected by what the eye sees, worries about what the ear hears, is absorbed in what the nose smells, indulges in the five tastes the tongue tastes and allows the body to give in to lust. It gives way to the selfish desires of the six sense organs and no matter if the action is on any path of righteousness, people will do anything to satisfy their self-interest at a particular time. That is exactly what the mind of man is. If you depend on the mind of man, it will turn out that you will ruin yourself, no matter how good it seems at first. In the end all will be a total failure.

An ancient poem speaks of this mind:

身ヲ思フ心ト中ヲタガハスハ身ニハ心ガアタトナルモノ

If you do not throw away your concern about yourself, your mind will do harm to you in the end.

Comments on the above poem:

To worry about yourself will be to do harm to yourself. This is because it offends heavenly principles.

A stupid man prays to the gods or the Buddha while he himself offends against heavenly principles and, therefore, that prayer will not be fulfilled.

Confucius says that a man who offends against heaven has no one to whom he can pray. Shu Zhu says heaven means principles and this is incomparably sacred. What is the meaning of the above words? It means, those in a high seat in power are nothing compared with the principles of heaven and if you offend against these principles, then you have no one to whom you can pray. How could you escape punishment by praying hard while in fact playing up to and financially eliciting the help of people in power? 'God'[10] dwells in an honest heart, so how could 'God' accept such discourtesy? Those with the mind of principle will not give heed to anything unrighteous and if they see lust in someone's eyes, or if they hear others they will let it pass, they do not do anything which is not righteous itself or not respectful and will not indulge in negativity. If you do not pay attention to your own desire, despite your self-interest, and follow your righteous nature, and have no selfishness, then it can be said that, in this way, you act with the mind of principle.

When you are consistent with heavenly principles it means you have taken a

---

10 In Japanese, the term is 'gods' with a lower case 'g'. However, for an English-speaking, predominantly Christian, audience the term 'God' has been used. In short, it means 'correctness'.

pledge with the gods and the Buddha. Kitano Tenjin[11] left the following poem:

心タニ誠ノ道二叶ナハ祈ラストテモ神ヤマモラン

*If your mind is singularly in accord with the way of principles, the
gods and the Buddha will protect you, even if you do not pray.*

No one is without flesh and blood, thus a wise and able man also has [the lower
mind, which is] the mind of man. On the other hand, no one is not provided with
heavenly ways; therefore, even a stupid man has the [higher] mind of principles.
Hence, whether it is the sages or not, the stupid or the incompetent, without
any difference, all people have in their mind an amalgamation of the mind of
principles and the mind of man.

Those who are going to learn the path of *kan* (spying) should carefully observe
their own mind whenever their mind is engaged in an activity and at every opportunity. This is done to find out if it is the mind of principles or the mind of man,
which will allow them to control their mind strictly so that the mind of man will
not interfere with the mind of principles. Remember that you should always try
to make sure that the mind of principles is always your lord in all things, and to
make the mind of man listen to and obey what the mind of principles instructs
or prohibits. That way, the mind of selfish desires will diminish gradually and
the precious mind of principles will come out as clearly as the moon comes out
from behind the clouds. Therefore, when you penetrate yourself into the way of
benevolence, righteousness, loyalty and fidelity, your mind should be nothing
but patient and in a state of self-restraint as in the ideogram for *shinobi* 忍.

When your mind represents the ideogram *shinobi* 忍 and is all patient, it is
even more undisturbed by external factors, so that you will not be perturbed by
anything and have a courage of righteousness. Furthermore, when the mind is
clear, like crystal, and if you can accord yourself to an opportunity with ease,
then no matter what the situation is, there will be nothing that prevents you from
getting into the enemy's castle or position and accomplishing a great achievement, no matter how firmly a place is guarded.

In ancient China during the reign of the Qin Dynasty, there were two lords
named Zhaodun and Zhibo, who were fighting against each other for the dynasty
of Zhao for an extended period of time. One time Zhibo was seized by Zhaodun's
force. It seemed that he could not help but be killed as a result of his capture so

---

11 Tenjin is the spirit name of Sugawara no Michizane. He was a scholar and a highly ranked
    government official in the ninth century. In 901 he fell into the trap of a rival aristocrat and
    was exiled as an official in remote Kyushu and died in loneliness. People in later times deified
    him as a god of scholarship to appease his angry spirit.

he summoned his two retainers Cheng-ying and Chujiu and said:

My time is running out now. When dawn comes, I am to be killed without fail. You two have served me with sincere loyalty. Therefore, I would like you to get out of the castle tonight, shelter my three-year-old child and when he becomes a man, ruin Zhaodun to revenge the humiliation I have been given before my death.

After hearing this, they said:

It is easy for us to be killed in battle with you, my Lord, as your retainers, whereas it is very difficult to shelter and bring up a three-year-old child and to survive. However, to keep our principles as retainers, how could we choose the easier way and abandon the difficulty? We will follow your order by any means that we can, my lord.

Then they escaped from the castle under the cover of night, and when dawn broke Zhibo was killed. Few of his soldiers were left and thus the dynasty of Zhao was finally overthrown by Zhaodun after many years of fighting. Meanwhile, Cheng-ying and Chujiu were trying to hide Zhibo's child, but Zhaodun knew of this and attempted to kill the child again and again. Then after a while, Cheng-ying asked Chujiu:

Our late lord entrusted his three-year-old son to us. Here is a question. Which of the following choices is more difficult: to beguile the enemy by death or to survive to shelter and support the child?

Chujiu replied:

Death is a choice made when aiming for justice, while on the other hand life is to live, struggling with hard work and pushes you to the edge of your wisdom. Therefore, I think to live is more difficult.

Cheng-ying then said:

If so, shall I choose the more difficult one, to survive, and you can take the easier way of being killed?

Chujiu readily agreed with this and they devised a stratagem. Their plan was [for Chujiu] to show his *own* three-year-old son, here and there and in his arms in public, proclaiming the falsehood that his own son was in fact his lord's child. While at the same time, Cheng-ying was raising their lord's true child in secrecy, pretending that he was his own son.

Chujiu was hiding deep in the mountains, while Cheng-ying went to Zhaodun to offer his false surrender. However, the enemy Zhaodun did not believe him or accept his surrender. So Cheng-ying said the following:

I served Zhibo as a vassal and saw his behaviour and now I have realized he deserved to lose the dynasty of Zhao. Opposed to this, I have heard about your virtue, you are better than him by far. So with all due respect I would like to serve you and make you a virtuous lord for our people, who are without a country. If you allow me to serve you as a vassal, I will tell you exactly where the three-year-old child of our late lord is hidden and cared for by Chujiu. You should kill the child and then the dynasty of Zhao will be stable for ever.

When Zhaodun heard this, he believed that Cheng-ying had in fact surrendered and truly wanted to join his vassals. He then gave him rank as a martial officer and bade him work as a close aide.

Next, he asked him exactly where Chujiu and the child were hidden and sent there thousands of his men to capture them. Then as Chujiu had prearranged beforehand, he stabbed and killed the three-year-old child, who was young enough to sit on someone's lap, and cried:

Our late lord Zhibo's son has come to his fate, and the conspiracy has been shown.

He then committed suicide through disembowelment. Zhaodun was pleased with the outcome, thinking nobody would threaten the future of his descendents. From then on he trusted Cheng-ying all the more for this event, gave him a large fief and a high rank and allowed him to take charge of politics. Consequently, the bereaved child of the lord Zhibo successfully became a man where he was hidden in Cheng-ying's family. At which point Cheng-ying raised an army immediately to destroy Zhaodun and the lord's child won back the Zhao Dynasty. Since this great achievement could never have been attained if it were not Cheng-ying's plan, the new king of Zhao praised him and offered him a large fief. However, he would not accept it, saying:

If I enjoyed the position and fief and remained alive, it would be against the principle on which Chujiu and I made all these stratagems.

Then, on the grave where Chujiu's body was buried, he killed himself with his own sword and was buried in the same grave covered by moss, together with Chujiu.

These two people can be called true and brave warriors of justice, they who act on principles. That is what a *ninja* should be. Because with only simple brute courage, which acts and is dependent on the mind of man, how could it be possible to attain such an achievement as in the above episode? It is not possible. Those who continue on my path should look up to Cheng-ying and Chujiu as their mentors.

Seishin II

The Correct Mind II

This chapter is titled 'Of Life and Death'. It is said that for *samurai* warriors the most important concept is the 'two word' idiom, life and death 生死, and this is because if warriors do not abandon the life-or-death issue, they will stick only to visible phenomena and thus cannot achieve utmost bravery. Therefore, warriors should detach themselves from the life-and-death matter without fail, hence the title of this chapter. Thinking more deeply on this matter, even if you have these two ideograms in mind, but do not realize when or where you should determine yourself to die, then it is tremendously shameful, and again we arrive at the title 'Of Life and Death'. Be aware that there are true and false ways to understand this. If you talk about the issue but do not deeply contemplate it in your mind or act in accordance with the principle, then you do not know any more than a parrot knows.

In the issue of detaching yourself from life or death, you should realize the root of your mind. If you want to know the root of your mind, you should first know the root of everything in the universe and the origin of your mind and body. To know what it is, you should be aware of the primary principle[1] in the universe. The primary principle has no shape and is emptiness, so it cannot be seen or taken in your hand but since the dawn of time and until doomsday, without flourishing or diminishing, it fills everywhere in the universe between heaven and earth, so there is nowhere it cannot reach. This certainly exists and though it cannot be taken in your hand or seen, it is there without doubt.

---

1 Throughout this chapter Fujibayashi talks of the primary principle 理 or the 'one' or 'oneness', and it must be stressed here that this is not the Christian or Western concept of a single orchestrating presence in the universe, but is in fact an Onmyodo concept and therefore a reader should come from that mindset. In short and cutting out the complexities, simply understand it as the essence of the universe.

Therefore, unless you see with the inward eye, it cannot be found. The wise know the principle of emptiness while common mortals do not. When this principle is felt and moved, it then changes to the 'one *chi*' 一気, which forms the flow of energy. When the flow begins to move, it is called *yo* (*yang*), and when it finishes moving and is quiet, it is called *in* (*yin*). The sun is composed of the energy of *yo* while the moon emits the energy of *in* and *yo*. Time is divided into five kinds of *chi*: wood, fire, earth, metal and water. They are called the Five Elements 五行. Wood and fire are *yo* while metal and water are *in*. However, earth is *in* but belongs to *yo* at the same time. The *chi* in each of the Five Elements generates or destroys the *chi* in the other elements and forms a yearly cycle. Thus, it is warm and pastoral in spring, as it is of the wood phase, fierce and intense in summer, as it is of the fire phase; in autumn it is windy and is of the metal phase, so that leaves turn gold, all the way to their stems and fall from the branch in the end. In winter it is the water phase; it is frosty, snowy and cold. Seventy-two days are allotted to each of these four seasons.

Doyo 土用 is the name of an eighteen-day period after each season; thus *doyo* adds up to another seventy-two days each year. The above five phases of the seasons add up to 360 days and rotate every year.[2] The earth itself is located in the centre of all directions, and so the *doyo* period that comes at the end of summer is the centre of the year and thus should be considered the most important. At this time the temperature reaches an extreme and is the hottest and most humid section of the whole year.

Just as the sea is filled with water, the Five Elements prevail everywhere in the universe. They have nowhere they cannot be, even in a tiny grain of foxtail millet or within a huge rock. The Five Elements make it cloudy, rainy, snowy or windy, they bring about earthquakes, thunder and lightning, rainbows and all other wondrous phenomena. All these occurrences are manifested by [the cycle of] either generation or destruction that occurs within the system of the Five Elements. Everything in the universe comes into being when the Five Elements are united in harmony with each other.

People are different from each other in a myriad of ways, yet originally are [made of] the Five Elements, which are born from the principle. Therefore, as human beings are born from the same principle, each individual being/body is merely a part of a whole being/body. It is just as water changes itself into snow, frost, rain, dew, fog, hail, or ice. They all look different but, when thawing, they all dissolve into water. Just like this, every part [of the body] is related to all the Five Elements. However, basically, the flesh of the body is of the earth element

---

2   That is to say that the four seasons and the seventy-two days of *doyo* add up to a full year.

and that which is moist in the body is of the water phase, that which is warm in the body is of fire and what is firm in the body is of metal. The elements that control each organ of your body are as follows[3]:

- Liver, gall bladder, eyes, tendons, nails – Wood
- Heart, small intestine, tongue, blood, hair – Fire
- Kidney, urinary bladder, ears, bones, teeth – Water
- Lungs, large intestine, nose, skin, breath – Metal
- Spleen, stomach, mouth, muscles, breast milk[4] – Earth

Mingmen 命門 is the right kidney and is of the water phase while, as for the 'triple burner',[5] details should be taught by word of mouth. The twelve standard meridians and fifteen channels are all under control of the five viscera and six entrails[6] so that they are related to the Five Elements.

As the Five Elements are taking shape, the heavenly principle develops. When it is endowed to people, it is called nature; when in heaven, it is called principles. This is understood by thinking that while in the area of Naniwa, reeds are known as *ashi* while they are called *hamaogi* in the area of Ise. The same thing is referred to with different names in different places. If something moves nature and thus triggers a feeling, it is called emotion. Nature and emotion are one at the root, just like people call it water when it is still, while calling the same thing waves when in motion. Emotion manifests itself in the five forms of benevolence, righteousness, propriety, wisdom and fidelity. Benevolence is of the wood phase, righteousness of the water[7] phase, propriety of the fire phase, wisdom of the metal phase and fidelity of the earth. As above, you should be aware that every part of everyone's body and mind has the Five Elements and the principle. The human mind and its workings are a product of the Five Elements and therefore the Five Elements are what the human mind and body are. The principles of the Five Elements are referred to as the principles of heaven and the *chi* of the Five Elements is referred to as forms of heaven.[8] Even on the path of heaven, there is nothing that does not belong to the Five Elements.

---

3 This section requires an understanding of Chinese medicine and space is not available to explain this in full.

4 Or 'milk-giving breast'.

5 The triple burner has various translations and according to traditional Chinese medicine is the idea of three areas in the body that regulate energy.

6 This is a concept in traditional Chinese medicine known as *zang fu*. *Zang* refers to the *in* organs: heart, liver, spleen, lungs and kidney; and *fu* refers to the *yo* organs: small and large intestines, gall bladder, urinary bladder, stomach and triple burner.

7 The text says metal twice. This is believed to be a transcription error.

8 In short, the final section rounds up the connection between the origin and the human and the great journey or path that is existence.

You should know that heaven and your body and mind are but one thing. Therefore, when you pledge any of your deeds or words to the principles, it is as if you pledge this promise to heaven. So, if you go against the principles, it is the same as if you go against heaven.

Xing-li-da-quan says that:

Heaven is a principle and human is also a principle. The principles cycle and make one together with heaven. The self is not the self but is a principle. Principle is not a principle but is heaven.

In heaven and on earth the Five Elements are found in the concept of *in* and *yo*, spring is followed by summer, summer by autumn, autumn by winter, then spring comes again. Everything is born, then grows up; when having grown up, it changes; when having changed, then it is settled; when settled, it then stores or conceals itself; then it is born again, just like a ring without end. Therefore, nothing continues to exist in the world forever but nothing ceases to exist forever simultaneously. When it dies, it only goes back to the Five Elements.

As evidence of this, think of when a man dies. Water found in the body turns back to water as it was, the body becomes dry, fire or heat turns back to fire again as the body gets cold with no heat emitting any more, metal turns back to metal so the body loses its strength, shrinks and does not function. After that, whether cremated or buried, it goes back to earth. The *chi* that connected the body will scatter and the bonds of nature will break down. You should be aware that your body will return to the Five Elements, the Five Elements return to *in* and *yo*, *in* and *yo* will return to the 'one *chi*' 一気 and the 'one *chi*' reaches the principle that is the core[9] of the universe itself. The principle then starts the cycle from the beginning, just like a ring and it has no end. Therefore, the principle of emptiness appears as the 'one *chi*', then as *in* and *yo*, and next as the Five Elements, just as water changes to snow or ice. The Five Elements temporarily take the image of a human being but it is not a complete life but is in fact life in non-life, and even though the body appears to die, it is not a complete death but death in non-death. Primarily, when you die, you will return to the principle of emptiness. Therefore, once you penetrate this principle completely, you will understand what looks like birth or death is in fact not birth or death in the true sense. Also births and deaths are repeated for eternity while there is actually no change occurring at all. This whole cycle should be left to nature and follows the turns of fate. If you keep the principle in mind and penetrate it, you will discover the very origin of the Great Path, which is a very deep esoteric truth and you will reach the status of 'no-birth' and 'no-death'. Common mortals who are confused

---

9 Not the centre but the central 'element' which forms the universe.

and fall do not know how this principle works.[10] They think that you live a substantial life, while in fact it is only temporary and 'life' is only the place where the Five Elements have taken shape as a human, and also, they assume that the body belongs to them though in fact it belongs to the Five Elements. Because of this, people hold on to their life and indulge themselves; or they think that death is a complete end, while it is in fact just a returning to the Five Elements, and they grieve and worry about it deeply. Thus people think birth and death are substantial, but of course they are not, and also that various aspects [of life] are real, while of course they are not, so people have doubt, hate to die, love to live and are therefore greedy by nature. People with doubt in mind, once facing the enemy, no matter how much they usually consider themselves loyal and brave, will be cowards in reality, forgetting all about their loyalty and act in opposition to the way they usually are or pretend to be. This is because they forget their intentions at normal times but act on their mind's inner intentions [in times of crisis]. That being so, they cannot achieve the true aim of a *samurai* but instead bring disgrace upon their name forever and thus will be laughed at by people for all eternity. Besides this, their family as well will be dishonoured. How could you have mercy on them? How could you have pity on them?

To live or to die is decided by heaven at the moment when you come into being, inside of your mother's womb. At the moment of conception it is determined according to whether the timing is good or not and whether the generating and overcoming cycles of the Five Elements are going in a proper order or not. Therefore, if you keep moving forward without fear of death, you may not die, while if you like to live too much and hate to die and run away through fear for your life, you may not survive. Thus, whether to advance or retreat does not matter as you will survive according to heaven's discretion, so why would you not take the chance to live by advancing, than trying to survive by running away? Likewise, suppose that if you are destined to die, why would you not make advances to the front and die instead of running away? In the same way, if it is your destiny that determines if you achieve fame, it would be better to do that in the vanguard rather than in the rear guard. Therefore, Confucius says that death and life have their determined appointment and that riches and honours depend on heaven. This means that whether you survive or die is determined by heaven when your life first sprouts inside your mother's womb. However, human affairs occur on the earth while the principles belong to heaven, so even though your path is marked out at the very beginning of your

---

10 The main point here is that 'life' or existence is eternal and that once you master the idea that your body is the manifestation of the principle of the universe in movement, then life and death no longer have any meaning.

life, if you do not do anything to preserve your health, take no precautions, or have no art of living but just sit back inattentively and leave all to heaven's will, you will die an unprincipled death and without fail. If you sow in the second or third month of the lunar calendar and re-bed, fertilize, and water plants in the fourth or fifth month, then weed, and guard the crops so that cows, horses, deer or such animals cannot feast, then it will yield a crop in the ninth or tenth month due to the natural course of things. Things are destined to be from the beginning of life and you should just grow and keep the mandate of heaven. If you do not take care, water, weed, fortify or fence against animals which eat crops, but do nothing, just saying it will be fine as it is determined by heaven, how could the crop hold out until the bleak season of the ninth or tenth month? The life of a man is just like this. It is commonly known how to take guard or to take care in normal times in order to die a natural and principled death in the twilight years of your life, so there is no need to mention it here. However, in an emergency situation, nothing is better than giving up sheltering yourself and to think that you are sure to die. Once you determine your mind that you are sure to die, it might allow you to survive the difficulty. Wu-zi says that if you are prepared to die, then this allows you to survive. Opposed to this, if you guard yourself with a mind to preservation, it will turn out that you will die anyway. Wu-zi also says that 'if you put your life above all, you are sure to die.'

This principle absolutely holds true not only for the path of *shinobi* but for all arts of war, be it *gunpo* military ways, *kenjutsu* swordsmanship, the art of the spear and so on, or even when you jump off a cliff or leap a ditch. This is because when you give yourself up to heaven's path and have an iron will, free from the 'three misgivings'[11] and give no attention to your life, you will be free from thinking or reasoning and have no indecisiveness and extinguish all earthly thoughts from your mind. Your mind will be clear and settled and determined, so that you would have the insight to tell the true essence of things with clarity, just as a mirror reflects things perfectly. Then you will not be disturbed by anything from outside and have no fear of the menace which lies in front of you. That would allow you to be free from all ideas and all thoughts and come to be aware of yourself. As a result, you would be able to change your way or take measures appropriate to the occasion in accordance with the principles, just like a ball rolls on a board or as a calabash floats on water [and adapts to its environment]. Consequently, you can win without seeking for victory, or survive a difficult situation even though you may have died. Alongside this, you will achieve such bravery that your name might be known to the world. Kukai wrote

---

11 From the *Shiji* manual: 'Forget your house when you are given an order to go to war, forget your parents when you go to war, and forget yourself when you are given the signal to fight.'

a poem that states, 'If you have a sword in your spirit to cut off your doubt, any dream may be realized in your life.' If you try to protect yourself to survive, you will have an indecisive mind from thinking and reasoning. Your mind will be inattentive, easily shocked and not stable so that you cannot have a clear idea of the way of things. That makes you more concerned with things from the outside and gives you fear of the menace in front of you. Consequently, you will be upset and hesitate, lose full control of your limbs, go pale, not speak properly, so that if you are on a *shinobi* mission, your tactics will often give themselves away, or you will lose in a battle. You should be fully aware of this.

The mind is just like water or a mirror. Water or a mirror does not move itself but is still and serene. However, it is stained by dust or dirt from outside, or moved by wind or men. It then loses its stillness and serenity and does not reflect anything truly, if anything should stand in front of it. This is how the 'original' mind is. If it is clear and stable, then it reflects exactly whether the one in front of you is right or wrong, good or evil, just like a mirror or water reflects in this way. There is nothing which cannot be reflected clearly. However, if any of the six kinds of impurity – shape/form, voice, smell, taste, feel and 'things which influence the mind'[12] – connects with the six senses,[13] through the six sense organs of eyes, ears, nose, tongue, body and mind, then the mind will be corrupt, unsettled and unclear, so that it cannot reflect anything clearly, just like muddy water or a dull mirror. The truth here is that you have an enemy and an ally nowhere else but in your own mind. Penetrate this principle thoroughly, so you will always be true to yourself. If you are committed to the principles completely, you will never fail to infiltrate when on your *shinobi* mission or once having infiltrated to achieve great bravery.

Poems which prove the ancient sages had no fear of death:

過去ヨリモ未来ヘワタル一ヤスミ雨降ハフレ風吹バ吹ケ

Now we are in a break between the past and the future,[14] let it rain or let the wind blow as it does and take everything as it comes.

Ikkyu[15] 一休

---

12 Literally 'law' 法 – the point here is that both lists match and this means any impurity that affects the mind.

13 The text says 'six colours' 六色, which is most likely an error and is thought to be 六識, which is a Buddhist term referring to senses of the past which have come to you via the six sense organs. In short, any dependency on the external world is a negative aspect.

14 In the original poem, it says 'between the world of earthly passions and the world of enlightenment'.

15 A famous Japanese Zen Buddhist priest, poet and painter (1394–1481).

借ヲキシ五ツノ物ヲ四ツ帰シ今ハ空ニゾヲモムキニケリ

Out of the five things I borrowed from heaven, I have returned four.[16]
Now I am on my way into the void.

Ikkyu一休

今マデハ生ラルル程生ニケリ　死ナルル程ニ今ハ死ニケリ

I have lived while I can so far. Now I will die while I can.

Ikkyu一休

生レケル其暁ニ死ニケレハ今日ノ夕ベハ松風ノ音

We were all born to die at last; it is like we hear the wind rustling over
the pine trees at the end of this day.

Ninagawa Shinemon[17] 蜷川新右衛門

カカル時サコソ命ノヲシカラメ兼テ無身ト思シラスハ

On such an opportunity you must value your life? [Dokan's reply:]
Not at all, as I have fully realized that my life is not mine to value.

Ota Dokan[18] 太田道灌

The above verse was written when in battle and when the enemy attacked Dokan
at spear point. As the enemy knew that Dokan liked to make verses, the enemy
said the first line. To this, Dokan responded with the second line on the spot [as
seen above].

露ノ身ノ消テモ消ヌ置所草葉ノホカニ又モ有ケリ

Life is as fragile as dewdrops but it will remain somewhere else even
after it floats away, other than in the grave.

Choshu[19] 聴杢

---

16 Earth, water, fire, and wind, which consist in the body.
17 A famous poet from the Muromachi period (?–1448).
18 A famous general and poet (1432–1486).
19 Iseno Sadachika (1417–1473), high-ranking politician of the Muromachi shogunate.

心ニモ任セサリケル命ニテタノメモヲカシ常ナラヌ世ニ

As life is that which you cannot decide, even a desperate situation may be interesting in the uncertainty of this life world.

Fujiwara no Motozane[20] 藤原元真

An explanation of the poems above:

Even an emperor is pathetically not free from his worries as a human and thus has no benefit [in this world] so, remember this, once you are born, there is nothing better than leaving this world and this is even more true for the mean and poor of this life, which, of course, goes without saying. Therefore, death should be congratulated, as death is a happy occasion and means that you will return to your *true* home and will finally be at ease. Those who are not aware that you will be at ease tend to worry about it or mourn death – how uneducated they are.

Those who rise above the life and death issues will pay as little attention to the boundary between life and death as a herd boy casually walking in the nearby mountains who blows his whistle even while all around him is in panic.

Once upon a time, there was a thief who had a son. The son thought that he had not learned how to steal correctly and wondered how he could live on stealing after his father died. Then he asked his father to teach him how to steal perfectly. The father thief answered that he would teach him. On that night they got into a house and the father opened a *nagamochi* large oblong chest and took treasure from inside, then he told his son to get in the now empty chest. His son did as his father told him and the father closed the chest and locked him inside. Then the father ran away with what he took, and what is even worse, he even cried out, 'Stop thief, stop thief'. The house master was woken up by this cry and found the thief gone already. Without knowing that he already was robbed, he went to sleep again. The son in the chest wondered why his father did this to him. He thought if he could not manage to get out that night, he would never have a chance again. After trying to find a way out, he thought out an idea and began making a loud noise like a rat gnawing. The house master noticed this and woke up the others to see what was going on. Someone said that there must be a rat in the chest and opened it without much care. At that point the son sprang from inside pushing the one who opened it over and ran away. While they followed him saying, 'Stop the thief', he came across a well where he took a deep breath and found and threw a big stone into the well and ran away. Because of this, the

---

20 A famous poet of the tenth century.

house-staff were perplexed thinking that he fell into the well while in fact the thief had managed to get back home. When he arrived home he asked his father why he left him and told him how he got out of there. His father listened and said that he had succeeded in the theft in the true sense of the word.

As you can see, because the father threw away his son, the son realized his father's intention and was prepared to give himself up [to fate] and put his life on the line by being caught or making good his escape. As he cast aside his worry about himself and put his life on the line, he succeeded in knocking down the man who was beside the chest. The lesson here is that it is your indecisive mind, which comes from thinking and reasoning, that gives you doubt. By throwing this away, you will become your true self, so that you can see reality very clearly and good ideas will come according to the occasion. That is why he could manage to get out of the troublesome situation.

Wang Zhene'e of Tang commanded a fleet with thousands of people to defeat the Qin Dynasty. They sailed all the way by way of warship to the region of Qin. When they arrived at Qingqiao of Qin and came ashore, he had his men leave the provisions and clothing on the ships and took out only their armour and weapons. They went up the mountain and he cast off the ships and left them to the command of the wind at night. After that Zhene'e said to his army, 'The ships, oars, clothes and provisions have all gone. Our home of Changan castle is too far over the ocean. Now unless we advance and fight to win, we will not be able to go back to our country again.' On hearing this, even cowards became brave warriors with desperate courage. They completely gave up their indecisive mind but rushed forward and won an overwhelming victory over the great country of Qin.

Long ago, some man of great bravery said:

When you are going to fight, you should always take out the sword hilt rivet of your wakizashi *short sword [so that it cannot be drawn in an emergency]. In this way if you take the rivet off, you will win the fight without fail. If you do not remove it, you will not be able to win.*

If you think of why he said this, you will notice that this is exactly what the core principle found inside the ideogram for *shinobi* 忍 means.[21]

Question: Now with the Confucian and Buddhist secret teachings, you state and are determined that you should not fear or hate death. Alongside this, you mention

---

21 The point here is that a *samurai* should fight with a long sword and use his short sword as back up, but by taking out the rivet in the hilt you can no longer draw the sword, making you fight with all your heart and perseverance. This is what the ideogram for *shinobi* means, to do things wholeheartedly and with faith and perseverance.

what ancient people said or did and are fully aware of these points, deep in your heart. However, while you know that very well, people sometimes lose their nerve. How can we avoid it?

Answer: That is the rust of your mind and you should polish yourself day after day. You should thoroughly comprehend the principles of the way of *in* and *yo* instead of having a vague understanding.

As a year has spring and winter, in spring trees and plants grow while in winter they conceal themselves, the sun and the moon rise and set, a day has day and night, the man wakes or sleeps, lives or dies. Spring is *yo* and of life, while winter is *in* and of death. Also, moonrise is *yo* while sunset or moonset is *in* and a man's waking state is *yo* while sleeping is *in*. This means that to live is *yo* while to die is *in*. If you hate and fear to die young, why would you not hate or dread winter to come, or the sun and the moon to set, night to fall or a man to sleep? As sleep is a small part of *in*, so death is a large form of *in*. What is the reason you hate only death but do not hate to sleep? You should be ready to die with nothing to fear.

Shochi I

A Guideline for Commanders I

About *ninpo*[1] – the *shinobi* treasure

If it were not for the great horse-judge Bo-le,[2] we would not have a horse that can run one thousand *ri*. Even a most excellent horse cannot run as far as one thousand *ri* if an ordinary man rides him. Even a falcon or a giant bird,[3] when flying against the wind, cannot fly at speed and even a huge fish which can swim in a vast river as it pleases could not be as good as sharks or trout when hindered by a small stream. Likewise, *shinobi no mono* who have achieved mastery should not serve an unprincipled general. If you work for an unprincipled lord, nothing will turn out as you wish, so that you will not be able to attain great achievements when on *shinobi* missions.

In the *Three Strategies of Huang Shigong* the wise do not make plans for an obtuse ruler. If one who has mastery of tactics meets a good general, it will be as Bo-le recognizing a fine horse and treasuring it. Or like Wang Liang and Han Ai, who once managed well-known fine horses with the greatest of expertise, so that they achieved the perfect accord with the horse and could ride it as far as one thousand *ri*.

---

1 This is not the same as the *ninpo* that is commonly used, as this version is constructed with the ideograms 忍寶 – *shinobi*-treasure.
2 A legendary Chinese judge of horses in the period of the Zhou Dynasty. Today, the word means generally a person with a first-class ability to recognize and develop talent.
3 This Japanese word means any kind of big bird that flies fast, such as a swan, crane or stork.

With a good general, a *shinobi no mono* can carry out what he wishes to do and obtain a successful result with ease, and build up momentum without difficulty, just like a falcon or a giant bird flying before the wind or a big fish swimming around in a vast river in a grand manner.

Similarly, if a general and a *shinobi* are perfect for each other and the *shinobi* is free to act as he needs, how could it be possible that he could not get into the strongest fortification? Sun Tzu says it is the enlightened lord and the capable general who are able to use the most intelligent ones from within their ranks, to be deployed as spies, so they can achieve the greatest and most complete victories in war. Thus it is apparent that it is essential for a lord or general to employ *shinobi*, hence this chapter is titled 'Shochi 将知 A Guideline for Commanders'.

Shinobi no ri 忍利

The benefits of using *shinobi*

This chapter shows that when a general utilizes *shinobi* very well, he will gain tremendous benefit and achieve victory in war without fail, and that *shinobi* are the key to the art of war.

The ten articles

I

When a commander-in-chief uses *shinobi*, it enables him to know all about the defences of the enemy's territory and its castle before he makes any plan, so that he will not be surprised nor will he fail and all will be as planned, which is a great benefit. When a lord or general is going to attack the enemy's domain, he should send an excellent *ninja* into the enemy's land to get information or send him into the castle to aid his plans beforehand. In this way the *ninja* will see and get all the information he needs in detail – such as the topography of the land, whether the castle is strong or not, lengths of roads – and then he can record these things as drawings and bring them back. The drawings should be redrawn precisely to provide the general with the details for his reference. With these maps the general can think on how to decide to arrange his people, what formation to be taken, where to set up an encampment, where the enemy may lay an ambush, where he should lay an ambush himself, how to attack the castle, preparations for the attack and everything about his plans. This allows him to launch his army and carry out his plans without question or trouble when the time comes. Also, through these ways you can find benefit in many areas.

Sun Tzu says:

The natural formation of the country is the soldier's best ally; but a power of estimating the adversary, of controlling the forces of victory, and of shrewdly calculating difficulties, dangers and distances, constitutes the test of a great general. He who knows these things, and in fighting puts his knowledge into practice, will win his battles. He who knows them not, nor practises them, will surely be defeated.

We are not fit to lead an army on the march unless we are familiar with the face of the country – its mountains and forests, its pitfalls and precipices, its marshes and swamps.

From Yoshimori's one hundred poems:

忍ヒ者ニ敵ヲ問ツツ下知ヲセヨ　只危キハ推量ノサタ

You need to inquire of a shinobi no mono *about the enemy when giving orders.*

It is dangerous if you give orders based on guesswork alone.

[A general] should consider this in earnest.

II

If you use *shinobi* you can know exactly whether the enemy is strong or not or what the enemy's commander-in-chief really thinks deep down, then this should provide you with the root for all the plans you need to make and it will bring you tremendous benefits. If *ninja* get into the enemy's domain or their castle they can find out: whether the enemy general is principled or unprincipled and to what extent; whether he is wise or ignorant; whether he is brave or not; whether their military orders are proper or not; whether the troop commanders, the higher commanders,[4] or even the soldiers are well trained in military skills or not; whether the morale of the entire clan is maintained or not; how many people there are; whether the lord has reinforcement forces from the neighbouring lord or not; how much food is kept in the castle; what ways the enemy lord likes or dislikes, etc. In fact a *shinobi no mono* records many things about the enemy, other than the above, and brings it back to the lord, so that it allows the allies to achieve enormous success in their plans, but note there are too many examples of such cases to mention of here.

From Yoshimori's military poems:

---

4 The ideograms used here are 物奉行.

計コトモ敵ノ心ニヨルゾカシ　忍ヒヲ入テ物音ヲ聞ケ

Whether a strategy works or not depends on what the enemy intend to do. Thus, you should send a shinobi *across the enemy line in order to pick up any sounds.*

軍ニハ忍ヒ物見ヲ遣ハシテ　敵ノ作法ヲ知テ計ラヘ

In war you need to send a shinobi-monomi *scout to get the information about the enemy's tactics before you make your strategy.*

Sun Tzu says that:

Success in warfare is gained by carefully accommodating ourselves to the enemy's purpose. By persistently hanging on the enemy's flank, we shall succeed in the long run in killing the commander-in-chief. This is called ability to accomplish a thing by sheer cunning.

The *Bingjing* 兵鏡 manual says:

If you wish to strike at the enemy then you must utilize spies beforehand. Do this to observe how many of them there are, and to judge truth or falsehoods and the present state of the force. Thereafter, raise an army so that you will attain great achievements and never fail to gain victory in battle.

III

By using *shinobi*, the lord should know exactly what formation the enemy is taking and where, whether there is a *kamari* ambush or not, etc., and thus can make preparations in advance and without confusion. This way you will never be taken at a disadvantage by a surprise attack and this method will be a tremendous benefit to you. This is because before the lord goes into battle, *ninja* would see what defensive measures are in place, such as formations or defensive preparations, or whether the enemy has ambushes or not, and he would bring this back and report to the lord. Because of this the general will have the formidable advantage of forward planning for proper arrangement of battle and in accordance with the information gained.

From Yoshimori's poems:

心ガケ深ク有スル武士ハ　忍ニヒカレ道筋ヲ知レ

A mononofu *who is highly motivated to do great deeds, should know the path to take, with the help of a* shinobi *as a guide.*

The *Three Strategies* say that the commander-in-chief should make changes and not be constant when the situation needs change.

Question: *As information about the enemy's formations or defences or whether they intend to ambush or not can be detected by* monomi *scouts, surely there is no need to have* shinobi no mono *also see these things? Why is it that you say a* monomi's *job should be done by a* shinobi *and thus assume there are advantages to using* shinobi *instead?*

Answer: *Monomi* scouts only see from a distant place and simply *speculate* on any given situation. Therefore they cannot see things so precisely and only have an approximation. *Ninja*, on the other hand, creep close to the enemy and observe things directly; therefore, they know the situation exactly and in all detail and because of this, intelligence reports will scarcely be inaccurate. In short, the benefits of the *shinobi* are completely different from those of the *monomi* scout.

IV

When your army is under siege in a castle, if you have *ninja* communicate secretly with those outside the castle or send information from outside of the siege into the castle, then the benefits will be tremendous. Suppose you and your allies are holed up in a castle and besieged by multitudes of enemies, so much so that you cannot get out through the siege, unless you were a bird on the wing. Even in such a tight case as this, *shinobi no mono* can get out secretly through the siege to ask the neighbouring domain for rescue forces, or to get through any siege and penetrate into a castle secretly and can then obtain signal instructions or other such information. As for this, further details will be described later on but there are more to be transmitted orally.

V

By *ninja* bringing forward information to an allied force of where its forces are not expected by the enemy or where the enemy are not prepared, an overwhelming victory can be obtained. This can be possible because, before the commander-in-chief arrives on the battlefield and takes up a position, *shinobi* have already been in the enemy's castle or camp. Therefore, they can inform the allies secretly from the enemy's territory where you are not expected to come from or the position where the enemy is not fully prepared and in this way a commander-in-chief can take advantage of any gap to gain victory. Also, this can be done with the minimum strength required and with the smallest number of casualties taking place, allowing for an overwhelming victory to be obtained.

Sun Tzu says:
Appear at points that the enemy must hasten to defend; march swiftly to places where you are not expected. An army may march great distances without distress, if it marches through country where the enemy is not. You can be sure of succeeding in your attacks if you only attack places that are undefended.

The *Six Secret Strategic Teachings* says:
He strikes like a sudden clap of thunder, which does not give time to cover his ears; strikes like a flash of lightning, which does not give time to close the eyes.

V I

When *ninja* send secret information to their allies, such as whether the enemy is advancing or withdrawing, you will gain the benefit of a massive victory. By *ninja* reporting whether the enemy is advancing or not, or whether withdrawing or not, in which direction and by which route they are advancing or withdrawing, in this way the enemy's plans will bolster the allied campaign, and then you will win a sweeping victory and there are numerous examples of this. Also, to strengthen this point, it is known that some military writings say you should ride in the same areas as the enemy [to understand their position and tactics].

V I I

Shinobi no mono working undercover on the enemy's side can bring internal discord among the enemy lord and his retainers by slandering them discreetly, which would enable you to take advantage of the discord and defeat them. Your *ninja* working on the enemy's side could carry out various plans or tactics to sour the relations between the enemy lord and his retainers, or they can cause doubt among the enemy troops so that they will not be working in accordance with each other. Or they can cause discord between the enemy and the neighbouring domain so as to isolate the enemy's lord. Then if you take advantage of these flaws, you could overwhelmingly defeat the enemy in this weakened state.

Sun Tzu says:
If the enemy's forces are united, separate them; also prevent their unification.

V I I I

If *shinobi* get information on the enemy's secret plans or tactics and bring it to you, it can bring you a great victory without expelling much strength. By *ninja* sneaking into the enemy's position, eavesdropping on its plans or tactics and informing the lord in secret, then the enemy plans or tactics will fail, which could bring you an overwhelming success. Realize that the benefit of this is tremendous.

Sun Tzu says:
The highest form of command is to balk the enemy's plans.

IX

If *ninja* infiltrate a castle or position and set a fire to it, the least amount of strength would be required to attain a complete victory. *Ninja* can get into the castle or position by using both *in-nin* and *yo-nin* skills and set fire from inside with the aim of burning it down to the ground, so the allies can attain the greatest victory with the least effort in attacking.

Si Ma Fa[5] says:
Use troops to attack from outside and use men to attack from within.

Question: *We have bows and fire arrows, firearms, grenades, fire arrows and so on with which to attack [a castle] from outside. Why should we have* ninja *burn it down from inside?*

Answer: How is it possible for you not to know that there is a vast difference between your trying to set fire from the outside with fire arrows or incendiary tools and the efforts of a *ninja* inside the castle, who can judge the best spot to kindle flames and the best time to set fires? That will determine whether it will be successful or not. Furthermore, as experts in handling fire, *ninja* are well trained with the kind of weapons that you talk about, which are fire arrows and such.

X

It is possible to kill the enemy general with *shinobi no jutsu* and if this is done the benefit will be immeasurable. There is a secret in *shinobi no jutsu* on the skills required to kill the enemy's commander. In a case where your *ninja* can kill the enemy general, then it will bring an enormous benefit, as the enemy will submit without fighting.

The *Three Strategies* says:
Without scheming and being unorthodox, you have no means to destroy evildoers. Without plotting, there is no means to be successful.

---

5   Writer of the *Methods of the Sima*, one of the Seven Military Classics of ancient China.

Question: *It seems to be utterly without fact that there is a way to kill the enemy's general. What kind of measure is that?*

Answer: There is a principle, which is extremely subtle. Therefore, I should remain silent on this issue at this point.

Alongside the above ten articles, the *Kanrinseiyo* manual says: *ninja* are the eyes and the ears of the art of war and the timbers of your plans and thus critical to a complete victory. Without using them, the general cannot know the terrain of the enemy's territory, how many people are there, or their plans or schemes, so they have no measure to plan for victory. If you make a plan on your supposition alone, it is just a stone thrown in the dark and it can easily miss the target, making it hard to hit the mark. Therefore, you will be in peril in battle, just like a blind person trying to defeat an opponent with a sharp sword. For this, a good general, if he wants to proceed, then he uses *shinobi* to see the topography of the enemy's land, how many men they have, if the army is strong or weak, whether they are advancing or withdrawing, their plans, and so on before he raises an army and sets out his plans. This way any event will constantly be successful, without fail.

Suppose a *ninja* is inside and sets fire and the general attacks from outside in response. The enemy, if trying to handle the internal fire, cannot defend against the external attack, or if fighting against the external force, then they will lose their castle. Thus they will be defeated without doubt. You attack castles, take to battle, win all battles, and defeat the enemy, with tremendous momentum sweeping all before one. With such little force, the greatest victory can be realized; remember, pushing a gate with the force of one thousand people is not as good as to remove the bar of the gate. This is why there have been no great generals since ancient times who have failed to use *shinobi* all through every battle.

Sun Tzu says:
Such is the intricacy and subtlety of espionage. Indeed, there is no place where espionage cannot be used. The enlightened ruler and the capable general are able to secure victories for their military campaigns and achieve successes that surpass those of many others. The reason is because of foreknowledge.

This foreknowledge cannot be obtained from the spirits, nor from the gods. It cannot be obtained by comparing with similar present or past events and situations. This foreknowledge must be obtained from men who have knowledge of the situation of the enemy.

When these five types of agents are deployed simultaneously, their complex modes of operation will be beyond the comprehension of the enemy. They are like mythical and divine schemes that can be deemed the most precious treasures and weapons of the ruler. Secret operations and espionage activities form an integral part of any military campaign, as the planning of strategies and the movement of troops depend heavily on them.

The ignorant general or the senseless general does not know how to win by using *shinobi*, so they do not use them. However, without using *shinobi*, scarcely is there a case where they will succeed.

Sun Tzu says:
Two opposing armies may be at war with each other for many years, seeking the ultimate day of victory. However, if one is reluctant to part with honour and ranks, money and gold, for espionage purposes and remains ignorant of the situation of the enemy, he is extremely inhumane. Indeed such a person can never be a general of men, can never be a good assistant to the ruler and can never be a master of victories.

As quoted above, Sun Tzu warns repeatedly and strongly against not using *shinobi*.

Many books or writings, Japanese and Chinese, have been left with the fact recorded that good generals in ancient times obtained great benefit from using *shinobi*. As a leader of people, the general should be aware that if he does not use tactics that include *shinobi*, let alone if he treats the subject with scorn, he proves himself to be seriously ignorant.

Question: *You mentioned earlier that using* shinobi *should bring you a victory and the general should not fail to use* shinobi, *and you quoted some ancient sages' words as proof of this. However, as castles or any fortifications are so firmly guarded these days, I cannot believe that* shinobi *could really infiltrate them. And let us consider the point that in the* **Questions** *and* **Answers** *between Tan Tai Zhong and his general Li Jing, Li Jing criticizes Sun Tzu for his usage of spies and says it is the worst idea. He says he once discussed the details of it and that 'Water allows boats to float on it but turns them over sometimes'. Likewise the use of spies may be successful but by relying on spies you may suffer a defeat. Considering these words, I speculate that the way of the* shinobi *is not a good method in the art of military command.*

Answer: It comes as no surprise that an ordinary-level *shinobi*, or *yonin* 庸忍, would think it too difficult to get into the firmly guarded fortifications of these modern times.[6] However, the basic principle of *shinobi no jutsu* has *in-nin* and *yo-nin* at its root, but it diversifies itself into ever-changing and countless styles,

---

6   The end of the Sengoku period saw massive changes in Japanese castle construction.

like that of the leaves and branches of a tree, so much so that not everything can be described here.

In essence, principles and performance should go together. If you are ignorant about principles, your performance will not mature. Also, if you cannot mature in performance, you cannot reach the highest of heights, even if you do in fact know the principles. Therefore, we cannot determine the pros and the cons by discussing with words what is right or not in the world of battle. In reality, if you fight with someone with a sword with the resolution to kill him, then two or three tenths of your attack is substantial – which is that which you *can* control – while seven or eight tenths is insubstantial – which is that which you *cannot* control. Even though you have substance and are keen at the start of your initial move, your attack becomes insubstantial when the sword is brought down on the opponent or when it is raised again. This is a metaphor for the baseline of *ninjutsu*, because *ninjutsu* is to avoid where the enemy is of substance and take advantage of their gaps and insubstantiality.[7]

Shinobi no jutsu has been mentioned in various writings, but in a way, you should not try to make ordinary people understand the principles of the art as the principles are beyond the reach of their intentions.

By quoting the above words of Li Jing it can be noted that he questions the need for *shinobi* spies and suggests that they are not a good measure in battle. However, know that [*shinobi*] are the primary way of tactics and this is with certainty. What Li Jing means is that it would not be right for an ignorant general to use *shinobi*. As he says, they are not a good measure for a stupid general. For a wise general, they are a good measure, because a stupid general cannot detect if the *ninja* is loyal to the lord or not, nor could he know if the *ninja* is competent or not. He may use [*shinobi*] recklessly because he has little sense of benevolence, is ignorant about tactics, not careful enough in using signals. Therefore, with luck he might obtain a victory with the help of a *shinobi*, but more than likely and without luck, he will go down to the realm of defeat as a simple matter of course. Therefore, while a *shinobi* is a bad measure for the stupid general, the wise general selects those who have mastery in tactics and bravery and firm loyalty and thus appoints them as *shinobi*, giving high rewards. Consequently,

---

7   The point to be understood here is that Fujibayashi uses the idea of striking an enemy with a sword to represent the true meaning of *ninjutsu*. When the sword strikes an attacker it is solid and has substance, but when the strike is past its central point it moves out of control and the swordsman is committed to the movement and therefore he is insubstantial and open; this then is when you should attack. In this way there is a connection between *ninjutsu* and martial arts. While different in many respects, both look for true gaps in the enemy's defences.

in such a case where a wise general retains a *shinobi* and that said general passes away, the *shinobi* could be loyal enough to sacrifice his own life to follow the lord into death.[8] Alongside this, the bright general takes the *shinobi*'s wife, children or others from his family as hostage, makes a deep plan, and arranges firmly for signals before sending the *shinobi* to the enemy. Thus, his army will not be defeated by any means. What is more, whenever he uses *shinobi*, the *shinobi* would never fail to infiltrate but attain great achievement and without exception. Therefore, a *shinobi* is a good measure for the wise general.

Figuratively, water and fire are treasures in the world but if they are used wrongly, they can do harm as well as good. Still there is no alternative for water or fire. Swords or spears are weapons to kill others with; however, if a stupid man is so stupid as to have his sword or spear snatched, it would kill him in the end. It all depends on whether the man is good or bad. Moreover, the extreme principle of *shinobi no jutsu* is so subtle that ordinary or stupid men cannot comprehend it. Thus, it should be passed down carefully by word of mouth.

---

8   This is an important point to note: *seppuku* or ritual suicide is the realm of loyal *samurai* in this context and shows the *samurai* side of the *shinobi* way of life.

Shochi II

A Guideline for Commanders II

About promises

Three points about the prohibitions within *shinobi no jutsu*

I

The name and identity of the *shinobi no mono* should be strictly hidden. The general, when employing *ninja*, should not reveal who his *ninja* are. You must be aware of this because it is the way of laying plans during normal times, before the *shinobi* are actually required at the outbreak of war. Without planning you cannot gain benefit but also it is possible that [a lack of planning] could be harmful to your own force. For this purpose there are certain [types of warriors] that aid [disguise] in *ninjutsu*. These are: *heishi* 平士 normal warriors; *tonshi* 遁士 hermit warriors; and *rishi* 離士 separate warriors.

The way of making promises should be passed down orally and in detail.

Sun Tzu says:
When using our forces, we must seem inactive.

II

The commander-in-chief should strictly prohibit the leaking of plans concerning his *shinobi*. If the plan is given away, it will not only fail, but even worse, it could possibly result in the defeat of your forces. Thus, this should be kept secret and should not be known to anybody, not even to a lord's senior counsellors. That is the code of the *shinobi*.

Sun Tzu says:
In no other business should greater secrecy be preserved.

The 'Colloquial Commentary' on the *Art of War* states: things should be from mouth to ear, the general speaks and the *ninja* listens and so knows his mission without a mediator. Also, one writing says 'if put in voice, it will resonate, so convey it not by mouth but by writing.'[1]

III

Those who are found to talk about any plans concerning the *shinobi* should be sent to their death immediately. As well as those who should not know about it by right, any of those who take part in such secret conversation about the said plan concerning the *shinobi* and who speak to someone else, giving the information away, should also be executed at once together with the one who has heard it. This is a part of the code [used for dealing with *shinobi*].

Even when universal peace has come in the country, there is still the law of keeping these things secret and not divulging to anyone that there are *shinobi* in use.

It is even more so when in a state of war and if *shinobi* have not yet infiltrated.

Sun Tzu says:
When espionage activities and secret operations have been leaked before their implementation, then the agents concerned and those whom they are in contact with must be put to death.

According to *I Ching* (Yi Jing):
If a secret is not kept, then things will come to harm.

According to *Shiji*:
A secret will work if it is kept, you will lose if words are given away.

Two points on secret writing

I

The secret letters between the general and a *ninja* should be written by way of 'water', 'fire' or 'ash'.[2] There are various other ways of writing them down which have come from ancient times, but it is not so easy to master them quickly. *Shinobi*

---

1   This is perplexing as the quote advises not to say things but to write them down. It is most likely an idiom implying secrecy and close communication without a 'middle man'.
2   The idea here is that a form of 'special' ink is used to hide the message or parts of it.

secret letters are written records of the promise given to the *ninja* by the general or offered to the general by the *ninja*, and should be written in 'water', 'fire', or 'ash' then and there and not sealed. As it is a secret communication, it should be made so that even a sage will not recognize it as a secret letter. Therefore, you should not expect to grasp the whole context simply from reading it.

Here, 'water' means iron mixed in water, 'fire' is *shin*[3] and 'ash' is the 'juice' from a soy bean, including the seed of a castor oil plant (*Ricinus communis*). You can use any of them depending on availability and on the time and place; further details to be transmitted orally.

According to one writing:
It should be put into shape or shadow and without ink, so you cannot see the mark.

II

Another way of secret writing

A secret writing should be cut into three so that three people can keep it separately and so that it will make sense only when the general and *ninja* combine it together. You should create further measures, such as dividing the characters[4] or such things and doing it according to the situation. Further details to be transmitted orally.

In the *Six Secret Teachings* Tai Gong says:
Whenever you have secret affairs and major considerations, letters should be employed rather than tallies. The ruler sends a letter to the general; the general uses a letter to query the ruler. The letters are composed 'as one unit and then divided. They are sent out in three parts, with only one person knowing the contents'. 'Divided' means they are separated into three parts. 'Sent out in three parts, with only one person knowing' means there are three messengers, each carrying one part; and when the three are put together, only then does one know the contents. This is then referred to as a 'secret letter'. Even if the enemy has sagacious wisdom, they will not be able to recognize the contents.

Also, tallies[5] are used by dividing them into pieces and are each kept separately by individuals. However, if overused, they can be confusing, complex and hard

---

3 Given only in phonetics. However, the *Giyoshu* manual states 'sake'.
4 I.e. make the secret system more complex, such as by cutting it into three parts but cutting through the ideograms etc.
5 Often tallies are items that are broken into parts so that when a messenger comes bearing one and it fits your own part, he is established as a true messenger.

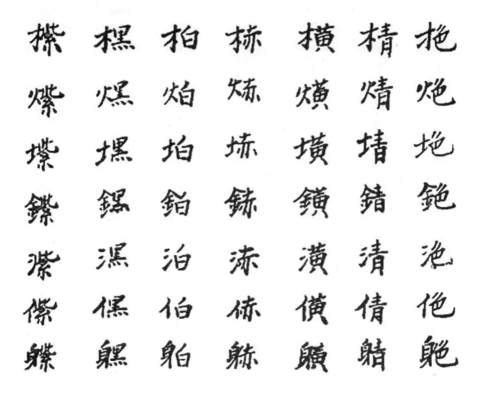

Figure 6. The *Shinobi Iroha*

to work out. Therefore, I[Fujibayashi] would use secret letters instead.

The way of secret writing in our school is very confidential, to be transmitted orally.[6]

In case the above code [see figure 6] is not useful in stopping the enemy's strength, write with normal characters.[7] To be transmitted orally.

---

6   This is one of the most commonly used sections of the *Bansenshukai* and has become known as the *Shinobi Iroha* or *ninja* alphabet. An *iroha* is a pangram (a sentence using every letter of the alphabet at least once) and here, in this version, an unusual mixture of ideograms is used. It is substitution code and a message would be written in the substituted letters. It is the same as using any given symbol to represent A, B, C, etc., and any two people who know the code can send messages to each other.

7   This appears strange, as it states that if the code is not working then use normal writing, which does not appear to be a logical step. However, as there is a subsequent reference to *kuden* or oral traditions, there may be a further layer of information about this skill, or it

Two points on *yabumi* secret letters, which are sent tied to an arrow

I

A *yabumi* is a letter sent over to the other side. In the process of manufacturing an arrow, the fletchings should be used as tags and the needed name should be written among the fletchings. The letter itself should be put in the bamboo arrow shaft or rolled around it. To be transmitted orally.

II

Before shooting, you need to know where the receiver will be.

When a *shinobi* is going to communicate with the general after he has got into the enemy's castle, he needs to let his allies know where he is, so that they will not shoot a reply from the lord in front of others by mistake. The *shinobi* should repeatedly shoot arrows then move backwards and wait for a response. It is essential to arrange for the time and place to do this. To be transmitted orally.

Four points on signals

I

Use signal flags during the day and *hikyakubi*[8] fire signals during the night. These are used when the commander-in-chief is in a distant position of five to ten *ri* away. To be transmitted orally. How to produce the *hikyakubi* signal fire is described in the fire tools section of the *ninja* tools chapter further on.

II

Use smoke signals during the day and use the *irekobi* adjustable torch or conch shell signals during the night. There should be arrangements for the conch shell signals made with the general beforehand. To be transmitted orally. Details for sending a signal by conch shell should be prearranged, such as how many sequences of three vibratos and how many sequences of five vibratos for a signal, and so on. Before sending a message with the conch shell, the three instruments of the gongs, the shell horns and the drums should be sounded to the utmost so that a *ninja* being in the enemy's castle or position can know that a signal is being sent to him with the following sounds from the conch shell. This also should all be arranged beforehand. This is done so that the agent in the castle or position who always hears the conch shell sounding will not miss the signal, as without such a prearranged format a *ninja* could miss the message. It should be arranged precisely beforehand that if he hears this warning signal that a signal will soon

---

could simply be a transcription error.

8 *Hikyakubi* means an express messenger or courier.

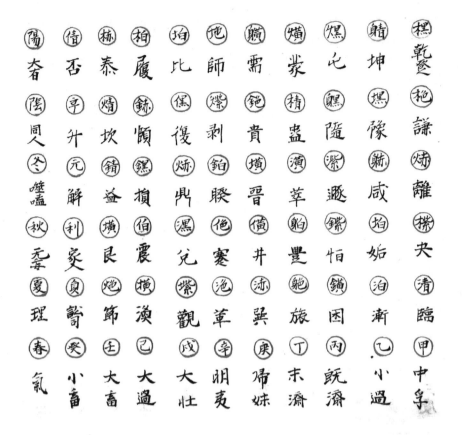

Figure 7. Conch shell table

follow which will explain future actions. Further details are to be transmitted orally.

The way to convey words by the conch shell

At the beginning of a word you are to signal, blow ● as the sign that the message is about to start. An example sentence is as follows[9]: 假○地○々ハ [unknown ideogram] ノ○々如是吹之.

Before you send a second message by conch shell, blow it intensely and take a rest for a short while, blow it three times in sets of three-section vibratos to signal the start of the next message. Then blow it sending out the needed message [in

---

9   This section appears to need the oral transmission to be fully understood. The black and
    white circles represent specific sounds that are to be sent and involve sections of code used
    from the table above. Therefore, without the oral tradition and with the words missing from
    the example, this sentence is too unclear to translate.

the code you have arranged]. [Alternatively,] as mentioned above, the gongs, the shell horns and the drums should be sounded loudly as advance notice to signal the start of a message. Otherwise it could be missed, as the *ninja* might mistake it for other usual shell sounds.

[Points on blowing:]
- Blow a little longer at the start [of a message].
- When lowering the intonation, blow only in a short burst and cut it off.
- Each word, letter or ideogram begins with one vibrato.
- When blowing a preparation signal before each word begins, add three vibratos.
- Note that when some words with lowering intonation are taken from the secret table [*see* figure 7] you should add one vibration.[10]

The above is a very important secret in communicating your words with the conch shell. It is good to ring the gong or sound the drum at the beginning. If the gong is rung at the start, drums can be good for the first word or ideogram. If the drum is used at the start, the gong would be good for the first word or ideogram.

For those words with falling intonation, only the conch shell should be used for sending messages. Full details to be transmitted orally.

Those who want to learn this path should practise this at all times, otherwise they will not be able to communicate with each other in an emergency. If you keep training with this faithfully, you will be able to understand it as if you are listening to someone speaking.

III

The signals of *iccho ikka* 一町一火の相図　or 'one fire for one *cho*[11] distance'. The above is to be transmitted orally.

IV

Marking your fire signal by using three signal fires[12]
A single fire signal might be confused with other kinds of fire, such as a smoke signal or travellers' torches. It is also possible there may be other fire signals sent

---

10 This sentence is highly reconstructed and is ambiguous and actually points to certain ideograms in the table in figure 7. However, some of the ideograms cannot be typed in a digital format as they are unique *ninja* codes. In these cases, one standard ideogram appears – 清.

11 A unit of distance equal to 109m and most likely a relay beacon.

12 The original says 'marks'.

by others in the area. Therefore, you should prearrange the number of fires to be used in your signals – hence it is called 'marking your signal by using three signal fires'.

According to one writing:

Signs should be transmitted from heart to heart, therefore you do not have to stick to ancient ways.

Six points on promises

I

If you want to infiltrate somewhere using the skills of *katatagae*[13] 参差 or *suigetsu* 水,[14] or such similar infiltration arts, you should make arrangements with the commander-in-chief so that he will draw the enemy out by using a form of bait.

If it is difficult to infiltrate from the start, you should use these skills and make a sudden attack on the castle or camp in a siege and toward nightfall with weak soldiers, while hiding an ambush troop at the rear. If the enemy soldiers are strong and they are given the order to chase off your raiding party, then you should infiltrate with such measures as the skills of *katatagae* or *suigetsu*, which allow you to smuggle yourself into the enemy troops. The bait used should not be strong soldiers because it is meant just to draw the enemy out. Remember, if it does not look like a true raid when they are chased away, the enemy will see through your intentions. Therefore, you should employ weak soldiers, encourage them keenly and give them an order to break through the gate. Then when the enemy thrust into them, as expected they will run. You should lay an ambush of stronger soldiers a little further away so that even those weak soldiers will not be killed. All these arrangements should be made between the general and the *shinobi no mono* in detail, very precisely and very firmly.

I I

When a *shinobi* infiltrates with *katatagae* or *suigetsu no jutsu*, a sudden attack should be delivered to aid his cover. On the cue given by the *ninja* to the com- mander-in-chief when he is entering, the attack should be intensified to a higher degree. This increases the pressure on the enemy side and the *ninja* can carry out his plan as he wishes.

---

13 This means 'to enter a place after someone has just left the position'. Further details are given in volume nine.

14 Literally, 'the moon reflected on water', or a homonym of the sixth month of the year. Further details in volume nine.

III

In performing *kyonin* 驚忍 or 'creating a gap by surprise', arrangements should be made both for your entry and your escape. When you want to infiltrate somewhere by way of the skill of *kyonyu* 驚入ノ術, that is, 'infiltration while the enemy is surprised', there should be arrangements made with the general to make sure that he shall sound the drums and make men cry harshly, all accompanied by a hail of gunfire, remembering not to kill the *shinobi* who is on his side.

I may say that in the case when a *ninja* needs to escape from the enemy's castle or position, he should carry a mark to identify himself, so that he is not to be mistaken as one of the enemy force. When undertaking his mission, he should hide the mark among his clothes and use it when he gets out. The commander-in-chief should make it known to all his forces at an appropriate time.

IV

When your allies deliver a night attack, there is a method where the *ninja* will not return with his allies but stay within the enemy side to then set a fire when the next and arranged attack comes. This is a useful measure to be taken in the case that it is difficult to infiltrate due to the enemy having very good tactics in defending against *shinobi*. Using this skill, you can stay [in the enemy camp] for a short while and then set fires as you wish.

V

Make arrangements to build a temporary or false camp but not too close to your own headquarters. This is done in the case where your *shinobi* have been detected and captured when trying to infiltrate the enemy lines with the above skills. On such an occasion, he should tell lies to make the enemy believe that he has been persuaded to join them and will work against his own allies for them. To prove himself true to them he should offer to set fire to a building belonging to his own side. He should offer this measure of betrayal when the time is right and after telling such lies.

VI

Concerning seals and tallies and ascertaining if they are true or false

A true communiqué will have the seal in the right position and/or have an odd number, while a false seal will be upside down and/or with an even number. This is done for when a *shinobi* has been captured and the enemy tells him to send a false letter to his lord and make him write as they would have it written. In such a case you should have an arrangement like the one above with your general. This arrangement should be made beforehand. If things are prepared thus, when the time comes, just think about the tactics you can use to destroy the enemy.

I may say that if the enemy captures a *ninja*, takes him close to the gate of his ally and forces him to speak as they want, the *ninja* should let his ally know if his word is true or false by coughing – that is, cough an even number of times if he tells the truth and cough an odd number if it is untrue. Further details are to be transmitted orally.

Three points on cooperation with the general

I

The *shinobi no mono* should give a signal to inform the lord that he is about to set fire on the windward side of the target. The general should attack from the direction of the wind.

Sun Tzu says:
When fire is burning in the windward direction, do not assault the leeward position. When the wind blows strongly, be aware that it tends to cease before long.

I say that you should have a good judgement based upon this quote.

II

When there is no wind, the general should inform the *ninja* of which direction he should set the fire by way of a flag or of the conch shell. The colours for the flag should be arranged depending on the four points north, south, east and west and the shell should be blown according to the 'five ways'. The point to be set alight should be determined depending on the direction of the wind. When there is no wind, it should be in accord with the formation that the lord has given and the *ninja* should be informed of his choice by flags or the conch shell, or by the code that has been prearranged for a mission of arson. The details are dependent on the time and the place and further details to be transmitted orally.

III

In response to the signal that the *ninja* gives to show that he has set the fire alight, an assault should be launched in perfect accord, just as divided pieces of a tally fit into one, and all will come together. Be warned, if the *shinobi no mono* has not given his signal, by using smoke, arrows, or fire arrows, etc., because the time is not ripe yet, do not launch the attack thoughtlessly – there will be no victory if you do. You should wait for the cue given with absolute confidence while making sure of the direction in which you should attack, and once the cue is given, you should start your attack with no delay and not prematurely but perfectly on time, just as pieces of a tally fit into one.

Sun Tzu says:

In assaults by fire, one must use the five ways of attacking interchangeably, depending on circumstances. When a fire breaks out within the camp of the enemy, prepare quickly to attack the enemy from outside. When fire breaks within the camp of the enemy and there is no confusion nor commotion among the soldiers, wait patiently and do not be eager to attack. When the fire is burning ferociously with opportunities to be gained, follow through quickly with your attacks. When there are no opportunities to be gained and followed through, cease immediately. Fire can be started from outside the camp of the enemy. There is no need to wait for the fire to start within the camp of the enemy. Fires can always be started at suitable times and occasions. When fire is burning in the windward direction, do not assault the leeward position.

Two points on the promise for the guarantee of the security of the *ninja*

I

Arrangements should be made for a *ninja* escaping from a castle as it falls, so that the allies will not kill him or them (depending on the number of the *shinobi*). During daytime any measure or sign can be arranged, while during night time a lantern with the crest should be the mark. Just before the assault, the arrangement should be made known to every soldier; however, it is not good to tell them too early. On the fall of the castle, the *ninja* should be in hiding in a closed place while the enemy are running away. After battle, the *ninja* usually comes out of hiding. So the above measure should be taken just in case the *ninja* cannot stay hidden but has to come out mixed together with the enemy soldiers.

II

It is common for a *ninja* to come out after all has settled down.

From the *shinobi-uta* poems:

忍得テハ敵方ヨリモ同士討ノ用心スルゾ大事ナリケリ

After you have slipped into the enemy's area successfully, you should give more attention not to fight among yourselves than to the enemy.

同士討モ味方ノ下知ニヨルゾカシ　武者ノ印シヲ兼テ
定メヨ

*Fighting among yourselves can always happen, depending on
what instructions you are given. You should always decide on an
identifying mark for your warriors beforehand.*

This chapter deals with the promises the general should make with his *ninja*.
Unless these promises are firmly arranged, it will be hard for the *shinobi no mono*
to infiltrate the enemy, or even if he can manage to do so, there will be no victory
or advantage. On top of that, it could cause a disaster. Be warned you must be
careful.

Sun Tzu says:
*The ruler must know fully how to use and operate the five different kinds of agents
and espionage activities.*

Besides the above twenty-two articles, no matter if it be *ad hoc* or with precision,
and no matter if there is a firm promise between the general and the *ninja*, those
performers of these ever-changing arts should not give out anything beforehand.
　Hereinabove is mentioned the established rules of signs and promises. This is
an introduction to this path.

Reasons as to why a *shinobi no mono* should be employed[15]

—

He must have five basic elements: loyalty, courage, strategy, achievement
(including worthy deeds) and fidelity – and on top of these a healthy body.

二

He must be gentle at normal times, and have a keen sense of righteousness but
little need of desires. He needs to be fond of learning the principles of things and
never forget his indebtedness to others.

15　The title here does not reflect the real content, which is more a list of what makes a perfect
　ninja or an instruction to a lord as to the characteristics to look for when hiring a *ninja*.

三

He must be fluent in speech, deep in thought, quick in communicating with people at normal times and difficult to deceive, especially by using logic to avoid falling for 'smooth talking' traps.

四

He should know heaven's will and have a grasp of Confucianism and Buddhism and be always aware that life and death have their determined appointment. He must aim at rising above his own self-interest at all times and bear the words of ancient sages in mind.

五

He should be earnest to know the morals of the *samurai* class and furthermore should learn much about the ways of Japanese and Chinese ancient warriors who had loyalty and bravery, dedicated themselves to their lord, and destroyed the enemy with tactics, and all in the service of their lord. Also, he should have a great interest in military affairs or the arts of war. His temperament should be that of a hero.

六

Usually he should not be argumentative with people. He must be gentle and dignified and, above this, have a name as being righteous and good. Within or outside of his domain, he should be reputed to be completely honest.

七

His wife, children and relatives must be of good descent, thus there should be little chance that he could be a reversed *shinobi* 反忍.

八

He must be well travelled and have a good knowledge of what the manners and customs are like in various provinces.

九

He must study hard and learn deeply the art of *shinobi no jutsu*, be competent in strategy, be talented at writing, skilled in all areas of *ninjutsu* to the highest degree and aspire to perform merits in battle.

十

As well as military affairs, he must also be accomplished in various arts, be poetic, musical, know how to dance, have the ability to impersonate others and be proficient in all other activities and can then use them to make up for any situation without blundering.

Those who have the above ten characteristics are very rare and should be called *jonin*[16] 上忍 or highly skilled *ninja*. It is difficult to find a *jonin* as mentioned above unless the lord has profound wisdom and completely understands people, just as if he can see into their mind. If he is not a sage, he cannot attain [the status of *jonin*].

Sun Tzu says:
Only those who are wise will be able to employ spies usefully.

As mentioned repeatedly in the chapters of this writing, the stupid lord if using *shinobi* cannot attain victory in every battle while the bright lord when using *shinobi* will win in all confrontations. The chances of winning are assured and his victory is sure-footed; it is as if he will never miss a hit one hundred times out of one hundred tries. Those *jonin* as mentioned above are difficult to find. However, it is not difficult to obtain satisfying results with *chu-ge no ninja* 中下 ノ忍者 – middle- or low-level *shinobi* – so long as they are employed appropriately and in accordance with the time and purpose. Every detail about how to use them will be mentioned in the subsequent volumes of this writing. Also, I will quote from ancient Japanese and Chinese writings as proof that middle- or low-level *ninja* can be made the basis of your tactics and that there are countless examples of this.

The wise general can make the best of *chu* and *ge*, that is middle and low *ninja*, just as a master hawker can make a first-grade hawk of a second-grade hawk. Why should they be abandoned? Besides, even an almighty *ninja* cannot

---

16 Alternatively pronounced as *jo no shinobi*.

carry out *hicho no jutsu* 飛鳥ノ術, the 'art of flying birds'[17] by himself, without leading or getting aid from ordinary *shinobi* of middle or low level. You should let them perform their duty properly so they will attain success. Therefore, when employing *ninja*, be sure that all the above matters should be considered very carefully. You should of course seek out *jonin*, but those ordinary *ninja* of middle or low level should not be thrown away. As mentioned in the chapters within this writing, that is this document the *Bansenshukai*, there is nothing better than using *heishi* ('normal warriors'), *rishi* ('separate warriors') or *tonshi* ('hermit warriors') [when using *shinobi no jutsu*].[18] The use of these people gives you countless benefits, uses that are endless. Further details to be given by word of mouth.

[Untitled list whose meanings are in pairs]
- Weeping willow (to descend) 柳
- Japanese willow (to ascend) 揚
- Praise 褒
- Criticize 貶
- Capture 擒
- Release 縱
- Give 與
- Take 奪

Details to be transmitted orally.

---

17 This is a common phrase and is used in different ways from one historical document to another. Here it has the connotation of 'skill' or *jutsu*.

18 *Heishi*, those who are employed normally; *rishi*, those currently not employed who are looking for employment; and *tonshi*, warriors whose identification is not commonly known.

Shochi IV

A Guideline for Commanders IV

How to protect against the enemy's plans I

Military schemes to defend against *shinobi* only function to block those *ninja* who have not reached the true principles of the *shinobi* arts. Seen from the viewpoint of those *ninja* who *have* mastered the true principles of *shinobi*, no matter how wide and deep the moat is, they could cross it as easily as if they were on flat land, or no matter how high the stone wall rises they could climb it as easily as pulling loose rope hand over hand in an open meadow. Even if you assemble your army with the [Chinese] Principles of Five, keep a guard strictly night and day, then try to question everyone, it is as easy as if prying on your neighbour. Also, even if you arrange passwords, identifying marks or certificates to stop the enemy from slipping in, that would only allow them to look like your allies so they could get into your army with as much ease as getting into their own camp.

According to Buddhist teachings, if you have doubt, the entire world is like a castle [and contains obstacles], but if you are enlightened then there is only emptiness[1] in the universe. This holds true; however, that being said, it is *almost* impossible to get into a good general's castle or position or serve with distinction under the orders of a stupid general. As the stupid general does not know how to use *shinobi*, even the most excellent *ninja* who has benevolence, bravery, tactics

---

1 This is loaded with connotation. Emptiness is a positive in this context.

and achievements, and is enlightened to the extent that there is only emptiness in the universe for him, even he would act awkwardly, just like a fine horse that can run as far as one thousand *ri* would be as a dog or sheep that has been fettered. If an ignorant general uses *shinobi*, it is the same as a slave trying to control the finest horse. Consequently, a *ninja* could possibly end up in dire straits and likely fail to attain his goal.

On the other hand, if ordered by a good general, bright and enlightened *shinobi* can steal into the enemy line with no more difficulty than when you get into your ally's camp. There he could move around among the enemy's forces of one million people freely and without being noticed by anyone. In this situation he can attain great achievements and practise his loyalty to the maximum, without any doubt. People do not know how masters with such skills have achieved so much, just like they do not know who has made the nature of the Five Elements in the universe. If the general's bravery is renowned even in distant domains or areas, then sooner or later the enemy will be destroyed, just like when the sun rises, frost or snow will disappear in time. According to the *Bingjing* manual, secret agents are requisite and essential in the art of war. However, it would be useful to write here how you can defend against *yonin* 庸 忍, that is ordinary *shinobi* of middle or lower level, and this should now serve as a paragon for a general, and also to provide those learners on this path with some hints for their way.

Six points on how to avoid employing enemy *shinobi*

I

Examine closely those who newly come into your service. They should be scrutinized so closely that even their past, their families and their homelands should be understood. Also, their wives or children, if any, should be made to move into your territory. If not, make him wed a wife that you offer and have children, so that you can take them as hostage.

You should have a reliable person stand guarantee for them. If there is no suspicion, then you can have them serve in your army. Be sure to check their references with their previous master exactly to see how or if he appreciates them, the reasons as to why they left their master and so on. Do this very closely and give it full consideration.

II

Be careful of anyone who surrenders up to you. You should suspect that someone who has surrendered might be *teki no ninja* 敵ノ忍者, that is an enemy *ninja*. If this is so, put *kakushi metsuke* or secret watchers in place and keep him under surveillance, giving any needed consideration. If you are in some provisional fortifications and you have no construction to keep new soldiers in, simply put him in an enclosure. If you are in a camp, you should place him somewhere in the outer area of the camp, outside of the first or second sets of troops.

Alongside this, have him make an oath to the gods on paper, and have him confess that it is not a stratagem and that there is no double-dealing. However, in such a case there are things you should be aware of in terms of the defence. If he surrenders under false pretences again, there are ways to expose his tactics. To be transmitted orally.

III

Merchants, monks, those who live in seclusion, *yamabushi*, *in-yo* diviners, Shinto priests, performers of music, dance or other types of entertainment, local villagers, beggars or anybody who looks suspicious should not be allowed into the castle or camp at any time. This should be strictly brought home to everyone by repetition.

A poem on military affairs says:

商人ヲ数多作テ敵陣ヘツカイテ内ノ体ヲ能看ヨ

Make up a number of merchants and send them into the enemy's camp where they can observe them.

From Yoshimori's poems:

番所ナドヘ乞食非人来リナバ　荒クモテナシ追返スヘシ

If a beggar or outcast comes near the guardhouse, treat them in a rough way and clear them off.

番所ニテ心ノ弱キ人ハタダ　不覚ヲ取ン基イナリケリ

In the guard station, a weak-minded person could make a blunder simply through his nature.

他国ヨリ来ル人ナラハ親類モ　番所ニ近クヨスベカラサレ

You should never allow anyone from outside of your province to come close to the guardhouse, even if he or she is a relative.

IV

You should bring merchants from your province. In the case where you use local merchants, you should have someone who stands surety for them. According to some writing, merchants who serve in your camp should be brought in from your own province. If you have to use local merchants, inquire into their background closely and have a reliable guarantor. If you accept merchants without much thought, the enemy *shinobi* may come in disguised as a merchant and seek information from the inside. In case the merchants are placed outside of your camp, they may set a fire and make a commotion so that they will take advantage of it and deliver a night attack.

Shibata's martial poems:

商人ヤ一銭刺ノ屋根アツク小部屋構ハ火付カハミヨ

If the small constructions for merchants or penny traders with thick roofs are set on fire, you should be aware it may be arson.

我陣ノ外ニ掛タル町小屋ハ火付ナルカト心ユルスナ

Keep vigilant eyes on the huts built outside of your camp so they may not be set on fire.

V

Detecting the possible conspiracy of a suspected agent

If you have those who seem to be directed by the enemy or those who look suspicious in any way, you should talk to their close retainers or relatives trying to determine if their words are true, or offer a deal that if they speak the truth, they will not be blamed but might be rewarded highly, even if they themselves committed to the conspiracy. Another way is to give a feast so as to loosen their tongues and to make them reveal themselves, or have them separate from each other, such as a master and his retainers, husband and wife, brothers, or other relations. This is done so that their plans will be found out with your own ingenuity. The methods you should employ should be varied according to the time, place and person.

VI

Not only courtesans or demimondaines but also maidservants, or any kind of woman, should not be allowed into your position. When you are defending a castle, a strict order should be given not to let any woman in the castle, even if she is from your province and has a reliable background.

I may say that warriors are *yo* while women are *in*. Therefore, if some women are within your force, the *chi* of *yo* will be degraded by *in* and it will yield. Zhuge Liang[2], when he encamped went up a high mountain every morning to look down onto his forces to see if they were of *in* or of *yo chi*. He once found his forces covered and distorted by *in*. Feeling suspicious about it, he investigated the troops. As a result he took out women from where they were hidden and executed three hundred of them. The spirits of the forces were regained at once.

Seven points on the discipline of the army

I

With newcomers mixing together with long-serving soldiers, the Principle of Five should be equally applied. The fivefold system is constructed in blocks of five people to make a force of twelve thousand five hundred people. This is because the formation should be arranged on the basis of the 'diagram of directions', which has the five directions of east, west, south, north and the centre. The beginning gives birth to the two fundamentals of *in* and *yo*, then from this comes the Five Elements, with which everything in the universe is built. Then conversely everything returns to the Five Elements, and the Five Elements are reduced to *in* and *yo*, and *in* and *yo* end up back at the 'one'.

Zhuge Liang's eight formations use five as a unit, which turns it into the eight formations, all of which are united into one. To be transmitted orally.

Use five coloured flags to show which formation is to be taken, and use the drums and the gongs to inform whether to advance or withdraw, or the speed at which this is to be done, according to the situation. Also, the five colours allow your men still to feel in control even with the formation's defeat or downfall. That is why it has been divided by utilizing each sign since ancient times.

[The Principle of Five]

- Five people make a *go* 伍 and each *go* has a *gocho* leader 伍長.
- Five *go*, put together, make a group called a *ryo* 両, consisting of twenty-five people, and each *ryo* has a leader.
- Four *ryo* make a group called a *sotsu* 卒, consisting of one hundred people, and each *sotsu* has a leader.
- Five *sotsu* make a group called a *ki* 旗, consisting of five hundred people, and each *ki* has a leader.
- Five *ki* make a group called a *shi* 師, consisting of two thousand five hundred people, and each *shi* has a leader.
- Five *shi* make a group called a *gun* 軍, consisting of twelve thousand five hundred people, and it has a *taisho* 大将 or the commander-in-chief.

---

2   181–234, prime minister of Shu Han and considered a good strategist.

An alternative system
- Two *go* make a group called a *ju* 什, consisting of ten people, and it has a *jucho* leader 什長.
- Ten *ju* make a group called a *sotsu* 卒, consisting of one hundred people.
- A *sangun* 三軍 is three armies, which means the *full force* consists of thirty-seven thousand five hundred people.

The above is how the Principle of Five works.

I may say the Principle of Five should be applied to a mixture of long-serving men and newcomers, because if there is any possibility of *tekinin* 敵忍, or enemy *ninja*, having slipped in among the newcomers, it will be necessary to have long-serving or hereditary vassals mixed with the newcomers.

From the six *bugyo* senior officers down to foot soldiers, servants, lower people, retainers of newcomers and low-rank *samurai* and newly employed *ronin* – every single person should be laid under this principle.

II

The first strict law that the unit of five people should follow is that if there is doubt with someone, they should not pretend not to see or not to hear anything or to ignore the situation. If something dubious is discovered by anyone from another unit, all of them should accept the same blame for such treachery.

The second law is that if even one of the five people breaks any of these martial laws, then they are all equally guilty as a group.

The third law is that they should check their weapons or belongings with each other in the unit.

The fourth law is that the unit should synchronize their steps and walk together.

The fifth law is that if one of them needs to leave the group he should get their leader's seal for permission to do so.

The sixth law is that if there is a suspicious man, you should tell the leader of the unit of that man and send him to the leader under guard.

The seventh law is that if you have found a suspicious person or you think that a *tekinin*, or enemy *ninja*, has slipped in, you should pretend not to notice but then tell the captain discreetly.

The eighth law is that anyone, even if it is a close relative of the suspect, who reveals information should be given high rewards.

This is the outline of the eight laws. These martial codes should be applied strictly with the greatest attention.

III

In each *ryo* of twenty-five, a *metsuke* overseer 目付 or *yokome* 'side-eye' spy 横目 should be secretly placed. The attributes a person needs to be a *metsuke* overseer are:

- to have little personal desire and a great sense of justice
- to have no favouritism to anything but always to be loyal to his lord
- to be from a respectable family

He should be given high rewards so that he will be more encouraged.

IV

Make sure that what is discussed and decided in a council of war, be it your formations or other such things, will not be discovered by the enemy *ninja*. You should work out an appropriate way of doing this dependent on the situation. The first thing is that the command from the general should be respected by *samurai* and soldiers above anything else and the army of soldiers should keep quiet. If the army is well controlled, every command for formation, attack on the castle, night attack or anything will be enforced throughout the army so quickly and they will be able to advance or withdraw freely.

The *Three Strategies* says:
When the general's plans are kept secret, enemy spies will not be effective.

Sun Tzu says:
The ultimate skill in the deployment of troops is to ensure that it has no fixed or constant formation and disposition. Without ascertainable formations, even the most deeply infiltrated and observant spy will not be able to probe and comprehend, and the wisest strategist will not be able to uncover your plans or plot against you.

I may say *shinobi* is not a matter of *in* but is in fact *yo*, which should be employed when you perform *shinobi* duties. You should be aware that *in-nin* infiltration is shallow, while *yo-nin*, that is infiltration by open disguise, is deep. This is what underlies the skills for defending against it.

V

How to detect that which is hidden outside the official listings[3]
Details to be transmitted orally.

VI

If *ninja* are imprisoned by the enemy and are offered paid service by the enemy general, they should answer that they agree to work for them but then inform their allies of this as soon as possible and notify them of the situation discreetly. In such a case, they should be rewarded by their original master with double the amount the enemy has offered, which should be arranged through someone in a close intimacy to the *ninja* and in secret.

VII

If someone brings information on the enemy's movements, whether advancing or withdrawing, or pertaining to their secret plans at least three days before the event, they should be rewarded highly according to how much he is devoted to his lord. As well as *samurai* or soldiers, merchants or peasants should also be informed of this offer but in secret – [that is away from enemy ears].

During the Genko era (1331–1334), when Kusunoki Masashige was defending Chihaya castle, there was a general of the enemy army of Kanto named Kanazawa Umanosuke who devised various stratagems to capture the castle. In order to hold out against this, Masashige made his two retainers, Kizawa Heiji and Munei Kofuji, pose as merchants and sell armour, horse gear, paper, lacquer-ware and so on, thus having free access to the enemy's camp. They successfully gained acquaintance with Umanosuke and he trusted them. Through this trust he was offered by the false merchants a scheme of treachery involving a way to defeat Onchi Sakon, who was a general of Kusunoki's forces. Because of this treachery, in the end, forty valiant warriors of Umanosuke were drawn into the castle under pretence and all of them were killed. Consequently, all Umanosuke's schemes were impaired.

Also a retainer of the Kusunoki clan named Hayakawa Kota was approached by Osaragi Mutsunokami with an offer to sell out and in reward to be given a certificate for land yielding two thousand *kan*[4] with the addition of one thousand *ryo* of gold. Upon this offer he immediately then told Kusunoki, who rewarded him with a land of five thousand *kan* and two thousand *ryo* of gold. Taking his cue from this, Kusunoki then used Hayakawa as a *shinobi* [employing him as a double agent] and succeeded in killing masses of enemies.

---

3 'Documents of arrival' 着到状 were given by a *samurai* to the lord when he joined the army – they listed his forces and his equipment. The manual has only the first two ideograms and appears to be an instruction on how to tell if there are extra and unwanted forces in the army.

4 A unit of fief, about one thousand eight hundred litres of rice.

Shochi V

A Guideline for Commanders V

How to protect against the enemy's plans II

Three points on watch fires

I

Instructions for constructing the main standing fires and the extra or expendable fires for your castle or camp

The main watch fires should be positioned on both sides of the gate on the outer fence perimeter [which is made of brushwood hedges or bamboo and surrounds the entire encampment]. Extra watch fires should be made, even five, six or seven *cho* away from the camp. To build these extra and expendable fires, you should dig a hole and crawl into it.

Some writings suggest that the main watch fires should be built thirty *ken* away from the fence with three sides built up as embankments and the right and the left embanked walls should be about seven *shaku* high.

The main fires should be lit before nightfall. The expendable and smaller external ones should be built thirty *ken* farther away from the main fires. These are not to be fed with more wood during the night, which makes it more difficult to keep a good fire going. However, on a quiet night, it does not matter how it is constructed. But, on a windy or rainy night, it can be difficult to light them, and the fires will not last until dawn. On such a windy night, you should pile wood at an angle with the extended ends on the leeward side and then light it from the windward side. These expendable fires should be burnt from midnight onwards.

Those in charge of a night patrol should be very attentive to both the main watch fires and the single-use fires. On a rainy night, it is better to put lots of straw on the main fires, as keeping the main watch fires burning is difficult. Also, you should have the proper knowledge on how to construct them. On a windy night, the single-use fires should have the flame toward the leeward direction [to prolong its life]. However, if the wind is blowing toward you, the wood should be piled at an angle, in a fan shape with the points facing you.[1] When the wind is blowing toward camp, then the distance between the one-use fires and the main watch fires should be longer than usual.

A martial poem says:

押寄テ先手ニ陣ヲ取ナラハ燎ヲタカセ夜ヲ明スベシ

When you are advancing and making a camp on the front line, keep watch fires burning until the day dawns.

A martial poem by Shibata says:

敵近キ里ニ陣取ル夜々ハ表ニ活卜燎火ヲタケ

When you encamp close to the enemy line, you should make large watch fires in front of your camp every night.

II

Hang large lanterns at every exit of your camp. Alongside this, put a lantern everywhere where needed. Such lanterns should not have the general's crest but some other one that is not in use anywhere else. It will aid you a little in your tricks. To be transmitted orally.

III

Hang a lantern down from the castle or camp walls or use *sarubi* monkey fire, which is fire on a rope, *kurumabi* cart fire or *mizutaimatsu* water-proof torches, to inspect the bottom of the moat area. When you defend a castle, as well as examining within the castle itself, you should watch for the enemy *shinobi* approaching; do this by using these lights and lowering them down the outer walls, especially paying attention to the recessed corners. This goes without saying when concerned with those castles that are not naturally fortified, and even those castles of strong fortifications should be guarded strictly every night with the utmost of attention. The tightest security should be carried out on a stormy night when the wind and rain are strong.

---

1 That way the fire has to fight against the wind and will burn longer.

A *ninja* poem says:

大雨ヤ大雨シケキ時ニコソ　夜詰忍ハ入者ソカシ

In heavy rainfall when the rain is at its most, you should take advantage of it for your shinobi *activities and night attacks.*[2]

One writing says that to see if the enemy *shinobi* has passed through your camp, there is a way of digging out a shallow two-*ken*-wide trench and applying fine sand on the bottom between the watch fires. This is done so that you can see the footsteps of someone who has infiltrated. However, as the *ninja* may be wise enough to manage to hide their footsteps, the sand should be raked very neatly and examined very closely so that it will be noticed if it is in disarray. Though this is actually a shallow tactic, it might help for defending against *shinobi* by making the enemy *shinobi* think that you are conducting the strictest guard.

Five points on passwords, identifying marks or signs or actions of identification

I

In some cases, passwords use a cue, like pulling the ear or blowing the nose to make your opponent give the code word; also there is a preset way of using matched pairs, which is easy for even lower-rank people to use. *Bugyo* commanders should invent good versions of these and change them from time to time and have their men say them to each other. If necessary, the password should be changed every night. Examples of these passwords are: 'stars to the moon', 'the moon to the sun', 'waves to water', 'smoke to fire', 'fruits to flowers', and so on. You should invent good versions so that everyone, even lower people, can memorize and say them with ease; change every night and have them say it. To be transmitted orally.

II

Though there are ancient ways for identifying marks, unless you invent new ones and rotate them, the enemy will manage to infiltrate by having similar or fake ones. Therefore, make sure to change them for every occasion. One of the commonly used ancient identifying marks was a white piece of silk of about one *shaku* two *sun* long which was put on the back of your helmet. However, you should arrange this ancient way according to the opportunity, like changing it to linen or cotton [to fool the enemy]. To be transmitted orally.

---

2   Or to defend against them.

One writing says, when in a battle camp, the passwords or identifying marks should be changed every day and night. If you use the same one for two days, the enemy will know this. You might have to change it even in the middle of the day or middle of the night. By using association between words, you should use one hundred different pairs for each one hundred-day period. Old pairs of words that everyone knows, like 'forest to mountain', 'water to valley', 'woods to village', 'waves to the sea', etc., are not desirable. Other instances, such as 'Yoshino to cherry blossoms', 'Miyagino to *hagi* flowers', 'Mount Fuji to snow', etc.,[3] could be created – as many as are needed. Alongside this, identifying signs like blowing the nose or holding the ear should also be employed.

III

When you are going in for a night attack, you should have everyone in your army wear the *dokagaginu* undershirt beneath his armour. To make this undershirt, white linen or cotton cloth should be used. Make the width of this double the standard width for normal cloth rolls[4] and the length should reach down to the hip and have no sleeves. To be transmitted orally.

IV

When your army has come back after a night attack or if you suspect that an enemy *shinobi* may have infiltrated the group, you should develop ingenious *tachisuguri isuguri* identifying signs as a basis, which are prearranged signals invented by Kusunoki Masashige as a way to find intruders. To be transmitted orally.

V

When your army is going in for a night attack, you need to make your troops take an identifying pass and check it at the gate when they come back, or make them repeat the passwords. However, it does not work well if your troops are very numerous or the enemy is very close.

Ninja poems say:

夜討ニハ敵ノ付入事ゾアリ　味方ノ作法兼テ定メヨ

During a night attack you may have the enemy follow you back, and get into the ranks of your allies. To prevent this, you should have a prearranged policy, a way to identify your allies.

3　These word associations are references to classical poetry.

4　Seventy-two centimetres.

我方ニ忍ノ入ト思ヒナバ　味方ヲカゾヘテセンサクヲセヨ

If you suspect that the enemy's shinobi may have infiltrated your side, discover them by counting the number of your allies.

A martial poem says:

夜討来テ引退トモ油断スナ火付ヲ残シ陣ヲ敗ルゾ

When you are the victim of a night attack, do not let your guard down even after the attackers have withdrawn. They may leave someone to commit arson and your camp may be destroyed.

Six points on behaviour in the guardhouse

I

Every gate of the castle or camp should be guarded whether day or night; everyone going in or out should be checked for identification with a pass. Especially when the enemy is close, arrange an identifying mark or password and have everyone of your army, of high or low rank, informed of it without fail. At every guardhouse, any of these three alternative ways should be strictly checked. Strict rules should be adhered to and in the case where there is someone who is not vigilant, he should be punished severely. Those on guard should be turned every two hours. At night everyone should be told to carry a lantern with the general's crest in the upper position and his own crest under it.

II

Whether in the camp or castle, guardhouses placed beside the outer wall should be guarded strictly day and night. Recessed corners of the stone walls, the inside of the water pipes of a floodgate, the rubbish disposal area, woods or bushes in the castle and any other suitable hiding places should be inspected with special care. These are where *shinobi* are likely to get in. Even if it is a well-fortified place or even if you are not in confrontation with the enemy, you should not lower your guard. On stormy nights of wind and rain, night guards or patrols should be even stricter. If there is someone who is not vigilant, he should be punished strictly, and this order should be enforced among all.

A martial poem says:

手アキトテ油断バシスナ夜討火付此方ヨリソ入ソ
トハ云フ

*Do not let your guard down even if you are not confronting the
enemy. Night attacks or arsonists may infiltrate from near your post.*

III

Concerning watch guards while in a battle camp
Halfway between the main watch fires and the expendable fires, ten foot soldiers
together with one or two mounted warriors should keep a strict guard at certain
points. They should follow the same rules as above for the lanterns with the two
crests and should take turns in two-hour shifts. Before taking turns, they should
perform scouting duties in no-man's-land.

IV

As well as the inside of the castle or a camp, the *tobari* outer area or the *kedashi*
area, which is immediately on the outside of your camp, should also be strictly
patrolled with night-time watch guards. Whether you are defending in a castle
or in a camp, night-time guards should be divided into groups, so that they can
sleep in turn, day and night. This should be done both for the inside and the
tobari or *kedashi* areas.

The *tobari* area, which is the area thirty to fifty *ken* outside of the castle or
camp, should be strictly guarded, and for the *kedashi* areas you should have
guards stationed at a distance of five to seven *ken* outside of the main camp.

A *ninja* poem says:

サハカシキ事アリトテモ番所ヲハ
立退去リシ物トコソキケ

*Even if there is a din outside, be aware that the guardhouse should
not be left completely empty [so that guards can] listen to sounds
outside.*

夜廻リヤ大事ノ番ヲスル時ハ　静リ居ツツ物音ヲキケ

*When you are on night patrol or have to stand guard in an
emergency, you should keep quiet so that you can hear any sounds.*

[Point V is missing from the text]

VI

Whether day or night, scouts for a far-distance observation should be sent out. To be transmitted orally.

Three points on night patrols

I

For the inside area, three foot soldiers at a time should be on duty in two-hour shifts, patrolling inward of the watch fires. Be sure to watch with utmost care the narrow alleys, rooms, latrines or any other places that are good as shelter.

For the outer area of the fires, five or six mounted warriors at one time should go round and keep watch closely and be on duty in two-hour shifts. In doing this, everyone should carry a lantern with the crests as taught before.

On night patrol, four or five people who are not carrying lanterns should follow those carrying the lanterns and at intervals. To be transmitted orally.

A poem says:

夜廻リノ心掛ニハ物音ヤ敵ノサハキト火事ト油断ト

When on a night patrol, what you should pay attention to is any sound or commotion among the enemy, the fires and your own gaps.

I I

Kamaritsuke secret scouting methods are used by those without a light following the night patrol, sneaking along at intervals. They go round in a stealthy way, trying to find enemy *kamari*.

From Yoshimori's poems:

夜廻リノ通跡ヨリ廻ハスヲバ　蟠リ付トゾイフ習ナル

You should conduct a thorough search, following behind the party of a night patrol. This is called kamaritsuke *or 'the detection of* kamari *agents'.*

夜廻リノ通ル跡コソ大事ナレ　蟠リ付ヲハイクタリモセヨ

It really matters that after the night patrol is conducted, be sure to conduct kamaritsuke *over and over again.*

蟠リ付ハ段々ニ行マワルコソ　敵ノ忍ヲ見ツクルトキケ

When undertaking kamaritsuke, *it is said that you should make multiple rounds at intervals to enable you to find the enemy's* shinobi *agents.*

III

When those on night patrol or undertaking *kamaritsuke* detection methods find a suspicious person then they should make him say the password or his name. If they still have suspicion about him, then in such a case they should pretend to be convinced that he is on their side and capture him alive, taking advantage of any gaps. Do *not* kill him immediately.

Yoshimori's poems also state:

夜廻リニ不審ノ者ヲ見付ナハ　知略ヲ廻シ生捕ニセヨ

If you find a suspicious individual while you are on night patrol, you should capture him alive by calling on all your resources.

夜廻リニ討捨ヌルゾ大事ナレ　ハヤマリ過テ味方討スナ

On night patrol it is inadvisable for you to cut someone down immediately. You should not be too rash – this is to avoid the risk of killing your comrades.

Two points on *togiki* listening scouts

I

Togiki scouting foot soldiers should be placed at intervals of thirty *ken* and mounted warriors should be placed at intervals of two *cho*.

II

Kagi [those who smell] or *monogiki* [those who listen] are hidden scouts. They should keep the following in mind:
- to head in the direction of *baikijin*[5]
- to make mental notes along the way
- to stretch a rope across the pathways
- to listen to how the dogs are acting

---

5   A variable direction based on Chinese astrology and used to decide a ninja's direction of attack.

When you are defending a castle or are in a camp, a number of people should be sent for *kagi* or *monogiki* scouting every night. *Kagi* or *monogiki* is to send people secretly along the roads where the enemy might come to attack or to places where the enemy's *shinobi* might infiltrate. Make sure to commit to a thorough detection sweep in every direction and secretly; front and rear and left and right. They are there to capture *shinobi*; however, if the enemy is too large in number then they should come back to inform the general as soon as possible. *Kagi* scouts go forward, while *monogiki* scouts follow the *kagi* scouts at a distance of twenty to thirty *ken*. Details are to be transmitted orally.

These are also called *togiki* or listening scouts. When going for *togiki* scouting, if you are not sure about the way to get back, you should make marks such as tying grass or placing a bamboo stick into the ground. When the wind and rain is raging and it is pitch black and the road is broad, you may not notice if the enemy *shinobi* has passed you. In that case, you hold a rope in your hand, stretching it out so that the *shinobi* will hit it when trying to sneak past.

In addition to this, when going for *togiki* scouting, you should choose the direction of *baikijin* – this is where a night attack of *shinobi* will come from. This is what those skilled in *togiki* scouting are aware of.

The direction of *baikijin* is:
- the twelfth direction on the time of the Rat, Horse, Hare or Cockerel
- the eighth direction on the time of the Ox, Ram, Dragon or Dog
- the fourth direction on the time of the Tiger, Monkey, Snake or Boar

One writing says that when you place people for *togiki* scouting, you should place foot soldiers at intervals of thirty *ken* and mounted warriors at successive intervals of two *cho* and this should extend halfway from the enemy's front line to your *hatamoto* headquarters. This is so that the information from the front line can be directly relayed back to the headquarters.

A martial poem says:

夜ルコトニ忍ノ者ヲツカハシテ敵ノ来ルヲ告シラスベシ

Send shinobi no mono *out every night so that they will see and inform you if the enemy is approaching.*

Two skills for defending against the enemy by using tools

I

Scatter bamboo caltrops and also scatter iron caltrops of two types[6] on those roads where you expect the enemy *shinobi* will come.

II

Set *harahatabarai* traps to knock the legs from under people or set *tsurioshi* traps beside the outer wall and camouflage them. Various kinds of front-line forts, fortifications, camps or castles which have no natural defence should have these traps around them on the roads where enemy *shinobi* may come from. Also, if the water gutter that is used to feed the castle is big enough for a human to get through, apply iron rope to it. The above tools are shown with illustrations later on.

These above are the 'hush-hush' sections of your tactics for preventing enemy *shinobi* from infiltrating. It is hard to tell exactly how to act according to the situation and the time and the place. If you have a set of fixed ways or use a constant form, how could even the greatest general obtain a victory?

As Tai-gong-wang says:
If a general's plan is leaked, the army will not be able to affect their strategic plans. If internal affairs are revealed, disasters beyond control will befall the army.

If enemy *shinobi* are in your army, it will bring about your downfall more than anything else. It is akin to having a griping pain in your stomach. Therefore, a commander-in-chief should keep the above measures in mind and enforce all these given disciplines among his men. Then how could ordinary *shinobi* of middle or lower level infiltrate your army? What are most subtle within the arts of the *shinobi* are the ever-changing angles which infinitely alter according to the situation, and there are too many examples to mention to help highlight this. However, the baseline of all stratagems or disguises is always the same, and that is the art based on the skills of the Five Elements. In order to defend against enemy plans or *shinobi*, or should an emergency arise, you may think it more desirable to have a large number of people. However, you should not hire more people into your army without careful consideration. Rather than leading a large number under your command with the enemy mixed up as your allies, it would be better to lead a small number of true allies. Even if they are a small number, there should be a way to win over a massive enemy force. You should not waste

---

6 Two different plants are mentioned: *Trapa japonica* and *Tribulus terrestris*. One is used for 'round' caltrops – small spikes formed into a 'ball' – and the other for twisted iron caltrops.

gold and silver to pay for useless people. That would be even more harmful. Save any expense and instead support as many full-time soldiers as possible, so that, when at war, you will not need to hire whoever you can find in haste, and this will prevent most of the enemy's spies from finding their way into your forces.

In order to stop enemy spies, do not fully believe what a newcomer says. Instead, you should think of making a converted spy of him, feeding him false information. Disguised *shinobi* can be detected by the five skills: certification with stamps; passwords; identifying marks and signs; the *dokataginu* undershirt; and *tachisuguri isuguri* signals and signs. Take note, mountain castles, outlying castles, fortifications and camps are subject to covert infiltration by *shinobi*. To defend against this, frequent night watches and guards should be carried out. To block converted *shinobi*, try to know their true intentions, and have a doubtful mind about what they say so that you will not be deceived. *Shinobi* always try to look for any small gap where you let your guard down. The character for *kan* 間 can be also read as *ma* (gap), *aida* (between) or *hedatsuru* (divide), and the ones for *cho* 諜 and *tei* 偵 can be read as *ukagau* – 'to peep' or 'to detect'. Thus everyone should be made fully aware that *shinobi* can arise by taking advantage of any gap in your guard. If strict discipline is maintained in conducting everything without negligence, *ninja* of the middle or lower level will not be able to get in successfully. However, a man cannot be alert all the time and also any army will have a gap in discipline no matter how strictly it is conducted. Therefore, a superior *shinobi no mono* will be able to take advantage of even the smallest opportunity when you are off guard or use the narrowest gap where you fail to maintain discipline. Therefore, he can infiltrate anywhere and, after infiltrating, achieve his goal without fail.

Yo-nin I

Open Disguise I

Infiltrating a long-term undercover agent

Shinobi no jutsu consists of *yo-jutsu* and *in-jutsu*. *Yo-jutsu* is to infiltrate the enemy in plain sight with elaborate plans of ingenuity, while *in-jutsu* is to 'steal in', hiding yourself from people's eyes. In this volume are written the techniques to infiltrate by inventing innumerable plans which should be ever changing according to the situation, and finding and taking advantage of any gap within the enemy while you yourself are in plain sight – that is why it is titled *yo-nin*.

Secret techniques to infiltrate without fail are deceptive ways which are varied and flexible and are done according to opportunity. Thus, as a basis, you should embrace the old ways of the *shinobi* who served under ancient great generals, but remember not only to keep to these ways but to adapt them, each dependent on the situation and the moment. Ignorant *ninja* are not aware of this principle but directly stick to ancient ways and do not even know the simplest of facts, like 'a ball rolls downwards if it is on a slope',[1] which means that when they see that a moat is deep and a stone wall is high, they do not know how to deal with the situation and even say there is no way to infiltrate such a place. It is folly to see something as unchangeable and stick to an old method without realizing that things keep changing and are in flux.

---

1   This is a direct translation of an idiom, it means that the lesser *shinobi* do not understand reason or consequence.

Six points on laying plans

I

Shihogami 四方髪 – **various hairstyles for each and every province**
Shihogami is one way to prepare yourself by changing your hairstyle according
to the place you are going. Depending on the time and the place, you should
choose an appropriate style. For example, *shukke* monks, *yamabushi*, *hatonokai*
conmen, *negoro mono* 'soldier monks', women, professional gamblers, and so on
all require you to change your hair. On top of that, you should employ a specific
way of shaving your forehead according to the province. These are all examples
of applying the technique of *shihogami* to prepare yourself – that is, according
to opportunity. When Kusunoki Masashige defeated Yuasa Magohachi Nyudo,
who was defending Akasaka castle, the tactics taken by Onchi Sakon Masatoshi
are recorded as proof of this.[2] Also, when Prince Takakura rebelled, Hasebe
Nobutsura used the trick of having the prince disguised as a female, and accompanied by a child-servant named Tsurumaru who handled the baggage. Also, a
man named Rokujo-no-suke Tayu Munenobu accompanied them with a parasol
over the prince. They successfully managed to get to Miidera temple without
anyone discovering them on the way.

II

Whether you disguise yourself as someone with a trade or just make a basic imper-
sonation, you should be skilled in the art of whatever you are going to disguise
yourself as. When you infiltrate using *yo-jutsu* 妖術 disguise techniques, if you
try to impersonate the appearance or the speech but have no skill in the trade,
your stratagem will easily be revealed. Therefore, you should learn in advance
not only how to look or speak like the person you are going to impersonate, but
also, the art of the trade they do. For example, if you intend to disguise yourself as
a monk, you should be familiar with that particular sect of Buddhism, frequently
visit a temple of the sect and closely learn its ways. When the time comes that
you need to carry out a secret plan, you should talk in secret to a monk of the
temple to make an agreement that, in the case where the enemy tries to find out
if your identification is true or false while you are carrying out your plan, the
temple will certify your identification without question. You should take any
measure to make your plan as flawless as possible, from the beginning to the
end, and before you take any action. Taking on the guise of a *komuso* priest as
an example, you should practise to play the *shakuhachi* flute very well and learn
to talk on Zen.

---

2 Presumably this is a reference to the war chronicle the *Taheiki*

Lord Mengchang of the state of Qi was captured by King Zhaoxiang of Qin. However, he managed to escape his bonds by bribing Zhaoxiang's wife with a snow-coloured fox-fur coat made from ten thousand foxes and escaped into the night without being noticed. As he reached Hangu Pass, the last checkpoint of Qin before returning back to his territory of Qi, he became scared that those on his trail might catch up if his army [were held] there until dawn. Now then, there was a man among the three thousand in his entourage who was good at imitating a cock crow and whose name was Tian Jia.[3] Tian Jia climbed up a tree and imitated a cock crow that woke up all the cocks in the area. Because of this the guard of the pass thought it was dawn and allowed Mengchang and his men to go through the checkpoint.

After Qin Shi Huang passed away and before the Second Emperor was in his full prosperity, a man named Chen Sheng put a piece of paper with the words King Chen Sheng[4] into a fish's belly[5] and released it in the sea. Also a man named Wu Guang[6] was good at imitating the call of a fox and called in a fox-like voice that the Great Chu would arise and the Qin Dynasty would collapse and Chen Sheng would be the king. People felt this was wondrous and thought it was a good omen that the Qin Dynasty was declining and, as a result, Xiang Yu of Chu and the founder of the Han Dynasty raised an army and Qin was ruined in the end.

Also in our country there have been a number of cases where the art of imitating did bring advantages to *shinobi no jutsu* and they will be mentioned later.

III

You should always try to learn the customs and manners of the people and the topography of various provinces.

You always need to learn and understand in full the following elements of various places: the customs and manners; the dialects and languages; the topography, such as the locations of mountains, woods, rivers, wetlands, steep, rugged or flat terrains; how long the distances are; and how wide or narrow the roads are – even the narrowest of roads. If you prepare such information beforehand, even when you are in a flurry or get lost and fall behind others, then with all this above information you can get to any given destination without

---

3 This name is most likely an error, as this person does not appear in the original story.
4 ?–208 BC, the leader of the first rebellion, known as the Daze Village Uprising.
5 A prayer or action for a future benefit.
6 This is not the correct name of the man who imitated the call, the correct name is unknown and does not appear in the original Chinese manual.

difficulty. Or when you infiltrate into the enemy province in the disguise of a person of that province, if asked about anything concerning the topography or the ways of the people, you can answer this correctly and in detail.

I V

You need to acquire and keep copies of the marks and seals of the lords of various castles.

You should always try to obtain the seals of castle lords or generals for the case where you need to forge letters to incriminate a target for a conspiracy. If the seal is different from the correct one, your plan may fail. Also you should approach someone who is good at copying others people's handwriting, which will enable you to forge the writings of the enemy lord or any of his generals freely as is sometimes necessary.

V

You should always try to learn in advance the flags, standards, helmet crests, screens, coats of arms and so on of many of the generals of your time. If you 'sneak in' with such information as above, it is useful, both in the case where you infiltrate under a stratagem and where you are asked about various points and need to answer appropriately, and also in the case where you infiltrate with *in-nin* hiding[7] skills or *fun-nin* 'slipping in' skills. This is important because if your cover is almost discovered while concealing yourself you may need to give an evasive answer.

V I

You should always hide your name or skills deeply.

Anyone who is a *ninja* should ask his lord to keep the fact a secret, which should also be the case even in a time of peace; as the fact that you are a *ninja* should be deeply hidden. Even to very close friends, you should never talk about how good or bad this art is in any way and when the land hits a state of turbulence it is often the case that the enemy will become your ally and your ally will become the enemy. It may happen that when you infiltrate with the intention of fulfilling a plan, there may be someone who is familiar with you on the enemy's side and who will be able to detect that you are *ninja*, which means that not only will your plans have to be aborted but also that you will be put to death – and remember that it could also do serious damage to your lord. Therefore, you should always keep your name and artistry a secret and guard it

---

7   Normally Fujibayashi uses the ideogram for *yin* from *yin-yang*. However, here he uses 隠, which means 'hiding'. He then adds *fun-nin* 紛, which means 'slipping in'.

with care, and on the outside you should look like a *tonshi* hermit-warrior or a *heishi* normal warrior. That is exactly the way you should be prepared, so you can use your *ninjutsu* when a period of turbulence arrives.

The *Six Secret Teachings* says:
When an eagle is about to attack, it will fly low and draw in its wings. When a fierce animal is about to strike, it will lay back its ears and crouch down low. When the sage is about to move, he will display a stupid countenance.

Lao-zi says that:
Great wisdom is no wisdom and great plans are of no plan.

Sun Tzu says:
A clever fighter has neither reputation for wisdom nor credit for courage.

All *shinobi no mono* should always keep in mind what these words actually mean.

Three points on *katsuraotoko no jutsu*[8] or the skill of the 'ghost on the moon'

I

This technique comes from the legend of Katsuraotoko, who lives on the moon.

In normal times, before the need arises, you should find someone as an undercover agent who will become the *betrayer*, an enemy you plant and thus make a *ninja* of him and have him within the enemy castle, camp or vassalage, exactly as the ghost in the legend, Katsuraotoko, is stationed on the moon.[9]

In choosing one to be planted as a *ninja*, you should not appoint a person whom you do not know very well in casual life or who is not very smart or trustworthy. When selecting someone from your family or a close relation, use one who has wisdom, faith and courage. On top of that, take a hostage from him and make him write an oath, so as to make sure of his pledge before you send him.

Remember, Zhang Yi of Qin successfully infiltrated the service of Wei and, while serving as a minister in Wei for years, he led Wei to ruin in the end.

---

8 A skill based on the Japanese legend of a ghost who was said to be very good looking and who lived on the moon to tend trees. According to the legend, if you gazed at the moon too long, unless the moon was full, the ghost would invite you there and you would die. Also, if you eat the blood-red leaves of his trees then you will become invisible.

9 In other words, in a far off province.

I I

You should make an *isoanaushi*[10] undercover agent of a girl from her childhood. If there is a child who is good looking among those close to you, you should create an intricate plan and then, when the time comes, use her to create false charges, or to murder by poisoning[11] or other such appropriate measures. However, this art will be discovered unless you have a *chitchu*[12] or *tonshi*[13] agent. *Chitchu* is someone who is given a fief by a lord but keeps it a deep secret that he is serving that lord and has thus made him a pledge. He is supposed to live in a place close to the capital (Kyoto), such as Osaka, and to do nothing at first. Then when the time comes, he is to be planted into the enemy after arrangement between the lord and the retainer. This undercover agent should not live in a remote area, as he will attract people's suspicion, so a busy area is better, as people tend to have less doubt about such people. The second term, *tonshi*, means a person who has retreated into a rural area of the country [in an enemy's province] and who has talents and intelligence, is faithful and does not lie. You should call on him and hire him discreetly with a promise to give him a high salary, so that you can ask him to act for you in the future when needs arise, and if such a need comes then he can be planted within the enemy without delay. Alternatively, you could use an *anaushi* undercover agent, which is a person who lives in a townhouse or private house close to the enemy castle and always tries to be on close terms with the vassalage of the enemy. When your army is going to approach or attack that province, he should display a want to serve the enemy expressing his great fortune to be there at such a time of need or something of that nature. They will show happiness to hear that, but what they do not realize or even begin to imagine is that in truth he is extremely 'violent venom'. Lord Nobunaga had a boy retainer of fifteen or sixteen years old who had excellent handwriting skills. The lord sent him to serve Imagawa Shinsuke, so that he could in time master the copying of Shinsuke's handwriting. Later he forged a letter from Shinsuke and made discord between Shinsuke and his lord, Yoshimoto. This caused serious disharmony within Imagawa's vassalage and was the downfall of Yoshimoto in the end.

---

10 An unknown term; however, it is most likely a generic term for an undercover agent. By combining the ideograms *ana* and *ushi*, it creates a compound for the ideogram for 'prison' or the first part of the word *ronin*, linking it to an undercover operative.

11 The sentence here is in code and at first appears to make no sense to the reader, but a closer inspection of the idioms used, 讒 and 毒殺, yields the above translation.

12 Literally, insects that live underground for winter.

13 A hermit *samurai*.

III

You should place an advisor or a liaison within the enemy

After planting such undercover people into the enemy, it is difficult for them to send a signal and to communicate with your lord without a liaison or contact. Therefore, there should be one who disguises himself as a merchant or monk and stays close to the enemy castle. The undercover agents should discuss things with this new liaison on any and all topics required or the liaison can obtain information from a child-agent who has been planted inside the enemy. Also, there should be another person who acts as a messenger between the liaison and the lord who comes and goes, to communicate and report on the situation. Remember, in the case where you have to plant a child, then you should be sure to have someone close to the enemy castle to pretend to be his father or brother.

Three points on *jokei no jutsu*[14] or shadow-like *ninjutsu*

I

Jokei no jutsu is to be like a shadow, following a thing that has form. If you catch any slight sign of hostilities or betrayal, just like a shadow corresponds to a form, you should go to the prospective enemy's castle-town and try to get employment within their vassalage, before the enemy starts their stratagem. If you arrive there too late, you will arouse their suspicion and your aim will not be fulfilled. For this mission, a *samurai* who is well known to many people will not do. Therefore, in this matter a *chitchu* 'worm agent' or *tonshi* 'hermit agent' would be appropriate.

II

The placement of contacts or liaisons

You should have as many contacts as possible in your group who disguise themselves as monks, merchants and so on and they should stay close to the castle so that they can bring back the information required or guide your allies into the area at the most appropriate time.

III

If the enemy has doubts or is suspicious of you, you should perform *karionna kariko no jutsu*, which is the art of a mock wife and child. This skill is to create a false wife and child and take them to the enemy with you and to offer them as hostages. In cases where the enemy will not allow you to enter into their service without taking hostages, you should use this skill. To be transmitted orally.

---

14 This term is also found in the *Shoninki* manual. The two ideograms are slightly different but share an etymology and are regarded as the same thing. The *Bansenshukai* version is 景 and the *Shoninki* version is 影.

[Two points on] *kunoichi no jutsu* or the art of the female agent

I

Kunoichi no jutsu is to send [a female] for a *shinobi* mission and this person is represented by one ideogram, which consists of three letters combined.[15] When it seems difficult for *tajikara*[16] [male *ninja*] to infiltrate, use this art. In general, *kunoichi* have a twisted and inferior mind, shallow intelligence and poor speech, so for example [*text blacked out with the number '2' left exposed*] you should not use those who you cannot recognize for what they are. If you have someone you have observed correctly, make them take a strict oath, educate them thoroughly and specifically about the signals and promises so that you can send them deep into the enemy by taking the appropriate measures. Alternatively, you make them a servant who is accompanying someone who has access to the enemy. Plans of this nature will be successful and without fail.

I I

Use *kakure-mino no jutsu* or the art of the invisible mantle to infiltrate
You will have to communicate with a *kunoichi* before you use this art. At a certain point, the *kunoichi* should tell the master's wife in a casual way and without importance that she wants to send for a wooden chest, which she has left with somebody. No one will suspect that she might have a stratagem, not at all – even an extraordinary warrior or one with the most resourceful mind in the world will not conceive of it, and it is even less likely that the wife in question will have any doubts so surely she will give her permission for the box to arrive. Then the female agent should tell the guards of the gate beforehand about the arrival of the chest. Before it arrives you should have someone hide within the chest, before it gets into the castle gate. This chest should have a false bottom and clothes should be put in the upper part. Also, it is fine to have it bottom heavy and it should be carried by two men.

Sun Tzu says:
At first, exhibit the coyness of a maiden, until the enemy gives you an opening; afterwards emulate the rapidity of a running hare, and it will be too late for the enemy to oppose you.

---

15 The ideogram for 'women', 女, can be broken down to three elements, which can be read as *ku no ichi* くノ一 or 'female'. See *In Search of the Ninja*, p.155.

16 A male *ninja*. The ideogram for man, 男, can be broken down to the two radicals of *ta* 田 and *chikara*. This point is of interest, as the term *kunoichi* has become famous in the Western world, yet *tajikara* has remained unknown.

The above-mentioned *kakuremino no jutsu* should be used when there are lots of people who know you and nothing else seems to be successful. This skill is of the highest secrecy and thus there are oral traditions to go with it. If this art is used properly during your *shinobi* mission, there is no castle you cannot infiltrate, no matter how strictly it is guarded.

Two points on *satobito no jutsu* or the art of the local agent

I

Place those local people from the enemy's province [inside the enemy castle]. When you intend to infiltrate the enemy castle, you should go to the enemy province before the allied forces have advanced, and find someone who is out of employment and ambitious and wishes to acquire fame or bravery, or someone who bears a grudge against or resents your enemy lord, also, commanders and so on, but who cannot express his grievance because of timing, or someone in the area who has a member of their family within your own allies. Taking the appropriate opportunity, you should approach such a person by using an appropriate measure and you should invite him to join your side. Sometimes, you should call on his place to bribe him with gold or *nishiki*, that is expensive brocade, and make this promise: if he achieves success in his tactics, he will be rewarded with a set amount of stipend. Do this with the guarantee of the lord's red seal. On that basis, you should take hostages from him and make him write an oath, and then place him in the enemy castle with a well-considered plan. The enemy lord will have no doubts about him as he is from his own domain, so it will be as easy for him as getting into his own house.

II

To infiltrate by becoming an attendant to the *satobito* or local agent
If the *satobito* or local agent in your plan is not good enough or is inexperienced, you should make yourself a servant to him and enter the enemy castle with him [as a part of their retinue]. You should have made arrangements with your lord for the signals needed and set fire at the most appropriate time.

[An example]
When Kusunoki Masashige went to defeat the clan head of Yasuda no sho of Kishu upon an order from Sagami Nyudo, he encamped at Katsuoji to observe the status of the enemy. After three days of doing this, he called for the *nobuseri*[17] bandits he was giving stipend to and asked if they knew of any other *nobuseri*

---

17 This word has a few possible meanings, including 'those who give ambush' or 'peasant bandits'. *Nobuseri* were used by some warlords as guerrilla fighters.

around there. One of the *nobuseri* bandits said he knew several of them and went out and fetched eight, to whom Masashige gave a lot of gold and silver. He told them to take his own *nobuseri* into the enemy camp to bring back information on the current situation. They took the job saying it was easy for them and took six of Kusunoki's *nobuseri* with them and infiltrated the enemy camp. Once in there, they mixed with the locals, stayed for one day and got back the next night. When hearing what they saw, Masashige inquired of each of the fourteen separately, and each one reported the same thing. Thus he judged there were no doubts and commenced a night attack, which of course ended up being a success. The above example is similar to this skill of *satobito no jutsu*.

Two points on *minomushi no jutsu* or the art of a worm in your stomach

I

You should judge an appropriate person to use as a *minomushi* or worm. A *minomushi* is someone who serves the enemy but is made a *ninja* working for your side. Thus the agent is exactly like a worm in the enemy's stomach, which eats its belly from the inside out. It is of extreme importance to have good judgement on who to employ for this job. If you judge it wrongly, it is obvious that it will cause a serious disaster, more so than it actually helps. Therefore, there are things you should be aware of for the purpose of recruitment. You should observe the following:

Find someone who has a predecessor from a previous generation who was punished for what he did not do or punished beyond his offence. Choose someone who is a descendent of such a family and has an ill feeling toward the lord that stems from the bottom of his heart.

Find someone from a family of such a good lineage that he should have been promoted higher than he has been or one of talent and ability but who is of a lower ranking than he should be and thus who feels bitter about his situation.

Find someone who has a strong loyalty and has made great achievements but has been given only a small stipend and who would rise to distinction if he was hired by another lord. Furthermore, it should be someone who feels that his lord is stupid as he is treating evil retainers who only flatter him but show no great deeds.

Find someone who is smart and talented but does not get on well with the lord and tends to incur his displeasure and is given only a low position.

Find someone whose skills or arts are superior in the world but is given only a low position. He might want to leave the position but not be allowed to do so. It could be possible that the man is being blocked from making a move, thus he may have to endure this situation.

Find someone who serves on the opposite side of a war to that of his father or sons and who regrets this fact.

Find someone who is very greedy and wants gold or silver or a high stipend or someone who is cunning and tricky and has little loyalty and is double-minded.

Find someone who has done something unworthy of his father and so has a bad reputation and who feels frustrated about that.

These eight kinds as mentioned above are only outlines that you should have in mind when choosing an appropriate person. Based on them, you should be tactful by figuring out a good way to know what the person thinks deep inside their mind, according to the opportunity.

I I

The art of making a *minomushi* or worm agent

If you have decided on a candidate for the above-mentioned *minomushi*, you should not inform him of your plan [at this stage] – it will be disastrous if you tell him your tactics without a thought or care. Therefore, once you decide in your mind who to choose, you need to think out a plan which will work so that the candidate cannot refuse to become a *minomushi* under any circumstances. It will depend on the situation at hand – however, here are one or two examples.

You should obtain lots of gold and silver from your lord and appear to be a rich *ronin*, a *samurai* for hire, then take up residence within five or six *ri*[18] from the candidate you have chosen. Then you should approach the target to get acquainted with him and make him think that you are richer than he is, so that you can quickly become friends. While trying to make the relationship closer, you should investigate his likes, so that you can take advantage of him and bribe him heavily. While making this friendly relationship stronger and stronger, you should cautiously induce him to talk about anything and investigate what he is thinking at his core by joking with him or something of that nature, so that you can have a confidential talk at the end of this humour. If this is successful, giving him a red seal which guarantees a high stipend, you should take his father, mother, wife, child or so on as hostage, make him write an oath, and arrange for the signs or signals before you use him. In general, whether young or old, few people think much of loyalty outside of their lust or greed, even more so with the above eight types of people. It is in no way impossible to bribe such people if you approach them with booze or sex.

---

18 The measurement of *ri* changed during the Edo period. Here we have used the Sengoku period measurement to make the distance more representative of the time when Fujibayashi was writing.

Three points on *hotarubi no jutsu* or the art of fireflies

I

If there is an enemy tactician who has overwhelming sway in the enemy vassalage, you should forge and transport a secret letter that has been created to imply his treason or create a letter from your lord to the retainer you have targeted. Also if there is anyone who has betrayed your side and defected to the enemy, take advantage of such a person and forge a letter that discusses specific signs or something which appears to connect the target retainer and this person who was once your ally; do this so that he looks like he is actually an enemy agent who has been planted and not a true defector.

Han Xin of the Han Dynasty and An Lu-shan (703–757), a retainer of Xuan-zong of the Tang Dynasty of ancient China, were similar to Yoshitsune here in Japan [and all three of these people were slandered and killed in the end]. Therefore, if there is a general who is excellent in tactics or wisdom on the enemy's side, and it is the case where people think that that excellent general may rise in rebellion and that the future of their side may be at risk, then you should look for the best opportunity and forge a secret letter and fake his treason. Or forge a secret letter from this distinguished general to someone on your own side, such as someone of his family, or a friend or someone who everyone considers that he would join forces with. When you make such a plan, send a man and make him a *ninja* with the reply to this fake letter sewn into his collar. He should wander around the enemy castle in a suspicious way, so that the enemy will question him, thinking that he is or might be a *ninja* and thus they will capture him. They will interrogate him intensively but he should not give in and answer at the beginning. After they get harsher in their questioning, he should pretend that he cannot help but confess everything and bring out the letter or the reply in such a way that he gives away the fake rebellion and incriminates the intended target. Understand the further details of this art; such as how to write the secret letter, what should be in the text, how to behave when captured by the enemy, how to confess when questioned and so on. These elements are difficult to explain in writing and should be transmitted orally.

Alternatively, you can employ *fukurogaeshi no jutsu*, the art of the reversible bag; this is where two different people should serve the enemy, the first should serve the enemy general and the second should serve his tactician. You have the one serving the retainer carry a forged letter which is addressed to the undercover agent's real general. On his way out of the enemy camp – with this forged letter – [have the agent who is serving the enemy general] capture him, so that the enemy lord will become aware of the happenings and get involved.

Alternatively, make someone wander around the enemy castle with a letter from a commander of your own side that is addressed to the target retainer. This letter should display the arrangements specifically for signals and other information on the structure of his 'betrayal' and it should be sewn into the operative's collar. When captured and questioned intensively, he should react as explained above.

A further method is: if there is someone who betrayed your own side and defected to the enemy, you should forge a secret letter which arranges for signals and plot details and make someone wander the enemy camp suspiciously with this letter, so that he will be captured by the enemy. When he is questioned, he should not answer at the beginning, but later after being questioned several times, he should bring out the letter and tell them of the target in question and how his defection was not true in intention and that he is going to double-cross them later or set fires and that it was all arranged beforehand.

This above skill of *hotarubi no jutsu*, the 'art of fireflies', should be performed only after you know everything about the enemy and in great detail so that you can construct your letter in accordance with the target's mindset.

When the Song Dynasty and Yuan Dynasty fought around the Yangze River, as many as three million people of the Yuan Dynasty were killed; the Emperor was so depressed that he could not function. Coming to his aid, a commander from a western tribe created a plan and was victorious in the end and he used an example of this above technique.

I I

Whenever you infiltrate with the techniques of *fun-nin*, 'slipping in', or *in-nin* 陰 忍, you should always forge a secret letter of conspiracy that is connected to a close retainer and carry it within your collar.

When infiltrating the enemy castle by *fun-nin* or *in-nin* without having *hotarubi no jutsu* embedded, that is, having an inside agent established, then you should always prepare a secret letter addressed to an enemy retainer and carry it sewn into your collar. This is because no matter how carefully you have made your plan, you may be discovered and captured, and in that case, the enemy will question you on the purpose of your infiltration. At the beginning of the inter-rogation, you should not show any sign of giving in, and after being severely inquired upon many times, you should say:

If you spare my life, I will give something of grave concern to you. If I do not inform you of this, then you will plunge into a crisis which will break out from inside of your allies and no one knows when it will happen – maybe it is even happening right now. If you give me quarter, I will tell you what it is. However, if I am to be executed, I will not give away anything no matter how severely you torture me.

Then the enemy will ask you to give away the conspiracy and they will spare your life. You ask them to give you a written letter of pardon, which says they will give you quarter for certain to secure the truth from them. Since it is a matter of grave concern, they will accept your request more often than not. Then you should ask the one in charge to take you out of the public eye[19] where you can bring out the secret letter from your collar. You should tell them that the target person on their side will create a rebellion with a promise from your own side and so while your army is attacking them on a certain date he will form a rebellion in concert with the *ninja*'s side, and that is why you have been sent as a messenger. Remember to be careful that it does not sound like you are contradicting yourself. The trick in carrying out this kind of art is to know very much of what the enemy is like and write a totally plausible letter using such wording as they might use. If the enemy does not believe you and says that it cannot be true that the target would betray his lord, they will claim that you are lying. In that case you should answer:

If you do not believe me, I know of a secret letter [which has been addressed to my lord from one of your retainers] and it is now being held by [insert name], so you should send someone to fetch it.

You should have prepared a letter of treachery exactly as if it were a real letter with the target's seal, and such arrangements should be made for it to be sent forward if the above situation arises, so that this plan will work well in such an eventuality. If things are going as you plan, he may be able to escape execution in most cases, and will cause domestic conflict among the enemy. Even if this plot does not work well, they will have doubts with each other, which should lead them to defeat in the end.

III

If you use someone who is not rewarded highly by your lord with the skill of *hotarubi no jutsu*, you should adapt this skill and feed him false information.

In general, the man to be sent in using the skill of *hotarubi no jutsu* should be someone who is rewarded highly by his lord, so that he would die for the mission, or a poor man who has many children to raise. If you have to use someone who is not obliged to the lord or someone ungrateful, he will change his mind and work out a plot that will ruin your own side – it is essential to keep this in mind.

Sun Tzu says:
Spies cannot be usefully employed without a certain intuitive shrewdness. They

---

19 It is unknown if this means 'away from the view of the general people' or if it means 'away from the view of the extended group of inquisitors' including the possible target.

cannot be properly managed without benevolence and straightforwardness. Without subtle ingenuity of mind, one cannot make certain of the truth of their espionage reports.

Hence it is that with none in the whole army are more intimate relations to be maintained than with spies. None should be more liberally rewarded. In no other business should greater secrecy be preserved.

Therefore, it is not recommended at all to employ someone who is poorly rewarded for this art. However, sometimes it may be the case that you cannot use the best man for the job. In such a case it is acceptable to use a [poor-quality] and poorly rewarded person; if this is so, choose someone who is restless, audacious, talkative, impatient and fickle. When you give someone of this type the details of the plan, you should tell him the direct opposite of your true plan. For example, if you intend to attack toward the west, you should tell him you are attacking the east, if north, tell him it is south, and you should give him all the information but in opposite and in a very plausible way.

When sending him out, you should make sure to arrange that this *ninja* will be captured[20] and without fail and when he infiltrates into the enemy, as he is of poor quality he will be careless. Because of this he will be caught soon after he is in position in the enemy territory, and the enemy will interrogate him to establish your side's plans. At this point they will try to make him confess what he knows. On such an occasion, if he gives them what he knows about his allies, his life will be spared and he may be given a high reward, but if he does not confess, he will not be rewarded and even worse he may be executed. Under such conditions, most people, even those who owe the lord greatly, but do not have enough righteousness, will become *hankan* or converted spies, and this is even more so with those who are only poorly rewarded and lacking in patience and thoughtfulness. Such people will divulge to the enemy whatever they know, such as the army's armaments, preparedness or anything of that nature. As the enemy will believe this story they will prepare their strategy based on your false information. This is the art of *reversing the reversed spy*, which will result in your side winning a glorious victory.

---

20 A clear example of the 'doomed agent', which, depending on his actions, makes him a reversed spy.

Two points on *fukurogaeshi no jutsu* or the art of reversing the bag

I

Fukurogaeshi means to reverse your mind in such a way as turning a bag inside out. A *ninja* should go into the enemy's land, create a connection and get into the enemy castle and declare the following:

I am from the province of Iga and I have practised ninjutsu *from my youth and I am skilled, I can infiltrate any castle or camp more easily than a cormorant bird dives in water. If you hire me, I will go and infiltrate for you any castle or camp you like.*

Also there is a special way to demonstrate how good you are, which should be orally transmitted.

He should also try to convince them with smooth talking, saying it is hard to show them the nitty-gritty of the arts here, as they are secret. If it is a time of war and if you promote yourself like this, your request for service will be accepted without fail. Later when [the *ninja*'s] original side advances, it will have prepared an unimportant hut or building that he can set fire to, as prearranged with his true lord. By taking such measures like this, he makes the enemy trust in him all the more. Therefore, he can take any chance he needs to come over to his allies and convey to his real lord as much information about the enemy as possible. When the opportunity arises, [with help from him] you should set fires to the enemy's castle, conduct a night attack by using tactics or surprise attack by way of ambush or have your allies follow the enemy forces when you lead the night attack back into the enemy castle and capture the castle directly by this method. This art is named *fukurogaeshi no jutsu* as it is like a bag turning inside out then turning back to its original form.

To do this art properly, it is essential for *ninja* always to try to stay unknown to people as much as possible. Nothing would be better than a *tonshi* or hermit *samurai* in this situation.

II

In case it is difficult to carry out this art, you should make yourself an attendant to someone who has access to the enemy castle or camp.

Those who have access to the castle or camp can be monks, doctors, blind musicians, *sarugaku* musicians, craftsmen, merchants and so on. You should investigate in detail anyone else who has access to the castle and become an attendant to one of them. If you can successfully get in the enemy castle or camp, you can lay various plots or make false charges or something of this ilk, which will cause domestic conflicts among the enemy vassalage or leave them having doubts with each other. Later when the time comes, you should set a fire as you have agreed with your lord.

In 1361, in Hakata, Tsukushi province, Echizen-no-kami, who was a retainer of Kikuchi Higo-no-kami, devised a strategy of night attacks against Matsura-to and won a complete victory, which has been proven and written in detail. In ancient times, people used to make false charges when doing this art, so, if you can infiltrate as an attendant to someone who has access to the castle or camp, there is no reason that you should not be able to do this. [If you infiltrate as an attendant,] the enemy will believe what you say without question, even false charges.

Two points on *tenda no jutsu* or the art of spitting in your own face

I

Tenda no jutsu is like if you cough or spit with your face upward, and letting the spittle drop down on your face. This art is to use the *ninja* sent by the enemy to your side and for them to come to harm.

You should keep strict control over your soldiers to have a keen eye for those trying to infiltrate your forces. To do this you should conduct various procedures, such as night patrols, to watch closely and to guard against *shinobi*. If a *ninja* is sent from the enemy and your allies capture him, you should say to him:

If you have intent to break faith with your lord, your life will be spared and you will be hired for a great reward.

Do this to persuade him. If the *shinobi no mono* says yes, you should give him a red sealed document from the lord to guarantee this, take his wife and children secretly as hostages and make him write an oath, so that any doubt should be cleared about his real intentions. Then you should ask him in detail about what the enemy's status is. If you have enough information about what is going on with the enemy, it will enable you to construct any kind of tactics you need.

In the case where you send him as a *shinobi* back to the enemy, they will let their guard down and consider him as being their own *ninja*, allowing your plans to work very well, which in the end will defeat the enemy with ease.

Sun Tzu named this art *hankan* or converted spy and said it is the best skill to use. He says:

Having converted spies, getting hold of the enemy's agents and using them for our own purposes – those enemy spies who have come to spy on us must be sought out, tempted with bribes, led away and comfortably sheltered. Thus they will become converted spies and available for our service. It is through the information brought by the converted spy that we are able to acquire and employ local and inward spies. It is owing to his information, again, that we can cause the doomed spy to carry false tidings to the enemy. Lastly, it is by his information that the surviving spy can be used on appointed occasions. The end and aim of spying in all its five varieties is knowledge of the enemy, and this knowledge can only be derived, in the first instance, from the converted spy. Hence it is essential that the converted spy be treated with the utmost liberality.

According to the *Chokkai*, the 'Colloquial Commentary' on the *Art of War*:
Everyone should know about the five types of spies; however, the arts of four of the kinds – local, inward, doomed and surviving spies – are all used in combination with converted spies. Therefore, in the use of converted spies [there is need for you to have] more intelligence and they should be rewarded most generously compared with the other four types. When you send a spy or use a spy, do not make a spy work for you or someone who is working for others, as there are always only a few who are of intelligence, while there are always plenty of those who have only a poor talent. It is always difficult to have anger at injustice while it is easy to take shelter in excuse. While in the enemy land, a spy has lots of money and beautiful women in front of him, swords and saws at his back and cauldrons to his side.[21]
If he double-crosses through fear of death or poverty, he will hide it from the lord but there must be someone who will inform the lord of this. In case he has more eloquence than others and does not submit, if led by elaborate questions, he will give away lots of secrets concerning your side, so any well-intentioned conduct of his will come to nothing. Thus, spies themselves will give out information without intent. The difficulty in using spies exists here, at this point. Sun Tzu knew this disadvantage very well, so he said it is of importance to make a converted spy according to the person in question.

These words are completely reasonable. Therefore, the lord should reward generously those *shinobi no mono* who have achieved the four values of loyalty, bravery, tactics and expertise.

I I

When the enemy *ninja* comes into your castle or quarters or to the foot of or around the stone walls or to a stone fort, then pretend not to have noticed him and let him hear you talk about the constructed and false tactics of your army, so that he will work as a *ninja* for you without his even knowing it.

If you notice that a *tekinin* or enemy *shinobi* has infiltrated your castle or camp, you should pretend not to have realized it and intentionally let him see or hear the things about your army. He will believe it is true and proper information and

---

21 Symbolic of punishment.

bring it back to his allies and inform them wrongly. The enemy general will take it as being true and make arrangements or lay plans for his army according to the report. In reality, this is a construct, since your allies know that he is an enemy *shinobi* and you have pretended not to know, by saying what is the opposite to the truth; for example, saying east for west, south for north and so on. As the enemy plans are all based on this false information, their intentions will backfire and fail. This art should be carried out when it is very hard to capture the enemy *ninja* even if you know he is just outside the castle or camp, or near a fence or stone wall, or when you know someone has infiltrated your quarters but you do not know who or where the *ninja* is. In such a case, you should let him hear you say such false information loudly or let him see what you want him to believe. This method is different from the previous mentioned art but the principle is the same.

When a general of the state of Qin was going to attack someone whose name was E Yu, as E Yu and Zhao She were in a very close friendship, Zhao She went to save E Yu, but after travelling as far as twenty *ri* he built a fort, with deep moats and secure walls and stayed still in the fort for twenty-eight days. Meanwhile a *kanja*-spy from the state of Qin came over to see what Zhao She was doing, and Zhao She knew this but pretended not to know and let him hear that it was very difficult to save E Yu. On top of this, he let the spy see how much they were trying to secure the guard as though they were digging in for a full defence. The spy went back and informed the general of Qin of this, so the general was very much pleased to know this and advanced his army saying that Zhao She was definitely not going to save E Yu, and so they could attack E Yu without any worry. However, at the same time as when the spy journeyed back to Qin, Zhao She retreated his army by thirty *ri* with their armour folded and flags down, and then climbed Hokuzan mountain and waited for the hordes of the Qin army. As the general of Qin did not expect anything, they were attacked by Zhao She's forces and Qin ended up in defeat. This is an example of where you can make an ally-*ninja* of an enemy *tekinin* – there have been so many cases of this.

Sun Tzu says:
All warfare is based on deception. Hence, when able to attack, we must seem unable; when using our forces, we must seem inactive; when we are near, we must make the enemy believe we are far away; when far away, we must make him believe we are near.

Two points on *shikyu no jutsu* or the art of relaxing your bow

I

Shikyu no jutsu, **the art of loosening a bow – this means when the bow is strung it is crescent-shaped but when loosened it goes back against itself**[22]

Normally, when a *shinobi no mono* is captured by the enemy, he will look like he is giving in and will follow the enemy on the surface while he will stick to his principles at his core; thus, he will not become an inverted spy, like a loosened bow.[23] This is the origin of the name.

At the point when a *ninja* is first captured, if the enemy offers to make him a converted *ninja*, he should take advantage of this. If not, he should take an appropriate chance to approach them with an offer like:

I have difficulties in my life owing to - there should be something inserted here but this is an oral tradition[24] *– and though I have been hired by the other side, they are against the principles of heaven and their high-ranking samurai are not respectable enough to serve as masters and therefore I do not feel secure about my future.*

Then, the enemy is sure to be pleased to hear this and willing to give you quarter. However, they will demand you to write an oath and to offer hostages secretly. To this, you should say:

I have had hostages taken by my lord so it is difficult to offer hostages here and now. In future I will offer hostages to you as soon as possible. [Also, it is not a good idea to take hostages] as if the slightest rumour of my betrayal is known to my side, our plan will not work successfully. As for the oath, I definitely would like to write it.

As an old saying goes:

One who is going to undertake a large project should be at ease with minor [and negative] things.

In the above situation giving a false oath that is born from loyalty for an end purpose is considered to be a reasonable measure. Do not hesitate at all in such matters.

As is said in the chapters of *Shochi – A Guideline for Commanders,* you should build a hut for newcomers at a distance from the main headquarters. The above *shinobi no mono* should also say to the enemy lord that he will set fire to the quarters of his own side to show he is not a double-sided agent, and if the enemy takes up this offer, he should go and set fire to a prearranged hut or something of the same nature; also, he should take the decapitated head of a newcomer and

---

22 It is possible this is based on the workings of a Chinese recurve bow.
23 Certain bows, when loosened, will invert on themselves.
24 Fujibayashi is saying that there is a secret skill for this.

bring it back. By such measures, there will be no way that the enemy will not relax its caution against you.

After this, the *shinobi* should take advantage of any chance to return to his allies, to make secret arrangements with his lord for the signs and for the best time to set fires; it could also be possible to kill the enemy lord in the end by this method.

II

Things you should keep in mind in a case where the enemy has captured you and brought you close to your castle and forced you to talk to aid their tactics
Sometimes the enemy captures you and brings you close to the fence or wall of your own castle or camp in order to make you give away a plot. You should say exactly what the enemy tells you to, but there is an ingenious and subtle way to do this. For these tactics, there is an established way where you should make arrangements with your commander-in-chief before you go into the enemy position [so that he will not be fooled if the above situation arises]. Even if you follow the instructions of the enemy, it will not upset or confuse your allies, as with these signs arranged beforehand between you and your lord he will understand your true meaning. In this way you can lower the guard of the enemy, and when the time comes you can return to your original side after setting fires in the enemy castle or camp, or after making false charges, or even after taking the head of an enemy.

Yamabiko no jutsu or the art of echoes

An echo is generated by clapping your hands but it echoes here and over there. The relation between the lord and the retainer should be like this when you undertake a *shinobi* mission[25] and this is how it is done.

From the beginning, which lord you serve is not a secret; therefore, any plea to serve the enemy may not be fulfilled. Even if you manage to serve the enemy with a hidden plot, it may turn out that your plot will not only be revealed but you will be killed and also it will be more damaging to your allies than anything else.

Therefore, you should make a secret arrangement with your lord, whereby you commit a serious offence and the lord reprimands you severely, throws you into prison, or confiscates your properties and exiles you from his domain.

Then there should be a constructed fight by force of arms so that you should

---

25 What does not come across in the English is that the man given such a mission is a relatively high-ranking samurai, who has the option of meeting with other high-ranking samurai in the enemy.

kill five or even seven lower soldiers before you run away. You should go to the enemy and tell them this false story to show that you are not lying and that you hope to serve them; if you do this they will allow you to serve them without any doubts. After becoming a retainer on their side, you should try to convince them by devoted service, bribe the counsellors or commanders with treasures, get into the favour of men close to the lord, according to their respective taste, or have discreet meetings with the enemy generals and infiltrate your own original side to set fires on unimportant buildings. By taking every chance to go back to your allies, you should inform your true lord of the status of the enemy, and, when the time comes, you should kill the enemy lord before you leave or set fires in his castle or camp while your allies are attacking from outside, or do anything you can according to the opportunity.

Takezawa Ukyo-no-suke killed Nitta Yoshioki by such a conspiracy; also, at the battle between the state of Wu and the state of Wei, a retainer of Sun Quan of Wu deceived a general of Wei with these tactics, these are written in the *Shogosho*[26] document and in detail.

The above chapter is about infiltrating in advance by *yo-nin* and has principles that are very profound and are deep secrets of *shinobi no jutsu*. They should be considered the utmost sections of wisdom, and are of a great subtlety. If an intrepid general and *shinobi no mono* work together in accord, spare no expense, listen to heaven's will, keep only loyalty and righteousness in mind, and when the time comes, use numerous secret skills, then even if a castle is guarded by any great commander and thought to be impregnable, there will be no way that they cannot infiltrate or capture it. There are more principles than are written in this manuscript which move by word alone, which should be conveyed from one mind to another and they cannot be passed down in writing no matter how much money is given.

---

26 This is most likely the Wakan Ninri Shogosho document, which is a missing section of the *Bansenshukai,* a copy of which is in the Iga Ueno Museum.

Yo-nin II

Open Disguise II

Infiltrating in haste

This volume is about how to infiltrate with *yo-jutsu* when you are confronting the enemy; therefore, it is titled *chikairi no jutsu* or short-term infiltration.

As it is natural that excellent tacticians make plans even when no sign [of war] is on the horizon, nothing is better than *toiri no jutsu*, that is to infiltrate far in advance. This is because while you and your enemy are confronting each other at a close distance, each side is highly alert – therefore, it is not easy to infiltrate. However, in the case where you have not put an agent in place with *toiri no jutsu*, then you cannot help but use the arts in this chapter.

Seven points on *ryakuhon-jutsu*[1] or information-gathering

I

As well as intelligence on the enemy castle or camp, you should try to find out the names of *roju* senior counsellors, *mono-gashira* troop captains, *bugyo* commanders, close retainers or esquires, tacticians, correspondence officers, messengers, gate keepers and so on, and also find out where they live, trying to talk to people as much as possible. Alongside this, you should try to collect information such as what kind of families they are from, where they are from, what kind of jobs they have been engaged in, etc.

---

1   From *ryaku* ('constructing a plan') and *hon* ('root', 'basis' or 'truth').

Sun Tzu says:
Whether the object be to crush an army, to conquer a city, or to assassinate an individual, it is always necessary to begin by finding out the names of the attendants, the aides-de-camp, and door keepers and sentries of the general in command. Our agents must be commissioned to ascertain these.

If you have such information as the above, you can utilize it as follows:
- To aid your operation and tactics and according to the situation.
- So that you can disguise yourself as a messenger from someone within their family.
- To use it to slander someone in the enemy so as to cause a breakdown among them.

Without this kind of information your plans will have no grounding.

I I
How to enquire for such information as described above
To get such information, you should approach those who have left the enemy side and are now masterless *samurai* (*ronin*) or monks, merchants, blind musicians, *sarugaku* musicians and so on – all of whom have access to the enemy side – and question them and record everything. If you need to do any further investigation, you should visit their relatives; note if they are peasants or town folk, or even *samurai* serving another clan. You should visit where they live and you should investigate thoroughly and talk to them closely and obtain precise information. In the situation where you have not obtained information beforehand, you should ask merchants or peasants around the enemy castle or your own prisoners fully.

In the case that you are besieged in a castle, or that both sides are facing each other in another province, you should go to a mountain village around the enemy camp and talk to mowers and loggers who are working for the enemy and lead them to give you the information you need. It is essential to obtain as much information as possible by leading them skilfully. It is good to carry a portable inkpot to write down everything.

A *shinobi* poem says:

墨筆ハ万事ノ用ニ立ツカシ 忍ヒニ行カハヤタテ放スナ

Japanese sumi *ink and a brush are useful for every purpose. You should not go on a* shinobi *activity without a* yatate *writing case.*

III

In the case where you pretend to come from another province, you should learn the manners or the dialect of the target province in full.

If you say you are from Iga or Koka, then the enemy will instantly go on to the alert; therefore, you should pretend to come from somewhere else, a place that you know well. However, if you cannot use the dialect or manners of the place proficiently, then the enemy will be even more suspicious, so you should master the language and the manners thoroughly.

IV

You should carry seals of the lords of other provinces.

I mentioned this earlier, but this technique is used mainly within the skill of *chikairi no jutsu* or short-term infiltration, thus it is included here again.

V

You should take a fake wife. If you do not, getting one while travelling will be acceptable. To be orally transmitted.

VI

All *ninjutsu* has the same principle, but this is especially so in the art of *chikairi no jutsu* or short term infiltration. You should take into consideration what the enemy wants, its ways of talking, thinking or acting – consider this when you construct your plan.

The *Three Strategies* says:

When neither the beginning nor end is visible, no one is able to gain full under-standing. Heaven and earth, like all things, also change and transform. You should keep changing your ways according to the enemy.

If things are not going as mentioned above, disastrous consequences will be brought forth in the end.

VII

As mentioned in the chapter of promises for *A Guideline for Commanders*, it is especially important when you use the art of *chikairi no jutsu* or short-term infil-tration to arrange passwords and signs without error.

Examples of night signals include *hikyakubi* fire beacons, *ireko-hi* adjustable lamps and *iccho-ikka* 'one fire for one *cho*'. For the daytime, signal fires, flags, conch shells, etc. are used. You should make arrangements with the general for the use of these signals – for example, by making very loud noises such as drum beats, cries, gun shots, etc. This may be done to inform you that they are going to attack. This is especially important for the times of setting fires – whether you are practising *yo-nin* or *in-nin* infiltration, it is hard to set fires successfully without this skill.

Four points on the art of passwords
I

Getting information about the enemy by asking their lower-ranking soldiers
Supplementary heading: three different ways to get into the battle camp, a night raid and the enemy castle.

Every *samurai* is normally prudent while lower people or soldiers are generally stupid and unwise, so nothing is better than talking to lower people to have them give away their secrets. Particularly, the young, the drunk or the rash are best. Lower people are not so closely connected with the higher-ranking members of the army so they are overlooked or not listened to more often than not and are rarely questioned. That is why you should involve yourself with the lower-ranking people and ask what you want to know.

Passwords are not strictly used when you are besieged in a castle; this is because there is no traffic going in or out. However, when you are constructing a battle camp or are going for a night attack, you should have a strict way of using passwords. Before the enemy constructs a camp, you should go around the back of the enemy's position or in any forests behind them or so on and ask lower soldiers or labourers for the passwords. The way to do this is passed on in oral tradition.

Also, when the enemy is coming with a night raiding party and you infiltrate them using the skill of *suigetsu no jutsu* or when you are going to perform a night attack on the enemy camp, in these two cases you will be able to move around side by side [with the enemy] and have a chance to ask and probe the people mentioned above.

When you are going to infiltrate with *in-nin*, you should discover the enemy passwords the night before. You should obtain the passwords while you investigate the present status of the enemy, or follow and blend in with the lower people of the enemy and you should talk about various things. There is a secret way to do this. Be aware that the way to execute this differs, dependent on if it is a camp or if it is a night attack.

II

If it is not possible for you to discover the passwords by such methods, there are certain words you can say in response to an enemy challenge which may work; for example, 'forests' to 'mountains', 'village' to 'woods', 'water' to 'valley', 'waves' to 'water', 'salt' to 'sea', 'fruit' to 'flower', 'smoke' to 'fire', 'green' to 'pine tree', 'edge' to 'tatami'. You should always be aware there are numerous variations of words and you should be prepared and have a good knowledge of them. When given a word by the enemy, be sure to answer in a way that appears to be a little careless and casual. If the word you have replied with seems to be wrong, it would be good for you to give another possible answer – for example, sometimes an analogy is used, such as 'Asama' (the name of a volcano) to 'smoke', 'Mount Fuji' to 'snow', 'Yoshino' to 'flower' (cherry blossoms), 'Miyagino' to '*hagi*' (Japanese bush clover), 'Sarashina' to 'the moon', 'Takasago' to 'pine trees', 'Namba' to 'plum flowers', 'Ide' to 'bush warbler' or 'frog', 'Mikusa' to 'quail', etc.[2] Thus, when you answer one as listed here, it would be better for you to answer in a way where you look careless because there is always a possibility that it may be a different password. If you give your answer without being timid, considering the above mentioned two points, then you will be able to get through the situation. However, the enemy may have an extra sign, such as one person picking his ear and the other person blowing their nose in response, and in such cases, sometimes you should not rush into saying a password in response. To deal with such a situation, it is good for you to transform your appearance and pretend to be an ignorant lower solider [who would forget such things]. In a military way of life, which is *budo*, there exists only danger. Therefore, you should have a calm mind when you face an emergency.

III

When you try to infiltrate with *suigetsu no jutsu*, sometimes the enemy general has his men whisper the password at the castle gate before they are let in; therefore, you should try to hear from the front or the rear.[3] If you cannot hear the password, withdraw without delay.

When the enemy withdraws after a night attack, you may follow and get into the enemy army. If the enemy castle is at a fair distance from your army, it will be the case that every soldier is told to whisper the password at the gate. If you are going to follow and get into the enemy or a castle and camp that are in close proximity to each other, be aware they are not likely to have this rule.

---

2 All of the above are plays on words concerning famous poetry. The point here is that there is a set of base pair passwords, which are taken from contemporary understanding, and that passwords may have a twist to them.
3 Fujibayashi is not clear on the position here.

IV

Try to copy whatever the enemy does
In the arts of war, there are techniques of passwords, *aijirushi* identifying marks and *aikei* identifying signs. These three techniques are all to detect those from the enemy who have blended into your army. Passwords and *aijirushi* identifying marks were mentioned earlier.

Aikei identifying signs include techniques of *tachisuguri isuguri* – that is standing and sitting while giving passwords – these were invented by Kusunoki Masashige. You should know there are a number of ways to perform these signs [not just standing and sitting]. For example, regardless of what the passwords are, or what signs and marks are given, the key is to do whatever the enemy does and say whatever the enemy says. This is the essential point in *shinobi no jutsu* and is there to avoid danger.

When Wada and Kusunoki were besieged at Akasaka castle in Kawachi, Monobe no Jiro, who was a retainer of the Yuki clan on the besieging side, successfully got into the castle by blending in with the enemy. However, he did not know the *aikei* signs of Tachisuguri Isuguri and was detected and killed. There is a detailed discussion about this in the *Teikairon*[4] – further details are to be orally transmitted.

Passwords should be changed three times every five days or once every three days, or if necessary, every day. If the enemy is going to commence a night attack, they will change their passwords even if it was decided as early as that morning; therefore, there is no use in your knowing old passwords. The primary elements [a *ninja*] should have are wit in a verbal exchange and a quick brain and eloquent speech.

Furthermore, unless you are skilled in the various techniques and have a calm mind, you will fall into serious trouble.

Four points on secret signs and marks

I

Take a *dokataginu*[5] undershirt with you. *Ninja* should prepare several *dokataginu* and dye them in different colours beforehand. To be orally transmitted.

II

Copying *aijirushi* marks instantly upon seeing them

---

4 This is most likely a supplementary section to the *Bansenshukai* that has been lost. However, it is believed by Ishida Yoshihito that one of the Okimori family versions may contain a transcription.

5 A form of underwear.

When the enemy is defending a castle and your army is attacking it, and the distance between the enemy castle and your camp is twenty or thirty *cho* or even forty to fifty *cho*, the enemy will send its guards as *togiki* listening scouts to the *tobari*[6] or *kedashi* outside areas of the castle.

When the enemy has established a camp, it will have guards outside the main watch fires and have single use fires burning in the vicinity. Also, it may send *kagi* and *monogiki* scouts [into the area]. *Ninja* should stealthily creep near to the guards, watchmen, night-patrol men, watch-fire men, *togiki* listening scouts and so on, that is those who defend the *tobari* or *kedashi* outside areas of the castle. This is done to discover the nature of the *aijirushi* marks, and when you have this information, go back and create one and use it to infiltrate the enemy. In such a case it is hard to succeed unless you are very courageous, talented in speaking and ingenious at invention and constructing plans.

忍ニハ三ツノ習ノ有ゾカシ　不敵ト論ト又ハ智略ト

A shinobi *should have three major principles, which are talk, boldness and strategy.*

On a rainy night, if a watch fire is dead, you may be able to sneak up to the watch-fire guard and kill him, or if you come across the enemy *togiki* listening scout, you may kill or capture him also. There have been many instances of such cases since ancient times. Although you should do this in some situations, it should most definitely be avoided if it is done when hot-blooded. Only do this if you need to, and if needed to succeed in infiltrating, or if you think you cannot get in there without disposing of them, in such a case you may kill that person. These two points hold true for the case where the enemy is not leaving its castle.

III

You should take an identification mark from a dead enemy soldier or take one from the enemy with stealth.

IV

A wise technique to identify the *aijirushi* mark is to ask an enemy behind you if he has one. At the siege of Osaka castle, a retainer of Todo Izuminokami had a narrow escape using this technique.

The above two points hold true for when the enemy is advancing an attack or fighting or when a battle ends and the enemy is withdrawing. To be orally transmitted.

---

6 Specific areas outside a castle or camp as explained in volume seven.

Three points on *mukaeire no jutsu* or the art of approaching the enemy for infiltration

I

While the enemy is advancing upon you, you should venture twenty to thirty *ri* out to see them and infiltrate a position where they take up quarters. Do this with both *yo-* and *in-jutsu*, so that you may set fires or cause confusion by supplying the enemy with misinformation. If you go out as far as thirty *ri*, the enemy will not expect you to be there, so you can take an advantage of this gap. Or you should go and stay there even before the enemy soldiers arrive, or in a nearby village, and while they are making a racket and settling down after arriving, you should leave your position and take a back road and set fire and burn their food, armouries, harness and horse tackle and so on, with the purpose to exhaust the enemy, or even to make false charges and to arouse doubt and cause discord among them. There are myriad secret ways to set houses on fire, or even markets or shops, etc. and also to practise the art of slander.

II

Make yourself up as a *goshi* or local *samurai* at five or six *ri* from where the enemy takes up quarters, then enquire if you can accompany them as a rear vassal and thus infiltrate this way.

III

Disguise yourself as a messenger from a relative or an acquaintance of someone in the enemy. With such an opportunity, you should use the technique of false seals. To be orally transmitted.

Two points on *bakemono jutsu* or the art of transformation

I

You should change your appearance to that of a *yamabushi* mountain pilgrim, office holder, monk, shrine keeper, merchant, monkey trainer, puppeteer, shrine worshipper, hermit, pilgrim, beggar or anything that is in accord with the opportunity.[7]

In doing this, if you only change your appearance, it will be like needlework without the thread knotted [and will unravel itself]. Therefore, if you want to disguise yourself as a *yamabushi*, you should carry a pass from a *sendatsu*, who is a 'mentor *yamabushi*' or if disguised as a monk, you require a pass from the head temple or other such things. This will work effectively. Of course, you should

---

7   The examples in this sentence have been written with the ideograms broken up into a simplistic code, so that, when put together, the correct ideograms can be read.

be prepared with the necessary tools, and know the manners or the arts of the people you copy.

In ancient times when Yoshitsune and his men fled to Oshu, the twelve of them all disguised themselves as *yamabushi* and a man named Musashibo at the Ataka no Seki checkpoint pretended to read from a random scroll and pretended it was a *kanjincho*, which is a prospectus to solicit funds for a temple. This ruse was purely derived on the spot and though they were planning to pretend to go with the order of the temple in Nara, it would have caused serious trouble if they had not created this *kanjincho* letter, but they should have been more prepared for this and given more attention. It was often the case that this technique would be used to infiltrate in those days, but it is not appropriate today. However, it is a way passed down from ancient times so I have written it here. This may still be applicable in a case where the enemy and your allies are distant from each other by tens of *ri*, or if you are following a runaway, or if you are trying to kill a criminal.

However, the cases of Tateoka no Dojun, who infiltrated the castle of Sawayama, and Kusunoki Masashige, who had Onchi Sakon infiltrate Akasaka castle, [are examples of these above skills and] still appear to have merit even today.

However, it can be difficult to use this skill of *bakemono jutsu*, as highlighted by the following cases: when Ise no Saburo Yoshimori went to Tosa-bo's camp disguising himself as a horse dealer, and when Shindo no Kotaro went to Arata castle pretending to be deaf and dumb. In these situations the ruse was difficult and you should only use these skills when the enemy is going to attack you. Also, when Echizen no kami – who was a retainer of the Kikuchi clan – infiltrated the camp of Matsura-to, he did so with this technique, as it was a case where both sides were facing each other and at a close distance. However, this will not work today. *Fukurogaeshi no jutsu* or the 'skill of reversing the bag' seems to be more appropriate for today.

I I

When you want to get into an enemy camp, you should go there stealthily the night before to record what the crests on their lanterns are like. Then you should go back and create a similar lantern yourself. When you get to the camp discreetly, quickly light the lantern and disguise yourself as a guard, night-patrol man or fireman or so on, according to the situation, and infiltrate with tactics.

A *ninja* poem says:

竊忍ニハ習ノ道ハ多ケレト先第一ハ敵ニ近ツケ

Though there are so many principles a shinobi *should learn, the first
thing of all is to get close to the enemy.*

However, it is difficult to fulfil this unless you have an absolutely fearless mind,
like that of iron. If you are easily frightened by the enemy, your plans will forever
be discovered and you will cause a disaster.

驚カス敵ノシカタニ騒ナバ　忍フ心ノアラハレゾスル

*If you are upset by the feints the enemy makes at you, your secret
intentions will be revealed.*

Three points on *katatagae no jutsu* or infiltrating the enemy while others are moving during a night attack

I

If you know – by using *monomi no jutsu* scouting techniques – that the enemy
is coming to perform a night attack, or even if you have not got the information but have just discovered that the enemy is going to attack your allies while
you are hiding during your regular duty as a *togiki* listening scout, then you
should send someone back to report it to the general while others should enter
the enemy castle just after the enemy raiding party has come out. Generally,
when the enemy is going on a night attack, you can see the lights in the castle are
different from those of normal times or hear dogs barking or horses neighing.
Or you can know that an attack force is coming when there is no sound of the
regular warning clappers or calls of the night patrol, or when you see a small
scouting group sent out from the camp, or even when flags or markers are
moving in disarray. In these cases, you should hide in a forest or deep bush
close to the castle waiting for the enemy party to come out. When it comes out,
you should infiltrate taking the advantage of the opportunity. There are three
advantages for doing this:

As the enemy is launching a night attack in an attempt to catch you off guard,
it is concentrating on outwitting you and is not thinking of being outwitted.
Therefore, it tends not to expect *ninja* to infiltrate by taking advantage of this gap.

At the time of a night attack, everything is busy and confused and all are
rushed, so much that they cannot finely interrogate someone in depth and on
the spot.

As so many people go in and out of the gates, it is easy to get in at this time.

Even if you do not know in advance where the enemy will sally forth from, you may see the enemy party come out while you are on *togiki* listening duty at night; therefore, you should take advantage of the chance and infiltrate just after it leaves on a raid. To be orally transmitted.

As *suigetsu no jutsu* has been well known to people in our country since ancient times, if the enemy army is properly disciplined, there are various techniques to counteract it so it is a dangerous task.

Katatagae no jutsu is totally unexpected by the enemy, and if you do this you can avoid the enemy passwords or *aikei* standing or sitting signals and therefore infiltrate easily and at your will.

Also, as there is only a lesser number of the enemy left in the castle [because others have left], then the advantages are as follows:

First, it is easy to set fires; second, it is not easy for the enemy to put out the fire; and third, if your allies are coming to attack the castle at the same time, the enemy will lose advantage as it will be undermanned. Therefore, there are so many advantages for *katatagae no jutsu* as seen above and it has an advantage over *suigetsu no jutsu* and is the best secret among the arts of *chikairi* short-term infiltration.

II

There is an advantage in the art of changing your appearance to that of a lower soldier and infiltrating as separate agents.[8] The advantage of this technique of changing your appearance to a lower soldier is that if you disguise yourself as a fully armoured *samurai*, you will be so conspicuous that it will not be long before you are questioned. Also, you will be most likely spoken to at some point, even by a stranger, thus, the chances of being suspected are quite high. If you show yourself as being in a fluster, the enemy will be even more suspicious. Therefore, to have an advantage in *fun-nin*, that is the art of 'slipping in', you should use the art of masquerading yourself as a lower soldier. This is because, first, lower people are inconspicuous; second, they will not attract people's attention; and third, if you make a blunder, people tend to overlook it. Thus, everyone thinks little of lower people. However, when there is no urgent situation and all is quiet in the enemy castle or camp, people tend to wonder about lower people. Because of this, you need to have good judgement on what situation you are in and change your ways accordingly.

In ancient times, in Omi province, at the battle of Anegawa, a man named Endo Kiemon, who was a retainer of Asakura Yoshikage, infiltrated Lord Nobunaga's army in conspicuous armour and with a decapitated head in hand.

---

8   The aim here is to have a group of ninja infiltrate a night raid but all as individuals, because doing it as a full group is suspicious.

He did this with an intention to kill Lord Nobunaga at the cost of his own life. He was searching for where the lord was but in the end a man named Takenaka Kyusaku guessed his intention, seized and beheaded him. This all happened because Endo did not know the arts of *fun-nin*, and that he should have disguised himself as a lower soldier. In this case, he should have got into the enemy as a lower ranking man.

Still, be aware that you should know well the banners and markings of the enemy generals beforehand or always try to mix into where people are gathering. To be orally transmitted.

Alongside this, the art of going separately means that if you go in a group you are more likely to be questioned and therefore cannot succeed, while if infiltrating as an individual, while some still may be questioned, others will likely succeed in infiltrating. This has been the case a number of times in our country.

III

When your allies are going to perform a night attack, *ninja* should go first and stealthily get as close as the *tobari* and *kedashi* outer areas, watch guards or single-use watch fires and so on. Then you should infiltrate the camp by taking advantage of the fluster.

Three points on *suigetsu no jutsu* or the art of the moon on the water

I

When the enemy withdraws into its castle, whether in a night attack or a daytime battle, you should infiltrate. Whether day or night, when the enemy comes to fight with your allies, both sides will mix in battle; therefore, while the enemy is withdrawing, it is most essential that *ninja* should *not* bother fighting with swords or spears at all, they should in fact concentrate on moving around to hear or see the enemy password or *aijirushi* marks.

II

After making an agreement with your lord, you should lure the enemy out with bait and use *katatagae* or *suigetsu no jutsu* to infiltrate.

In this technique, you should lure the enemy with tempting bait, like fishing in the sea or a river, so as to make an enemy who will not normally come out in fact leave its defences.

When attacking a castle, you should attack from three sides and leave one side open. From that open direction, you should make up a false messenger from the allied general, someone who is expected to reinforce the enemy and who is expected to lead an attack on the besieging forces from the rear. You should forge a letter with a false seal, which should say that the general will send his army to attack from behind and send food and other things such as this, but it is important that the letter should give a specific date of their arrival. Then, at night on that specific date, you should disguise yourselves as baggage train handlers and pack cattle groups or horse trains with false loads, then enter the position in a large number. To support this, make an arrangement with your lord that he should start attacking just after you have entered. There are more things to be orally transmitted.

When Masashige made Yuasa surrender Akasaka castle, this technique was used.

The second technique is as follows: when your allies surround the castle at the start of the besiegement, you should build an annex camp at night and after dusk [while the enemy is unaware] and build this quite close to the castle.

Third, your allies should depart for a night battle but be small in number [which will attract the enemy].

Fourth, your allies should go forward in a small number to build a camp at a place that has limited defence qualities.

Fifth, use false flags, false screens and false rations, etc. [to attract the enemy and make them move so that a gap is created].

According to the time and place, you should perform these above techniques in an appropriate way for the status of the enemy forces, so that you can lure them out of the castle to perform *katatagae* or *suigetsu no jutsu* and infiltrate them. Further secrets are passed on orally.

When you sneak in using *katatagae* or *suigetsu no jutsu* as stated above, the three[9] points you should keep in mind are:

- When in the enemy castle or camp, in order not to lose your way, be it north, east, south or west, you should fix onto someone, remember him and follow along. This is done to help you remain calm and also if you are questioned by the enemy. This is the reason for it being mentioned here in this section.
- Be sure not to forget the enemy password or miss *aijirushi* marks and always try to follow the ways of the enemy in both action and speech. The techniques of passwords or *aijirushi* marks [previously described] are meant for such cases.
- It is essential to make a signal fire out of the way of people as soon as possible so your allies can know that you have infiltrated successfully. If it is too late, it will cause a serious problem, so the sooner the better. Details are to be orally transmitted.

---

9   The original manual states 'four points'.

Five points on *taniiri no jutsu* or the art of 'eating deep into the enemy'

I
To capture someone by tying and binding them

I I
To kill someone

I I I
To set fires

I V
To communicate with other *shinobi*

V

In using this art of *taniiri no jutsu*, the enemy is likely to be doubtful of you, therefore you should use the technique of a false wife or a false child. If you think it is not enough, there are techniques such as going to your allies to burn huts which have been built for newcomers and so on [to prove your trustworthiness to the enemy], or to kill someone and return [with their head]. For these, details are to be orally transmitted. You should not take them lightly.

In ancient times Hosokawa Akiuji and his army of thirteen thousand was in a battle camp at Fujiidera of Kawachi with the intention to defeat Kusunoki Masatsura. Masatsura collected more than three hundred people from Takayasu and Honzawa, divided them into groups of five to ten people and sent them into the enemy troops in a scattered way called *taniiri*. They got in here and there by making up plausible stories, saying that they wanted to change sides and talking about Masatsura's disgrace at Chihaya castle. Afterwards Masatsura sent a messenger to the opponent saying he would like to surrender. Then suddenly he raised the flags in attack – at this point the three hundred people on the inside attacked.

This art worked well by itself in ancient times and you will not fail to infiltrate if you perform this skill with a false wife or child and other such stratagems.

Two points on *ryohan no jutsu* or the converted prisoner
I

There are various techniques to make *ninja* of the enemy by using a prisoner as your *ninja* or to make a messenger of the prisoner.

If you get a prisoner in confinement, you should win him to your side by promising that you will give him a high reward. Also you should take his wife, children or someone in his family as hostage and make him write a *kishomon* pledge so you can use him as your *ninja* and get him back into the enemy castle or camp.

There is also another way. If the prisoner has his parents, children, friends or someone close to him on the enemy side, you should make up someone as a messenger from the prisoner to make a *ninja* of that person.

When the enemy castle or camp is falling, no matter if the enemy general is dead or if he has fled, if he has parents or sons in another castle, you should falsify a messenger from the general to tell them to surrender or think up another stratagem according to the situation. This art was used by Ise no Saburo Yoshimori in the middle of the first month of 1184, when he made Tauchi Saemon Noriyoshi surrender, who was a son of Abe Minbu Shigeyoshi.

I I

When you have a prisoner in confinement, you intentionally release him back to the enemy without making him realize your true intention, so that he will become a *ninja* for you.

While keeping a prisoner in confinement, your army should do everything opposite of what your lord really plans to do. Then let him hear things without letting him know your true intention. Then you should pretend to let your guard down so that the prisoner can run away back and tell their lord this false information. At the same time, you should send a *metsuke* surveillance operative to see if the enemy lord has fallen for your stratagem or if he has not. If he has taken it in, you will have a great number of advantages over him as he is thinking of your plans in reverse.

In ancient China, when Ling Peng was attacking Qin Feng, Qin Feng placed a part of his army in Xian while he himself stayed in an impregnable castle called Deng to defend against Ling Peng. After Ling Peng spent a few days staying in position without attacking, his army became very noisy and busy one night because he gave the order to get prepared to attack Xian early the next morning. At the same time, he let a prisoner run away, pretending to let the guard down so that he would bring what he heard to Deng. The prisoner told Qin Feng that the enemy was going to attack Xian the next morning and that they should be prepared. Qin Feng got most of his army back to Xian that night, but Ling Peng had sent a scout to see what was going on. After making sure the false information had got through, in the hour of Tiger of that night he had his army cross over the river and attack Deng. Though the castle was so strongly fortified, they had too small a number of people in defence and the attack was not expected, and it ended up being captured. Alongside this, they went to attack Xian after gaining the advantage and Qin Feng was defeated.

Two points on *fukurogaeshi zen jutsu* or the complete art of reversing the bag

I

In this art, you should forge a letter to the enemy lord or someone connected to the enemy lord, senior counsellors, troop commanders, common *samurai* or anyone on the enemy side, who lives in another place or in another province. You should bring the forged letter to the said relative and get a reply letter from him. In the meantime, you should see or hear as much information as possible and you should not deliver the original and true reply but falsify a letter and take it to the enemy.

II

When the enemy defends a castle while you are surrounding it and hostages are taken from the people of that domain, in this situation have the relatives, wives, children, brothers or so on of someone who is being held as hostage [write letters] so that you can fully use the skill of *fukurogaeshi no jutsu*.

The above are outlines only and in a real situation, when facing the enemy you should keep these things in mind. The essence of these mental techniques should be explored to a great depth, and thus be used appropriately. Be sure not to execute them lightly. At the same time, if you think about them too much, you will lose sight of the gaps, and you will not succeed. You should be aware of this thoroughly.

Yo-nin III

Open Disguise III

In three sections:
1. On gauging and measurement
2. On distinguishing
3. On observing from a distance

On gauging and measurement

Two points on gauging mountains and valleys
Supplementary: eight points on what you should keep in mind when describing and reporting the features of mountains.

I

When you do not exactly know the shapes of the mountains, you should try to describe them according to the Five Symbols used within the Chinese Constellations. This is done to easily assess the difficulty or ease of a mountain.

The Five Symbols used for describing mountains are:
1. If high in the north and flat in the south then use the symbol Black Tortoise 玄武, representing Water.
2. If high in the south and flat in the north then use the symbol Vermillion Bird 朱雀, representing Fire.
3. If high in the west and flat in the east then use the symbol White Tiger 白 虎, representing Metal.
4. If high in the east and flat in the west then use the symbol Blue Dragon 青 龍, representing Wood.

5. If the mountain has a raised centre and is predominantly flat in all four directions – for a long-term camp[1] – then use the symbol Ascending Serpent 騰蛇 , which represents Earth.

Alongside this, you should be resourceful according to the place or the time and remember there are more oral traditions here.

II

You should examine the enemy province to establish if the mountains are large or small, high or low, steep or gentle; also assess the flora and whether the rivers and valleys are deep or shallow, or wide or narrow, long or short and so on and so forth.

As well as observing the area around the enemy castle, you should look for a possible battlefield or a possible camp site for your army, you should also examine closely other places that appear at first to have no use to you. Collect precise information such as what they are like or their measurements, etc. This is done on the assumption that you will establish a battle camp on a mountain; therefore, you should investigate the area where your vanguard should be placed, on which crest your headquarters should be set, considering every possible way for the best fit.

Generally speaking, it is not appropriate for a small army to take up position on a large mountain or a large-numbered one on a small mountain. Therefore, the first thing you should do is approximate the size of the mountain. More is taught by oral tradition.

Also, a high mountain is good for you to take up a position on while a low mountain is not so good. Therefore, you need to estimate how high the mountain is. You also need to consider how steep the mountain is, as a steep mountain is good for you to defend if you are a small number and when using foot soldiers but is of no advantage when using mounted ones. A gentle mountain is good when you are manipulating a large number of men or using mounted soldiers, while not so good when you are a small number or using foot soldiers. Therefore, you should give careful consideration to how steep the mountain is. There are more oral traditions here.

It is advantageous if there is a forest or bush behind your camp because you can get firewood or feed your horses with ease, it is convenient when you lay an ambush, and it enables you to pretend to have a stronger military force than

---

1 The text simply inserts 'long-term camp' in the middle of the sentence.

you actually do have.[2] Details are to be orally transmitted. On the other hand, it is not good if there is a forest on either or both sides or in front of your camp – more traditions are found here – therefore, you should know the exact locations of forests and bushes. Alongside this, the strategy to be taken should vary according to the valleys and rivers if they are deep or shallow, wide or narrow, long or short, and their exact make up. So you should try to know all of this as precisely as possible.

Eight points you should keep in mind when examining a mountain

I

Estimating the measurements of a mountain in relation to the size of your army

You should try to have a specific picture of where each of the vanguard, the second troops, the side troops, the rear, or the headquarters will be located, according to the exact topography of the mountain or valley area. It is difficult to investigate it thoroughly without being trained in military strategies. Further details are not to be described here. The way of taking a position varies according to how extensive, what shape, or how steep the mountain is, but the camp should be in accord with the following:

For ten thousand people you will need a square with a fence constructed around the perimeter to a measurement of three *cho* and forty *ken* on each side. The quarters should be built at a distance of seven, eight or nine *ken* from the fence and it should be divided as follows: three *cho* for the quarters (huts) and forty *ken* for the pathways among the quarters. There should be six pathways and each way will be seven *ken* wide. This principle can be applied no matter how large the number of people is. To be orally transmitted.

The basic principle in understanding quarters is that you will need two *ken* for each mounted warrior. However, you can also calculate the number by the amount of fief for each *samurai*; in this case it should be worked out as one *ken* wide for one warrior of a salary of one hundred *koku*. However, if it seems to be too small to live in, you should calculate it as follows[3]:

- Two and a half *ken* for two people with one hundred *koku*.
- Two *ken* for those with two hundred *koku*.
- Two and a half *ken* for those with three hundred *koku*.
- Three *ken* for those with four hundred *koku*.

---

2 Here Fujibayashi uses Sun Tzu's theory of the 'substantial and insubstantial' with a reference to trickery.

3 The issue here is for a *shinobi* to measure the land he is scouting to check if the area he is observing will be big enough to encamp the entire army on.

- Three and a half *ken* for those with five hundred *koku*.
- Four *ken* for those with six hundred *koku*.
- Four and a half *ken* for those with eight or nine hundred *koku*.
- Five *ken* for those with one thousand *koku*.

For people with more than one thousand *koku* you need to reduce the measurement by three tenths. For example:
- Six *ken* for those with one thousand five hundred *koku*.
- Seven *ken* for those with two thousand *koku*.

If you have a fully manned army, there should be no more than two mounted warriors for each [text missing] square or a maximum of twelve foot soldiers per *ken* square.

II

Investigate if there is water or not. Even if you find mountains that seem good for a battle camp, you should not build a camp on the mountain where there is no water, making it essential to know if there is water or not. Therefore, pay attention to the area for rivers or ponds and also you can identify a water vein to some extent by observing the formation of the ridge line. Even on a high mountain, you can find water by looking in a ravine. Also, some writings state that you should try to look at lower land when seeking water, looking especially for arrowhead plants,[4] iris, reeds or any other marsh plants or willow trees. Or you should also look for the holes made by crickets and ants and dig around the area to find water.

One trick to see if there is water in an area is to put a bird feather in a standing position by sticking it two or three *sun* into the ground; if there is water, you will see dew drops form on the feather. An alternative way is to put a cotton cloth into a hole and leave it for one night; if there is water it will be heavier. One more method: dig the ground about two *shaku* deep and put your ear to the ground; if you hear a sound like drumming, there will be water in the area.

III

Estimating the distance to a river

You should know how far or close the nearest river is as well as its depth and width. It is desirable for you to take the rivers near your camp into consideration when thinking out tactics. Even when not in a camp, you should always

---

4 *Sagittaria trifolia.*

be careful about this. Even a small stream can be good. Further details are to be orally transmitted.

I V

You should be careful about *kamari-ba*,[5] which are *fields of the kamari*, forests or other areas of dense plant growth, which can hide *kamari* ambushes, whether for your army or for the enemy. The *fields of the kamari* include: forests, thickets, valleys, the shades of mountains, banks, ditches, rivers, dense growth of Amur silver grass, reed grasses, fields of high grass, wheat, hemp and so on. You should be careful about such places and consider if they will work as the enemy's *kamari-ba* or your own.

V

Investigating where a fort is to be constructed

Both in attacking a castle and defending a castle, sometimes you build a fortress and position a number of people there. Therefore, you need to check the topography of the land near the enemy border and your own territories and find an advantageous site for a fortress. To be orally transmitted.

V I

You should look for an appropriate place for the commander-in-chief to give his orders by torch signals in a night battle. The lord should give orders with a torch from a good vantage point. The position of the lord should be where he can look over the site in all directions; again, there are oral traditions that accompany this.

V I I

You should investigate from both angles, your own and the enemy's. Considering the advantages of terrain, forests and bushes, rivers and the sea, or other such things, you should also be aware that some can be beneficial for the enemy in one aspect and others can be beneficial for your side from another aspect. It is essential for you to determine this precisely. It is difficult to write down every detail in advance as it all depends on the time and the place; therefore, more information shall be explained in oral form.

V I I I

You should look for mountain tops where you can establish *hikyaku-bi* fire beacons or *hikyaku-bata* flag stations. When *shinobi no mono* sneak in the

---

5   Literally, *kamari*-field. *Kamari* are considered as ambush troops.

enemy castle or infiltrate the enemy domain, you should use the techniques of *hikyaku-bi* at night and *hikyaku-bata* in the daytime in order to communicate what you have found to your lord. This does not work unless the sites you choose are on a high mountain top. Therefore, it is essential for you to see how this relay can be done successfully at the relay points of high mountain tops or ridges. To be orally transmitted.

There are oral traditions for each of the above points. While you may think there is no difference between the skills above and simply drawing what you see, such as mountains, rivers, fields, streams and so on, if you have no knowledge of military strategy and just draw them without proper method, you will not fulfil your lord's intentions. This is why I have tried to mention the outlines of military tactics alongside the subject itself and not only in this matter, but in everything. If you want to be a *ninja*, you should be well trained in the arts of war.

Four points on investigating seashores or rivers

I

When observing the sea coast, you should decide if it is a good landing place or not. To do this you should estimate how deep or shallow it is, how sandy or rocky it is, if it has enough depth to it and if the waves are gentle or not, if it is a bay or an open sea, and how much difference can be found in the tide levels. You should investigate these matters with absolute certainty. More given in oral tradition.

II

Estimating sections of a river which are deep or shallow
To know where a river is deep or shallow, be aware that you should consider if it is wide or narrow, if the stream is divided or not, if the water is moving or still and if there is a ford to cross. Also, if it is a coastline, you should record the difference in tide levels thoroughly and with certainty.

A poem by Ota Dokan[6] reads:

ソコイナキ淵瀬ハサハク山川ノ　浅キ瀬ニコソアダ
浪ハタテ

*The depths and shallows make noise in a mountain stream but it is
the shallows that make wild waves.*

Also there is a poem that instructs how to gauge the difference in tide levels or if a river is deep or shallow by hearing a plover bird's call.

---

6 A *samurai* poet, 1432–1486.

遠クナル近ク鳴海ノ濱千鳥声ニテ汐ノ満干ヲハシル

If the calls of plover birds are retreating or advancing, you can know the tide by their cry.

In the case where the tide is high or you do not know how deep the river is, there is a way to discern it by driving cattle or horses into the sea or river. This method was invented by Sir Kiso Yoshinaka[7] and is an oral tradition.

III

You should know if a river floods to a great extent or not, if it floods quickly or not, and, once it floods, if the floodwater recedes fast or not, among other points. To know these things, you should identify the nature of the river upstream; that is, if it is near or far [from its source], if it is narrow or wide, high or low, and so on. In addition to this, you should observe waterfalls and consider the wind.

IV

When the river is overflowing, you should know where is flooded with water and where is not. You should know this by noting the colours of the stones on the riverside or by observing the plants or trees. To be orally transmitted.

Four points on how to estimate the depth of mud in a rice field

I

You should know if the mud in a rice field is deep or shallow by quickly observing the field from a distance. You can gather quite an accurate estimate by observing the contours, whether the fields are high or low,[8] by observing the surrounding area, how steep the valley is, etc. You should note whether there are banks, culture ponds, wells or trenches that are in a higher position than the fields themselves and you should be aware of whether the fields are irrigated or not and how deeply they are irrigated. Take note, you should remember that scarcely no field that has spring water is a shallow one. More details to be given orally.

II

To know the depth of [water and mud] in a rice field by observing grass stubbles or the ridges between the fields from a distance of four or five *ken*

Generally, there are two ways to do this:

In a shallow field, the stubbles are short and look equal in height, while in a

---

7   A twelfth-century warrior.

8   Presumably as water descends, lower fields become deeper.

deep field some are long and others are short, they are not of the same height and appear a little slanted. However, you may mistake stubbles that have regrown, which would give once equal stubbles an uneven appearance. To avoid this, you should judge them by their size and have an understanding of the difference between cut and regrown versions.

In autumn, winter or early spring, ridges are not embanked properly; therefore, those ridges between deep fields are low, narrow and crooked, maybe even collapsing in some places. If it is from late spring to late summer, when the ridges are properly embanked, they will look a little different; however, not all details can be mentioned here. The ridges between shallow fields are generally high, wide and firm without any collapsing present.

III

To know if a field is deep or shallow by getting close to it and observing the colour of soil, the colour of the ridges and whether or not the water is fed from a spring

If you inspect a field up close, there are three things you should consider:

1. The colour of the soil: if it is a deep dark black and loose in consistency, then it is a deep field; while if it is whitish, heavy and sticky, it is a shallow one.
2. Those fields with a spring are most likely to be very deep.
3. The outer side of the ridge of a deep field is most likely wet and the soil is never dry, while that of a shallow field is dry and whitish. To see if there are any deep spots in shallow fields, or where it is shallow within a deep field, you should consider if there is a spring or not or if the rice plants grow well or not in those places. However, if there has been a long spell of dry weather, the plants will grow well and have fruitful ears in deep fields while if it's a year of cold weather, the ears in deep fields are generally bad and shrink.

IV

To identify if a field is deep or shallow, by observing the plants when they are young

There are two points: first, in a deep field, plants look slightly crooked and the base near the root will be skewed because of deep mud, whereas in a shallow field, the plants are upright and look firm. Second, some plants in a deep field can grow high while other plants do not grow very well. However, it also depends on what the weather of that year is like, especially the level of rain or sun. To be orally transmitted.

With the above points in mind, always try to integrate the information around you and keep your eyes open and vigilant.

Five points on the art of knowing the depth and width of a moat

I

On observing the outer perimeter of an enemy castle situated on flat land and how you should estimate the depth or width of the moat around the castle by observing the earthworks over the moat

At night time, even if the moat has only a small amount of water, it tends to look as much as seven or eight tenths higher than it actually is. To avoid such a miscalculation, you should carefully observe the embankment on the opposite side.

II

You can estimate by rope, by observing how the enemy constructed their defences, or by the colour of the water.

When using a thin rope, you should make white wooden markers at intervals of five *sun* or one *shaku* and secure them to the rope. Place the rope in the water and draw it tight to establish where the wet mark appears.

By seeing the way the enemy fortifies itself, you can know, for example, if the moat is shallow, where the enemy has taken special caution by constructing a fence, or spiked defences, or defences with thorny branches or has attached branches to the fence.[9] As well as this, you should pay attention to any other measures the enemy has taken to guard itself.

You should be aware that the water of a deep moat looks dark blue, while water of a shallow moat will be pale blue or whitish and rippling. Shallow water often has grass protruding from it, which can be seen dotted around; however, remember that it is sometimes the case that the enemy will place grass which has been tied with a rope [and stones] as if it grew there naturally. To avoid being misled, you should inspect the colour of the grass.

III

You should estimate the measurement across the moat from the corner. When you estimate how wide a moat is, you should discover where the moat is curved or bent at a right angle and measure it there.

---

9 Branches and thorn bushes which are tied to the fence – probably inverted – to prevent people climbing over the fence.

IV

You can measure a moat by using an arrow and thread when you infiltrate stealthily on a moonless night. By doing this you will be able to get the exact measurements of the width of a moat or the distance from the very bottom of a moat to the edge of the roof on the opposite side.

The above-mentioned arrow with a thread is *ukisu*[10] and the arrowhead should be *kiwada mochi,*[11] [that is, with a sticky substance on its point,] while the thread should be a little thinner than three [unknown measurement]; to be orally transmitted.

V

Knowing the height of a stone wall or earthwork
The same process can be used to estimate the height of a tree. There is also a method to do this by using a form of triangular ruler, which can be used to assess the height of a tree. Another way is to estimate this is by looking through your legs. This should be passed down directly.

Understanding how strongly a castle is fortified or not

There are various ways to know if a castle is well fortified or not. In performing this art, you should always try to know the ground plan[12] and layout of the castle, and the topography or anything of the surrounding area, even up to around five, six or even seven *ri*. This can extend as far as twenty or thirty *ri* from the castle if needed. What you need to consider when in the field are the following three things:

1. what the land is like
2. whether the mountains are high or not
3. water, firewood and food

With such information, you can be creative in many ways. However, there are countless possible cases so that it is difficult to write down every case here; more will be passed on in oral tradition.

---

10 This text is in phonetics only.
11 Possibly a sticky mixture of the plant *Phellodendron japonicum* which may be used as a substance to allow a lightweight arrow and string to stick to a roof so that you can use the string to measure the distance or height of the castle wall.
12 *Nawabari.*

Two points on how to estimate topography, distance and elevation

I

Uramittsu no justu is the art of estimating the distance of land; there is the art of using a map, a carpenter's iron square which measures five *sun* and then applying the art of *uramittsu*. This art is described in writings on gunnery, so its method is not written here.

I I

Using an iron square to understand the difference in height between two points

To use this skill you need to know the distance between the two separate points. You can do this by stretching a rope to measure it or do it by using the art of estimation of distance as precisely as possible.

Hang two strings one *shaku* apart and identify a true level with an iron square and mark the strings at those two points. With the iron square, measure the difference in height between the two separate points that you wish to measure in the distance, which will give you a starting point to work out the height by using the following ratio.

If one point in your view through the strings is one *sun* higher than the other point at the distance of one *shaku*, then it will hold true for six *sun* at six *shaku* or at six *shaku* for ten *ken*, and so on.[13] Further details are to be orally transmitted. Also, this art is shown in the illustrations.[14]

This technique to know the difference in height between two points is very useful, especially when you are going to use flooding tactics on low-level ground, or when you want to shoot a fire arrow into a high castle and need to make a correct estimation.

Three points on how to identify if the enemy is strong or not

I

You should collect as much information on the things listed below as you can and report it to your lord:
- If the enemy lord is principled or unprincipled.
- If he is wise or stupid.
- If he is brave or a coward.
- If the codes of the army are righteous or not.
- If the vassals such as troop commanders, captains and soldiers are well

---

13 It should be noted that these are going up in increments of ten and become obvious when you are familiar with Japanese measurements.

14 Image missing from text.

prepared in military ways or arts (*budo*).
- The manners of the entire vassalage.
- The number and size of the army.
- If their neighbouring lords will send them reinforcements or not.
- If their food is ample or not.
- What, if anything, the lord has a special liking for.

Anything else you can discover about the enemy should be reported to your lord. In order to know the enemy lord's way of thinking, you should try to establish an understanding of this: by observing the way of the mind of his most trusted retainer(s); by considering the lord's favourite things; by listening to people talk about the way the lord governs the land; by reading and observing notice boards; by approaching those people who have access to the lord, such as blind musicians or *sarugaku* musicians, and making them speak by putting them at ease; or by listening to *samurai*, soldiers or other people talk. In ancient times, Onchi Sakon asked Kusunoki Masashige and Masashige replied as mentioned in a different volume of this writing.[15]

II

You can know the quality of the enemy by looking at how its quarters and formations are built. Battle camps should be built in accordance with the 'method of Hoen', which means they will be defended on all eight sides, but those that are scattered here and there over a village are not proper defences and this improper way is called *hagun* or the *defeated army*. Further details about how to build a position are difficult to be transmitted unless they are transferred fully from person to person.

The way to see if a formation is good or not is hard to understand, unless given from person to person. However, the method is as follows: if [the enemy forms up in] sections according to the 'method of Hoen' and is prepared to hold position during the first stage up to the third stage of battle, then know this should be regarded as a good formation. If the formation is a single mass without any division or assignment of tasks or if there is no way to break up or reform the troop, then know that this is a poor way of control. It is difficult to write every detail down here, as the way of making formations should be transmitted from person to person.

---

15 This is exactly how the sentence is written in the text; it appears to be referencing an earlier quote.

You should gauge if the enemy army will win or lose by the minds or words of their *samurai* or soldiers.

Liu Tao (the *Six Secret Teachings*) says:

If the army is excited and the officers and troops fear the laws, respect the general's commands, rejoice with each other in destroying the enemy, are proud of each other's courage and ferocity, and praise each other for their awesomeness and martial demeanour – these are indications of a strong enemy.

Also:

If the army is startled a number of times, the officers and troops are no longer maintaining good order, and if they terrify each other with stories about the enemy's strength, speak to each other about the disadvantages, anxiously listen and talk to each other, talk incessantly of ill omen, spreading doubts and confusing each other, fear neither laws nor orders, and do not regard their general seriously – these are indications of weakness.

On distinguishing

Two points on making a rough estimation of the number of the enemy force

I

Constructing an estimation of the number of the enemy and any adjustments needed – by observing what the enemy province is like or the mindset of the enemy lord

In the case where the enemy province has high mountains or coastlines, or covers a large area, or there are large cities or towns in the neighbouring provinces, in these cases there tend to be a large number of unseen warriors[16] in the mountains or on the coastlines or there may even be *ronin* gathering in the larger cities of the neighbouring provinces; therefore, you should be aware that the enemy army will be larger than the dimensions of fief can tell you. Also, you should consider the mindset of the enemy lord when estimating the number of his army because:

1. A good general always has many men who will serve him and they normally have a larger number of people compared to the number expected for his fief size.

---

16 This appears to allude to warriors who did not make up standard armies and were those who lived in unemployed or hermit states, and who could be called upon to fight and invalidate a *shinobi*'s estimation of enemy army size.

2. In contrast an evil general will be the complete opposite.
3. Also it [the number of men a general has] depends on what kind of battle he is going to fight.

One military writing says that for each ten thousand *koku* [someone is in control of] the following is true:

A high-grade general or province will have twenty-six or twenty-seven mounted warriors.

A medium general or province will have twenty-two or twenty-three mounted warriors.

A lower general or province will have fifteen or sixteen mounted warriors.

For the high-grade general, the whole army adds up to twenty-five or twenty-six lower people for each mounted warrior, including *ashigaru* foot soldiers and those under direct control of the general. For a medium general, there will be twenty-one or twenty-two lower people for each mounted warrior, and for a lower general there will be fifteen or sixteen lower people for each mounted warrior. You should calculate the entire army according to the above ratio.

Writings on the art of war show the following list and estimation for an army with fifty mounted warriors:

Fifty mounted warriors, each attended by four people, adding up to 250 including the warriors themselves.

Fifty musket and archer foot soldiers with two troop commanders for the archers and musketeers, each attended by five people making twelve in number [and adding up to sixty-two overall].

Fifty spearmen will include thirty pikemen and twenty spearmen[17] *[with shorter polearms] under the formation commander (samurai-daisho), adding up to fifty in total.*

Two spear captains or yari-bugyo, two banner organizers or hata-bugyo, one troop captain or kumigashira, and one musha-bugyo, add up to six, who are each attended by six, adding up to forty-two in total.

Four message officers attended by four, adding up to twenty.

Thirty samurai on foot and fifty chugen or komono servants.

Five people carrying two matoi and umajirushi standards, and five small flags.

The above adds up to 509. These are all those who go out on the battlefield.

---

17 The type of spear mentioned here is *mochiyari* 持鎗, which is a shorter spear than a pike, measuring around two and a half *ken*, according to the rules issued by the Takeda clan.

Two people to run the kitchens for the samurai-daisho.
Two or three squires.
Two secretaries.
One monk.

The above adds up to [seven or] eight people, each attended by two, adding up to twenty-four.

Also included are:

Twenty labourers for working in the kitchens for the samurai-daisho.
150 labourers supplied by the samurai (so-samurai).
Three fresh horses for the samurai-daisho [with drivers].
Fifteen workhorses supplied by the samurai [with drivers].
Five workhorses for the samurai-daisho [with drivers].
Approximately thirty pack horses with thirty drivers for them.

The above adds up to around 250 people and if you combine all of the above, they add up to more than 750 people in total.

The above list shows the composition of an army with fifty mounted warriors including lower soldiers. This is an estimation that was true in the Warring States period, when there were fewer soldiers, but this is not the case today. In this estimation, fifteen lower-class soldiers are counted for a single mounted warrior, but it is different now because any war now will be the first war after a prolonged period of peace and the situation is now different from that time of incessant wars.

II

Based on the estimation above, you should estimate how many are defending a castle, how many have come to the camp, or how many are going to the battlefield, etc. Generally, about one third of the number is left to keep a castle. However, it is not the case if there is a special issue of worry in the castle, but details are to be orally transmitted.

Also, about two thirds of those in the camp go out to the battlefield; however, it depends on the time, or the number of castles or fortresses, and this is also to be orally transmitted.

By considering the estimated numbers as above, you can estimate the number to be in a formation on the march.

Four points on estimating the number in a formation

I

Knowing the number of your allies, you should proceed to a vantage point and estimate which is larger, your army or that of the enemy.

II

Round off numbers to the nearest ten or hundred to calculate an estimation of the total.

III

Make an estimate by using the topography and the dimensions of an area with the supplementary information of how densely the army is formed.

As mentioned earlier, it is not possible to have more than two mounted warriors for every two-*ken* square or twelve foot soldiers per one-*ken* square.

IV

There is a possibility that you may miscalculate the enemy number depending on where the enemy is located or how it divides its forces. You should carefully consider this fact.

If an army is located on a mountain top, or divides its force into more than two, it tends to appear larger in number than it actually is. If the army is located in a valley, or gathered together in one single place, then it looks to have a smaller number than it actually has. To be passed on by oral transmission.

Three points on estimating the number of the enemy's army while on the march

I

A method to estimate an army when it is in a normal state[18] is to observe the flags, *umajirushi* standards and so on. These will be in the front and at the rear and you can use them as a guide to your estimate. Choose two flags and count the number between them to get a total. There are further secrets and there is an illustration to help [image missing].

II

To measure the width of a road and estimate the number of an army[19]
You should know the distance of the road [you are observing] and set up three

---

18 A 'normal state' means when the army is not in an alarmed state or in an emergency.

19 The aim here is to have three points along a large distance and know how many men will fit between the points.

control points along the way: the first control point should be close, the second point should be far off, and the third point should be even farther than that.

You can gain an estimation of the number [of the enemy by observing them reach] each waypoint.

III
To estimate the enemy number by counting the number of mounted warriors
As mentioned earlier, this varies according to how good the lord is or how large the province is, be it large, medium or small, or if it is a battle after a time of peace or one in wartime or even in the middle of successive wars that have continued for years. To be passed on by oral transmission.

Ten points on observing a castle or camp by external observation
I
Investigating if there is a double wall or fence
A double wall is a wall or tied wooden fence constructed inside a permanent outer wall [for extra defence when the enemy breaches the fortress]. Also, to add to this defence system, some castles are provided with a hidden enclosure near to the castle gate.[20] Or even if the castle does not normally have a hidden enclosure, there may have been one built at a time when there was a need to defend the castle.

II
Investigating if there is a false suspended wall
A suspended wall is a wall that is outside of a double wall. The defenders will weaken the foundation of this wall so that it will collapse easily when required. To construct this wall, pieces of wood or stones are used as weights on the inside of the wall, and towlines are fastened to the inner wall or secured by spikes in the ground. If enemy soldiers ascend such a wall the towlines are cut and it will fall on them.

III
Investigating if there are any 'stone arrow' defences[21]
These are appropriate-sized stones hung from six-*sun* square windows that are bored along the ridge of the fence. This is done so that when the enemy forces are climbing the wall, you can cut the rope and let the stones drop on them. Wood

---

20 This is so that when the enemy is trapped between the two walls, soldiers may attack them while in this space from a hidden compound.
21 Literally 'stone bow', *ishiishi-yumi*, meaning shooting stones.

and stone are both used for this.

I V
Establishing if there is a *sarusuberi* sliding cart

A *sarusuberi* is a cart loaded with large stones or wood that is set on the top of a hill and fastened with towlines. If the enemy advances, cut the towlines or put stone and wood connected with towlines on the top of a steep hill, so that you can cut the rope when the enemy climbs the slope.

V
Investigating if there is a *horinuki* ditch or *komagaeshi* defence against horses

Horinuki is a technique of digging a ditch of six or seven *shaku* in depth somewhere on a slope with the width depending on the area of the place itself. Drive [a mass] of spikes into the bottom, and cover the ditch with thin pieces of bamboo and soil, leaves and so on. It is sometimes the case that such a pit is dug in the shallows of a river.

V I
Investigating to know if there is a fence, spiked bamboo fence, trip rope, riverbed rope, etc.

Fences are built with wooden stakes seven *shaku* and five *sun* high from the ground, at an interval of three or four *sun* and with cross beams at five *sun* from the top. Sometimes *karatachi*[22] branches, which are thorny, are tied onto the fence. You often see this kind of fence in a dry moat or in the shallows of a river to prevent an opposing army from crossing over.

Yarai are spiky defences made of bamboo seven, eight or nine *shaku*, or even up to one *jo*, high; these are secured by lashings.

Sakamogi defences are made of big tree branches with branches stretching out in all directions; they are arranged with the sharp edges pointing toward the enemy.

Rangui are spikes put in the ground in a random fashion; these are commonly known. The *sokotsuna* or riverbed rope is a rope that should be stretched across the river at an angle with the current. Fix the rope below half of the depth of the river. These measures for defence are usually placed where the enemy does not have very strong fortifications. So you should identify where such things are built. There are various things you should keep in mind, though to find *rangui* spikes with ropes you need to be very careful. This is also to be orally transmitted.

---

22 Of the orange family.

VII

Investigating if there is a *hikibashi*[23] retractable bridge

A *hikibashi* is often built between the *honmaru*, which is the main castle enclosure, and the *ninomaru*, which is the secondary castle enclosure. It is built with hinges on the front. A drawing is provided as to how to construct it [image missing].

VIII

Investigating the waterway for the castle and assessing whether the enemy has a shortage of water

As well as the position of the waterway in the castle, and the level of the water supply, you should be aware of the possibility of the enemy drawing water from the moat at points on the *yagura* turrets. You should also fully investigate the water gates, and other such things.

In ancient times Kusunoki Masashige used great skill to take control of the water at Akasaka castle and to save water at Chihaya castle. You should be mindful of the lessons from these episodes.

If the enemy is short of water, it will attempt to take water from a valley or moat stealthily or drink dirty water – or even try allowing you to see its men washing their horses with water, with the intention of deceit. An example of this was at Tottori castle in Inshu, where they pretended to wash horses with white rice [so it looked like they had plenty of water].

IX

Investigating if the enemy is well fed or starved and exhausted

If the enemy is running out of food within the castle and is exhausted, those *samurai* or soldiers of the castle will try to take any vegetables or plants that they can; therefore, you should look at the leaves or branches of plants and trees in the area. Also if they seldom cook, you will not see smoke from the castle very often, or they may kill and eat horses; therefore, the neighing of horses will gradually decrease. People's voices will be weaker, the face colour will become paler, they may stagger or even walk with a cane and a rice bowl in hand. If they take to pillage even though it is prohibited by the codes of the army, it is because they are lacking in food. This is what you can know by observing from outside.

An alternative method is to open the belly of someone who has come out on a night raid and whom you have killed; this is done to see what they have eaten. In doing this, you should be careful to see what is digested in the stomach, as they

---

23 Possibly wheeled.

should have had some food before they came out for the night attack. Also, if you give white rice to prisoners and they vomit, you should be aware that this means that the enemy is running out of food.

You will never fail to know what is happening in a fortress if you go close to the castle wall and try to see or hear. Remember, Sun Tzu says 'those who stand with a cane are starved'.

In ancient times, when the Nitta clan defended Kanegasaki castle in Echizen, they ended up eating all the horses so that there was not a single neigh heard.

X

Judging if the enemy is strong or weak

If the army in a position is booming with noise, then discipline is not well administered and the lord or troop captains are not so competent. If those *samurai* or soldiers are moving around and not in an orderly fashion, you should be aware that the leaders do not have leadership skills or dignity enough to control the army. If five, six or even seven people are gathering to chat, you should know that they have doubts among themselves.

There are multiple variations of the above that you should observe. A strong army should look the opposite of the above; observe the enemy with this in mind.

Three mistakes you are likely to make when observing at night

I

Differentiating pillars from human beings

When you are sneaking outside the enemy castle, pillars if seen in the moonlight can look like the enemy in silhouette. To avoid making this mistake, you should be aware that pillars are still whereas people move, and that pillars are arrayed in orderly lines and have the same height whereas people will not appear to be in straight rows and they will have differing heights. These pillars are normally for flags or pikes to be rested against.

II

Differentiating between the fire of the enemy and the fire of those on your own side

When a fire breaks out on the enemy's side, if you observe it from behind your own army, it often looks like your vanguard is attacking. However, there will still be a gap between the two sides, though the distance between them is not so great.

Essentially, at night a fire looks closer than it actually is.

III

Differentiating between a fire signal and spring field-burning
Generally, fire signals are high while bush fires are low.

On observing from a distance

In this chapter you will find techniques for how to investigate enemy formations by watching them from a distance.

Three points on how to judge if the enemy is advancing or retreating from a castle or camp

I

Observing if the enemy is sallying forth from a castle or camp by the flags or *chi* of the people
If the enemy is exiting, whether for a night attack or a dawn raid, you will see flags or *umajirushi* standards move. If observed closely, an army when going out for battle will take a formation and it will line up in the following way: first the vanguard, then the secondary detachment, the third detachment and two flanking detachments, and finally the rear guard, all of whom will arrange themselves in this order and this will be done step by step. However, if the enemy is arranging to get the first and second detachments ready and put them in assembly just before a night raid, there will be particularly loud noises and any besieger should understand the situation if they hear such noises as these. Therefore, it is often the case that the enemy will prepare each detachment during the day, this is done to avoid its tactics being discovered. In such a case, the flags or *umajirushi* standards of the enemy may be relocated, but also remember that they may furl the flags and move them unnoticed. In any case, you need to be very careful about any point about flags that is different from the norm.

Some writings on military affairs say: when departing for battle, the vanguard will go to the rear while the rear guard will go to the gate. Therefore, you can tell if the enemy will come out or not by watching the positions of the flags.

When coming out for a morning raid, if the enemy is not so competent it will prepare a meal late in the evening after it has already cooked once for its normal evening meal and because of this fire or smoke can easily be identified. If the enemy is competent, it will cook any food needed for the next day or even the day after the next at the same time as the normal meals are cooked, making it difficult to notice if it is preparing to move out or not. However, you should observe very carefully and see if there is more smoke than normal. Also there are things you should keep in mind in case you are observing a battle camp in summer.

Even such a general as Takeda Shingen had the army's food for the day of a battle prepared on the evening before; at the Battles of Kawanakajima, his enemy Kenshin, who was observing from Mount Saijo, [was so good that he] noticed the situation [by the smoke of the preparation fires].

II

You will know that the enemy is going to make a night raid by observing the fires and lights, *komonomi* or small scouting groups, the absence of night patrols, the neighing of horses or barking of dogs, or by their being quieter, and so on. When enemy forces are going to perform a night raid, you may notice the following:

- They will send messengers among themselves to make advance arrangements, to prepare their equipment or for other various reasons. Thus you will see more lanterns, torches and other lights than normal.
- They will send *komonomi* or small scouting groups beforehand to investigate the ground and footings, the topography and what the formations of the enemy are like.
- Normally they will perform strict night patrols where you will hear the clapping of wooden warning clappers or the night guards' safety cries. However, when they are going to make a night raid, you will not hear the wooden warning clappers or the night guards' safety cries while they are patrolling.
- As they will need to gather horses into a group, you will hear more neighing than normal; and also, as people are busy and noisy, dogs will bark more.
- Or you may find the opposite, that the enemy will be quieter than normal, maybe even clamlike and silent.

You should consider all of the above things and judge if they are commencing a night raid or not.

III

Understanding if the enemy is in the castle or camp by observing birds, flags or fires

If the enemy has already withdrawn from the castle or camp but pretends to be there, it may leave flags or *sashimono* markers standing, or torches, lanterns or *hinawa* matches lit for you to see. If this is the case, you will notice that the flags or fires are still. Or you will see birds perch at very low points and close to where people should normally be, such as on towers or quarters and furthermore they will be feeding in a relaxed fashion or even flying in a relaxed way. To add to this you will see no smoke. If the enemy is there, you will see flags and fires moving and birds will stay away and pay attention to the ground while flying high, or even flushing in all directions nervously. However, this also depends on the kinds of birds in question. Pet pigeons, sparrows, kites or other tame birds tend not to be very afraid of people. However, it is possible to see the differences in the location of these birds and the way they fly; also, if the enemy is present then you will see smoke rising.

Two points on how to judge if the enemy is taking up position or retreating

I

To judge if the enemy is taking up position or retreating, you observe its loading and scouting activities.

If it is unloading and handling goods needed to take up a position, or if many *bushi* warriors are riding around and partaking in *monomi* scouting, then you should be aware that it is going to take up a position.

If the enemy is not unloading or handling materials for establishing a position but is in fact staying still, you should know that it is withdrawing. You should know that if it does not send out scouts but builds an embankment or stands pillars at equal intervals, then it is concerned by your forces and has decided to fight in defence against you.

II

Identifying the way the enemy sets up a position when it is waiting for support from its allies

Even if the enemy forces do not unload or take out materials for establishing a position, but in fact stay still and look like they are retreating, and it appears that the rest of the army is not joining them, but they are actually paying careful attention on not losing formation, then in this case they are waiting for the rear forces to arrive. To establish if this is the case, you should watch out for any soldiers repeatedly looking to the rear and also you will notice that, as they wait for the rear forces to arrive, there will be multiple people being sent away as messengers or arriving as messengers from the rear forces.

Five points on judging whether *fushi-kamari* ambushes[24] are present

I

Probable places where *fushi-kamari* ambush troops will hide
Possible places where there may be *fushi-kamari* are: forests, bushes, valleys, the

---

24 *Fushi* appear to be larger ambushes, while *kamari* are smaller ambushes.

shade of mountains, behind embankments, in trenches or rivers, in clumps of reeds, in deep grassy fields, wheat fields, and so on and so forth.

Sun Tzu says:

If in the neighbourhood of your camp there should be any hilly country, ponds surrounded by aquatic grass, hollow basins filled with reeds, or woods with thick undergrowth, they must be carefully rooted out and searched; for these are places where men in ambush or insidious spies are likely to be lurking.

I I

To establish if there are *fushi* ambushes in *kamari-ba*, that is 'fields of *kamari*', as mentioned before, you should observe: birds or animals, *chi*, fires, grasses, flags, smoke, dummies, fake birds and so on and so forth. As mentioned above, you should judge if there are *kamari* ambushes or not by observing if birds are present or not and by the patterns of their flight.

Sun Tzu says:

The rising of birds in their flight is the sign of an ambush.

The *Six Secret Teachings* says:

If there are soldiers in a field, wild geese will fly out of the formation. As for animals, you should judge by observing the way of running of such animals as foxes, racoon dogs, deer, rabbits, cats and so on. If there are troops in ambush or waiting to attack, you can see animals running out of the mountains or field.

Sun Tzu says:

Startled beasts indicate that a sudden attack is coming.

Also you can always see *chi* above forests or woods if there are any troops hiding within. If there are more than one hundred people, there will be *chi* without fail. Compare the sky above a forest within land where you know for sure there are no *fushi-kamari* and that same space above those forests where there will likely be *kamari*, and you will understand the difference and be able to tell if there is an ambush or not. Also you can observe smoke from *hinawa* matches; even though it is only a small amount, it can still be seen due to a number of people gathering in one place.

In addition, it is said that on a cloudy night the clouds above an ambush look white,[25] while on a clear night there will be many stars visible;[26] also see the shimmering lights of *hinawa* matches. However, if these lights are still, you

---

25 Probably due to smoke from musket fuses.

26 This sentence is not qualified and does not specify if this is 'magical', as with the *chi* of army, which is discussed earlier; it simply is as it is in the text.

should be aware they will be *hinawa* that are being held in bamboo[27] sticks and are war tricks. Once, a group withdrew from their position with some *hinawa* looped over the branches of willow trees to make the enemy think that there were people there. It looked like people were holding these fuses; however, if held by a real person they should move around up to five *shaku* or one *jo*, but these fake ones could only move up to one or two *shaku* [as they swayed], thus you could tell that they were false. Remember, if they are held by real people, the lights will come in and out of your vision.

When observing grasses you should judge if there are people hiding in a deep grass field, a wheat field, a hemp field or so on. If there is an ambush waiting, those grasses will not look neat but will have a skewed look, like after a storm. If no one is there then the tops of the grass will look neat. If you have a closer look by approaching, you will see traces where *fushi* ambush groups have made their way in. This will take the form of pathways or grass that has been pushed over, or if it is after rain or early in the morning, you will see no dew drops on the grasses as they will have been brushed off.

As for flags, *kamari* actually take flags or *umajirushi* standards with them and lay them down. Therefore, if you see flags or *umajirushi* standards standing among the trees of a forest or such a scene, you should judge that these are fake flags that have been left there to make you think there is an ambush. However, if you see people watching sneakily from the shade or if you see small back-pennants [as opposed to larger flags], then it will most likely be a real ambush.

Also, the enemy may make smoke by burning pine needles in a valley or over a mountain to mislead you into thinking there is an ambush. Be warned, this is definitely not an actual ambush as an ambush party will never purposely make smoke.[28]

The enemy may make dummies and falsify an ambush with the intent to draw you out. You should know these will not move, and if you see these dummies in the shade of a tree or far away on a mountain you should know that there is no ambush. This method was invented by Kusunoki Masashige a long time ago when he defended Chihaya castle. There is also a form of making fake birds, but these also do not move, and you should judge there must be an ambush under where those birds are placed.

These things are actual events in ancient times and have been passed down

---

27 It was common practice in Japan to split bamboo down one side and prop open the length with a smaller twig. The *hinawa* would then be placed in the gap and the twig removed, trapping the *hinawa* match in place.

28 It should be mentioned here that Fujibayashi does state early that smoke will be present if there are enough lit fuses among the ambush party, but only a slight amount.

as they were; however, remember sometimes the insubstantial can actually be insubstantial and substantial can be substantial.[29] Further details are to be passed on by oral transmission.

III

Judging if there is an ambush or not in the fields of the *kamari* by watching or listening

In performing this technique, if it is in a forest, you should stealthily go to the leeward side so you can hear any sound the enemy makes as it will travel on the wind or you may even smell their *hinawa* matches. If you need to investigate a valley, you should go down to a field or riverside [and just outside of] the valley and look up to the valley sides from there. If it is a valley close to the sea, you can get a boat and investigate the valley by looking up the valley from the sea. In some cases you should climb up to a high mountain top. You should judge the best method according to the opportunity.

IV

Knowing if the enemy is retreating with deceptive tactics while they lay ambushes

It is not true defeat if the enemy has a consistent plan and retreats in a proper fashion and formation.

Li Jing says:

If the flags are in order, the drums respond to each other and the commands and orders seem unified, then even though they may be retreating and running, it is not a defeat and must therefore be unorthodox strategy.

In some cases a formation may get into a state of confusion and some may run in a panic and retreat in a non-unified fashion or others return to the fight or run scattering in random groups of five, ten, twenty or thirty people; this is true withdrawal.

Li Jing says:

Whenever the soldiers retreat with their flags confused and disordered, the sounds of the large and small drums not responding to each other and their orders shouted in a clamour, this is true defeat, not an unorthodox strategy.

If those troops retreating look to the same place, know that that is where an ambush is laid.

---

29 This implies that sometimes things *are* as you see them and that you do not need to look for tricks in everything – all may be as it actually appears.

One of Yoshitsune's military poems:

逃テ行足輕ドモノ脇ヲ見ハ其見ル方ニ伏アリト知レ

If those ashigaru *running away all look to one side, be aware there must be an ambush in that direction.*

V

Judging the enemy intention by observing how it fights or retreats

It is strictly prohibited in *gunpo* military rules for regular troops to approach the enemy side after the hour of the horse (one o'clock in the afternoon), so you should be aware that if the enemy makes an approach to your side near dusk then it must have tactics.

Whether large or small in number, it is the norm to take up a position on high ground, such as a hill, when near the enemy castle or camp. Therefore, if the enemy takes a position in the middle of a field and in a small number, you should be aware it has tactics. In addition, if the enemy goes where it is not supposed to go, retreats when it is not supposed to do, or it does what it is not supposed to do, you should be aware it has tactics in place.

You should keep all the above points in mind and have good judgement so that you will know the enemy's plans and carry out your own plans to outwit its tactics.

To determine if the enemy is going to cross over a river or not

If enemy soldiers are going to cross over a river they may take off their *aori* saddle skirts and archers will untie their arrow quivers. Generally those who are [mounted] and crossing over a river are not attended by those on foot, or if there are any on foot there will be only a few. Also those on foot often use a hemp rope (*koshinawa*) around the waist, one *jo* four or five *shaku* in length, which they put around the waists of the people crossing with them. If people on foot take out this rope and put it around their waists, you should know they are going to cross over a river.

Seven points on how to judge the enemy by observing the dust or[30] flags

I

If the standard bearers are positioned at the front of the army, then the enemy is going to take up a position. If they are moving back into the middle of the formation, then know that the enemy is going to advance.

---

30 The original text says 'of', which is presumed to be a transcription error.

II

If the flags are moving in a small amount of confusion, the enemy has not settled its formations. If the flags are in great disorder you should be aware that arguments are taking place.

III

If *kofu* or small banners and flags are leaning forwards, you should be aware that the enemy is going to fight, while if they are leaning backwards, he is not going to move forwards.

IV

If the front forces are moving while the rear forces are stationary, you should be aware the enemy is making formations.

V

If you can see dust from horses rising at the front, you should be aware that the enemy is advancing, while if you see it in the rear the enemy is withdrawing. If you can see no dust, no banners moving and the flags still, you should be aware the enemy is building up a secure position.

VI

If the enemy has marched for a long distance and its warriors create lots of dust and are disordered, you should know that there are more mounted warriors and fewer foot soldiers, while if you can see only a little dust, which rises low, there must be more foot soldiers and fewer mounted warriors.

VII

You can judge if the enemy army is massive or not by observing the location it occupies, its fences and so on. Also you should be aware that if an enemy army takes a position in a forest or bush-land that means it is small in number and will be easily thwarted and it will retreat.

There are further details for the above articles that are to be orally transmitted. Those who are studying this way should always devote themselves to this path, and if the time comes, you should keep your mind determined and construct a plan, paying attention to refinement and details. Doing it thus will allow you to see into the heart of the enemy and you will be able to perceive with excellence that which is substantial 實 and that which is insubstantial 虛.

In-nin I

Hidden Infiltration I

Infiltrating a castle I

Those who hide or the 'great hermits'[1] always stay in an urban area. Though *in-nin*[2] is not as good as *yo-nin*, if you have only *yo-jutsu* but no *in-jutsu* you cannot gain any benefit from it. Therefore, this volume deals with the ways to take advantage of the enemy's gap, to perform *ongyo-no-jutsu* hiding skills and how to infiltrate with the help of tools. Also, how, when in need, to change your way in order to deal with any situation at hand, and how to switch between *yo-nin*[3] and *in-nin* with fluidity without fixing only on *yo* or only on *in*, just as the seasons change. Thus there are variations, such as setting up with *in-nin* at first and then using *yo-nin* later, or infiltrating with *yo-nin* at the beginning and performing *in-nin* at the end, or even using *in-nin* in the middle of *yo-nin*, or going with *yo-nin* in the middle of *in-nin* and so on and so forth. The changes or shifts must be made extremely fluidly, just like a ball rolling on a platter or a gourd skating on ice.

In old times, Dojun infiltrated Sawayama castle by disguising himself as a lumberjack. Once inside, he changed methods and hid under the floor; that is to say, he performed *yo-nin* first and then switched to *in-nin*.

---

1 The context here is someone who hides from and eludes society, to hide himself from the world – literally 'great hermit', *inja*, a person who hides, but in this context the word 'hermit' gives the wrong connotations for a Western audience, as this agent operates in inhabited areas.

2 The original script has a transcription error at this point and says *yo-nin* twice.

3 Fujibayashi drops the *nin* at the end of each *yo* and *in* here. However, they have been inserted in this volume for the sake of consistency.

When Suyama and Komiyama infiltrated Kasagi castle, they chose a night of heavy wind and rain, climbed up the rocks stealthily with grappling hooks and penetrated the castle. They were questioned by enemy soldiers who were following a night patrol; at this, Suyama Yoshitsugu made an *ad hoc* reply, saying that they were from the Yamato division and on a night patrol for fear that there might be a night attack or that a *shinobi* might infiltrate as the rain and wind were heavy. Then he continued and said that they had not found anybody who had infiltrated the castle, but then told each group they encountered to watch out; they did this while they were marching calmly toward the main building. After finding out where in the building the Emperor was stationed and what its status was, they set a fire to the buildings. This is an example of using *in-nin* at first and *yo-nin* at the end.

Furthermore, Kotaro,[4] when he infiltrated Mineoroshi castle in Sanagu of our domain of Iga, was questioned and chased by his enemy. While running away, he threw a rock into a well, so that the pursuers were misled into thinking he might have fallen in. Gaining time by doing this, he made good his escape.

Also, when Magodayu[5] infiltrated a house, the enemy heard him and thrust a spear into his hiding place. Magodayu whispered to himself, as though he was accompanied by another agent, and he said: 'The master of the house seems to have woken up, *we* should retreat.' He then made a second voice in false reply, 'All right.' In this manner, the enemy thought that 'they' were hiding behind the wall and leaving their hiding place and so the enemy went out to capture the 'pair'. As a result of this Magodayu went deeper into the house.

The above two examples are of using *yo-nin* in the middle of *in-nin*.

Yamada Hachiemon once argued with a man about his skills. During this argument the man challenged him and asked if Yamada could steal his sword or not. In response Yamada Hachiemon offered a bet and stated that he would take the man's sword in broad daylight on the day of the festival in the principal shrine of Iga.

On that day, Yamada Hachiemon put on a straw raincoat and a straw hat to draw his target's attention and walked ahead of him. He did this so that the target would believe his sword was safe as long as he had him in sight. Hachiemon then ran into a house in a village called Nagata, where he had prepared a disciple who was wearing the same disguise as his own. When he entered, the disciple went out from the back door and moved to a hill top which was five *cho* away from the shrine. The sword owner, thinking the one on the hill top was in fact Yamada

---

4 Shindo no Kotaro, one of the eleven great *ninja*, mentioned in volume one.
5 Nomura no Odaki Magodayu, another of the eleven great *ninja*.

Hachiemon, waited and waited at the bottom of the hill but became bored as the man would not come down. As time passed he instructed someone to keep an eye on the opponent while he himself visited the shrine. Meanwhile Yamada Hachiemon disguised himself as an old hag with a large cloth hat and mixed into a crowd under the main gong – in this way, he waited for his opponent. As it was a festival day, there were lots of people scrabbling for the cord of the gong and beating the gong with enthusiasm. In this confusion he drew the target's sword out of its scabbard from across the opposite side of the offertory box and took it from the man unnoticed. Not realizing his sword had been stolen, the man pushed his way out of the crowd and boasted in the horse arena in public, showing how his sword had not been stolen, but in fact it was not there.

This is the art of using *in-nin* in the middle of *yo-nin*.

There were numerous tactics carried out by ancient people using *in-nin* first and *yo-nin* later, *yo-nin* first and *in-nin* later, *in-nin* inside of *yo-nin* or *yo-nin* inside of *in-nin*, the outlines of which are mentioned above. The point here is to instil the idea that you should use *in-nin* and *yo-nin* alternatively and freely according to the opportunity, without placing a disproportionate emphasis on either one, with the aim of winning an overall victory.

Ten points to consider before the mission

I

You should investigate exactly what the enemy castle or camp is like by collecting information from people or observing it in detail. You must decide on the best skills and measures to fulfil your mission, and deliberate on where you should infiltrate from or retreat from and so on. Those who are engaged on this path should travel around the castle towns in various provinces at times of tranquillity and, while always trying to have good judgement in distinguishing truth and falsehood, you should observe with attention any information, such as where to get in from or where to retreat from and, after doing satisfactory investigation, create a drawing recording this information. Even when you happen to pass by a strange village, you should always investigate as many paths as possible, by walking the bypasses or narrow routes, and by observing where they are steep or flat, how wide or narrow they are, the distance from one point to another point, where they begin and end, etc. You should try to know as much as possible, even such things as animal trails. Do this by asking and observing and then write it down.

I I

You should take a nap before 'stealing in', as sleep is a human behaviour just as day and night are a part of the sky. No matter how encouraged you feel, you cannot perform anything without sleep.

I I I

You must consider the time of the rising and setting of the moon. It is best to infiltrate before the moon rises or after it sets. This is called *tsuki no daiji* or the principle of the moon. Ancient *ninja* named this skill 'before Yakushi and after Jizo' and it was kept secret. This is because moonlit nights are usually disfavoured by those performing the art of *in-nin*. The method of knowing the time of moon rising and setting is mentioned in the chapter on astronomy in the section called Opportunities Bestowed by Heaven.

I V

When infiltrating at night, you need to know the time by observing the star Polaris or the star cluster Pleiades, or by using a weight[6] or a sandglass.[7] These are also mentioned in the chapter on astrology.

Someone[8] says you can know the time by observing your breathing through your nose.[9] If you are breathing through the left nostril in the hour of the Rat, it will alternate every hour.[10] I have tried this but have so far failed to master it.

V

Before 'stealing in', you should have firmly worked out any arrangements with your lord to make sure that no mistakes will happen. This should concern everything, including *hikyaku-hi* fire beacons, the *ireko-hi* adjustable lamp and smoke signals, etc.

Details on the arrangements of signals are mentioned earlier in the subsection 'Concerning the agreement between your lord and the *ninja*' in the volume; A Guideline for Commanders Part II.

---

6   This is echoed in other scrolls.

7   The oldest recorded Japanese sandglass appears to be dated 1616.

8   Literally, 'some-person' – interestingly, this is also backed up by Natori-ryu.

9   Unknown to the *ninja* at that time, this phenomenon was first described in detail in 1895 by the German physician Richard Kayser, who called it the Nasal Cycle. The air intake in each nostril shifts in percentage of volume as blood periodically swells on alternate sides of the nasal cavity. The average cycle time can vary.

10 Approximately 120 minutes in Western time. However, this would depend on the season at the time.

VI

When you decide the time is right, you should get close to the enemy castle or camp by using both *in-* and *yo-jutsu*, wait for the correct time and infiltrate. Remember to give careful thought to the place where you should 'steal in' and retreat from. It is often the case that you become lost when coming back, so you should put various kinds of marks or use signals such as *iccho ikka* – 'one fire for one *cho*' – or the *ireko-ju*[11] 'adjustable lamp'. *Iccho ikka* is mentioned in the volume on *shinobi* night attacks; however, there are some differences in using the above method when infiltrating, but this is to be orally transmitted.

VII

If you are not very selective about the squad to be picked for the mission, the infiltration in question will be unprofessional, so as well as an agreement about the way of signals, it is essential for every member to be well informed on all matters. Be sure not to select those who you think are cowards, careless or unskilled as those who go together on a mission. On top of that, you should make a written oath among yourselves that no one will fail to live up to his word or the agreed way of signals and all should stand or fall as one mind, be it dead or alive.

Supplementary to the above, if you cannot cut out those who are cowards, careless or unskilled and have to take them onto the squad, then assign them to the role of signals. If you have to take them with you to the place of the mission, make them follow behind you while 'stealing in' and go ahead of you on the way out.

Two *shinobi* poems say:

唯人ヲ連テ忍ニ行ナラハ　先ツ退口ヲ記シ覚ヘヨ

*When you steal in with an ordinary person, the first thing you should
do is mark and show him the way out and how to escape.*

忍ニハ二人行コソ大事ナレ　独忍フニウキコトハナシ

When going on a shinobi *activity, venturing out in a two-man
team is difficult. However, on solo* shinobi *missions there are no
such concerns.*

---

11 This uses the same first ideogram as the 'adjustable lamp', but also uses 'gun' or 'shot' as a second. However, the tool itself is not explained and may be a transcription error due to its context. Therefore, here it has been translated as 'lamp'.

VIII

When infiltrating a castle, all of your squad should infiltrate there from one point together and become scattered after you have entered.

IX

When infiltrating a mountain castle, fortress or *tsukejinya* which is a camp close to the enemy castle or fortress, your squad should enter in a scattered formation.

Supplementary to this, be aware of the fire signals and the three kinds of marks. The fire signals and the three kinds of marks are mentioned in the chapter 'Concerning the agreement between your lord and the *ninja*' in A Guideline for Commanders Part II.

X

Be fully aware of the possibility that you may be detected while discreetly collecting information on the happenings within the enemy army. With that information you should forge letters from someone on the enemy's staff and address them to your lord. Leave one or two of them at the place you stay at and also hide a letter from your lord in your collar. This technique is mentioned in detail in the previous chapter *Yo-nin Jo*.

A *ninja* poem says:

目付者又ハ窃盗ニ行時ハ　書置ヲセヨ後世ノ為

Before you go out on a metsuke *secret surveillance or on a covert* shinobi *activity, you should leave a note for future benefit.*[12]

Further details for the above points are to be orally transmitted. You should not take them too lightly.

Twenty points on the art of infiltrating while the enemy is off guard

I

Concerning the night when the enemy lord departs from his castle to attack your province

Although most people know that guarding your own castle is more important than attacking an opponent's castle, there are four advantages, as listed below, when infiltrating a castle on such a night.

1. When a massive army departs from its castle, everything is busy and noisy and everyone is distracted by their tasks.

---

12 Fujibayashi here slightly changes the poem. For a full explanation see the author's work *Secret Traditions of the Shinobi.*

2. They tend to be preoccupied by the thought of beating the enemy so that they are not attentive enough to make an inquiry into every detail [of defence].

3. At such a time as described above there will be many people going in or out of the castle.

4. It is the time people least expect the enemy *shinobi* to infiltrate.

I I

Infiltrating between the first and third nights after the enemy has arrived at its position

1. Although people tend to be sharp and attentive at the beginning, they are so busy with multiple and miscellaneous duties and sometimes they become confused through hardship. It is as though human beings, birds and animals relax during spring.[13]

2. The enemy forces are not prepared or determined at this time.

3. They are busy building quarters or setting up their camps.

4. They have less fear so thus have less vigilance.

Infiltrating between these nights is beneficial because of the above four advantages.

I I I

On a night after the enemy has travelled over a long distance, especially if double the usual distance, or has crossed a steep area, on a sunny and warm or even hot day in spring or summer.

I V

On a night after the enemy has travelled across ice or snow, or even crossed deep water or also, when the enemy has been freezing, has toiled and is exhausted, on a stormy day or on an extremely cold day in winter.

V

If the enemy arrives and takes up a position after sunset, when he is still busy building quarters, preparing meals, washing horses with hot water and has not settled down to a set routine.

---

13 This statement is ambiguous and unexplained but is possibly a reference to how people relax and let their minds drift after the hardships of winter, i.e. relax in spring.

V I

On a night when the enemy is tired after he has had a battle or disputed all day long. As man is not made of iron, it is always the case that men let their guard down when they are tired.

V I I

On a night when the enemy is getting ready to advance an attack on your side. Under any circumstances, when [troops] leave a fortress their minds are not in their usual state – and this is even more true when they are going to battle. The enemy troops at this time are busy preparing food, outfits, orders, agreements, last wills and testaments and so on and their minds are wandering from one point to another. Also it is the time the enemy least expects *shinobi* to enter.

To discover when the enemy is to advance, you should listen to the conch shells. One military manuscript says that in the case where the conch shell is blown at certain time intervals, then it sometimes means that the enemy is preparing to advance or for a battle. Examples include having a meal at the first shell signal, getting ready with your war gear at the second signal, and having the vanguard depart on the third signal and so on. In this example, the shell is blown nine times at each command, so if there are three signals as described above, it adds up to twenty-seven blows of the conch shell. The time is not definite and all is dependent on the enemy's way of signalling.

V I I I

Finding a gap on the night after the enemy wins a clear victory in a night attack against your own side or even in a daytime battle
If the enemy army secures a victory and you are beaten badly, it will be conceited and overconfident – this is a certainty. There is no one who does not know the saying, 'Stay on your guard even after you have won.' However, though people often repeat this saying and remember it, if they have control of a situation then they get carried away and flippant. Do not miss this opportunity.

I X

Infiltrate when your allies are victorious and the enemy has been soundly defeated and is retreating into its castle and is still in complete confusion and fright.

X

It is difficult to steal in if the place is quiet, while it is easy if it is noisy. This is how to judge the right time.

It is always the right time for you to infiltrate when any unforeseen accident takes place, such as a fire breaking out, horses being released, or enemy soldiers fighting among themselves, because people are in a state of surprise or in commotion or confused. Do not hesitate too much and take the chance while you can.

A *ninja* poem says:

大勢ノ敵騒キハ忍ヨシ　静マル方ニ隠家ハナシ

You can find a way to creep in when a number of the enemy are distracted. When they are quiet, you may find no place to hide.

The enemy general may be a sage and have planned to catch you through confusion. You should judge this carefully. However, if it is an enemy trap, it will be fine as long as the *shinobi no mono* are skilled enough.

XI

With signals having been prearranged with your lord, you should approach the enemy from the opposite side: when attacking from the front, you infiltrate from behind; while if from the back, you go from the front; and you should always remember this principle even if there is no signal. *Ninja* should refrain from being impulsive in any way. If you see a fight with spear or sword, even if it is next to you, you should leave and focus on judging the situation with your trained eye. The only thing you should keep in mind in your mission is how to take advantage of a gap within the enemy, how to infiltrate the castle and capture it, or how to destroy a camp. Otherwise, how would it be possible for you to infiltrate a strictly guarded camp or an impregnable castle[14]?

A *ninja* poem says:

忍ニハ身ノ働ハ非ストモ　眼ノ利クヲ肝要トセヨ

Even if a shinobi *does not have impressive physical abilities, remember the most vital thing is to have acute observation.*

XII

If a large number of soldiers are defending a small castle, infiltrate from where people are gathering; while if a small number are defending a large castle, infiltrate it from a steep and difficult area. The reasons for going where a number

14 The message is that you should not get into any form of hand-to-hand fighting, but continue on your mission of infiltration.

of people are gathering together in a small castle defended by a large number of people are as follows:

- As it is noisy, it is hard to hear any sounds.
- It is easier to blend in with the enemy.
- Where there are many people, they tend not to put everyone under scrutiny.

You should go to a steep and difficult area[15] of a large castle that is defended by a small number of people because they pay attention only to where it is not naturally fortified and tend to neglect where the fortification seems to them secure enough.

XIII

On a night of heavy wind and rain

On a night of heavy [rain and] wind, it is very likely that a night attack will occur or that *shinobi* 竊盗 will steal in. It is a well-known fact that nobody likes being drenched by the rain or swept by heavy winds. Even if the lord gives strict orders, it is often the case that the guardsmen are not fully alert during a night patrol. This is an enduring secret principle for *in-nin* and it holds true even if there is only drizzle or slight breeze.

Therefore, it is essential for every *ninja* to foresee the wind and rain. How to forecast the wind or rain is mentioned in the chapter on astrology in the volume called Opportunities Bestowed by Heaven.

大雨ヤ大雨ノ降時ニコソ　竊盗夜討ノ便リトハスレ

In heavy rainfall when the rain is at its most you should carry out a shinobi mission or a night attack.

雨風モ頻リナル夜ハ道暗ク　竊盗夜討ノ働トナル

In the dead of night when the wind and rain are raging, the streets are so dark that you can execute a shinobi mission or can deliver a night attack smoothly and with ease.

---

15 *Nansho.*

– 175 –

XIV

When the enemy calls for reconciliation, you need to consider whether it is a trick or the truth and converse with your lord to determine this [before you go to infiltrate]. Whenever you are going to attack the opponent, you will be negligent; it is essential for you to consider this.

Sun Tzu says:

Peace proposals unaccompanied by a sworn covenant indicate a plot.

XV

When your army is attacking a castle, if the castle is too hard to capture or you want to deceive the enemy with a ruse, then you sometimes raise the siege and depart. On that night the enemy will be tired and they will relax their attention because of fatigue – this is a certainty.

XVI

Concerning a castle or camp without a commander or general in charge, or one that has a single commander but is defended by a conglomerate of clans

If a position is defended by a conglomerate of forces, even if it has a universal commander, the forces tend to take liberties and they find it hard to pull together; whereas if the vassalage for a single lord is used to defend in one place, then it is difficult to infiltrate. Therefore, even if the castle or camp is led by one commander, it is reasonable to investigate which areas are defended by a collection of troops from different clans and infiltrate from there.

XVII

Prolonged battle and weariness

Generally, people are keen and attentive at the beginning of a campaign but if it becomes prolonged, then they will become tired and negligence will ensue. Also, if you observe the enemy throughout a prolonged period of battle, you will certainly find a gap you can utilize.

XVIII

When the enemy lord is not competent in military administration and greatly relies on the number of his army, underestimates his enemy and is not very vigilant

Those who do not pay much attention to military strategy and are not careful and prepared usually do not know how wise other people are as they are too arrogant to fathom others but rely instead on the size of their army, and are too arrogant to exercise sufficient caution in their defence.

XIX

Be fully aware of the principle that man is a lazy creature
People get conceited and take the enemy lightly when they have victory, yet they
are disgusted and become lethargic when they lose.

When having an easy time, people are indulged, at ease and negligent, while
during a difficult time, they become exhausted and fall into laziness. In summer
most people are lazy because they are exhausted with the heat, while in winter,
because they hate the cold, frost, snow or the gale, you will find very few who
are always keen and who stay attentive. Unless you are fully aware of this fact, no
shinobi mission will be fulfilled.

In a fight with *tachi* long-swords, those who can discern the direction of the
opponent's sword and understand his gaps 虚 will win, while those who cannot
see this will lose. Even in a sword fight you should be aware of what is substantial 實 and what is insubstantial 虚. This is even more important when a larger
number are involved and the time span is over several days. If you can identify
when and where they relax and make your plan based on this, then there is no
chance that you will fail to infiltrate.

A *ninja* poem says:

忍ニハ危ナキヲ良トセヨ　前へ疑ヒハ臆病ノ沙汰

For a shinobi *it is desirable not to have any anxiety or hesitation.*
Doubts beforehand come from your own cowardice.

XX

The arrival of enemy reinforcements, be it day or night
When reinforcements arrive, the enemy feels it is almost guaranteed success and
always becomes negligent. However, the forces that have just arrived have not
been fully informed of the military orders of the army, so they are quite unfamiliar
with the situation and they are not strong in their defence yet. Therefore, you
should consider the best plan to take advantage of this opportunity.

The above points are concerned with when and where the enemy will be
negligent and weak, therefore a *ninja* should not have any anxiety or hesitation
but plunge into the enemy's gap at these points. A *shinobi no mono* who knows
the theory behind this but who has anxiety and hesitates at the crucial time, will
not be able to infiltrate a target even if he spends a thousand years on the task.
This means that if you are very close to the enemy but lack determination, you
will have too much anxiety and miss the correct opportunity and end up being
detected by the enemy or, even worse, imprisoned.

Wu Qi says:

If the soldiers are committed to fighting to the death, they will live, whereas if they seek to stay alive, they will die.

When in a difficult situation, think nothing of your body and your life but stay serene and still as you would at normal times. You should also firmly keep in mind the principles: '*death and life have their determined appointment*' and '*nothing is born, nothing is destroyed*'.[16] If you do this, even danger will turn out to be good luck.

I really think that even the smartest and best-reputed man will let his guard down at some point – this is even more so with ordinary people. If people think of the front, they will forget the rear; if they focus on their right, they are not thinking about their left – this is the way of life. It is especially so when they are in a state of anxiety or difficulty and when all around them is bustling; because of these factors they will be nervous and make more mistakes. As a rule, *ninja* avoid where the enemy is substantial and take advantage of where it is insubstantial.

A *ninja* poem says:

竊盗ニハ時ヲ知ルコソ大事ナレ　敵ノ疲レト油断有トキ

For a shinobi *it is essential to know the proper time. It always should be when the enemy is tired or has let their guard down.*

Eight points on the art of infiltrating by taking advantage of the enemy's negligence

I

Shinobi no jutsu should be performed according to the time and the place. However, first of all note that the things you should keep in mind are different for daytime and night time.

In the daytime, go to where there are many people and where it is noisy; while at night, go to where it is quiet. You should first whisper as a test and see if the guards are asleep or not. If they are asleep, no voice or sound will be heard. However, if they are snoring, then know that there is a method to understand the various kinds of snoring. Details are to be orally transmitted. You should stay quiet, listening for one hour or so to know if they are keeping quiet as a ruse or if they really are asleep. If they feign sleep, after a little while you will always hear them say something in doubt. If the guards are attentive and they

---

16 Quoted from the *Heart Sutra*.

pay keen attention to your whisper and become vigilant, you will hear them whisper among themselves, get ready with bows, spears, swords and so on, or you will hear other movements like sitting down or standing up in preparation, and as a result they will make very small sounds. In such a case you should leave as soon as possible. If they become startled, flustered or make noise in reaction to the small sound you made as a test, then they are a mere group of unskilled people not in order. Therefore, if you leave them for a while and come back later when they have settled down you can try to find a gap within them and you will never fail to infiltrate from that direction.

The mindset of people varies according to whether they are at the beginning, in the middle or at the end of [a watch]. At the beginning, they are keen and energetic; in the middle; they become slack and lazy; and at the end they get bored and want to leave or even fall asleep at times. Therefore, experienced *ninja* avoid the time when the guards are keen and energetic but wait for the time when they get bored and sleepy. Taking advantage of the time, they immediately get in there without delay and there is no chance of failure.

Sun Tzu says:

Now a soldier's spirit is keenest in the morning; by noonday it has begun to flag; and in the evening, his mind is bent only on returning to camp.

You may think the above principle holds true only with military tactics and not those used by *ninja,* which may make you neglect it. However, where on earth can the essence of *shinobi no jutsu* be found outside of this? Further details are to be passed on by oral transmission.

II

While observing a guardhouse you may encounter the following:

Those who appear to be *togiki* listening scouts who investigate stealthily and carry spears, halberds, *tachi* long-swords and so on, hiding themselves behind fences or walls. There may be whisper of warning in the guardhouse [if they suspect you]. Also, you may find that when a commotion takes place two or three out of a guard of ten come out to investigate.

These above are signs of a strictly guarded station and *shinobi* should leave as soon as possible. When retreating, be sure to have a plan and avoid catching their attention, as though you are the sound of frost forming on a cold winter night.

III

While observing a guardhouse, if you hear the guards speak loudly, engaging in friendly chat, having a drinking party, singing etc., it is often because only young and inexperienced guards are working on that shift without old and experienced ones. This is exactly where you should get in. Do not hesitate.

I V

Though sometimes guards look like they are in idleness and not conducting vigilant precautions, be warned that it may in fact be a deception and they may intend to draw *shinobi* into a trap. Be sure to have good judgement as to whether they are actually inattentive or whether they have a stratagem to lure *shinobi no mono* in and capture them. If it is a stratagem, there will be scrupulous guards somewhere around, often with *togiki* listening scout(s) beside them. You should have very watchful eyes to see if the situation is true or false and do not enter without careful thought.

V

After getting in the enemy castle or camp, *ninja* should act after the night patrol has passed as it has been done since ancient times. As for the distance that they should keep between them and the patrol, this should be worked out by observing the way the guards are acting and with reference to the points on places that you should not enter (as mentioned earlier).

V I

Hints on how to infiltrate a position and bypass a secure guardhouse:
- Draw them out and have them follow you.
- Make them fight among themselves.
- Use grenades and shots.[17]

There is more to be orally transmitted to accompany the above points.

Supplementary to this, there is an old method of applying sleeping powder, but I have not tested this.

V I I

There is no difference between the principles of *ninjutsu* and the principles for *kenjutsu* swordsmanship. When the enemy is not going to close in, it is difficult for you to strike at him with a sword because you should strike on the moment that the enemy closes in on you. Or you should dodge the path of the enemy's sword and strike when the sword is brought down or take advantage of the moment that the enemy raises his sword. These examples are based on the

---

17 Literally 'throwing-fire and shooting-fire tools', most likely forms of Chinese firecracker.

principle of striking when the enemy closes in on you. Those who are stupid try to strike when the opponent is not going to close in – therefore, they cannot kill the opponent. What is worse is that this may end up not only as a failure but also may result in their being cut. The same holds true in *ninjutsu*: when the enemy does not move,[18] you should not move either. You should infiltrate at the exact moment that the enemy moves in and do not try when they do not move – this is a way of principled people. Unskilled people tend to try to get in when the enemy is not on the move; therefore, their infiltration ends in failure and also they are often destroyed in the end. Thus, when the enemy is not moving, *shinobi* have no way to infiltrate. Even an impregnable castle or strictly guarded camp can be infiltrated without exception, if you take advantage of the enemy's movement. This all depends on whether the enemy moves or not. If the time comes when the enemy is on the move, you will be able to infiltrate smoothly and without any difficulty, unless you are possessed by an unreasonable urge. This is the method by which only accomplished people operate.

VIII

The three diseases of *shinobi no jutsu* are:

1. To fear.
2. To take the enemy lightly.
3. To think too much.

By removing these three, you will be able to infiltrate as quickly as lightning.

First, if you have a fear of the enemy, you will quake, feel nervous, become confused as to which is the correct procedure, forget the tricks you have mastered and can perform at normal times, tremble in both hands and feet, lose colour, slur your words and give yourself away and be detected.

Second, if you make little of the enemy and think they are stupid, you will prepare only a shallow stratagem and be flippant and thus you will sometimes fail.

Third, if you think too much and transcend reason it makes you doubt what you should not doubt. Also, if you have too much anxiety, you cannot determine your mind and will become confused and end up failing.

Therefore, you should overcome these three diseases, have a deliberate

---

18 Fujibayashi plays on the word *iru* 入 or 'to enter' – he says 'when the enemy enters'. However, the context is 'move' or 'movement'. Fujibayashi is playing on this ideogram as a principle of a swordsman moving in and the enemy opening gaps as they move. The idea is that in hand-to-hand combat there are gaps when an enemy moves, and similarly in *ninjutsu* gaps appear and allow a *ninja* to carry out his art of espionage. Here he is trying to instruct the student by using an analogy to a different art, which is the martial arts in this case.

strategy, and when the time comes, infiltrate as quickly as lightning and without any delay.

The *Six Secret Teachings* says:
Of disasters that can befall an army, none surpasses doubt.

A *ninja* poem says:

得タルトソ思ヒ切ツツ忍ビナバ　誠ハナクト勝ハ有ヘシ

Make yourself resolute with the idea that you will win whenever you go on a shinobi *mission, and you can succeed even if it is not so achievable.*

Yin Jing says:
If a falcon enters into a heavy forest, there is no trace of him and if a fish moves into deep water, there is no way to pursue him. Even Lilou[19] could not see a shape if he bends his head over it and even the music-master Kuang[20] could not hear the shape if he concentrates on it. How subtle it is to fly and disturb only the slightest dust, a brave and death-defying one will see [codified text[21]].

---

19 A character in ancient Chinese folklore who has superior eyesight.
20 A character in ancient Chinese folklore who has acute hearing.
21 Here the text breaks into a code, similar to the code used for *kunoichi* or female agents. However, the meaning is unknown.

In-nin II

Hidden Infiltration II

Infiltrating a castle II

Twelve points on appropriate places for infiltration

I

1. By a steep area if it is a mountain castle or a castle on a hill.[1]
2. By the sea or a river if it is a waterside castle.
3. By a marshy area if it is a castle beside a marsh.
4. The above three areas are where the enemy neglects to guard correctly. The same holds true with a temporary fort.

II

The roof of a castle gatehouse
A castle gatehouse is usually most strictly guarded, but the roof is the most convenient place for you to attach a hooked ladder.

III

Where *shinobi-gaeshi* spiked defences are beside a castle gatehouse
As well as *shinobi-gaeshi* spiked defences, you should be aware that any place where a special precaution has been taken is not a naturally fortified area, so it can be a convenient place to enter.

---

1   The original says 'flatland castle'. However, as this would not fit the text it is presumed there is a missing ideogram for the commonly known, 'lesser mountain castle', which would fit with Fujibayashi's writing.

IV

If a section of the outer moat leads directly into the main enclosure or to the second enclosure at any point, use a bridge that connects the second enclosure and main enclosure or use the *komayose*, which is an area just outside of the main enclosure where people dismount and leave their horses, as these are convenient places for you to infiltrate. If there are no bridges or *komayose* areas but the moat still leads in, then consider it still accessible.

V

As well as castles beside the sea or a lake, any castle that has a moat should also have a protruding section at the base of the stone foundation wall. Go there first and take appropriate measures in accordance with the situation.[2]

VI

Through the gutter of a waterway
In ancient times someone named Shimotsuge no Kozaru infiltrated Takura castle of Ise through this point and set the castle ablaze, to its ruin.

VII

When you climb up a stone wall, external corners or flat surfaces are not desirable. Recessed corners such as *yokoya*[3] indented corners, *byobuore*[4] or triangular indents in a wall, human waste chutes or rubbish dumps are convenient for you to infiltrate; however, it depends on the place.

VIII

Get in through a shooting port. Ports for muskets are not desirable; however, ones for shooting arrows are.

IX

Sometimes, it is possible to infiltrate by extending and opening up: through *yokoya* outlets, which are side arrow ports, or *chiriotoshi* outlet holes through which castle waste is thrown out; or by removing some stones from the stone foundations beneath fences of wood and earth.

---

2 Fujibayashi does not actually state what to do here.
3 *Yokoya*: literally 'side arrows'. This is where defenders shoot arrows at intruders on the wall from the sides.
4 *Byobu*: an outer wall in the shape of a 'folding screen'.

X

During castle construction,[5] a special enclosure is sometimes built to hold hostages made up of people from the province; this is used when the enemy defends a castle. The location of the enclosure varies, but in most cases it is placed at the back of the main enclosure, often in a steep area. If you know of this, you can make use of it. You should make a point of going to a nearby village in that province to ask about such enclosures, so that you can obtain correct information.

XI

In an entire castle area, the outer enclosures or the third enclosures are usually surrounded by earthworks and bamboo thickets, or it may also be the case that the moat is dry, making it easy to infiltrate. However, there is little benefit in getting in at that point. If at first you move to the third enclosure, then the second one and then to the main enclosure, you will have too many difficult obstacles to cross over; therefore, it will exhaust you and, if you are not well enough equipped, it will take too much time and trouble, which makes it very likely that you will be detected. Therefore, you should figure out the best plan using all kinds of ingenuity with the intent to infiltrate the second or main enclosure directly.[6]

XII

To infiltrate temporary forts, approach from the back as they are usually strongly guarded from the front.

The above points are convenient places for *shinobi* 竊盗 to infiltrate a castle or camp. As mentioned in 'Eight points on the art of infiltrating by taking advantage of the enemy's negligence', the main idea is that you should infiltrate by exploiting carelessness. However, if you think of the enemy's negligence alone but do not understand these twelve points on convenient places, you will not always succeed in infiltrating. You should steal in 竊盗入ル at the appropriate *time* and *place* and when the enemy is careless in one of these places mentioned above; this aids the way of both *in-* and *yo-jutsu*.

Fifteen points on the art of using tools

I

If a mountain is too steep to climb, use a *tsuribashigo* hanging ladder. To be passed on by oral transmission.

---

5   *Nawabari.*

6   The point here is that there are certain gaps in castle defences that connect through to the main enclosure; it is best to use these to bypass heavy security.

I I

For the roof of a gatehouse, use a tied ladder, cloud ladder, flying ladder and so on. Put it onto the wall and climb up. Be sure that it makes no noise. To be passed on by oral transmission.

I I I

To climb straight up to a *shinobi-gaeshi* spiked defence, a *komayose* dismounting area or a bridge, or from the bottom of a moat to the upper wall straight up, it is best to use the spider ladder. To be passed on by oral transmission.

I V

To cross over from the outside of a moat to the top of a fence on the other side, use the *hiko* or flying [tool[7]]. To be passed on by oral transmission.

Supplementary to this, remember to lift up [with rope] the tools you will need to use after climbing up, including the *yakigusuri* or gunpowder for arson.

V

To climb up a small fence inside a castle, the roof of a building, or a tree, use the *shinobi-zue* 竊盗杖 or *shinobi*-cane. To be passed on by oral transmission.

If you cross over with any of the above mentioned tools, there will be no place that you cannot pass, no matter how high or steep it is, particularly if you use these three major tools: the spider ladder, the *hiko* [tool] and the *ninja*-cane. I invented [and modified] these, which took years of effort. These three are handy and enable you to climb a high wall or cross a large moat with ease.

Of all the numerous climbing tools, nothing is as comparatively small-sized or valuable as the above. However, though there are no better tools of *ninjutsu* than these, you cannot utilize them to the full without practice. Those who learn *ninjutsu* should not neglect to train themselves with tools.

V I

For crossing a sea or a river, use the water spider tool or a war boat. If you do not have either of these, or if you need to get a large number across, you should prepare the appropriate craft, such as a willow basket raft, jar raft, reed raft, bamboo raft, floating bridge, etc. You should choose an appropriate craft in accordance with the opportunity. If the river is rapid and sweeps away such a raft as above and thus makes it difficult to use, put a thin rope around the waist of a

---

7 Possibly the flying ladder. However, Fujibayashi states that he invented this particular tool, and he did not invent the flying ladder; also, he does not name this tool a ladder. Therefore, it could be an unknown tool.

good swimmer and have him swim across the river. When he gets to the other side, he should tie the rope onto a tree or to bamboo at the correct height, then on your side stretch the rope and do the same thing so the rest of the people can cross over while keeping hold of the rope. Further oral traditions are within.

VII

If you need to go to underwater, but it is difficult, then use the 'U' or cormorant tool[8] for this. In the daytime you should hide at the bottom of the water so that you will not be found by the enemy. There are more things to be passed on here.

VIII

For a marshy area, use flat, boarded shoes.

If you use the above selection of tools to cross over a sea, a river or a marsh, you will be able to cross over them without fail. Of those, the 'U'-tool, that is the cormorant tool, was invented with my ingenuity. It is very useful when submerged under water.

IX

According to ancient methods, when infiltrating a castle you should use a floating bridge to cross over a moat. Get a good swimmer to take the end of a floating bridge across the moat to the side of the stone foundation wall and tie ropes to bamboo or trees; otherwise, fix *kunai* digging tools firmly into the ground and use them. Next, stretch the bridge and secure it to your own side as well, then cross over it. According to one theory, take two long pieces of bamboo and hitch temporary spacers out of rope, so that the width of the ladder is one *shaku*, four or five *sun* wide and then put it across the moat. Next put two bamboo latticed mats on the two bamboo supporting beams and alternate with them as you cross. Alternatively you can lash wooden rungs as you cross over. There are further details.

X

According to ancient methods, when climbing up a stone wall, use a tied ladder, and where the tied ladder does not reach, then insert *kunai* digging tools into a crevice and use two rolled ladders, hooking one onto each *kunai* alternately, so that you can climb up the wall step by step. To be passed on by oral transmission.

---

8   Possibly a snorkel.

XI

According to ancient methods, when you get to the bottom of a fence that is set atop a stone wall, set a *kunai* firmly into the base and step up onto the tool, then stab the wall with a *sagurikane* or probing iron. When you decide where to bore a hole in the wall, hang a *nagabukuro* or long bag at that point and dig the wall out with the *kunai*. Drop the soil through the bag and keep digging until you make a hole large enough for you to sneak in.

Also, there is a way of crossing over the wall with an *uchikagi* hooked rope – do this without digging the hole. The long bag is used because it absorbs the sound of the soil dropping into the water.

XII

According to ancient methods, when you are on a stone fort or wall, do not use a high ladder but use the same tool(s) over and over, repeatedly. You should retrieve the tool(s) each time they are used.

There is a way called the flowing bridge and this is used for defending a castle; its benefits are questionable. Further details are to be passed on by oral transmission.

The above four points are those methods of infiltration that were used when our province [of Iga] was self-governed and every fortress was not so heavily fortified. As the castles or fortresses were not so impregnable at that time, *shinobi no jutsu* and *ninja* tools from those days are not good enough any more. On top of that, quite a large number of tools existed but they are too heavy and offer little advantage. Thus they are outdated for infiltration into a modern castle, like the castles of our time.[9] However, there may be a chance that you will want to use those old methods, so I have recorded them above. Reviews on whether they are good or not were mentioned in *Shinobi* Questions and Answers.

XIII

There is a tool called the folding ladder from another clan. It seems to have been well designed but it is too heavy, thus it is not so good. On top of that, if there is no stone wall outside a moat, it is difficult to hook this ladder onto a point. Also, it bends in the middle so it is not easy to climb up. There is another tool called the *tsugihashigo*[10] jointed ladder; this also is not so useful for *shinobi* 竊盗. Generally no matter how well devised it is, a heavy tool should not be used.

---

9 The end of the Sengoku period and start of the Edo period saw a massive leap in Japanese castle technology.

10 This appears in the *Gunpo Jiyoshu*.

XIV

Breaking *mogari* fences, *sakamogi* thorny branches and *shinobi-gaeshi* spiked defences etc.

There is no set method for this, but you should twist and break them off or tear them off, with a thick rope in each case, but this depends on the situation. Remember, if you use a *ninja* tool, be sure to use it when the wind is whistling so as to hide any sound, so when you break off a defence with [missing text[11]], you should keep this in mind.

XV

When you break or cut through a wall, fence, *mogari* fence, *sakamogi* thorny branches etc. and get in, use a thread so that you can follow it on your way out. Be sure to use this thread. To be passed on by oral transmission.

A *ninja* poem says:

道筋ニ目付ヲセント心掛ヨ　出処忘レテフカクハシルナ

> *Always try to make a mental note of the way you have come, so that you will know how to get back; if not you may make a blunder of it.*

How to use the above tools is to be orally transmitted.

Although it is essential for *shinobi no mono* to know where and when the enemy is negligent and the convenient places within a castle or camp where you can infiltrate, if you are not skilled with the use of tools, it will be like a Zen monk who knows very well the principles of swordsmanship but is poor at actual sword-fighting. Every *ninja* should always endeavour to train himself in the use of tools.

Ancient people said that, among all 23,000 words of the *Analects*, you can become enlightened by just a single word. Likewise, when you learn you should not just comment or discuss but concentrate on every word and the details. Whether you can infiltrate an impregnable castle or not depends on how hard you train before the need arises.

Two points on *chakuzen no jutsu* or the art of infiltrating before your allies arrive

I

The period of six days before the lord arrives
Once your own army has advanced toward the enemy castle, it will be difficult to

---

11 Probably rope.

infiltrate. Therefore, you should infiltrate one to six days before your lord arrives. This is the technique of infiltrating before the enemy sees any signs of attack. In conducting this, it is of vital importance to have arrangements or promises regarding the *hikyaku-bi* fire beacons, smoke signals, *ireko-hi* adjustable lamps, flags, conch shells and so on.

I I

When you carry out this *chakuzen no jutsu*, you should make use of *yo-kei*, which is the tactics of open disguise. Examples include *eikei*[12] shadowing, *minomushi*[13] 'the worm in the enemy's stomach' and *kunoichi* female spies, etc.

Further details are secret for the above. You should not approach this art lightly.

Two points on *osoi-iri no jutsu* or infiltrating by using the cover of your allies' raid

I

Assaulting the enemy, day or night, for at least five to even eight days before you intend to infiltrate
Generally, when people are mentally fatigued they will be inattentive and let their guard down. However, you should go after you have made all the required arrangements with your lord, which is a standard preparation.

I I

While having fire arrows shot successively, approach from the direction where there are no arrows, or after several nights of your side shooting them every night, use the next night for infiltration. More details are to be orally transmitted.

Kakure-mino no jutsu or the skill of the invisible mantle

Kakure-mino no jutsu is *in* within *yo*, and is the deepest secret of *in-nin*. Therefore, its methodology is not simple and further details are secret.

When you steal in with the secret skills from the *kakure-mino no jutsu* invisible mantle skill, you should employ *yo-kei* open disguise tactics, such as *katsura-otoko* undercover agents, *kunoichi* female agents etc., or use *bakemono-jutsu*, [which is the art of copying the enemy] and so on. If you infiltrate by

---

12 *Eikei*, literally 'shadow shape'. This is assumed to be the same as *jokei*, 'shadow-like *ninjutsu*', as mentioned in volume eight, or *jokei*, 'hiding from the light', which is most likely comparable to the skill of *joei* in the *Shoninki*.

13 Possibly *shinchu*.

conducting this art completely, there are no castles or camps that you cannot infiltrate, no matter how impregnable they may seem.

Four points on *kakure-gasa no jutsu* or the art of the invisible hat

I

When you infiltrate the enemy castle or camp for the first time, you should take cover temporarily: in woods or a bush, in a place where people are gathering and making noise, under a bridge, upon a roof or in a tree etc. While hiding in such a place, observe the status of the enemy and overhear his passwords. Also, there is a technique where after learning someone's name you call out to him as if you were acquaintances.

I I

You should go on further with resourcefulness according to the opportunity. To be passed on by oral transmission.

III

Use resourceful ways when you are suspected by the enemy. Still more points to be passed on by oral transmission.

I V

If an enemy suddenly chases you, you should throw *hyakurai-ju*[14] fire crackers, or use *torimono-somakuri*[15] and so on, to surprise him so that you can run away while he is startled.

There are further details to be passed down on the above skills. Explanations of *hyakurai-ju* fire crackers and *torimono somakuri* are in the volume on fire tools.

Six points on the art of arson

I

As mentioned in 'Concerning the agreement between your lord and the *ninja*' in volume five, A Guideline for Commanders Part II, even if you get into the enemy castle or camp, arson cannot be properly done without prior agreement on how to convey signals with your lord. If a *ninja* sets a fire without such a signal, the fire will be extinguished by the enemy, and what is worse, the *ninja* will be caught in eight or nine cases out of ten. So make sure this does not happen. On top of

---

14 Chinese fire crackers.
15 Unknown skill or tool but most likely used to hinder someone.

this method, it is essential for you to weigh up the timing for setting the fire by considering how fast or slow your lord is when arriving and attacking.

For when *ninja* return from the castle, it is of vital importance to have an advance agreement on a sign so that your allies will not kill them on their return from the enemy position. In most cases *ninja* escape with composure after the castle has fallen.

Two *ninja* poems say:

忍得テハ敵方ヨリモ同士討ノ用心スルソ大事ナリケリ

After you have slipped into the enemy's area successfully, you should give more attention to not fighting among yourselves than the enemy.

同士討モ下知ニヨルソカシ　武者ノ印シヲ兼テ定メヨ

Fighting among yourselves can always happen; depending on what instructions you are given, you should always decide on an identifying mark for your warriors beforehand.

II

If you need to return without setting fire, as opportunity dictates, you should bring back absolute evidence with you when you return. If not, write your name on a pillar or wall or in the castle or camp.

Here are some *ninja* poems:

敵城ニ竊盗フ印シヲ取ナラハ　紛レヌ物ヲ肝要トセヨ

If you take evidence of your entry in the enemy's castle, it should be an object that would cause no doubt.

敵方ノ旗馬印ヲ取タラハ　味方ノ為ニ悪キトソ云フ

Getting the enemy's hata *or* umajirushi *and bringing it back with you is said to be bad for your allies.*

敵方ノ城ヤ陣所ニ名ヲ書テ　竊盗印ヲ人知セヨ

You should write your name within the enemy's castle or camp. This is so that people will know that you have achieved success in your mission.

III

When you are going to set a fire, split the men in your squad into various directions and set fires at different points.

Supplementary to this, you should change the points you set fire to according to whether or not there is wind and taking account of the direction of the wind. Though you have an arrangement with your lord, you should make judgement on exactly where you should set the fire by observing the enemy status from the inside.

IV

It may not be necessary to mention this, but the places you should set fire are: gunpowder storehouses or those of saltpetre, firewood or wood stores, food storehouses or military supply depots, or the bridges from the second enclosure to the main castle enclosure.

V

There are appropriate measures or timings for when you set fire to a castle or camp, or to the gunpowder or saltpetre storehouse, or to bridges. To be passed on by oral transmission.

According to the *Taiheiki* war chronicle, on the eighth day of the fifth month in 1333, when Akamatsu Enshin, Ashikaga Takauji and Chigusa To-no-Chujo Tadaoki attacked the *rokuhara tandai,* who were official agents of the Kamakura government in Kyoto, those soldiers from Houki of Izumo connected two or three hundred[16] carts by their shafts and piled broken houses and rubble on the connected carts, which approached the height of the base of the watchtower. This episode ended in breaking through the wooden gate by burning it down.

This is an example of the above points.

VI

How to burn down town houses or farmhouses
If a village is set on fire at only one or two points or at only a few town houses, the fires will not burn fiercely or spread. Furthermore, with only a small number of points alight, the people will be able to extinguish the fires. The modus operandi in *shinobi no jutsu* is to burn down a village or town in one 'burst' by setting fires in many directions and from all the cardinal points at the same time.

---

16 Not literal.

In-nin III

Hidden Infiltration III

Infiltrating a house

Though it is easier to steal into a house [than a castle], if you do not know exactly what the internal layout is like, you will often fail in your infiltration. Even after you enter, if it is not so easy for you to find where the enemy is sleeping and you spend precious time trying to figure the issue out, the enemy will detect you and your infiltration will end in vain. Therefore, if you intend to infiltrate, you should conduct a thorough investigation beforehand, concentrating on the following points:

- what all of the gates and entrances of the enemy house are like
- whether the road is wide or narrow, straight or curved
- the make-up of the house
- the house design
- the bedrooms
- whether it is difficult to open or close the doors and the gates
- what the *joshi* locks, *kakegane* hooks and eyes, *kuroro* latches, *shirizashi* locking bars etc. are like
- whether the floorboards squeak or not
- most importantly, whether the enemy is wise or not
- what arts or skills the enemy is accomplished in when their situation is undisturbed
- the names of the men and women in the house

You should go and look around the target house, and/or go and investigate the inside of it by disguising yourself and deluding the enemy. After bringing back the required information, you should talk among all of your squad to figure out the best plan and agree on the passwords and *aijirushi* identifying marks, to decide where to regroup after being dispersed, and, lastly, to make sure you have flawless arrangements on any points such as signals, so that you are perfectly prepared on all points before the infiltration in question.

In this situation, using *amadori no jutsu*, or the art of the rain bird, would be desirable. Also, if you have a *minomushi* worm – which is an undercover agent in the enemy house – you should bribe him enough and make sure he is not going to turn traitor. If you are not sure of his loyalty at any point, you should take someone, like his wife, child or relative, as a hostage and make him write an oath. As mentioned in the chapter *Yo-nin Jo*, it is essential for you to have correct judgement on whom to recruit as a *minomushi* undercover agent.

Li Jing says:

Water can let a ship float but it can turn it over.

Do not disrespect his words.

A survey on how to distinguish people's sleep patterns according to the season

In spring, the weather is warm and calm and people feel relaxed and easy and their bodies are loose and weary. Especially from the middle to the end of spring, the temperature increases, so people tend to sleep more and more.

In summer, the day is long while the night is short. Particularly from late in the fifth to the sixth month of the lunar calendar, it is extremely hot during the daytime and people are very tired and slack. Toward the end of summer, the heat and humidity do not decrease, even at night, and people cannot sleep in the early hours of the morning, which makes the short summer nights even shorter [for purposes of infiltration]. Especially during the *doyo* period [at the end of summer], the heat and humidity running up to the change in season makes it even more difficult [to infiltrate].

Generally when the body is dry, people sleep less; while when it is wet, they sleep more. This is why the old sleep less while the young sleep more. Therefore, toward the end of summer, everybody tends to sleep as it cools down and par-ticularly after the hour of Boar (nine to eleven o'clock at night) they feel easy and relaxed, which makes them sleep deeply. On a night when it is drizzling, the humidity increases making the temperature decrease and therefore people sleep more deeply.

Autumn is ruled by the *chi* of metal and the *chi* of dryness. Therefore, the leaves and grass turn yellow and fall, and the wind sweeps all away. As mentioned above, when people are dry they sleep less. Also, as it is cold at this time the body, muscles and bones are trim and in good health; therefore, people are not likely to feel tired. On top of that, when the day is short and the night is long, people sleep less. However, in the seventh month,[1] the summer heat still lingers, making it little different from the end of summer.

Winter has the *chi* of water and it is so cold that the body is stiffened and people do not become tired easily. As the night is very long, people tend to have trouble getting to sleep and wake very quickly.

The common principles for the four seasons are as mentioned above; still, as all depends on the individual person, you should consider further details.

Two[2] points on how to detect if people are asleep or awake according to their age, disposition and behaviour

I

How to detect if people are asleep or awake by observing whether they are old or young, or thin or fat

You should be aware that the old have less moisture or warmth in their body so they are dry and cold and sleep less. It depends on the person, but most old people do not go to sleep until after midnight and tend to wake from around the hour of Tiger (three to five o'clock in the morning). This is the way of those aged forty and above. Younger people have so much energy that they 'sleep tight' in the dead of night or even late into the morning. This is where older and younger people differ from each other. Generally, thin people sleep less while fat people sleep more; this is because the thin have less moisture than those who are fat.

II

How to detect if people are asleep or awake by their disposition or behaviour

Generally, those who are alert, quick-tempered and spirited sleep less while those who are gloomy and sluggish sleep more. Those who have a firm body and kneel down or squat on their haunches most of the time and who never lose their composure will sleep less. On the other hand, those who are of ill character or of bad behaviour, who like lying down and are licentious about everything, tend to sleep deeply.

Those who sleep less and wake quickly have the following characteristics: they are always well prepared and aware; they do not loosen their *obi* sash even when lying down; they are scantily clad and resistant to the cold; they refrain from

---

1   In the old calendar, this means the beginning of autumn.
2   The original manual states three.

drinking or eating heavily; they abstain from being lewd and they are discreet about everything. Those who are always self-indulgent, who like to be warm at night, are addicted to heavy drinking or beauty, wallow in lewdness, or spend their time in idle amusement, will sleep more.

You can also detect if someone sleeps deeply or lightly by observing whether his mind is in a state of joy or sorrow. Those who have nothing to worry about and have an easy life sleep more, while those who have much on their minds, who feel low-spirited and depressed, normally sleep less. Those who are motivated to learn and devote themselves to seeking the truth also sleep less.

The above is how to gauge people's sleep.

Two points on dealing with dogs[3]

When you sneak into a house with a dog it is difficult, as the dog will bark at you and make the enemy suspicious. Therefore, you should go there two or three nights before you want to infiltrate and make toasted rice balls with one *bu* of strychnine powder mixed in each and put them here and there – it is best to place them where the dog is likely to venture. If a dog eats one, it will soon die.

Four points on the way of walking

I

Use a flat, boarded shoe for deep marshes or *nukiashi*[4] tiptoe walking for shallow marshes.

A drawing[5] of flat, boarded shoes can be found in the Water Tools volume of the *Ninki* section.

Nukiashi steps should be flexible like a willow branch; there are oral traditions here.

II

When you infiltrate the enemy house or mansion, you should use *ukiashi* or floating steps, as a running fox or a passing dog. *Ukiashi* steps should be executed nimbly like a monkey swinging through trees, or like the running of a fox or the passing of a dog and should be as fast as lightning. To be passed on by oral transmission.

---

3 The original table of contents states 'two points'; however, only one point is given.
4 The foot is 'pulled out' of the water vertically and with care.
5 The original drawing is missing.

III

When you walk on a floor, wear *itazori* sandals, which have cotton, padded soles, or use the art of *shinso*[6]-*no-uho* steps[7] in either the proper way or the 'makeshift' version. A drawing of the *itazori* silent sandal can be found at the end of the Opening Tools volume in the *Ninki* section. *Shin-no-uho* steps should follow the principle of a leaf floating on water, and when doing these steps you should walk along the edge of the wall. To be passed on by oral transmission.

IV

Zasagashi or probing the room

This technique is used when you get into the enemy house and you do not know if the enemy is waiting for you or if you have not formed a mental image of the place of infiltration.

Walk along the edge of the room, either on the right or the left, depending on the situation. This should be done with your sword [taken out of your belt and the blade] drawn one or two *sun* from its scabbard. Probe forward with the scabbard to see if it hits someone; if it does then you must thrust forward and remove the scabbard as you pull back from the thrust, then cut the person immediately. This is called *zasagashi no jutsu*. This art is included in the seven arts of the cord but it is an important technique when you walk around an enemy house; therefore, I have put it here.

Six points on *jokei jutsu* or the art of projecting no shadow

I

Staying out of the moonlight or firelight

The moonlight shines from the outside to the inside, while indoor illumination shines from the inside to the outside. When you sneak in on a moonlit night, be sure to stay out of the moonlit areas. When the moon is in the eastern sky, avoid walking on the east side. If someone inside a house is watching the outside and trying to detect abnormalities, he will not be able to see into the areas beyond where the firelight shines. This is the same with moonlight.

6　In this context, *shin* means 'a proper way' and *so* is 'makeshift'.

7　The document simply says *shinso-no-uho*, which translates as 'proper or makeshift rabbit steps'. There is a form of *uho* step found in the magic art of Onmyodo, which is a ritual walk, moving the feet side by side. The ideogram written for this word is 兎歩 (*uho*), which means 'rabbit steps'; however, presumably this is an attempt to phonetically 'spell out' the ideogram 禹歩 (*uho*), which is the above-mentioned way of magical steps also known as *henbai* and commonly used in Onmyodo magic. For a full discussion see *In Search of the Ninja*.

II

Avoid the 'legs of moonlight or illumination'. The basic idea is the same as the one above, and it is called *hikari ashi* or legs of light.[8]

III

Do not walk on the windward side but approach on the leeward side. If you pass or stay on the windward side, the enemy may hear any sounds you make or smell your *hinawa* fuses or other such things. Also it is hard for you to hear any sound that the enemy makes or to tell whether they are asleep or not if you are on the windward side. Therefore, positioning yourself on the windward side should be avoided. If you cannot avoid this but have to walk or stay on the windward side, be sure not to make any sound at all. If you are on the leeward side, you can hear the sounds that the enemy makes and they cannot hear any sounds that you make. Therefore, being on the leeward side has lots of benefits.

IV

When there is no wind, you should avoid bushes or forests beside a house. If there is wind and noises are being made, then the above is acceptable.

V

Do not go into dry hay or grass or ash[9] close to the enemy. However, if it is after rainfall or when dew is forming late at night, then it will dampen any noise if you do venture there.

VI

Avoid disturbing the surface of water. When you cross over stagnant water, even if the enemy cannot see you, ripples will form and the enemy will be suspicious. For this reason you should cross without causing ripples.

Eight points on the appropriate night for infiltration

I

On the night after a wedding

On a wedding night people indulge in large drinking parties and dancing and do so until late; therefore, they will certainly sleep deeply the following night. If on the night of the wedding things calm down and finish with people going to sleep around two o'clock in the morning, then it would be even more desirable for you

---

8   Presumably these are rays of light.

9   Probably placed there so that intruders' footfalls may be heard as they pass through and tread on charred sections of wood.

to infiltrate that night as everyone will have joy in their minds and will tend to forget vigilance. To be passed on by oral transmission.

I I

On the night after someone's illness
[It is desirable to infiltrate] on a night after the master, his wife or one of his children has been ill and people have kept a vigil, with the result that the stricken person recovers, making the family relieved and joyous, or on a night when the patient suffering from a serious disease shows a little sign of recovery. Furthermore, infiltrate on a night when someone suffering from 'fever shakes' has an intermittent period of recovery. In all these situations, those in the family should sleep heavily on such nights as these.

III

On a night of amusement
On a night when the target has a party of dancing, a village party or any other form of social gathering, people may stay up as late as the hour of Tiger (around four o'clock in the morning). When they go to sleep after that hour, they should sleep very heavily. This is definitely an appropriate time for you to infiltrate. However, you should avoid the season for fresh tea (which is in May or June).

I V

On the next night after a fire or another unusual event in the neighbourhood
If a fire or fight or any serious event has happened in the neighbourhood on the previous night, the neighbours in that area will have lost sleep and will be exhausted, so, in most cases, they will sleep well the next night. You should take advantage of that night and infiltrate. However, consider the possibility that it is a ruse and part of their tactics – that is, assess whether the situation is real or fake. To be passed on by oral transmission.

V

On a night of a labour when the enemy is engaged in construction or labour duties
You should steal in on a night when the enemy is exhausted – such as after a stressful day or after physically working hard or walking back after a long journey; at such a time, the targets will sleep deeply. Particularly in spring or summer, as it is warm or hot, they will be exhausted even more so and it will improve your chances of infiltration.

VI

Two or three nights after a tragic event

If a parent, wife or child dies, the family will have an intolerably hard time and pass a few nights in tears, but because they are tired from having taken care of the deceased in illness, they will sleep well two or three nights after the day of the death. Within the first seven days, men or women from the family will spend time there talking and lamenting during the early hours of the night, but they are only human and should sleep very well after midnight, normally without fail; this is even more the case with the servants or lower people.

Also, on the evening of the tragic event, most people make a fuss over it and are not vigilant, which gives you a chance to infiltrate by disguise 紛忍. It is difficult to write down every detail on how to determine the truth of a matter – that is, whether the 'event' is a ruse or not. Important points to be passed by mouth only.

VII

On a night of wind and rain

It is hard to hear sounds on a night of wind and rain. Therefore, such nights have been used by *shinobi* infiltrators since ancient times. On top of that, on a rainy night it is cool in summer and warm in winter[10] and people sleep comfortably and so it is the right time for infiltration. This is called *amadori no jutsu* or the art of the rain bird, as *amadori* rain birds come out when it is rainy and windy. When you are going to steal in, be sure not to wear a hat or other such things.

VIII

On a night of a commotion

When a turmoil or commotion has happened in the enemy house or in the neighbourhood, you should take the chance and infiltrate. Details have been given earlier in the infiltration into a castle and so are not mentioned here.

In old times, there was a *suppa*[11] in Yufune village of our province whose name was Kubo Uemon. One early evening he went to a mansion that he was going to infiltrate and found a huge pile of firewood in the yard. He hid in the mountain of firewood while observing what was going on inside the house. Suddenly, it began raining and men and women began taking some of the firewood indoors, carrying it up onto the ceiling by putting a ladder up to the upper sections of the

---

10 This could be a reference to cloud cover: if a winter day is fine then the night will be colder due to lack of cloud cover; if there is rain the cloud cover retains the sun's heat and thus makes the night warmer. However, this is just a theory.

11 Considered to be an alternative word for a type of *ninja*.

house. Kubo Uemon took advantage of the chance and following a little distance behind them, with firewood on his shoulder he mixed in between them. After getting into the house, he followed the men and women up to the loft with firewood and lay down in hiding and remained there. Later on that night when people became quiet, he decided to make his move and got up, but made some noise as he brushed against the firewood; furthermore, the bamboo ceiling creaked. There was one person in the house who was still awake, who heard the sounds and became suspicious. The person then woke the master and told him of the noise and the master brought out a spear and stabbed it up through the ceiling. The spear hit the centre of Kubo's forehead but he grasped [and wiped] the spear neck with the sleeve of his kimono. The master said that he felt it hit something but if it was a human then it should have left blood on the spear. So they checked the spear with a light but as Kubo had wiped it with his sleeve, it did not have any blood on it. When the master and his servants went back to sleep, the *suppa* came down from the ceiling and stabbed all five of them to death: the master, his offspring and his retainers. After his head wound healed, he was forever called Ana Kubo Uemon.[12] Generally, it is essential for *shinobi no mono* to be resourceful according to the situation, even if you encounter something that you did not expect.

As for a rainy night, it is said that in ancient times, a *ninja* from our province went to the house of someone who was very cautious. He took an umbrella with him as it was rainy on that particular night and had another person stand directly in the rain with it in hand, while the first *ninja* went to the back door and concealed himself in stealth. The guard heard raindrops fall on the umbrella and tried to drive the stranger in the rain away. Taking advantage of the commotion, the *ninja* got into the house easily and successfully stabbed the master to death. In *shinobi no jutsu* it is fundamental to make changes and produce movement. Whether it is windy or rainy, or moonlit or pitch black, the most amazing point in the arts of the *shinobi* is the skill of provoking a change in the enemy status. To be passed on by oral transmission.

Four points on the appropriate place for infiltration

I

From the rear door
There are six advantages to stealing in through a rear door:

1. Whether in a house or a mansion, the front entrances are heavily guarded while the back doors are not defended to the same extent.
2. As not so many people use the back door, it is convenient for you to hide there.
3. While the front entrance is usually secured by guardsmen, a back door

---

12 The nickname 'stab-hole' became a prefix to his name.

tends to have less security as they are less careful than they are with the front entrance.

4. It is likely that there will be somewhere you can hide yourself for an extended period at the back door.

5. It is possible that people may leave the back door unlocked even when they go to sleep, while the front will always be secured.

6. To get deep inside a house, you need to open many doors if you infiltrate from the front. However, if you get in from the back door, you can come straight into the inner rooms, as they are much closer. Generally, it is less likely that you will be detected or questioned. On top of that, it is closer to where the enemy is sleeping.

With the above advantages, it is an established way for *in-nin* to infiltrate from a rear door.

II

Entering from the rear to the front
There are three advantages in your getting into a mansion from the rear and going straight to the enemy's sleeping quarters:

1. As mentioned in the segment above, one advantage is that you do not have to open many doors to get close to the room where the enemy is sleeping.

2. In the case where the enemy is not where you expect them to be, you should ascertain the position of their room and infiltrate from the rear of that room. Here you do not have to bother to unlock a *kakegane* latch to enter, as it is usually unlocked.

3. If you enter a room from the rear and if there is someone in the room who is not asleep, then they will not suspect you as an intruder. It is because those who come from the rear are not considered to be *nusubito* thieves or night attackers.

For the above three advantages it is best to come from the rear. More oral traditions are to be told.

III

Entering from the *zashiki* drawing room[13] rather than the front entrance
Though it is not desirable to steal in from the forward direction, if there is no

---

13 Normally covered in *tatami* matting, this may have an open and private garden next to it; therefore, the *shinobi* should enter this way.

way to get in from the rear, it is better to go in through the *zashiki* drawing room. This is because the *zashiki* room usually has only a single door – in most cases it is a *fusuma* or *shoji* sliding door, which is easy to open. Even if the door has a *kakegane* latch or a *shirizashi* locking bar, it is still not difficult to open. The *zashiki* drawing room itself is inside the house complex, and thus it does not have enough security on the doorways to the rear and deeper areas. Also it is rare for anyone to be present in the *zashiki* drawing room. Therefore, in the case that a door to private areas is too securely locked for you to open, you should withdraw for the moment and steal in from the *zashiki* drawing room; this is a tradition from ancient times. However, it depends on the time and place. To be passed on by oral transmission.

IV

Entering from below a *mado mushiro hashiri* or the straw mat window cover
This is a good place to get into a house. *Shitajimado*[14] or *senshimado* latticed windows are easy to cut through or take off. *Inufusegi* – small portable fences for stopping dogs, which are situated below the *mushiro* straw covers – are usually similar to bamboo blinds; therefore, you can take them away and infiltrate through there. Or some places, such as below the *hashiri mizudana* washing troughs, are easy to get in from.

It is a common way of *in-nin* to make use of the above methods, rather than entering by opening doors.

Four points on *yo-chu-in jutsu* or the arts of *in-nin* inside of *yo-nin*

I

Put *kunoichi* in place in advance, or infiltrate when there is no sign [of a threat] or, if the enemy is vigilant, encourage them to become inattentive.

Even the smartest person on the path of *in-nin* sometimes does not know in which room the enemy is sleeping, especially if he is an extremely high-ranking person and has an extensive mansion. It is also the case that the enemy may be so tightly secured that you cannot infiltrate. In such a case you should employ the tactics of *yo-jutsu* at the beginning and then sneak in later. This art is the art of entering by using the skills of *in-nin* inside of a *yo-nin* scheme, thus it is called *yo-chu-in jutsu* or the art of *in* within *yo*.

The technique of sending *kunoichi* female agents beforehand is useful when the enemy is high-ranking and his quarters are unknown or if he has a number of security guards and it seems difficult to kill him only with *in-nin*. You should

---

14 A type of latticed window found in tea-ceremony houses.

have a *kunoichi* placed within, as it is a move that the enemy will not expect and it will enable you to enter the enemy area under her guidance. If you conduct this art to its full effect, there is no mansion that you cannot enter no matter how high-ranking or heavily guarded the enemy.

Ordinary people easily give themselves up to lust or greed. Of all people, high-ranking men tend to wallow in sexual desire, so this art of the *kunoichi* female agent is one of the most effective tactics of all the *yo-jutsu* arts. As mentioned in the volume *Yo-nin Jo*, there are things you should consider deeply when conducting this art. To be passed on by oral transmission.

Another point is to infiltrate the enemy before he notices any signs that you are preparing to penetrate. Generally, the longer it takes to infiltrate, the longer people have to think, which will cause the enemy to fathom your plans in time. Once they become attentive, it is difficult for you to achieve any further goals. Therefore, it is of utmost importance for you to be quick enough to infiltrate with tactics before the enemy has time to think.

Also you should infiltrate an alert enemy by causing them to drop their guard; this is for those who guard themselves very heavily, keeping safeguards day and night, with every gate or door locked securely, changing sleeping quarters up to two or three times a night. If this is the case, you should have them let such measures slide into neglect, allowing you to take advantage.

In older days, someone from another province killed his colleague and ran to Edo. He sought shelter with a *hatamoto* warrior, and the warrior carefully hid him. The victim's son came to Edo to look for his father's killer and searched for a few years. However, the enemy was securely protected and there was no way to kill him. After all the years, [the victim's son] eventually worked out a plan, in which he wrote a letter saying, 'Though I have sought after the enemy for a few years, I have had no luck and have no clue where he is. As all of my effort has come to nothing, I am bitterly disappointed and therefore will kill myself by disembowelment';[15] he then sent this letter together with his short sword, to his mother, wife and children. Then he hid himself, while his mother, wife and children grieved deeply, a fact that became known. This resulted in a message from the enemy family being sent to the killer in Edo, who did not doubt the validity of the letter or suspect that it might be a stratagem and fully allowed his guard to slip, going out here and about. This then ended with the son killing him without difficulty.

This is an example of making the enemy become less attentive and taking advantage of the gap. Learning from such an example, you can think of countless

---

15 *Hara wo kiru.*

ways to make the enemy let its guard down. The deepest principle of *ninjutsu* is to avoid where the enemy is attentive and strike where he is negligent.

I I

Infiltrating by two men going and one man coming back

One way to achieve this is to go in a pair to the enemy house at night. One member calls on them at the door while the other hides close to the door itself. When someone answers, the visitor says that he is a messenger and stands at a distance of two or three *ken* from the door. The person from the house will come out of the door to listen to him better, while the one hiding by the door will get in at that point. He should take shelter around a stable within the house complex or behind equipment for the moment. This is how to get in a house without a gate. If it has a secure gateway, you should infiltrate after all in the enemy house have fallen asleep. In this situation, one agent hides beside the gate while the other knocks at the gate door. When someone opens the smaller door of the gatehouse and asks who it is, the *ninja* should reply and instruct him to listen very carefully so as to draw him out. The moment that he comes out of the door, the agent who is hiding near the gateway gets in through the gate and also in through the door of the house. Then when the servant who answered comes back into the inner sections of the house to tell his master of the message, the agent follows him inside and after the servant leaves with his master's answer, then the agent may kill the enemy [master]. Another way to enter a residence with a gatehouse is to cross over the wall and hide inside the grounds while the other member calls on the occupants and waits for someone to answer the gate. The hidden man should slip into the house behind the servant and do the same as above. It is essential for you to be resourceful according to the opportunity or the place and not stick to the same measures. This technique is a plan to be completed late at night. It does not work very successfully at an early time during the evening when the [residents of the house] are not yet asleep. If you use this technique when they are asleep, it will work very well and normally without fail. There have been successful instances of the use of this art in ancient times.

I I I

Kakure-mino and *kakure-gasa* **or the arts of the invisible mantle and the invisible hat**

These are arts that include *in* within *yo*. For example, a pregnant woman visits a target place and when she leaves it looks like she has left the target area; however, in fact she has not. Be careful, this is not the same as the *kakure-mino* or *kakure-*

gasa no jutsu that are mentioned in the chapters on infiltrating a castle. This is expanded on in oral tradition.

IV

Kyo-nin no jutsu **or the startling technique**
Place someone beside the back door where he should enter in secret, while his partner agents stage a fake fight in front of the front entrance of the house. They do this by: shouting, pretending to be crazy, pretending to attack someone by yelling, telling the enemy that the house of someone from their family is burning or someone from the family has suddenly died or they can set a fire somewhere in the neighbourhood. If you startle the enemy in such a way, the people of the house will come out of the front entrance without fail, which means the one hiding by the back door can take advantage of this situation. Thus this is called *kyo-nin* or startling *ninjutsu*.

Further details and other ways of doing this art should be kept as an oral tradition.

This art is appropriate when done at night and when the people are not yet asleep. However, depending on the opportunity, it can sometimes be used in the early evening or even in the daytime. This art is mentioned earlier, in the volume on infiltrating a castle, and it has almost the same usage, but there is a little difference because of the difference in structure between a castle and a house, so I have mentioned it here as well.

Five points on the art of listening to snoring

I

It is best to use a *kikizutsu* listening cylinder in most cases. There is no special way to produce this tool, it is simply made in the normal way. It is necessary for you to know if the enemy is asleep or not by listening to their snoring. This is done when you come to the wall of the house or to the room next to where the enemy is sleeping – do this before you enter. Sometimes, the snoring in a room is very quiet or the sound of the rain or wind is so loud that you cannot hear very well. In such cases, you should use a *kikizutsu* listening cylinder by putting it through a window or from behind any point that allows you to hear well. More secrets are found in oral tradition.

II

Knowing if the enemy is still awake
If someone is awake, the person will move if you wait.

In summer, there will be the sound of mosquitoes or the mosquito net that gives away movement; while in winter, it may be the sound of a *fusuma* sliding door, bedclothes, breathing and so on. When you need to know if someone who does not snore is asleep or not, you may mistake the sound mice make as the enemy not being asleep and as their movement. You can tell if it is mice or human if you continue listening for a while, but there are more skills to this passed on in oral form.

In older times some *suppa* from our province went to a house whose master was very alert. This *suppa* infiltrated the house in the sixth or seventh month of the year, and when he got into the front yard, the chirping of insects around the area stopped. Thus the master noticed this and sneaked out of his mosquito net with a sword in hand. The *suppa* knew that he had come out by the sound of the mosquitoes [moving off] the net and withdrew secretly. Therefore, as you can see from the above, you should be very attentive to sound.

III
Knowing if people are pretending to snore to deceive you
It is sometimes the case that someone realizing that you are coming pretends to sleep by snoring, while in fact he is actually awake. Fake snoring sounds false and high-pitched and is irregular in length and loudness. Also, you can hear individual breaths between the fake snores.

If you listen carefully for a while, you will hear the person swallow saliva or sigh or draw a long breath. On top of that, he will try to move himself with as little sound as possible, his body, bones or joints will squeak. You should be aware of these points.

IV
Knowing if the enemy is fully asleep
If someone is deeply asleep, you can hear his snore regularly and quietly but there will be no other sound [such as those outlined above]. However, be aware that there are additional elements that should be considered and that the above is not always failsafe.

You should be aware that there can be a difference in the way of snoring between those who live an easy life and those who are suffering hardships. Those who have an easy life may have a regular snore without irregularity in length or loudness while those who suffer hardships may have an irregular and suffocating snore. Considering these points, you should judge if they are truly asleep or not. Some people say that those who have a lung disease or leprosy have an irregular snore even if they have an easy life. That seems to be quite likely.

V

Knowing if people are in a deep sleep or not in the case where they do not snore

Some people usually do not snore and even those who normally snore may not be snoring because they simply cannot get to sleep. Therefore, it is difficult to judge when it is the case that you can hear no snoring at all. There are ways to know if the enemy is truly asleep or not. [codified text[16]] distribute this [substance] in the air so it will fall onto the target's face and if the person is awake and has his eyes open, he will get suspicious and thus you can know if he is asleep or not.

Second, apply ash by putting it in or mixing it with the above item.

Third, blow rice,[17] foxtail millet or common millet with a blowpipe.[18]

By doing any of the above, you can tell for sure whether the person is asleep or not. There are more methods other than these if you are very resourceful. Also there is more information in the points below on how to observe the enemy.

Four points on the art of observing the enemy

I

Before you use fire to see where the enemy is sleeping, lock the doors

If you get close to the wall of the room where the enemy is sleeping with stealth to establish the enemy is in fact asleep, you may need to observe with a light exactly how the enemy is positioned or how many people there are in the room, what the room or the house is like etc. If the enemy is not asleep, they will notice any fire you display and your plan will fail as they will come out of the room and do you harm. Therefore, traditions of the ancient *shinobi* say you should lock the doors before you have a look at the enemy with fire.

The tool shown below [*see* figure 8] should be made of tempered iron, of two or three *bu* in thickness. If it is a single door [which can be stored in a recess and on tracks], then put the tool at the bottom [on the side of the post]. If the doors have two or more screens, put it at the places where doors overlap each other. It should be put in by inserting one end into the vertical gap between the doors and then allowing it to hook at the door edge while the other end should be hooked on the *hotate* part of the *toyose* door stopper.[19]

- The hooks on both sides should be five, six or seven *bu* in length.

---

16 By the context of the text this appears to be a light powder or mist scattered in the air by an unknown means with the effect of making a target move and react if he is awake. The text is codified; however, its full meaning is unknown.

17 In the text this is in a form of code like that of the make up of the word *kunoichi*.

18 Either at the person or into the room to test if the person reacts.

19 A thin strip of wood attached to the inside edge of one sliding door and when this tool is in place the sliding doors cannot be opened.

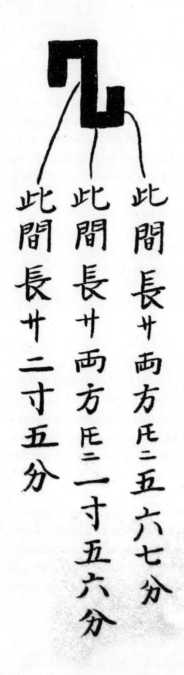

此間長廿二寸五分

此間長廿両方卍二一寸五六分

此間長廿両方卍二五六七分

Figure 8. Door clasp

• The very end straight is one *sun* and five or six *bu* in length and is equal at both ends.
• The centre length is two *sun* and five *bu*.

With this tool applied, people cannot open the doors immediately. Therefore, you should use this door clasp when you intend to set fires or when you do not have enough men and cannot place someone at every entrance. Also, if you rush in and attack from one single entrance, the enemy cannot run away. Screwing the door(s) will not work as it makes sound and you cannot fix them at a multiple number of doors. Therefore, this door clasp is recommended.

11

Four techniques to observe the enemy sleeping in a room while you are outside of it:

1. blowguns
2. *tagaemi* (observing them while lighting the room from another direction)
3. the fire on the end of a rod
4. the *ganto chochin* or the gyro lantern

You should prepare a short blowpipe and darts with gunpowder applied[20] and light one, then blow it from behind cover so that you can have a good look at where the enemy is sleeping.

In the technique of *tagaemi*, look into a room from the opposite side [from the

---

20 Presumably mixed with glue or resin.

fire] because you cannot observe the internals very well if you look from the same side as you have put the light in from. If the enemy is awake, they will stab at you with a *tachi* sword or a spear. Therefore you should look inside a room from the opposite side from the side you put the torch in, to avoid this reaction. This way you can see those inside while staying safe.

Thirdly, fire on a rod means tying a light onto the end of a thin rod to have a better view.

Fourthly, the *ganto chochin* or the gyro lantern does not serve unless there is enough room to fit it in through, as you have to point the light into a room through any available gap to see the insides. As you can see in the drawing of this in the volume on fire tools, it is too big and not appropriate for this use.

III

Four arts for using fire to see into the room where the enemy is sleeping after you get into the house:

1. Look with the *torinoko* fire egg.
2. Look with the *ireko-hi* adjustable lamp.
3. Look with the *shinobi taimatsu* that is the *shinobi* torch.
4. Look with the *fumetsu taimatsu* that is the long-lasting or the immortal torch.

When you get into the enemy house and sneak into the room next to where the enemy is sleeping, you should not carry any long or heavy, or many tools. Be sure to take handy lightweight fire tools as these above.

The *torinoko* fire egg should be held in your palm. When light is not needed, you should close your hand over it and when you need to look at the enemy, you should open your palm and blow on it so that it will flare up again, and then turn it toward them to have a better view. To be passed on by oral transmission.

In using the *ireko-hi* or adjustable lamp, when you want to 'extinguish' it you should lift the cord up, while when you want it to 'burn', you should lower the cord.[21] In the case where you want to look at the enemy while not allowing them to see you, hold it at the bottom and turn the end toward them.

When using the *shinobi taimatsu* or *shinobi* torch, if you hold it with the burning side put on the scabbard of your sword or any other similar object, it will not flare up. When you want it to flare up, swing it upwards and it will burn very well. This torch is also called *yawara taimatsu*. To be passed on by oral transmission.

---

21 This is not to actually extinguish but more to hide the light.

In using the *fumetsu taimatsu* or the long-lasting torch, if you hold it with the opening of an incense box away from you and swing it several times, do this so that you can see what is in front of you as it swings and passes. I have not tried this.

With the above tools, you can see the enemy situation without fail, even if they are in the darkness. You should take any of the above with you when you infiltrate an enemy house, and observe what the house or a room they are sleeping in is like; this is to dismiss any uncertainty before you sneak in. The drawings of these tools are in the chapter on fire tools in the *Ninki* volume.

I V

There is a tradition passed down that if you are not familiar with where the enemy is sleeping and have no light to look with, you should obtain such information by the imitation of animals.

If you loudly imitate the noises of dogs, foxes, cats and so on, the enemy will awake and verbally express irritation, thus you will know where they are sleeping. An ancient tradition says Kozaru – known as the small monkey of Shimotsuge – imitated dogs fighting so that the enemy would become angry at the sound [of the fake skirmish], allowing Kozaru to know where the enemy was [sleeping] so that he could kill them.

I personally think if you take such measures as placing *kunoichi* or such in position beforehand, then it is improbable that you will not know where the enemy is sleeping. What is more, unless you imitate the animals with expertise you will not succeed. Even though it is an ancient tradition, if you are not so good at imitating, it will end up with you being killed by the enemy. Even if you are good, it is best during *in-nin* for the enemy to be asleep, meaning that the above skill is not such a great method, as there is no point in waking them up before you infiltrate. If your intention is to lure them out to kill them, you can do that easily by using *kyo-nin no jutsu* or the art of startling them. Therefore, imitating animals is not appropriate as a measure simply to find out where the enemy is sleeping.

Five points on *ongyo jutsu* or the art of hiding

I

Where you should hide when you get into a house or within grounds where you have not been before
It goes without saying that when you get in a house for the first time, you should take temporary shelter. This can be under the *mushiro* woven straw mat of the toilet, in a bamboo thicket, in shrubbery, among piles of wood or firewood or behind anything that is appropriate. Then, after waiting for the opportune

time, you should get into the house. However, there are some things you should consider before hiding in a toilet.

When you get into a house, you should take temporary shelter in the stable,[22] in the loft space, behind or in a big pot,[23] under the floor, behind any tools or so on and observe the inside of the house and wait for the people to go to sleep. When you are to sneak into a complex or a house, it is advisable to infiltrate at dusk when people cannot see each other's faces very clearly and are busy and distracted with preparations. Do this to see how you should get to the above mentioned places and to see where to take shelter. Then just before they light the fires, you should get in and take shelter in any of the above mentioned places.

I I

Kannon[24]*-gakure* or 'deity of mercy' hiding
Kannon-gakure is for when you come across the enemy guardsmen. If this happens you should stand by a wall, fence, tree, a pile of wood or firewood or anything such as these and without being in a state of panic. You should cover your face with your sleeve but leave a little of your eyes exposed and make sure not to breathe with noise or allow the enemy to feel your breath. You should stand there, dead still while chanting the spell of *ongyo* [inside your mind], which is the spell of hiding. It is also good to stand with your back toward the enemy. If you do this the enemy will not be able to detect you. There have been a number of cases since ancient times where this way of hiding has worked successfully. Those who do not know how advantageous this is and have the enemy coming upon them, rush to hide and run away. As a consequence, they will make their footsteps or breathing heard, hit something by mistake, step on some rubbish or such and end up being detected. The important spell of *ongyo* is to be chanted with a *mudra* hand sign of *houbako* or the treasure box *mudra*.

I I I

Uzura-gakure or quail hiding
Uzura-gakure hiding is to get close to anything and draw in the arms and legs, pull in the head, crouch with the face down and with a serene mind, as though you are listening to frost fall on a cold night, chanting the spell of *ongyo* hiding in your mouth.[25] Be sure not to turn your face toward the enemy. There are

---

22 This is a small animal enclosure in the entrance to larger houses.
23 The text says *kama*, which is a form of larger cooking pot. The idea is to get low and almost under the pot, as far as the *shinobi* can, or to get inside it.
24 Buddhist deity of mercy.
25 Inside your head or in silence, i.e. 'captured in your mouth'.

five advantages in crouching with your face down and five disadvantages in crouching with your face up.

If you turn your face toward the enemy, it looks white.[26] If you cover your face by crouching with your face down, it does not look white, so it is hard for the enemy to detect you.

As men are *yo*, turning your face up is conflicting while turning your face down is also *yo* and therefore complementary to your hiding. When you have your face up your breathing will be harder and the enemy will detect you, while when your face is down it will be shallower and faster, so they will not detect it.

Third, if someone's 'breathing' and your breathing correspond,[27] then this other person will not fail to realize you are there. Therefore, turning your face upward is disadvantageous while turning your face down is advantageous.

Fourth, when you turn your face up the body will naturally tend to extend instead of contracting, while when your face is down it will always contract, thus making it harder to be detected and more advantageous.

Fifth, as you cannot see the enemy when you cover your face, your spirit will be as tough as iron or stone. However, when you hide on your back, you can see the enemy. Tradition says 'eyes are cowards'. If you see the enemy, you will become inevitably fainthearted and anxious to run away before the enemy detects you. As you will then be in a state of panic and start moving, it will be easier to be discovered. In case you cannot crouch with your face down, cover your

Figure 9.
The spell of hiding
'ON ANICHI MARISHI EI SOWAKA'
Details are to be orally transmitted

---

26 This is superb evidence for the absence of the classic *ninja* mask, which may have been the guise of later Edo period thieves wishing to disguise their identity.

27 His meaning is not clear at this point – however this could be *sound* or the *moisture* in the air?

face with the sleeve. If the enemy is searching with suspicion and using a light, you should leave. However, even in this case, if you are in a good hiding place you should remain there, steadfast. It is even more so if the enemy is simply on a routine night patrol and they are not carrying a light; here you should keep on hiding with this art and with strong nerves. There have been lots of examples where people have hidden well using this skill, many since ancient times. [People of other provinces] say that the *ninja* of Iga become like a stone and the above points are their ways.[28] If these points are conducted properly, the body and heart should be like a stone, which makes the enemy overlook you, as they would overlook a stone.

In older times, a *suppa* of our province sneaked into a castle and was standing at rest when people on night patrol came by. He immediately rushed into the dry moat besides and crouched using the art of quail hiding. They vaguely saw the outline of the *suppa* on the bottom of the moat and made a stab at him with a spear and the tip of the spear pierced his belly.[29] However, the *suppa* did not move in the slightest and the people on night patrol left saying it must not be a human being as it did not move. Later, the *suppa* came out quietly and set fire to the castle and burned it down.

When Prince Daito stayed in Han'nya-ji temple in Nara and in secret, a warrior monk of Ichijo-in temple, Azechi no Hogen Kosen, found out he was hiding within and advanced on the temple leading more than five hundred people before dawn, in a raid. There was no one attending on the prince and it was not possible to run away or make a defence against the raiders. Also, as the soldiers were squeezing into the temple there was no way to get mixed in with them and hide. Therefore, the prince decided to kill himself and stripped to the waist; however, to kill himself would be the simplest way out, thus he looked for another option. The prince decided to take a chance by hiding and looked around the Buddhist sanctum where he found three chests full of *sutras*. Two of them had the lids closed while the other was left open with more than half of the *sutras* left out beside the chest. He squeezed himself into the open chest and covered himself with *sutras*, chanting the hiding spell of *ongyo* in his mind. He thought intently that if he was detected he should kill himself and thus drew his sword and put it onto his stomach, and waited, expecting soldiers to say 'here he is!' The soldiers rushed into the sanctum and searched everywhere from beneath the altar to the ceiling but could not find him. Finally, they said the chests looked suspicious. They opened the two with the lids closed and took out

---

28 Grammatically, Fujibayashi is not implying that he is not an *Iga no mono*, allowing him still to be from Iga himself.

29 For this to happen, the *suppa* must have been pierced through his back and into his stomach.

all the *sutra*s in them, right to the bottom, but found the prince was not there. The prince wondered how amazing it was that his life was saved and felt like he was in a dream while he was in the chest. However, he thought that they might come back and do a more thorough search and so he moved into one of the other chests that they had ransacked. As he expected, the soldiers came back into the sanctum, noticed the open chest, and examined it by taking all the *sutra*s out. At last they laughed and joked that Prince Daito was not there but Xuanzang[30] the Chinese nomad was. Then they all left the temple laughing.

I V
The three methods of escape when the enemy has awoken
First, imitation; second, false conversation; third, staying while pretending to leave.

If the enemy catches any sound that you have made and are straining their ears to hear you, you should imitate a dog or cat by flapping your sleeves or by biting wood, or copying the sound of a dog or cat in a fight so that they will think it is only a dog or cat. To be passed on by oral transmission.

Second, fabricate a conversation so that the enemy thinks that you are going to move outside when you are in fact staying inside the house, or so that they think you are on the inside of the wall when you are on the outside, or even so that they think there is another man hidden out of sight, while there is not. It is important to note that you should make up a situation so that the enemy will act in a way that is contrary to what they should do, as they will take the conversation as fact, even though it is actually false. This is the art of *yo* within *in*.

In old times, Shindo no Kotaro went to Sanagu castle and performed this above art. Also in the Correct Mind chapter, this art is mentioned in an old incident which shows that if you are committed to death, in actuality it will allow you to survive.

Another example is thus. A *shinobi no mono* from our province stole into a house to kill the master. He waited for his chance but the master was very careful and kept a night guard while he himself retired to his bed. After waiting for an extended period of time, that is until the hour of Ox, the *ninja* realized that the guard had fallen asleep due to tiredness and everything was dead quiet and the fire was out and all was dark; therefore, it was time to make a move. He tried to open the door but the *kagi shirizashi* lock was firmly secured and would not open. Then he dug a hole in the ground beneath the threshold with a spade and squeezed through so that his face was on the other side in order to observe

---

30 Famed for discovering the 'wisdom *sutra*'. As the soldiers found only *sutra*s, they are linking them to the Chinese sage.

the status of the house internals. He found that the guard had just opened his eyes; this was because as the *ninja* came through he made a faint sound with his breath, bones or joints or the floor or something such as this. The guard became attentive and tried to listen as quietly as listening to frost rise on a cold night. After a short while, footsteps approached the *ninja*, forcing the *ninja* to escape from the hole. The guard stayed beside the hole so that he could stab at anyone if they came through the hole. To counter this, the *shinobi no mono* whispered this following and false conversation:

'*The guard seems to have awoken, so we cannot get in from here. Let's leave and get in from around the storeroom toward the back.*' Then the response was given in another voice: '*OK, let's withdraw. [Insert name*[31]*] has already opened the door near the storehouse.*'

Hearing this, the guard thought that the *ninja* agents were multiple in number and that it would not be easy to drive all of them away and that he should call for support to attack the *shinobi no mono* when they broke through. Therefore, he retreated quietly and woke the master. After he had woken him, the guard moved to the back door and waited there. Having realized this, the *ninja* stole into the house quickly through the original hole and went to the master's sleeping room, where he saw the master getting ready by the light of the night lantern. The *ninja* said to him, 'Please get out of here as soon as possible,' and the master thought it was his guard and did not suspect him in the slightest, at which point the *ninja* stabbed him to death and extinguished the fire and ran away. The guards heard the sounds and shouted, 'Intruder! Come here!' All the people in the house and the neighbours as well came running to aid the master. As the *ninja* had expected this to happen he was prepared with *hyakurai-ju* or the one hundred fire crackers, and left them lit on the edge of a bamboo thicket. Hearing the loud noises of the *hyakurai-ju* fire crackers, the chasers thought there must be a number of people shooting muskets and spent a while making their mind up about what to do. While they did this the *ninja* escaped to a distance of more than one *ri*. The people besieged the bamboo thicket all that night and examined it thoroughly when dawn broke and found there was no one there and only the *hyakurai-ju* crackers remained. They all left in anger as they had been outwitted.

In older times, someone had a grudge against a low-ranking retainer. He intended to kill him and went to the enemy house, where he tried to open the door carefully. The master heard the sound, woke up and got out of the room in secret and moved to the inside of the door that the *ninja* was opening. The *ninja*

---

31 The text says '*dare, dare*', which is used to mean 'insert the required name'.

entering noticed this and said to himself, 'The master has woken so we cannot succeed. Let's retreat,' and also replied to himself, 'OK,' as if there were in fact two men. He pretended to withdraw by retreating about one *ken*, and quietly came back to the door and stayed by the wall. The master of the house, not realizing it was a trap, opened the door and came out to catch 'them'; at that moment the *shinobi* – who was waiting for him to come out and who was by the door – killed him with a single strike, and attained his objective. This is the way to take advantage of the enemy's intention to wait for you and to kill you by surprise. Though there have been so many cases other than these, I cannot mention every one so have put the above two as examples.

The third art is pretending to run away while staying behind. If you are in the enemy house and the enemy awakens, you should pretend to run out of the house by making noises at the exit but in actuality you stay inside the house; this is in the case where you are alone. When they exit to chase you, you should go deeper and take any chance to kill the enemy.

If you are two in number, one should run away and make the enemy follow while the other member goes deeper inside the house. This is for the case when the retainers or guards of the enemy wake up and come out.

If the enemy [target] himself wakes up and comes out, you should wait for him and kill him at the door. You should agree among your squad beforehand on every arrangement for every case, such as what to do if you wake up the enemy – who should run away, who should stay, etc. – and all in detail. This technique has been used successfully in many cases since ancient times.

V

If you are chased by the enemy and it is hard to beat them, there are eight useful methods of withdrawal:

1. *Tanuki-noki* or the racoon dog retreat
2. Retreat by *Hyakurai-ju* or the one hundred fire crackers
3. Retreat by caltrops
4. Throwing wood or stone into water
5. Disguising yourself as an enemy pursuer by shouting as he would
6. Having the gate door closed by announcing that something unusual has happened
7. Having the gate door opened by announcing that the lord needs to leave urgently
8. *Tanuki-gakure* or racoon dog hiding, and *kitsune-gakure*, which is fox hiding

Whether a large number or a small one, if the enemy is chasing you and there is no chance of victory if you fight back, you should just run away with the following tactics:

1 *Tanuki-noki* or the racoon dog retreat
If you are being chased and are about to be cut down from behind, you should suddenly stop on bended knees so the opponent will crash into you and collapse. Then you should kill him immediately. If a single enemy soldier is chasing you, fall on your knees so that he will not collide with you but will in fact pass by you with momentum. At this point you should hit his waist with your *tachi*. Even if he tries to cut you as he passes by, there will be little chance of his sword hitting you successfully as you are kneeling down – this works on both sides. If there is three to five *ken* between you and the chaser, you should hide yourself somewhere, such as beside a gatehouse, or any place you can hide along the street, so the enemy will think you have gone further and keep chasing after you. After the enemy goes four or five *ken* away from your position, you should head back, and if you come across them later, you should invent a plausible story such as, 'the *enemy* ran that way and one or two are following him. If the *enemy* fights back *our* allies will have difficulty. Hurry up!' while you yourself take another way out. It is said that an old racoon dog will do the same thing when chased by dogs; therefore, it is called the racoon dog retreat.

2 Retreat by *hyakurai-ju* or the one hundred fire crackers
In the case where you are fourteen or fifteen *ken* or even twenty *ken* away from the enemy or if you are closer and are hiding by using *uzura-gakure* quail hiding and the enemy cannot find you and they are running around in the area, then, here you should light *hyakurai-ju* fire crackers in a bush or thicket or in an abandoned hut or house. By doing this the enemy will think that a night attack squad is there and rush to intercept it while you evade and retreat. How to construct *hyakurai-ju* fire crackers is mentioned in the chapter on fire tools in the *Ninki* section.[32]

Various traditions to use this tool have been transmitted.

3 Retreat by caltrops
You should take bamboo caltrops with you and scatter them on the route you expect to retreat by or place them in front of each door before you infiltrate. This is done because normally you are too busy to scatter them when you retreat; however, it is sometimes possible to scatter them when withdrawing. In older times they sometimes had caltrops trailing on strings when retreating.

---

32 It is in fact omitted from the volume in question.

To avoid stepping on the caltrops you yourself have scattered, you should pass where you placed them without lifting your feet and with the sole of your foot kept on the floor.

4 Throwing wood or stone into water[33]

When the enemy chases you on a dark night, you should throw wood or stone into water so that the enemy hears the sound as it approaches, thinking that the stone was you who entered the water, while in fact you have retreated. This is the skill that Shindo no Kotaro performed when he went to Mineoroshi castle of Sanagu.

In old times, a *ninja* sneaked in a house and was detected by a servant. While being chased, he lifted and threw a stone the size of a teakettle over a fence. While he stayed on the inside of the fence, performing the skill of *uzura-gakure* quail hiding, the pursuers on hearing the sound of the stone thought he had jumped out and over the fence; therefore, they opened the gate and gave chase. At which point he then went back to the house, penetrating deeply and killing the house master, who had come out upon hearing the ruckus.

Another *ninja* sneaked into a house, where the master woke up and gave chase. The *ninja* ran into a thicket in front of the house and the master thought that he had cornered the *ninja* and stood off for a short while, waiting. Then the *ninja* threw a lump of earth from within the thicket and out in another direction, making the master think that he was sneaking out from his hiding place. This made the master give chase, taking the side route around the thicket, while in fact the *ninja* left the thicket from the other side and infiltrated the house with stealth.

5 Disguising yourself as an enemy pursuer by shouting as he would

When the enemy notices you and makes fuss by shouting loudly, if you try to run away without saying anything this will attract people's attention even more. On the other hand if you do not intend to hide but show yourself in plain sight, disguising yourself as an enemy in pursuit while running and shouting, 'Night attack! After him!' people will not suspect you at all. In doing this art there is a method to misdirect them. If you intend to retreat in the west, you should tell every person you meet, 'I heard the thief going to the east. Follow him in the east.' This is called *tagae-no-jutsu* or the art of misdirection. To be prepared for such a case, you should wear a *haori* jacket of a persimmon colour[34] on the outside and pale grey on the inside. When you sneak in, wear it with the persimmon side out,

---

33 The text has an ideogram that is unidentifiable before the term 'water'.
34 A dark brown.

then, when disguising yourself as a pursuer, reverse it and have the grey side out. The *ninja* of old would – in some cases – use this art with success.

6 Having the gate door closed by announcing that something unusual has happened

In older times, someone infiltrated a castle and killed his target. When people around there heard the sound they came out shouting and ready to cope with him. He immediately got out of the building and found the gate was open as it was early in the evening. He then thought he should prevent his followers from chasing him, which would allow him to withdraw with ease. Therefore he said [to the gate guards] at each gate, 'A fight is taking place in the castle now: close the gate – no one should be let out of here. This is an order from the lord. Get prepared and never let your guard down.' As he was shouting these words and running around, the guards thought it was true and closed the gates at once. Meanwhile he retreated without difficulty.[35] This technique should be used during the daytime or early evening when the gate doors are open and you think the enemy will chase you.

7 Having the gate door opened by announcing that the lord needs to leave urgently

In the case where you infiltrate the house of a high-ranking person or a castle and you retreat to find the gate doors are closed, you should say to the gate master in a haughty fashion, 'The lord is going out to (insert place) and at haste. Open the gate doors,' or 'I have to go to (insert place) by the order of the lord,' or 'A fire has taken place, I was told to find out its origin by the lord,' etc. There are things to be orally transmitted for this technique. Also, there are various ways according to the situation. You should have a well thought out plan for your retreat before you sneak in, or think out how to retreat before you kill someone. There is more to be orally transmitted.

8 *Tanuki-gakure* or racoon dog hiding and *kitsune-gakure*, which is fox hiding

If you are chased by a large number and think it is difficult to manage an escape, you should climb up a tree and hide; this is called *tanuki-gakure* or racoon dog hiding. This works very well and you will not be found in most cases. A leafy big tree is desirable. Another way is if the enemy is collecting more and more people on the hunt and escape seems hard, you should dive into water, with yourself in water but your face out, covering your face with duckweed, water grasses,

---

35 Presumably on the other side of the gate.

lotus leaves, foliage, etc. This is called *kitsune-gakure* or fox hiding. It is named so because, if a hunter shoots a fox and it is injured but not killed, the fox will run but will not be able to escape in full because of pain; therefore, it will dive into the deep place of a stream. If any hunter approaches it, it will hide itself in a cavity or such with only its nose and mouth out of the water and covered with weeds. This is called *kitsune-gakure*.

In older times, in Nagoya of Bishu, someone held a grudge against a high-ranking *samurai* and sneaked into his mansion at twilight. As it was summer, he thought the enemy might be taking a bath or may come out to urinate and thus he hid around the bathroom so that he could kill the *samurai* if he got the chance. As he expected, the enemy came for a bath and he killed him without difficulty. However, when he was escaping the mansion, all in that area as well as those in the mansion gathered raising a clamour and chasing him. The killer thought he might not be able to escape and dived into a moat with willow trees on the bank and hid himself in water with his head covered with the leaves of willow branches. Those pursuing lit torches and tried to detect him along the riverbank but could not find the intruder and gave up in the end. At dawn he got out of the moat and escaped without difficulty. There were many such cases in ancient times; therefore, it became the case that a good general would have his men remove all grasses or leaves from the moats, or willow trees, so that there would be nowhere to hide.

Here is another example of *tanuki-gakure*: in older times, two *nusubito* thieves sneaked into a house and someone in the house woke up and cried out, waking up others who gathered from all directions. One thief ran out beyond the fence but the other could not make it and found a large *yuzu*[36] tree and climbed up and hid among the leaves. The chasers searched everywhere but they could not find him up the tree and gave up the search, returning to the house to sleep at last. Meanwhile, the one who escaped on the ground was waiting for the other but his partner did not join him so he went back to the mansion. He tried but could not hear anything from outside the fence so he went into the ground and searched around for his collaborator and heard a sound up a tree. He whispered to the man, 'Come down quickly,' but he answered that he could not because the tree was too thorny and was trapping him. The thief below told him that he was a dire coward and that he should come down immediately, but the other could not. So, the man below had the idea and shouted out, 'Thief, a thief is up the tree! Come on!' Those from the house heard the voice and came out. Then the thief in the tree jumped down forgetting the spines and hurt and both could escape. This was very smart of the thief beneath the tree.

---

36 *Citrus Junos.*

Three points on how to arrange your men when infiltrating a house

I

Watchmen

You should place your men as watchmen on every route from the quarters, rooms or neighbouring houses to the target house. Watchmen do not have to be experienced or well trained but should be preferably coolheaded. Generally, for any job, those who are cowards, careless and lacking patience are not good. But remember, as watchmen they are capable of causing especially serious harm [to your plans]. As ancient methods tell us, there are three devastating disadvantages to having those who are cowardly, careless or lacking in patience as watchmen:

1. Watchmen who are not coolheaded and lack patience cannot wait for their allies who have infiltrated a position to come back. They get nervous and walk around or get upset, making them fail to hear or see the signs and signals given to them; therefore, this will result in ruin.
2. When the cowardly watchmen's comrades withdraw from a room, the cowards will not give the required password but mistake their comrades as the enemy and try to kill them or run away at the first sign of trouble.
3. Cowardly watchmen might mistake those enemy coming from outside as their allies, or those allies coming from outside as the enemy. They are always careless and cannot be relied upon. If even a single man in your squad is like that, then all in your squad will be confused and make mistakes.

As you can see in the above three points, if you think anybody will suffice and you then use those who are not coolheaded, nor careful and lacking in perseverance as watchmen, then it will not bring you any benefit but instead cause you a devastating defeat. Therefore, tradition from ancient *shinobi* principles says you should be careful. It is essential for you to choose appropriate people for each job with careful consideration of their disposition and then have a strict agreement for the signal or arrangements, so that no mistake will ever occur.

Taking into account the natural disposition of each person, generally the young are hot-blooded and strong but careless or not so good while the old are calm and good while sometimes they think too much and miss the chance. However, those who are tough and smart by nature and are between thirty-four or thirty-five and fifty years old are good both as performers and watchmen.

II

Main performers

Supplementary to the above: Place people at every door or if you do not have enough men, then lock the doors.

The role of the main performers is of the most importance. Therefore, it would be disastrous if they were not proficient with courage, tactics and performance. One of the two performers is the person who should unlock the *joshi*, *kagi*, *toboso* and the *shirizashi* locks or employ various other measures to sneak in. The other [the supporting performer] listens to the enemy snoring or any other sounds and informs his partner – the performer who is doing the unlocking – of anything he needs to know and he also informs a further member of the squad who acts as a liaison for the information, and the liaison in turn tells the performer any required information that he needs [from the outside].

The liaison man is one of the watchmen, he goes deep into the house where *samurai* are or even close to the place where the performers are working, and passes on the orders or information from the supporting performer to a signal man outside or alternatively what the signal man says to the supporting performer. Details should be orally transmitted.

In addition, you should put your men at every door. This is done to kill every person in the house. The following are three techniques to be used by those stationed at a door.

The first is to stretch a rope across the doorway at a height of eight or nine *sun*. When the enemy soldiers rush out of the room, they will trip and fall down over the rope and you should kill them at that point.

[The second is] to scatter caltrops at every doorway so the enemy will step upon them.

[The third is] to stay at the doorway and stab with your *wakizashi* short sword. Generally, stabbing with a sword will be fine when you are in the house or in an external corridor. More should be orally transmitted.

How to lock doors is mentioned earlier and not here. Shutting doors with a drill will also suffice.

III

Signal senders

Supplementary to the above: Marks, bells or fires that are to be used as signals.

The signal sender should be on a slightly elevated place with a bell or fire, so he can be seen from any direction. He should communicate information from those inside to those outside, or information from those outside to those inside.

Also, you should have a mark to identify your allies from the enemy for after you have dispersed – for example, all of the squad might wear a *tenugui* headband of white. As for passwords, they are mentioned in the chapters on *yo-nin* and not here.

The signal sender should carry a wind-bell[37] and a *shisoku-bi* paper torch.[38] The method for making the *shisoku-bi* is mentioned in the chapter on fire tools. Light the *shisoku-bi* torch and put the number of these torches you need – according to the prior arrangements you have made – onto a long bamboo stick. This stick has a one-*shaku* split at the end and the watchmen will be able to see the number of paper torches fitted to the end of the stick and will act according to the arrangements made for that specific signal.

Signalling at night will not work without something that makes sound or fire. If it is a night battle, lanterns, drums or conch shells will be used, but they are so large that they will attract people's attention because the sound they make is too noisy, so they are not good as a measure for signalling when infiltrating a house. That is why the above tools should be used. The sound of a wind-bell is not loud and the enemy will not notice it ring, but it can be heard from a distance and is appropriate as a signal in infiltrating a house. The *shisoku-bi* paper torch is a little bluish and hard to identify if people see it. Nothing is better than the wind-bell and *shisoku-bi* as signal measures when infiltrating a house. One writing says: signals should be considered and they should be varied according to the arrangements and each opportunity. It is essential to have a strict and firm agreement so that no mistakes will be made as to the signals.

The above three major points are of extreme importance and all should be arranged appropriately according to the situation. There are more secrets beyond writing.

Two points on caution

I

Do not light the lamps that are already in a sleeping room. Keep fire with you and light the above-mentioned *shisoku-bi* tool. If you light any light, you should use a *katou* pottery lantern [which covers and directs light], the *ireko-hi* adjustable lantern or the *ganto chochin* gyro lantern etc.

If you use a light that is already in a sleeping room when you arrive, it will allow the enemy to see you clearly. Therefore, you should not use the enemy's light or any lights of the house. If you need light, there is a way to light a lantern.

---

37 *Furin* – a small bell held on a string, similar to wind-chimes.
38 Paper layered with glue and gunpowder and rolled around bamboo; when the bamboo is removed the tool is ready to light.

Place pliers[39] on the open top of a lantern and rest a plate on top of them. Then place the lantern beside a wall with the illuminated side facing the wall so the light will not be seen. As for the *ireko-hi* adjustable lantern or the *ganto chochin* gyro lantern, they will be mentioned in the chapter on fire tools.

The above tools give you light but do not allow others to see you.

II

To avoid sleeping by not avoiding hardships or by splashing your face with cold water or by using *kakushinsan* awakening medicine

If you want to train yourself to stay awake as much as possible, it is essential not to avoid hardships for yourself. You should sleep with your kimono on and *obi* belt tightened, wear as little clothes as possible even in the cold, do not eat too much, keep yourself from lying down but sit up correctly, do not avoid mosquitoes in summer and do not use a fan or so on. If you do not avoid hardships like these, you will sleep less. It is of primary importance to avoid lewdness. If not, you will be exhausted and cannot help but sleep deeply. Washing your face with cold water or moistening your ears with your spit will also do. The recipe for the *kakushinsan* wakening medicine is mentioned in the chapter on fire tools in the *Ninki* section. Further details on how to avoid sleeping are orally transmitted.

The seven ways to use the *sageo*[40] sword cord

Make an *obi* belt with the *sageo* cord if your own *obi* is cut by the enemy or you are in an emergency situation or [disturbed] while sleeping and you do not know where your *obi* belt is. To make one, split a *sageo* sword cord [and tie the ends together].

The *tabimakura* or the 'travel pillow' – tie the ends of the *sageo* cords of both your long and short swords [while they are still connected to the weapons] and lie down on them, so that you will not be robbed of your sword or your *wakizashi* short sword while you sleep. Also, in an emergency, it is convenient if you take the *sageo* cord with both swords attached and put it around your neck while you are on the move and tying your *obi* belt.[41]

The skill of *zasagashi* or using your cord and sword to probe the room is mentioned earlier in the chapter *In-nin Jo*.

Climbing up a wall by using your sword as a foot rest is also mentioned earlier

---

39 While ambiguous, this appears to be a method of creating a temporary and directional light from a standard household light, so that the *ninja* may control the light emissions.

40 The cord used on sword scabbards to attach them to the waist.

41 The idea here is that if you have to move for any reason and with haste you can wake up and sling your weapons around your neck as you run and get dressed.

in the *In-nin* section.

Making a screen in a field – this is mentioned in the chapter on *torimono* or capturing people.

Making a binding rope from a *sageo* cord – how to bind people with the *sageo* cord is an oral tradition.

The *yariyose* or the 'spear catcher' – tie the end of the *sageo* cord onto your short sword.[42] Draw the sword out fully and hold it in your right hand and the scabbard in your left hand, with the rope hanging between. When a spear is stabbed at you, catch it and wrap the *sageo* cord around the spear and take the enemy's weapon. Details should be orally transmitted.

[Seven points on traps to injure the enemy]

I

The *harahata-barai* or 'shank sweepers'
Harahata-barai shank sweepers should be prepared on the inside or the outside of your own mansion and on every route you expect the enemy *shinobi* will come from. If the enemy *shinobi* sneak in from where the *harahata-barai* trap is placed, it will hit their shanks badly and they will think it must be a human strike and therefore they will withdraw.

1. Set out a trip wire as seen on the next page [*figure 10*].
2. The bent whip is made of long bamboo.
3. On the left are two wooden spikes. Stand these two spikes in the ground as in the drawing and tie the bamboo tightly between them.
4. Make a grid of wood as in the bottom of the drawing by lashing it together. Put thin bamboo[43] at the end of the thick bamboo and put it between the horizontal bars so that it can spring off easily.
5. The vertical bars have fasteners.

II

The *tsurioshi* or the dead-weight trap
The *tsurioshi* is a weight hung from a *kamoi*[44] beam in a house. This is used to keep a strict guard or to protect any route where the enemy *shinobi* are expected to come from. If the enemy *shinobi* open the door where a *tsurioshi* weight is set, the weight will fall down and the *shinobi* will be injured or startled. To set it,

---

42 One end is already attached to the scabbard; therefore, you now have the scabbard and the sword with the cord hanging in the middle.

43 In the picture this appears to be rope.

44 A narrow section continuing around a Japanese room, containing the top slots into which sliding doors fit, acting as a lintel.

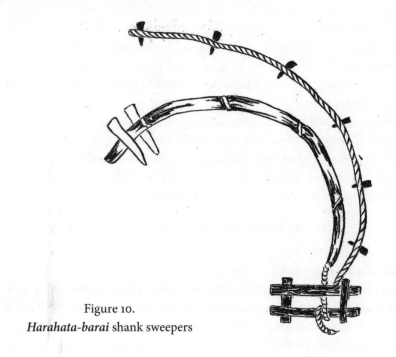

Figure 10.
Harahata-barai shank sweepers

Figure 11.
The *tsurioshi* dead-weight trap

tie a rope onto a heavy weight such as a mortar, a stone mill, stone board, heavy wood or so on and hang it up so that the weight is outside the door and the rope is stretched through to the inside of the room. Put a nail on the vertical edge of the door and put a fastener or hook at the end of the weighted rope and hook it onto the nail. If the enemy *shinobi* open the door – even by just a slight amount – the hook will slip off and the weight will fall down. *See* figure 11, left.

III

Caltrops

You should scatter caltrops outside the house and where the enemy *shinobi* are expected to come from.

IV

Startling the enemy while you yourself are asleep

Put a nail onto the vertical frame of a door and put a thin rope onto it, pass it around a vertical door post and stretch it to your bedside. Attach this end to a box or a bucket of around two to four *shaku* in size, and then put a smaller bucket on top of that; fill this upper one with beans or pebbles or anything that makes a noise when spilt over. If the enemy *shinobi* open the door, the smaller bucket will be pulled down and pebbles or beans will spill over, making a loud noise. The enemy will be startled and you will be woken up. There are various techniques that fulfill the same function, see the example in the drawing overleaf (figure 12).[45]

V

The large bamboo trap

Stand two spikes into the ground on the inside of an [external] door and tie a horizontal bar onto the two spikes in the ground [making a gate]. Put the base of a section of bamboo between the gate and the other end between the vertical pillar and the *tozashi* framework by bending it. Also attach a rope at the middle of the bamboo and around the vertical pillar to bend the bamboo further. If the enemy *shinobi* open the door, the bamboo trap will hit their face and they will think they have been struck by someone and will be startled.

---

45 Note the drawing here appears to be incorrect as it does not continue from the vertical post to the door, possibly the fault of the transcribers.

Figure 12.

Figure 13. The large
bamboo trap

VI

Stretching a rope or standing up the *tatami* mats

In case you cannot have secure locks on the doors, such as when travelling, stretch out a thin rope or stand the *tatami* mats against the *shoji* sliding doors. There is more to be orally transmitted here. There are many other creative ways to get the same effect according to the situation. Also locking doors with a drill will be fine.

VII

Tsurioshi **traps that are to be prepared on all routes**

- Use two trees as posts, as seen here on the left and right of the drawing.
- Hang a weight of wood in the centre.
- How to lash the rope to the anchor point is orally transmitted.
- The *otoshi* bamboo at the bottom is the trigger to the trap.

Figure 14. The *tsurioshi* trap

In-nin IV

Hidden Infiltration IV

Gates and doors

Three points on the preparation for opening doors

I

To open a door, you can discover – by using a *toikagi* probing tool – where the *joshi* padlocks, *kakegane* hooked latches, *shirizashi*[1] locking sticks and so on are located and also their construction typology. It is also possible to discover the positions of padlocks, hooked latches, bolts,[2] locking sticks, wooden pegs[3] and so on, by utilizing your practical experience and feeling where a door is locked. However, it is absolutely essential to collect this information by observing the locks directly or by inferring information about them through what you hear. You should glean information about the target house you wish to infiltrate by talking to people or by observation and then take the appropriate tools for the opening of the doors.

II

Mark with your nails the positions of wooden pegs, latches and so on, while passing by them.

---

1   A small stick of wood the length of the width of the door. As the doors slide in Japan they place the stick between the door post and the side of the door, acting as a blockage which stops the doors from opening; these are still used today.

2   Known as *kuroro* or *toboso*, they are similar to the modern door bolt and are bolted into the threshold or door frame.

3   Small wooden or bamboo pegs that are wedged between the ring and the hook of a latch so that the latch will become locked tight.

III

To open doors, it is essential to work with the wind and sound. If there is no sound or wind to use or to take advantage of, urinate on the threshold and open the door with care. There is another way called *wata-ake* or floss opening but this is to be orally transmitted.[4] In particular, it is essential that opening tools make no noise or as little noise as possible.

Six points on discovering the position of *shirizashi* locking sticks by touch

I

There are five types of locking sticks. If you try to open a door and you feel something is blocking the pathway, you should be aware that there is a locking stick in position. You can identify which of the five types it is by following these rules.

II

Locking stick in the groove of a doorway
If you try to open the door and it is stuck at the bottom but opens at the top then it is blocked at the lower groove.

III

Cross-shaped[5] locking stick
If you try to open the door and it is stuck both at the bottom and the top and has no margin of movement, then the locking stick is the cross version.

IV

San shirizashi locking stick (a bar positioned in the centre of the door)
This type of locking stick is found with the *oitate-do* type door. When you try to open the door, it will be stuck in the middle and make noises around that area. Also, bamboo locking sticks are sometimes used and if that is the case, then the door will not make any noise when you try to open it.

---

4   This skill appears in the Shinobi Hiden manual and is the art of twisting floss from plant life onto door or gate hinges to extract the oil to use as a lubricant.

5   This appears to be two sections of wood that form a cross 'X' and are placed between the sliding door and the door frame. Also, they may be tall and fit in the space of the door or they may be squat and the 'X' may fit across the band of the doorway; the latter is most likely correct.

V

Deba shirizashi **or a protruding locking stick for an** *oitate-do* **style door**[6]
This is fixed in the middle and if you try to open it too hard, it will feel like it is bending and furthermore, if you try to open the door, it will squeak.

VI

Shirizashi **locking stick found on** *oitate-do* **style door**
This one will also be stuck in the middle and if pushed, will squeak a little.

For each of the above, there is a small amount to be orally transmitted. Unless you try to open them for yourself, you will not be able to know exactly what each is like, so you should try whenever you can.

Four points on how to unlock locking sticks

I

For locking sticks in the groove of a threshold or cross-shaped locking sticks, use a *toihazushi*[7] probe[8] to find the position of the stick and knock it out of place. If the locking stick cannot be knocked off with the *toihazushi* probe, you should put a pair of closed pliers through the gap [between the two sliding doors] and open the tips of the pliers when they reach the other side [to take the pressure off the stick], and then take the stick away by thrusting it out of place. In the case where *shoji* inner sliding doors are in the way and you cannot push the stick out because they are blocking the path, then use the *toihazushi* probe or the pliers to open the inner sliding door [bit by bit]. Then, after you have opened them, knock the stick off the track in the way described above. If the bottom of the door is boarded, use a round drill then open it up and then use the pliers [to knock off the locking bar].

II

For a *san shirizashi* or central locking stick on an *oitate-do* door, pull the two doors apart with strength and knock off the locking stick by lifting it with the *toihazushi* probe, then you can open the doors freely.

III

Do the same as above for the protruding locking stick. Also you can unlock the latter by lifting it up with a *yarigiri* drill or even the *yubikagi* finger key.

---

6 An unknown type of door.
7 Sometimes known as *toigaki*; however, analysis of the ideogram within the whole of the text leads to the above reading.
8 See the image in volume twenty.

IV

For the *muso shirizashi* locking stick,[9] use the *toihazushi* probe or a *yarigiri*[10] drill. Also, it can be taken off by opening and joggling the door.

For each of the above points there is more to be orally transmitted. However, if you learn only by mouth but do not try with your own hands, then the locks will not come off neatly.

Five points on how to find the position of *kakegane* hooked latches by touch

I

If a door is stuck fast to the vertical framework around the door then you should be aware that there must be a *wakakegane* ring latch[11] or a *tsurikakegane*[12] vertical lintel latch. If you try to open a door that is secured by a *wakakegane* ring latch, then normally it is stuck firmly and if you push or poke the latch, you can feel it 'joggling' [on the other side]. However, even if you push it hard, it will not come off.

II

Tsurikakegane or vertical lintel latches

If you try to open the door and it rattles then you need to understand deeper issues which are passed on by oral transmission. But if the door has a *tsurikakegane* vertical lintel latch, then the door will always have a second supporting [piece of wood] on the inside of the door's vertical frame.[13]

III

Joshi-kakegane or the locking latch

If it is this version of latch, the door will not have a second vertical support as described above and if you try to take the latch off or unhook it, it will not come out[14] and will hold fast.

---

9 *Musomado* is a form of window and could be what Fujibayashi is referencing here.

10 Refer to the image in volume twenty.

11 Instead of a swinging hooked latch that goes into a ring, as with the standard model, this appears to be a bar with a ring end that fits onto a fixed hook.

12 A latch that goes from lintel to door or a latch that goes from a window ledge to the window frame but not on either of the vertical sides of the opening. In essence, it is a vertical hooking lock that attaches at the top or bottom of a door.

13 Japanese doors have a solid edge all round, here it means there will be a second strong beam directly next to the edge of the door.

14 Most likely this is a wooden peg in the latch to secure it.

I V

The *senkakegane*[15] hooked latch on an *iaido* or single-track door[16]

If you try to open the door and it feels like it is connected and is pulling on the other doors with a margin of movement, then it is this lock.

V

Tsurikakegane **or lintel latches**

In this case, the door will stick at the top and have a vertical latch, and in most cases it will be a ring latch.

For each of the above points, there is more information to be orally transmitted. However, unless you try these things with your own hands, you will not be able to master the skills required. There are a number of types of latches and the drawings are not included here.

Eight points on how to unhook latches

I

For ring latches, if there is a gap between the vertical frame [and the door], use the spiked edge of a *toihazushi* probing tool to unhook the latch by lifting up the string[17] that is connected to the wooden peg which is locking it in place. If it does not have a string, use the reverse side of the *toihazushi* probe and dislodge it by hitting the peg from the bottom. If it does not come out by hitting it or if the peg is too short and does not have any of its length protruding, making hitting it of no use, then push and pull at it and cut it off with the blade[18] section of the tool and then take it out by lifting it, if you can. Within all of the above three skills, you should take out the peg and thrust forward to unlock ringed latches.

I I

If there is no gap between the vertical frame of the door and the wall, which has a ring latch attached – or even if there is a gap and you put the *toihazushi* probe into it – it is sometimes hard to get to the latch with the door closed. If it is an *iaido* or

---

15 A standard hooked latch.

16 A form of external door where all the sliding doors are on the same track.

17 The sen peg is a small peg that is jammed into the ring of the latch to fix it in place; the string is attached so that the peg is not lost during the daytime when the window is open, and simply hangs by the window during the day. Therefore, when the peg is in the string droops down in a loop and if a ninja pushes this upwards, the peg will spring out and the latch can then be opened.

18 This tool appears as an image in the tools chapter, it has a small blade attached near the handle.

oitate-do type of door, then you should use the *nobekagi* extendable key[19] from [the hole you make] at the top, bottom, left or the right of the door. Also, remember that the methodology for using the *nobekagi* extendable key is the same as with the *toihazushi* probe, but there are some additional oral secrets to be understood.

If it is an *ippon-do*, that is a single door on its own, use the *hamagari* collapsible saw with a nail at the end as in the drawing above [*figure 15*] and remove the wooden peg with the three spikes on the end of this tool. Do this

Figure 15.

by going through any gap between the wall, pillar or door. Then remove the nails [holding the latch in place] by force.

III

How to unhook lintel latches

To gain entrance, use a gap if you can find one, but if there is no gap because it is covered by an extra board on the framework, then you should use the *nobekagi* extendable key on single-tracked doors or on an *oitate-do* style door. Put a nail on one end of the *nobekagi* extendable key and then put another nail into the first [making a hook that you can grab with]. With this nail hook, strike the bottom of the *kakegane* latch from underneath so that it will come out. If it is a single door, then use the collapsible saw in any gap next to the wall to flip the hooked latch up and out. Also using a *tekagi* hook will be fine. If there is a supporting beam on the vertical line [of the door], then it is acceptable sometimes to remove it by chisel, according to the situation of course.

IV

Concerning hooks and eye latches on a sliding door or on vertical lifting shutters: try to force the door forward by joggling it and the hook may come out.

---

19 This is a thin iron rod used to hook latches.

V

Lintel latch

Using a collapsible saw, *toihazushi* probing tool or a hook, reach in through any opening in the wall above the door or by going through the *kamoi*, which is the open latticework above a door.

VI

Kusari-kakegane or latch chain on single-track doors

Whether there is a supporting frame or not, use a *nobekagi* extendable key. The method of its use is mentioned earlier.

VII

Joshi-kakegane or locked latch

If there is an earthen wall around the lock, use the *tekagi* hook. If there is a wooden board, then use the *otsubo-giri*, which is the larger round drill and then use the *tekagi* hook [to reach in]. Or there is another way, which is to burn through the board first.

VIII

Concerning hooks and eyes on paper or silk *shoji* sliding doors

Unhook the latch by breaking or cutting through the [paper or silk] of a *shoji* sliding door or by dividing [the hook and eye] by force. Or you can enter without unhooking the latch by dividing [the doors] by force.[20]

The above are the secrets on how to unhook latches and open doors. Further details are oral tradition. Do not take this information lightly. Again, if you are taught by mouth alone but do not try to discover with your own hands, you will not be able to achieve mastery in this art.

Two points on how to detect door bolts[21]

I

When you try to open a door softly and it is stuck at the bottom, you should be aware there must be a bolt in place. If there is a bolt, it will rattle at the bottom when you try to open it. Especially if there is a hole for a bolt to fit into, you should know this.

---

20 Fujibayashi appears to repeat himself; however, the first point could mean divide the latch from its eye and the second could mean divide the doors.

21 A *kuroro* is a simple bolt that is fixed to a door and bolts into a hole in the framework or floor, as with modern bolts. This stops the door from sliding open or, if it is on hinges, from swinging open. The name of the *kurorokage* tool comes from this and translates as 'latch key'.

II

Usually bolts are exactly halfway across any door. One in ten are at the leading edge of a sliding door or occasionally you may find one at the opposite end. Therefore, check where it rattles and is stuck, as that is where the bolt is situated. There are three types of holes for these bolts to fit in. The first one is in the groove of the threshold, the second is on the higher track just above the groove of the threshold, and the third is a hole which reaches below the threshold.

Three points on how to unlock bolts

I

To lift up a bolt, force a chisel between the threshold and the door and try to lift up the bolt shaft repeatedly. If you perform this action, up to ten times at most, most bolts will come out no matter how deep the hole is – even if it is the third type of hole described above. Remember to do this exactly where the bolt is and to know its position, be it halfway across, on the left or on the right. If you try to lift the bolt up at a different point from where the bolt actually is, then it will not come out. Generally a lock at the non-leading edge of a sliding door is hard to take out. A bolt on a door where the bolt fits into the upper groove of the door frame and a bolt that has a stopper on the door when it is in the locked position is hard to bypass. It is sometimes the case that a wooden length is placed in the upper groove of the door frame; this is done so that the door cannot be lifted upwards. This type is hard to open by the above method – that is, by lifting the bolt with a chisel little by little.

II

If a bolt is too hard to open with the above techniques, or if it would make too much noise to do so, use the collapsible saw. You should put the spiked edge of the tool into the keyhole 鑰穴, if any, and cut through the bolt which is attached to a vertical-lifting window shutter. If there is no keyhole, attach a nail or needle to the end and put it through the wall on either side of the bolt and push it in deep enough to hook the bolt. Then use the attached nail to lift up the bolt so that you can release it.

III

Most bolts are positioned exactly in the centre of the door and at an equal distance from both edges. If you test this in various ways and discover that the bolt is somewhere around the middle of the door, then you should take the measurement of the entire width of the door by using something long, such as a piece of straw or string, and fold it in two – this way, you can measure exactly where the centre is. The next step after finding this centre spot is to measure one *shaku* up from the bottom and then drill – at any point along that line – through the door with a spear drill and lift the bolt with force, utilizing the leverage of the drill; this is done so that the bolt will come out and the door will open. It goes without saying that you can use a *kotsubogiri* small round drill on the base part of the door so that the bolt will come off.

Further details are secret. You should learn all of the above by trying it for yourself and exercise your ingenuity.

Two points on how to know if there is a *sen* wooden peg in the latch

I

You should be aware that most push-up shutters or hinged doors have a wooden peg inserted into the latch. A door with a peg cannot be opened if you try to lift the latch up and and it will not feel loose if you try to move it forward. If you try to move it forward bit by bit, it will not make any sound at all, or if it does make some noise it will make a soft sound that only wood makes.

II

Some push-up shutters, hinged doors or even vertical lintel latches or locked ring latches have this peg. If you push a shutter that has a vertical lintel latch forwards you will notice that you will feel a slight margin of movement and if you push a hinged door then it will slightly bend. Those with ring latches will rattle when you gently push the door inwards. Although generally most of the above do not make much sound, those with ring latches make a *comparatively* loud noise, while those with vertical lintel latches are comparatively low in volume.

For each of the above there are oral traditions. Again you will not master or know the subtleties without practising it for yourself.

Two points on how to release a *sen*[22] wooden peg

I

To remove a wooden peg from a vertical push-up shutter or from a hinged door, if there is a gap along the vertical framework take out the peg with a short sword or knife, or with the spear drill and so on. If there is no gap, you should gently rattle the door little by little and it will sometimes come off.

---

22 The ideogram used is 鑿, which normally means 'drill' or 'spike'. However, at this point the text states 'sen' in phonetics next to the ideogram, meaning 'peg'.

II

If the above does not work, make three or four holes in a line on a door with a spear drill then pull the peg out by force with the drill. There is more oral transmission here. Also, you can use a large round drill to do the same thing.

Further details are to be orally transmitted for the above.

Six[23] points on how to identify *joshi* padlocks[24] [and their workings]

I

There are five types of padlock
   1. The *ebi joshi* or shrimp padlock
   2. The *mimitsuki joshi* or tower padlock
   3. The *hineri joshi* or twist-key padlock
   4. The *se joshi* or rear-sliding key padlock
   5. The *hikidashi joshi* or guided[25]-key padlock

There are also five ways to unlock them. Although there are various ways to open them through the keyhole, the tricks for opening the *hane* internal prongs are divided into five versions, according to whether there are one, two, four, six or eight prongs.[26] There are some small variations between them, but you should focus on learning these five basic ways and using them without mistakes and not get bogged down or become confused with extra information.

II

The shrimp padlock is normally built into the external parts [of the locking structure] and in this drawing below [*figure 16*] you can see that it has no tower section on the upper part. The prong will have a square nodal built onto the end [so that it can lock into the internals[27]].

This style of padlock is called the shrimp padlock and is used in most cases for larger padlocks (*figures overleaf*).

---

23 The original says sixteen.
24 See introduction.
25 To guide, tug, draw or pull.
26 Fujibayashi here is saying that padlocks are classified according to the number of internal prongs they have. These prongs need to be manipulated to open the padlock.
27 This point is highly ambiguous, and this sentence should be taken as a reconstruction.

Figure 17.
The keys that are needed for the left two keyholes can be seen in the two following images [figures 18. and 19.]

Figure 16.
If it is a four-pronged padlock then the main chamber of the lock is very thin and the keyhole will be like one of the images right [figures 17–19].

Figure 18.
[This is for the bottom keyhole.]

Figure 19.
[This is for the top keyhole.]

Figures 16–19

The internal prongs[28] [of this lock] are normally in sets of four,[29] but sometimes they can come in sets of six or eight. If it is a four-pronged padlock then the main chamber of the lock is very thin and the keyhole will be like one of the images left[30] [*figures 17–19*].[31]

In the case of a six-pronged version, the chamber is a little thicker than it was in the case of the four-pronged version and has the following keyhole [*figure 20*].

For such a padlock, there is an internal prong called a *haribane* or needle prong. The keyhole is a little different but the basic trick of opening is the same.

Figure 20.

Figure 21.

If the main body of the padlock is diamond shaped, the keyhole will be like this [*figure 21*].

It is rarely the case that this above keyhole is for a type of padlock that is small [and most will be large].

---

28 The text names these as 'feathers' or 'wings'. In reality these are thin metal prongs that are connected to the central shaft and form the main locking mechanism. As the two sections of the lock are closed together, these prongs try to spring outwards. As they approach the deepest part of the internal chamber of the lock they spring into small cutouts and thus become 'hooked'. This is how the lock works at a basic level. The key simply follows the same pathway as the prongs and forces them inwards, which unlocks the padlock.

29 These sets are the number of prongs that the lock has in its internal mechanism. If it is four pronged, then four individual prongs spring outwards and fall into four separate cutouts. The same goes for the other variations.

30 The point Fujibayashi is making here is that a ninja could tell the internal make-up of a lock by looking at the keyhole. The two images in question here are side views of a padlock, as some padlocks of the time had their keyholes on the side.

31 This key does not appear to have the correct profile for the lock. However, different versions of the Bansenshukai show this keyhole as thin and flat, a shape that matches the key. Therefore, it must be concluded that this is a transcription error in the drawing.

Also, shrimp padlocks for large gates can be built into the large wooden gate bar.[32] This will be a four-pronged version and the prongs will be square in shape. The shrimp padlock on this defensive beam [and its key] look like figure 22.

I I I

Tower padlocks[33] have two 'tower' fittings built onto the top of the main body of the lock. This type of padlock can also be four, six or eight-pronged. In the case of a four-pronged version,[34] it should be opened like this [and also here are examples of the keyholes; [*figures 23–24*].

In the case of a six-pronged version, the keyhole will look like the following image [*figure 25*].

In the case of an eight-pronged version it is thus [*figure 26*].

If the lock is thin, flat and square [or rectangular], then it is the same as the above mentioned for the *ebi joshi* or shrimp padlock.

---

32 This is the large wooden bar that slides across medieval gates to bar them shut. The 'shrimp-like' arm of the lock closes over secured fittings and the bar is locked in place. This form of lock can still be seen on some castle gates.

33 Literally 'ear padlock'; however, in English it is more appropriate to name these 'tower' after the tower-like fixtures. As can be seen in Fujibayashi's illustration, there are towers at the top of the lock so that the locking bar can slide through and into place.

34 This first image (figure 23) is a relatively poor illustration of the inner workings; however, it serves to display the prongs, which are mentioned frequently in this chapter. The arrow shape on the right represents these prongs, and when inserted the prongs try to force themselves outwards, which results in them catching and creating the lock.

Figure 22.   Figure 23.

Figure 24.   Figure 25.   Figure 26.

IV

Twist-key padlocks have a keyhole on the flat side of the main lock. No matter how many variations of this padlock there are, it always has only two prongs in the internal mechanism. The twist-key padlocks for letterboxes and ink-stone boxes are the same internally and should be opened in a twisting fashion [*figure 27*].[35]

V

The *se joshi* or the rear-sliding key padlock has a long keyhole on the rear[36] of the main body [and the key slides over the prongs to open the lock]. It can be four or eight pronged, but the way to open it is the always the same [*figure 28*].[37]

VI

The guided-key padlock always has a one-pronged key. The keyhole is small and round and always found on the opposite end to all the other locks [*figure 29*].[38]

The above information on internal lock mechanisms is based on observing the external casing and the keyhole of the padlock. Although there are other variations for the internal prongs and workings, there are not many variables outside of the above five principles, no matter how many padlocks there are. Always observe the keyhole carefully; this is so you will know the internal workings. Even if a padlock looks like it has a completely unfamiliar form you will still know the workings of the inside of the lock.

Eight points on how to open various padlocks

I

To open the shrimp padlock use [the skill of] *ichibyoshi* 'single rhythm' or it can also be done with a toothpick. There are oral secrets for how the lock internals are made and their typology.

---

35 The lock looks similar to a Western lock: however, it uses exactly the same internal prong-and-catch system as the rest. The only difference here is that the key is angled and requires a twist motion to open the lock instead of the standard side-entry method.

36 Possibly underneath.

37 The point here is that the lock, even though the keyhole is on the back of the main body, still opens out in the same motion, as illustrated in the drawing (figure 28).

38 Japanese keys enter from the same side that the prongs enter, so the key can move the prongs together; in the case of the guided-key padlock, the key enters from the opposite side.

Figure 27.

Figure 28.

Figure 29.

Although a shrimp padlock on a gate can usually be opened with the above techniques,[39] if you cannot unlock it you can open it with a toothpick or sliver of wood or bamboo.

II

Tsukibiraki joshi or the thrust-and-open padlocks – including the shrimp lock – are opened with the skill of *watagaminuki*[40] or the 'pulling out'[41] motion. According to how large the padlock is or how strong the prongs are, you should vary the strength with which you probe the lock.

III

Thrust-and-open forms of padlock, in most cases, should be opened with a *kikominuki*, which is a long wooden shim. Knowledge on the methodology is required.

IV

[You can also] open a thrust-and-open lock by making a key on the spot – that is prepare 'pig' iron or tin [text missing] to form a temporary key.[42]

V

Twist padlocks should be opened by prising off a *kikuza* chrysanthemum-shaped metal nail cover[43] [and then removing the nail from the wood]. Then use the nail to pick the lock.[44]

VI

For a rear-sliding or shrimp padlock, nip off the neck of the *kagiire*[45] with a

---

39 To do this the shinobi must be on the inner side of the gate, meaning he has already got into the enemy house or castle and does not need to open the lock for himself. Therefore, he must be doing this for others to follow.

40 *Watagami* is the shoulder parts of armour connected to the breastplate with straps, or it can also mean the hair on the back of your head.

41 This appears to be a skill where, once pressure is applied to the internal prongs, a *ninja* would need to apply a motion to the locking bar (the sliding bar) in order to coax the internal mechanism out of the external chamber.

42 The concept here is that once you have identified the internal workings from observing the keyhole, you can prepare a makeshift key to fit the pattern.

43 This is a form of washer shaped into a flower that is fixed to the door and acts as a nail-head cover.

44 It appears that Fujibayashi is saying this lock and these covers are often found together, thus you can easily find a temporary lock pick.

45 Literally, 'key enter'; however, keyhole is often written as *kagiana* in this manual.

pair of pliers and then take it off by force with a chisel and open the lock with bamboo.

VII

Generally, locks with internals of six prongs[46] have variations or multiple types of keyholes. Such keyholes should be opened by force with a chisel,[47] pliers and so on; then use the art of *watagaminuki*, which is 'drawing out', or use wooden shims to open the prongs [and the lock].

VIII

If the lock mechanisms are wide and the internal prongs of the padlock will not retract from their locking positions within the casing and are stuck, then put a chisel into the gap of the handhold of the padlock and push it forwards. Doing this with a pair of pliers will suffice.

Further details are secret. You should not take all of the above too lightly. You should practise these skills by yourself after being taught by mouth so you will be able to do it with a smooth mind.

Two secret points on how to open various padlocks

I

Use an iron toothpick to open a rear-sliding, twist or thrust-and-open padlock when speed is needed. There are more oral traditions to be passed on here.

Supplementary to the above: the pick should be very thin for a twist padlock that is found securing a *kakesuzuri bunko*, which is a box for storing writing materials.

II

Generally, the key used to open a thrust-and-open or twist padlock has a single channel if the internal mechanism is two-pronged and has a double channel[48] if the internal mechanism is four-pronged.

There are more details to be orally transmitted for each of the above points and these together are the deepest essence for opening padlocks. With those tools mentioned above, there is no padlock that you cannot open. However, this all depends on how skilled you are, therefore you should always get hands-on practice.

---

46 This uses a different term and may not be prong.
47 This is to widen the hole in order to access the internal system.
48 Each 'U'-shaped channel pushes together two prongs.

In-nin V

Hidden Infiltration V

Shinobi night attacks

The night raid is a military tactic to defeat a large number with an inferior force. This is especially true of a *shinobi* night raid,[1] which can dramatically defeat a large army with the smallest of numbers. In the period of Iga [that is when it was self-governing] they used to specialize in this form of warfare. The arrangements for this form of warfare such as organization and the allotting of duty assignments are similar to those for a daytime battle. Therefore, those who want to learn the way of night attacks should first learn, in full, how to organize, divide or allot jobs to their men.

Two points on *monomi* scouting

I

Before you depart for a night attack, you should send *shinobi* to closely investigate the enemy situation and then construct your plans based on this information. Sometimes they should stay there within a castle or camp and communicate the situation back to your side with various signals, which should be arranged beforehand. The details for signal fires are to be orally transmitted.

---

1   It is important to note that there is a difference between a standard night raid and one executed by *shinobi* or in a *shinobi* fashion. A *shinobi* raid appears to be a more clandestine attack with specific tactics that are not fully explained in the text. It is important for the reader to understand which version Fujibayashi is referring to at a given point, as he switches between the two.

II

It is essential to send *shinobi* to investigate the topography of the area, how densely populated[2] the enemy army is or the status of its camp, and to share this information and give instructions accordingly. Oral traditions follow.

A *ninja* poem says:

夜討ニハ忍物見ヲ先立テ　敵ノ案内知テ下知セヨ

For success on a night attack, send shinobi *in advance to know the details of the enemy's position before you give your orders.*

Four points on the outfit to be worn on night raids

I

Do not wear a white *kosode* jacket,[3] the reason why is to be orally transmitted. On secret attacks wear a black *futae*, which is a double-layered black top.

II

Do not carry a *sashimono* warrior's banner and wear no armour but only a set of *kikomi*, which is a sleeved chain-mail shirt.

III

Kasajirushi **helmet marks**
Put a strip of white silk of the length of one *shaku* and two *sun* on the back of your helmet. However, it should be changed each time.

IV

If you have to travel a long distance and need to go by horseback, perform *wariguchi*[4] and tie the bit. Supplementary to this: avoid cream-tinted, dapple-grey, plain[5] grey or cremello horses. Details are orally transmitted.

---

2 This concerns not the number but how densely packed the army is into a given area.
3 A jacket with thinner sleeves as opposed to a broad-sleeved kimono.
4 This is the action of tying the mouth so that no sounds are made by the horse.
5 Ashige.

Seven points on the instructions to be given during a night attack

I

Passwords

Take up such passwords so that even lower people can easily remember them and teach them. For example, moon, sun, star, water, wave, door, *shoji* sliding door, etc.

Supplementary to this: sometimes, a set of signs such as pinching the nose or holding the ear should be used with these passwords.

II

Passwords should be changed at the beginning of a raid and when change is required. Remember to check that your men can say them correctly.

III

You should tell your men that if they kill an enemy they should not cut off and claim the head but just leave the body as it was when they killed him. Supplementary to this: carry a small wood tag with your name and leave it where you have been. This is the same concept as when you put identifying marks on arrows.

IV

You should tell your men that when your team withdraws they should bring back any [enemy] weapons that have fallen on the field.

V

You should tell your men that, even if they are in sword combat with the enemy, they must strictly withdraw at the first opportunity upon hearing the signal and that they should retreat. More oral traditions.

A martial poem says:

夜討ヲハシタルク討ヌ物ソカシ一村雨ノ降コトクナリ

Night attacks should not be performed sluggishly. They should be done as quickly as a murasame *passing rain shower.*

VI

For a *shinobi* night attack, you should not carry a pike, but any weapon you can use with skill. If you do carry a pike, you should fight by sweeping horizontally and hit the enemy, then withdraw it and stab in a straight line.

A martial poem says:

夜討ニハ長柄ノ鎗ヲ嫌フ之太刀長刀ニ弓ヲ用ヒヨ

For night attacks, pikes should not be used. Use tachi *and long swords and bows and arrows.*

VII

On a *shinobi* night attack, do not make the war cry of '*Ei! Ei!*'[6] There are more traditions here.

From Noma's martial poems:

忍取ノ城モ夜討モウチトキヲ早クアクルハ越度ナリケリ

When capturing a castle by shinobi-*stealth and conducting a night attack, it is a mistake to raise a shout of victory too early.*

Four points on the tactics to be used before a night attack

I

Build a fortification on a border, have faithful soldiers under a good formation commander (*samurai-daisho*) and when the enemy commences an attack, conduct a counter night attack upon them.

II

The following is not an established way – after pretending to withdraw you should conduct a night attack. Also, *koya kamari* or ambushes from a hut are meant for the same purpose as above. Also, there is another way, which is the art of setting fire to a building and retreating.

One of Kato's martial poems says:

敵ヘヨラバ昼ハ色々逃敗リ暮ニ掛りテ一シマイセヨ

If you advance on the enemy, you should repeat withdrawing and beating in various ways during the daytime and finish off when darkness falls.

---

6 This is pronounced 'A-E' but with a long 'E' as though they were single letters said together.

III

During the day before you intend to conduct a night attack, you should keep those troops for the night assault in the rear or even in the reserve troops so that they will not have had to work hard all through the day.

IV

Deceptive night attacks

While securing the guard for your own castle or camp and laying *fushika-mari* ambush troops at several appropriate points, you should conduct night attacks with a small number and withdraw lightly, expecting that the enemy will follow you and infiltrate your troops. If they do take the bait, you should then lure them to a *nansho* or difficult section of terrain or to a *sessho*, which is a dangerous place, and defeat them by enveloping them on all sides. This is not a regular method, so if you have only smattering knowledge, your men will be in confusion when withdrawing. Sometimes you will conduct night attacks against the enemy vanguard as many as three times a night; if so, you should use fresh troops each time.

Four points on the appropriate time for a night attack

I

Concerning the night that you infiltrate your *shinobi* within the enemy side

This is called the *kaeshiuchi* or turn-back attack. The *shinobi* should use the *ireko-hi* adjustable lantern or the *hikyaku* beacon fires. In the case of a castle raid, you should have the team carry lots of tools, such as cloud ladders, spider ladders, floating bridges, etc.

This way [your normal forces] can approach the target by unexpectedly covering double the usual distance by pushing them so that they can attack when the enemy least expects or is least prepared.

The art of *hikyaku-bi* signal bacons is to put one or two lanterns or torches on the tops of high mountains on the route to the enemy castle. The infiltrator who gets into the enemy castle will then send a message with the *ireko-hi* signal tool to the nearest mountain-top beacon, then [the operator of] that beacon relays the signal by raising his torch to the next beacon on the next mountain top. In this way a message can be conveyed ten *ri* or even twenty *ri* in a very short time – thus it is called *hikyaku-bi* or express messenger fire. More oral traditions.

II

You should attack on a night of heavy wind and rain. Oral tradition. Also, attack on a very quiet night, when the enemy least expects it.

III

Attack on the first to the third day after your first sighting of each other.

IV

You should attack a massive enemy army when it is worn out and tired, such as when it has travelled across a dangerous place or has been in a battle camp for a prolonged period.

Eighteen points on the ways of *shinobi* night attacks

I

Whether the target is a castle or a military camp, put *shinobi* inside before you commence a night attack. If you cannot get *shinobi* in beforehand, send and position *shinobi* in an area of difficult and naturally fortified terrain and then attack in a large number from easier terrain [this will give the *shinobi* the gap he needs].

II

Attack heavily, retreat smoothly.

III

You should use reserve troops.

IV

Use *iccho-ikka*, which are 'one *cho*, one fire' relay signals. Reserve troops, lanterns and torches.[7]

V

The way of musket shooting.

VI

How and when to make your war cries and raise them in accord.

VII

The art of *shinobi* horses.[8]

---

7 These three items are given without explanation.

8 This is a reference to the preparation needed to make ready a horse for scouting. This involves dampening the sound of the horse's footsteps and neighing and also understanding how to bit the horse correctly and when to uncover the horse's eyes.

VIII

The formation of one troop to the front and the second troop to the rear of the enemy. Supplementary to the above: use the *mawashi-zonae* or the formation of surrounding the enemy.

IX

To use a large number of fire drums.[9]

X

The use of 'fire hair'[10] in accordance with the situation.

XI

Arrange for a meeting place where your men can gather after defeating the enemy.

XII

When withdrawing, use the *okunomori* housekeeper.[11]

XIII

There are various ways[12] to detect the enemy agents who infiltrate your force after a withdrawal.

XIV

Use the method of successive attacks. Supplementary to this: leave one man from the first raid in the enemy camp to set fires [within the enemy during your next raid].

XV

A night attack is to be followed by an early morning attack.

XVI

You should understand the formations of men and troops. Supplementary to this: know how to have them shoot muskets or how to plan a raid.

---

9 An unknown skill or tool; however, it implies a fire tool that is drum shaped or other variations on the connotations of the drum as a form.

10 An unknown skill or tool.

11 Unknown skill, with an alternative name of *yamori*, which can also mean a form of amphibian.

12 Examples are markers, password and movement combinations, a secret command to duck down on a given word, the use of certain coloured undergarments etc.

XVII

Remember to have as many men as possible to throw hand grenades and fire weapons.

XVIII

When a small number is defending a large castle, mount a stealth raid from the direction of a naturally fortified area. Take tied ladders, *tsuribashigo* hooked ladders, spider ladders, etc.

Further details for each of the above should be orally transmitted.

These points above are outlines of how to conduct *shinobi* night attacks. There are a few differences between attacking a castle and a camp that you should keep in mind. Therefore, there are deep secrets to be orally transmitted.

Night attacks, if done with proper measures – even if they are known to the enemy – will result in benefits for your side. You should always make tight arrangements among yourselves for the methods, the assemblage and the ending, with extra caution at the moment before you attack. You should not let any other *samurai* know the arrangements for night attacks no matter how close he is, unless you are fully sure of his determination and single-mindedness; this way the attack will be totally unexpected.

Twelve points on the *gando* burglar raid

I

Send *meakashi* scouts beforehand to observe the enemy ground, houses, roads or anything else needed and have tight arrangements among you for extra security.

II

Think deeply of the direction [of advance], taking note of the following four points: stars, mountains, wind and fire. Also have an estimation of the times of the rising and setting of the moon.

Supplementary to this: *shakuhachi*[13] flutes and such should be used at times; more oral traditions.

III

At the time of the attack, send *meakashi* scouts, dog-scouts[14] etc., to see how many people there are in the enemy and if they are asleep or not. *Meakashi* scouts should carry an *ireko-hi* adjustable lantern or *gando chochin* lantern or

---

13 Possibly for signalling.
14 The text literally says 'dogs'. However, this is a term held over from Chinese warfare and refers to a clandestine infiltrator.

similar to look inside enemy places. If they do not have one and have to look inside with a normal torch, then they will be illuminated due to the torch light that it emanates. Details and drawings for the *ireko-hi* adjustable lantern and *gando chochin* lantern are given in a later chapter.

IV

For each door at the rear of the target building, place a hidden attacker, or fix a drill and seal the doors, or stretch a rope across the doorway or scatter caltrops outside.

Supplementary to the above: hidden attackers, when waiting for the enemy to come out, should not stay too close to the door but be at a distance of four or five *shaku* from them. If they get too close to the door, they might miss their chance to strike the target.

V

Of 'big dogs', 'small dogs'[15] and how to open the doors

VI

Koshi fire performers
Light your *torinoko* [straw] 'fire eggs' with a *donohi* fire lighter, at a distance of one or two *cho* from the target area. When you are in front of the door, place twelve torches under your arms in a bundle and with the ends together, light them with the *torinoko* 'fire eggs' and blow upon them so that they will ignite.

VII

Hizoe fire assistants
[The fire assistant] should stand on the right side of the fire performer and throw six of the torches from under the performer's right arm while the performer himself throws the six under his left arm.[16]

Although the above is the way passed down from ancient times, in our school of this modern day, torches with powder should be used and two or three forward members should rush into the building with these torches tied onto their spears.

---

15 As discussed in the footnote above, this is an infiltration agent. However, here the prefixes 'big' and 'small' are given, the precise meanings of which in this context are unknown.

16 Presumably this is done consecutively, with the assistant throwing his six torches first, then the fire performer throwing his own six immediately after.

VIII

Dozei **or the main combatants**
Lightweight spears, bows, swords and so on are appropriate to be carried. Do not carry a long spear because if there must be close fighting in a building they will not be suitable.

IX

Hari **watchmen**
They watch for the enemy coming from outside and inform those inside of any change in situation, or they defend against the enemy from the outside. Therefore, they should be placed at the mouth of every route. In *shinobi* attacks you should also have them. Although you should choose courageous and cool-minded people for every job, it is particularly important that your watchmen be calm and patient people. If you choose the wrong person as a watchman, it will have devastating effects. If you chose the wrong person, the following will happen:

- If you have sneaked into a place and yet do not come out very soon, he will not wait for you and will wander from his post.
- If you need to flee from the inside [of a compound] in haste, he may panic and fight against you mistakenly.
- If you are pushed back and have to withdraw, he will run away as fast as he can without paying heed to either enemy or allies.
- If people come from the outside, he will not inform those inside or defend against them [but instead will flee].
- If you have such a man as a watchman, it will be extremely damaging to your raid. Therefore, watchmen should be selected very carefully indeed.

Question: Now it is understood that watchmen should be selected with special care, can we use those who are restless and impatient for other jobs instead?

Answer: It goes without saying that proper selection is the same for *meakashi* scouts, *oinu* 'big dogs' and *koinu* 'small dogs', fire performers, fire assistants and other such jobs, but only watchmen are mentioned specially, because as watchmen stay outside, people of this world think that it is an easy job and do not select people carefully but use even cowards, without due care and attention, which often ends in a catastrophe. Therefore, I have given emphasis on watchmen here.

X

Depending how large the enemy number is, you should use ambushes.

XI

Make arrangements beforehand for a meeting point in the event that you become scattered. Supplementary to the above: use signals such as *ireko-ju* signals, arrows, fire arrows, etc.

XII

Scatter caltrops and put *hyakurai-ju* fire-cracker diversions in place.

There are more oral traditions for each of the above.

Twenty points on capturing people

Although capturing people is not a primary job of *shinobi*, every *ashigaru shinobi* 足軽忍 is engaged in this task these days. Those who have studied in our school should not serve for this task. If you are employed only for this job, know that it is totally outside the traditions of our school.[17] However, it may be appropriate for you to capture people on occasion when needed, even though you are not fully retained for this task alone. For this reason alone I write about this subject here. However, as it is not the main path, you should not consider or pursue the details too much. People of future generations should be made fully aware of this point.

I

Six things you should know beforehand

You should consider these six points: social standing, the number of people to capture, the relationships between the group, the place they are situated, the gravity of the crime and the weapons that they carry.

1. Different skills should be used for *samurai* from those skills used on lower people. *Samurai*, when time passes by, usually increase in strength and resolve, therefore it is best to make your move to defeat them as soon as possible. The reasoning behind this is the same as attacking a castle quickly while the enemy is not fully prepared. In contrast, the energy of lower people will dwindle and dwindle as time passes by, as normally they only have blind daring at the start. Therefore, take your time constructing your plan to capture them.

2. The number of people [to capture] will determine your preparation. If

---

17 Interestingly, Fujibayashi does not name his school; he simply says *toryu* or 'our school'.

only one or two people are holed up somewhere, you should storm in there to kill or capture them; however, it does depend on who is present within. If they are more than two in number, you should have a plan to bring a person who has caused medium or lesser offence on to your side [and have them betray their comrades]. If the plan does not work, have the same mindset as attacking a castle.

3. If those holed up are a number of people, the skills to be used should be varied according to whether they are from the same family or not. If they are, you should make a plan assuming they are in accord. If they have no blood relations between them, you should make a plan to divide them or get them to betray each other. This is almost the same skill as for those who have committed medium or lesser offences.

4. The skills to be used should be changed according to exactly where they are, such as if they are on the ground floor or the first floor,[18] what fortifications they have built, etc. If they are on the first floor, then you should select the tactic of 'one team from the front, the other team from the rear', and should use a ladder to ascend to the first floor. However, if a large number is contained within, you should follow the same principles as when attacking a castle. Also, putting a pan on the head may be useful at times.[19]

5. Your tactics should vary according to the gravity of the offences [of those to be captured]. Even if there are a number of them, you should consider closely what kind of crime each one is blamed for. Persuade those who have committed lesser offences that some circumstances may be taken into consideration. For those who have committed major offences, you should not tell them their life may be saved or anything like that but that they should die properly as *samurai* should. If there is a mixture of major and minor offenders, the same tactics should be adopted as for a group of people not from the same family who have no blood ties.

6. According to what weapons they have, you should be prepared with different things. If they are armed with projectile weapons, you should protect yourself with a shield or bundled bamboo, or even a *koromo* cloth shield. Also making a shield of *tatami* floor mats will do.

The above six points should be considered when you decide what skills to use.

---

18 In the British tradition of ground floor, first floor, second floor, etc.

19 It has to be remembered that this was the Edo period and they were probably without armour; therefore, some form of head protection was needed.

As well as this, you should have different plans and skills according to the situation presented to you.

II

Put someone who has committed murder into the enemy group[20]

III

Build emotional rapport within them and capture them.

The above two are measures to be taken when you know what the members of the enemy group are accused of, but they do not know that you know this. However, there are more secrets to be known in the case when they are not acquaintances.

IV

If the criminal runs into a temple or a *samurai* house and the chief priest or the house master will not turn him over to you, you should tell them that the target is insane. Also, the above holds true even for the case where you are chasing a criminal who has broken free and is on the run.

V

When you are chasing a criminal whom you have failed to catch, do not follow him directly on the same route but take another one. If you carry a sword, take a left route while if a spear, take a route to his right.[21]

A passage by Yamamoto Kansuke says:

There are two things to be considered when chasing someone:

When attacking a fleeing enemy, there is the principle of ukiashi *or 'floating steps' and be sure to sweep and attack him at a low level.*[22] *Sometimes, you may miss the strike if you are too close. If he fights back, you should act defensively and force him to lose his vigour.*

You should be aware of when to advance and when to retreat. This is an oral tradition.

---

20 While ambiguous, it is possible that the idea here is that you plant someone within the group with the promise of letting him free from his sentence.

21 If you approach from the left with a sword, then your right hand will be in line with the opponent's body, making it easier to cut him. If you approach from the right with a spear, then the spearhead will naturally aim at the enemy's back as you come upon him.

22 Gedan. This term is ambiguous: it could mean 'take his legs from beneath him'; however, this is not a certainty.

VI

If a criminal target is being followed by another group or person and if that target rushes out in front of you, the pursuer may ask you to let them kill the target [and to not get involved]. By using *on-yu no jutsu*,[23] a very skilled man will not kill him nor will he fail to catch the target and will also then let the pursuer kill him instead. However, if the target attacks you with force and you have to kill him, you should seek out the pursuing agent [to confirm your story].

VII

In the case that there are those who have committed a major crime cornered in a building, if you try to use a stratagem by telling them there is a way to save their life, they will not be persuaded and will realize it is only a stratagem, which will make the situation even worse. Therefore, you should go unarmed (there is a deeper secret within this) and tell them the following:

As you have committed such a grave crime, one that means there is no way of escape, I am here upon our lord's order. If you follow what I say and give your katana *sword and* wakizashi *short sword to me, I will take you to a temple and let you commit* seppuku *ritual suicide there. If you do not follow what I say and then kill us in this conflict, then you will have committed a grave offence as we are innocent and even if you are killed after that, it will remain a totally injudicious incident. It will not only be to your dishonour in this life but will also do you harm in the afterlife and even though it may benefit your aim at present, eventually the walls around you will be torn down, bamboo and wood will be thrown at you and you will be captured with* tsukubo, sasumata *and* kotoji *criminal catching rakes etc. If this happens you will be beaten to death or bound with rope and beheaded, which is the death of lower people and villains. If you act like this, it is obvious that you will have to be disgraced in this life and will flounder in the six lower worlds.*[24] *Therefore, it is time for you to make up your mind: whether to reject our suggestion, stick to your pride and die a death of lower people and villains, thereby suffering a stigma that will last forever; or whether to accept our suggestion and die the death of a* samurai *and obtain honour in this world. Again, rather than dying as a lower person or a villain, you had better die in the way that should be. If you do not follow our words and injure or kill us, you will still die a foolish death. Thus, there is no reason for you to injure or kill us, those who you have no grudge against.*

You should persuade them with logic as much as possible, thinking about how they feel, then take them to a temple and let them kill themselves by ritual

---

23 An unknown skill, literally 'hide and play' 隠遊 also, in-yu no jutsu.

24 Rikudo, the six lower worlds, one of which each human being must go to after death according to his or her deeds in this world.

disembowelment. If you swear that you are telling the truth and urge them to respect justice, it might be probable that eight or nine times out of ten they will give you their weapons. To do this, there are important things you should keep in mind that are to be transmitted.

The above technique should be used for people who are holed up, who are in a close relationship with each other, such as parents and children, brothers etc., no matter how many people they are, and also, this skill is for those people who do not have a very strong agenda. In these cases, you should use reason to get the enemy to surrender.

VIII

If a number of people who are not in close relationship are holed up, you should consider how grave the crime for each one is and go unarmed and call one of a lesser offence. You should fix an agreement and confirm that the both of you should work together to kill both from the inside and the outside of the situation, then you should capture him at the end. Details are oral traditions.

IX

In the case that a person (or people) of a lesser offence are holed up, or if the gravity of their offence is not known or is unclear to anyone but your master, you should speak earnestly to them and state that they had reason for their actions and tell them to come out by convincing them. However, this is all deception and you should seize them in the end.

X

To capture those who are holed up, you should tie a torch onto the ring of your *kagiyari* or hooked spear and move forwards, observing with care. The torch to be used should be made of cherry-tree bark that has been soaked in oil, completely dried and bound with a circumference of four *sun* and a length of two *shaku*. Also, if you do not know exactly where the enemy is, you should sometimes throw in *kuma-bi* bear fire. The recipe for *kuma-bi* is in the chapter on fire tools.[25]

It is written that to capture those who are holed up late at night, you should scatter *tama-bi* ball fires within the enemy; this seems to me very appropriate. The recipe for *tama-bi* ball fires is in the volume on fire tools. Also, *gando chochin* lanterns are used at these times.

---

25 The recipe is missing.

XI

If fire is not available, use the art of *zasagashi* or probing with the sword and sword cord – this is oral tradition.

It is also written that in night combat, you should take *jodan no kamae*,[26] with *both* of your swords and have the two scabbards on both sides of your waist held vertically, this is to protect you from being cut horizontality by the enemy.

XII

Entering through a door

There is a technique to be used when those who are holed up might wait for you at either side of the door, or when you do not know if they are there or not. More oral traditions are to be found here.

Some writings say that there are three principles for entering through a door:

If the enemy has no room on his left, then he should have his sword above his head, while if the blockage is on his right side, then he should take a *chu dan* or the middle guard with the intent to thrust at you. If he is straight ahead and maybe has a barrier in front of him, remember that estimating the distance is essential.

The above is how to predict the enemy's movements in advance.

XIII

If you cannot capture the enemy with a stratagem, then you should use the following skill of mounting a surprise attack from the front and secretly attacking from the rear or attacking from the left and entering from the right. Trying to enter from the rear will work well in most cases. Generally, avoid getting in from where a lot of people are gathering.

XIV[27]

Shirahadori or ensnaring the opponent's sword.[28] Use the art of *murasame* or 'sudden shower'.

XV

Use *ganseki-kuzushi* or the 'cracking rocks'.[29]

---

26 A guard where the sword is held above the head.

27 The following appear to be skills or tools for attack and defence in this situation.

28 This is most likely a tool or skill but not the popular bare-handed sword-catching technique. It is highly unlikely that an armed man would give up his weapons to choose an unarmed defence against a sword.

29 Possibly a skill and most likely the art of dividing the group. Alternatively, it could be a form of hard attack or a tool for hard attacking.

XVI

Use the *tora-zume* or the 'tiger claw'.[30]

XVII

Use the *torimono-dama* or 'capture ball/bullet'.

XVIII

The art of *zetsunyu-san* or 'noxious gas'. Infuse the room with this powder by shooting it from a musket.

The recipe:

- Blister beetles [*Meloidae cantharidin*] – five *momme*
- Arsenic – three *momme*

Alternatively:

- Bury a *mamushi* venomous pit viper in the ground and cover with horse droppings. When mushrooms grow there, take them and make powder of the mushrooms; this is said to have the same effect.

The *haibukuro kiri tan*[31] or noxious ash in a paper 'bomb', can be used and more secrets are to be orally transmitted. It is written that you should keep this powder in a paper handkerchief and disperse it over the enemy. I say if you sprinkle this powder, it can turn out badly as it may also spread toward yourself; therefore, using a musket is the best method.

XIX

Use the art of *hayanawa* or quick-rope criminal binding.

There are oral traditions for each of the above points.

For close combat or sword fighting, there is no way to describe how to do such things at length here. Therefore, just be sure to always train yourself with *kenjutsu* swordsmanship, *iai*[32] sword-drawing and so on. Tactics always depend on the time and place, thus guidelines are mentioned here for your reference.

---

30 Probably a form of clawed catching weapon, possibly hafted on a shaft. It is highly unlikely that it is the common unarmed combat strike, where the hand takes the form of a tiger's claw, as it is improbable that an armed man would favour unarmed combat. Further, it may be close to the *teko-kagi*, or over-hand claw, which is a tool strapped to the back of the hand. The idea would be to grip the enemy in some way.

31 It appears to be the ash of a spindle tree or *Euonymus sieboldianus*.

32 Note that this does not include the Do character used in *Iaido*, the way of sword-drawing.

XX

The *torimono somakuri* tool – a deep secret for oral transmission only. With this tool, even a single person will not fail to capture any criminals holed up, no matter if they are a large number or not. This art of capturing is truly a deep secret. As the art is of great value, do not pass it down to any more than one person.

Tenji I

Opportunities Bestowed by Heaven I

Tonko – auspicious ways

Including:

- A general survey on how to choose a date or a direction
- The Five Precepts and the times of the day
- Knowing a lucky day or direction by the generating and destructive cycles of the Five Elements[1]

You should not use with total faith the way of choosing a date, time or direction nor should you ignore it in its entirety. The reason you should *not* rely on the art too much is because the date or time is universal to all, thus if a date is lucky for your forces it is also lucky to the enemy as well. The *Hikekyo*[2] *Sutra* says 'there are no lucky or unlucky days in Buddhism' and also, the *Nehankyo* or *Nirvana Sutra* says that 'in the teachings of Nyorai,[3] there is also no way of choosing a lucky day.' Furthermore, in addition to this, you should *not* rely on how to choose a lucky direction because Mencius says the following:

Here is a city, with an inner wall of three ri *in circumference, and an outer wall of seven* ri. *The enemy surround and attack the city, but they are not able to take it.*

---

1 In Chinese thought, the Five Elements interact in both a positive and negative way and they have specific connections with certain times and dates.
2 Presumably, the *Karunapundarika Sutra*.
3 The teachings of Buddha – in Sanskrit, Tathagata.

Now, to surround and attack it, there must have been bestowed to them by heaven the opportunity of time, and in such case their inability to take the castle was because the opportunities of time given by heaven were not equal to the advantages of the situation afforded to them by the earth.

If one thinks of how to play *Go*, you will notice that those who are good win even if they go in an unlucky direction, while those who are poor players lose even when going in a lucky one. However, that said, you cannot say that this art is totally useless because the art of war is the way of deception. If you ignore and take no heed of the teachings of this chapter, that is of luck or bad luck concerning a date, time or direction, then there will be no way to make those who are cowards advance with courage, nor will you be able to manipulate those who are stupid and sceptical.[4]

Confucius says:

The people should be made to follow a path of action, but they should not be made to understand it.

Concerning the above, on such an occasion it is of vital importance for you to focus on dealing with earthly matters in a correct way.

Wei Liao Zi says:

Punishment was employed to attack the rebellious and virtue was employed to stabilize peace. This is not what is referred to as 'Heavenly Positions', auspicious times, yin *and* yang *and the appearance of comets. [It must be remembered that] the Yellow Emperor's victories were a matter of the effort of man, and that is all they were.*

In the matters of man, you should handle them as best as is possible after giving thorough thought to the nature of the issues at hand and exercise your power according to the time and place and what is needed. If you excel in handling 'the matters of men' then it can be said that you are correct in your principles and correct principle is the way of heaven. Xing-li-da-quan says that heaven is a principle and also that human is a principle. Therefore, following principle and devoting yourself to heaven is regarded as unity, and you will be in a place where the self is not the self but is in fact a principle. Also, principle is not just a principle but is in fact a way of heaven. Thus, if you obey principle, you will

---

4   It is important to keep this section in mind when reading the rest of the volume. All the information within this section and its use in the context of *ninjutsu* is designed to deceive others or foresee what an enemy will do and is not considered directly or wholly a *ninja* subject.

be protected by the spirits and deities,[5] even if you do not choose a lucky day, direction and so on, and you will live long and in peace. Tai Gong said that what happens in the lower world and the laws of heaven change accordingly; so if you do correct actions it will be a lucky day, while if you do incorrect actions it will be an unlucky day. Also, if you do the correct thing it can be said that it will be a lucky direction, while if a wrong thing it will be an unlucky direction. These words tell all. Thus do not rely on fortune-telling but work to test these things yourself.

In ancient China, Tai Zong of the Tang Dynasty said:
Divination to determine a lucky date, time or direction is nothing you should employ. Why should we not do away with this?

Li Jing said this in reply:
This should not be thrown away because the art of war is a path of deception, so by divining for a date, time or direction you will be able to use the coward and the stupid. These kinds of people are not confident when identifying a lucky date or direction, so you should tell them that if you attack immediately, you will be able to defeat a massive enemy or strong enemy without difficulty. Therefore, it is a measure for encouraging them to fight and you should not discard it.

Tai Zong also said:
My lord always says a bright general does not employ astrology or divination for the date or time but that an ignorant general is involved and attaches himself to this art. Therefore, I think it should be thrown away.

Li Jing replied:
In ancient times, Zhou-wang of the Yin Dynasty went to battle on a day of Kinoe-ne and was defeated and killed by Wu-wang. Therefore, this means that the victor Wu-wang of the Zhou Dynasty also went to battle on a day of Kinoe-ne and won a great victory and took hold of the country. Both went to battle on the day of Kinoe-ne. Also Wu-di Liu Yu of the Song Dynasty raised his army on the inauspicious day of Oumounichi[6] and defeated the Southern Yan Dynasty. His generals said that Oumou is an unlucky day so they should not go to war but Wu-di said that Oumou was in fact a lucky day because the enemy will be ruined, the reason for this is that we are going to fight them.

---

5   The Chinese word here also means 'wrathful' or 'fierce' and while it directly translates as 'demon' in Japanese, in the original Chinese it has the broader meaning of 'spirits'.

6   One of the twelve unlucky days on which people should not go to battle, according to the ways of Chinese *in* and *yo* 'magic'.

He then advanced his army and won a great victory and the Southern Yan was ruined in the end. So, if we think of such an event, it is obvious that the divination for the date or time should not be thrown away.

[He then continued:]

Also when Tian Dan[7] was defending a castle in Mo with a small number and the massive army from Yan surrounded the castle, the people of Mo [defending in the castle] looked dispirited and flustered, saying they were very likely to end up surrendering to the army of Yan or even running away. Therefore Tian Dan made a plan [with a retainer] and sealed a promise with a person who was told to falsify the divination. As promised, he divined that the army of Yan would sustain an imminent and crushing defeat. Hearing this, the defending army regained their spirits and advanced, and, taking advantage of this momentum, Tian Dan performed the fire-cattle columns skill[8] and drove away the army of Yan and won an overwhelming victory. This shows how warfare is a path of deception and you should not throw away those things but use them.

Then Tai Zong said in return:

Tian Dan defeated the army of Yan with tactics using the spirits, whereas Tai Gong ruined Zhou-wang of Yin with fortune-telling by burning turtle shells. What is the difference between these two?

Li Jing replied:

The tactics of enlightened generals are identical. They use them in one way or in the opposite way depending on the time. However, either way is meant for the same purpose [of victory]. In ancient times, when Tai Gong went to war, assisting Wu-wang in advancing to a place called Mu-ye, a roaring thunderstorm came on suddenly and struck them, destroying the flags, the bells and drums of the army, thus they were all frightened. At which point San Yi Sheng[9] said they should withdraw the army and perform divination to establish a lucky time to go to war because the phenomenon looked like an ill omen for the coming battle and would arouse suspicion or fear among their army. So to prevent it from being a bad omen for the coming battle and to end the confusion within the army, he insisted they should divine with turtle shells and see what the spirits would say about the matter.

In reply, Tai Gong said, 'How could useless divining sticks or the shells of dead turtles tell you if a situation is lucky or not in relation to an army? Wu-wang [the leader of the army] is a retainer of Zhou-wang, who is his king. Therefore, here the

---

7 A Chinese general famous for his use of fire-oxen.
8 Cattle with burning brands attached to them.
9 San Yi Sheng and Tai Gong were both famous retainers of Wu-wang.

case is of a retainer going to kill his king, so if we win, it will be against [heaven's] principle. If the upcoming divination for this battle tells us that it is unlucky, it will mean we will have to retreat, if that's what the divination shows, but then how could we then go to battle again after we have retreated?' Because of this they retreated without divining at all.

This above episode seems reasonable. San Yi Sheng performed divination and used it to end the confusion among the army by telling them that the date was auspicious, while in the other case Tai Gong spoke with the intention to return at a point when he could achieve an absolute victory. Thus, the deep reason underlying their actions is identical and both of them aimed to overcome the hesitations of the soldiers. Therefore, divination for a date, time or direction is reasonable and here I [Fujibayashi] am going to describe below, in the remainder of this chapter the outlines of the [major] methods of divination used [in Japan today].

Auspicious times that are considered as times of *tonko*[10]

On a day of Kinoe or Mizunoto[11]
The fifth hour from the position of the hour of the Rat is the hour of *tonko*.

On a day of Kinoto or Mizunoe
The fifth hour from the position of the hour of the Monkey is the hour of *tonko*.

On a day of Kanoto or Hinoe
The fifth hour from the position of the hour of the Dog is the hour of *tonko*.

On a day of Tsuchinoe or Tsuchinoto
The fifth hour from the position of the hour of the Tiger is the hour of *tonko*.

On a day of Hinoto or Kanoe
The fifth hour from the position of the hour of the Dragon is the hour of *tonko*.
The above are considered the luckiest times.

---

10 *Tonko* are arts of magic to aid 'hiding' and 'deceiving people's eyes'.

11 The following list of names for days are names that are in accord with the original Chinese calendar and rotate continually and add up to sixty. In the time period in question, the public would understand fully which day was represented and this would be common knowledge, just as the Gregorian calendar is understood by us today. Therefore, days of Kanoe, Hinoe, Tsuchinoe, etc. were well understood by the average person, making this volume less confusing to them than it is to a modern reader.

[An alternative way of establishing] lucky times:

On a day of Kinoe or Kinoto
Count to the tenth hour clockwise from the animal-zodiac allotted for that day to find the lucky time.

On a day of Hinoe or Hinoto
Count to the eighth hour clockwise from the animal-zodiac allotted for that day to find the lucky time.

On a day of Tsuchinoe or Tsuchinoto
Count to the sixth hour clockwise from the animal-zodiac allotted for that day to find the lucky time.

On a day of Kanoe or Kanoto
Count to the fourth hour clockwise from the animal-zodiac allotted for that day to find the lucky time.

On a day of Mizunoe or Mizunoto
Count to the eighth hour clockwise from the animal-zodiac allotted for that day to find the lucky time.

You can discover the above auspicious hours of a day by counting the stated number of slots [clockwise] from the Chinese zodiac sign that is used for that day.[12] For example, if it is a day of Kinoe that is also the day of the Rat then the auspicious hour for that day will be the hour of the Cockerel (6pm to 8pm), and if a day of Kinoto and the day of the Ox, then the hour to use will be the hour of the Dog (8pm to 10pm).

The Five Precepts and the times of the day

立 – this ideogram represents wood in this context
命 – this ideogram represents fire in this context
罰 – this ideogram represents earth in this context
徳 – this ideogram represents metal in this context
刑– this ideogram represents water in this context

---

12 The Chinese systems of Ten Heavenly Stems and Twelve Zodiac Signs or 'Earthly Branches' run side by side, meaning that a single day has two labels. Each day has a designated 'Heavenly Stem' and an animal representation. The two systems run in a sixty-day cycle.

[Understanding the hours and how to know what to do at those times:]

立

The hours that correlate to the ideogram 立 are good for celebrating rituals, for gods, for deciding upon issues, for making armour or weapons, for standing posts or for raising the framework on a house and such issues.

命

The hours that correlate to the ideogram 命 are good for praying to gods or the Buddha and serving one's lord or any other kind of service. However, they are extremely unlucky times for the punishment of crimes, for killing someone and other such issues.

罸

The hours that correlate to the ideogram 罸 are times that you should not pray to the gods or to Buddha or start a lawsuit and you should generally avoid doing anything. However, killing is acceptable at this hour.

刑

The hours that correlate to the ideogram 刑 are generally unlucky for everything that you do.

徳

The hours that correlate to the ideogram 徳 are generally lucky for everything that you do.

[The following is a list of how the ideograms mentioned above correlate to the hours for certain days. With this list and the guidelines above, you will understand which hours are beneficial for certain activities.]

The auspicious hours for the days of Kinoe and Kinoto
On these days the time of 立 is in the hours of the Tiger and Hare.
On these days the time of 命 is in the hours of the Snake and Horse.
On these days the time of 罸 is in the hours of the Ox, Ram, Dragon and Dog.[13]

---

13 It says 'Snake' in the original text; this is presumably a transcription error and should read 'Dog'.

On these days the time of 刑 is in the hours of the Monkey and the Cockerel.
On these days the time of 徳 is in the hours of the Boar and Rat.

The auspicious hours for the days of Hinoe and Hinoto
On these days the time of 徳 is in the hours of the Tiger and Hare.
On these days the time of 立 is in the hours of the Snake and Horse.
On these days the time of 命 is in the hours of the Ox, Ram, Dragon and Dog.
On these days the time of 罰 is in the hours of the Monkey and the Cockerel.
On these days the time of 刑 is in the hours of the Boar and the Rat.

The auspicious hours for the days of Tsuchinoe and Tsuchinoto
On these days the time of 刑 is in the hours of the Tiger and Hare.
On these days the time of 徳 is in the hours of the Snake and Horse.
On these days the time of 立 is in the hours of the Ox, Ram, Dragon and Dog.
On these days the time of 命 is in the hours of the Monkey and the Cockerel.
On these days the time of 罰 is in the hours of the Boar and the Rat.

The auspicious hours for the days of Kanoe and Kanoto
On these days the time of 罰 is in the hours of the Tiger and Hare.
On these days the time of 刑 is in the hours of the Snake and Horse.
On these days the time of 徳 is in the hours of the Ox, Ram, Dragon and Dog.
On these days the time of 立 is in the hours of the Monkey and the Cockerel.
On these days the time of 命 is in the hours of the Boar and the Rat.

The auspicious hours for the days of Mizunoe and Mizunoto
On these days the time of 命 is in the hours of the Tiger and Hare.
On these days the time of 罰 is in the hours of the Snake and Horse.
On these days the time of 刑 is in the hours of the Ox, Ram, Dragon and Dog.
On these days the time of 徳 is in the hours of the Monkey and the Cockerel.
On these days the time of 立 is in the hours of the Boar and the Rat.

The Five Treasure Days

By the ten celestial stems
The days of Kinoe and Kinoto are days whose element is Wood.
The days of Hinoe and Hinoto are days whose element is Fire.
The days of Tsuchinoe and Tsuchinoto are days whose element is Earth.
The days of Kanoe and Kanoto are days whose element is Metal.
The days of Mizunoe and Mizunoto are days whose element is Water.

By the twelve signs of the Chinese zodiac

The days of the Tiger and the Hare are days of Wood.

The days of the Snake and the Horse are days of Fire.

The days of the Ox, Ram, Dragon and Dog are days of Earth.

The days of the Monkey and the Cockerel are days of Metal.

The days of the Boar and the Rat are days of Water.

The above information is based on the Creation and Destruction Cycles and the Ten Heavenly Stems and the Twelve Earthly Branches.

Distinguishing a lucky direction using the art of *tendojin*[14]

In the first lunar month, south is the lucky direction.

In the second lunar month, south and west[15] are the lucky directions.

In the third lunar month, north is the lucky direction.

In the fourth lunar month, west is the lucky direction.

In the fifth lunar month, west is the lucky direction.

In the sixth lunar month, east is the lucky direction.

In the seventh lunar month, north is the lucky direction.

In the eighth lunar month, east and north are the lucky directions.

In the ninth lunar month, south is the lucky direction.

In the tenth lunar month, east is the lucky direction.

In the eleventh lunar month, east and south are the lucky directions.

In the twelfth lunar month, west is the lucky direction.

The above are lucky directions that can be used in connection to anything.
For performing military affairs, the directions of Saikyo 歳刑 and
Ouban 黄幡[16] are also considered lucky.

The lucky directions of the Sankyo Gyokujo 三鏡玉女[17] or the Three Goddesses of Taoism

In the first lunar month, the directions of Kinoto 乙, Kanoto 辛 and Inui 乾 are lucky.

In the second lunar month, the directions of Kinoe 甲, Hinoe 丙 and Kanoe

---

14 This is a method to determine auspicious directions, based on the Chinese system of *in* and *yo* (also known as Onmyodo).

15 In this section there are pairs of dates; what is not known is whether the meaning in this case is 'south or west' or 'south and west' (in other words, 'southwest'). There are multiple ways to say 'southwest', such as having the ideograms for 'south' 南 and 'west' 西 next to each other or it can be expressed as the direction of Ram-Monkey 羊申, or the direction of Kon 坤. Therefore, it is not clear what Fujibayashi means here.

16 Saikyo and Ouban are two of the eight gods who govern the luck of directions in the Chinese system of *in* and *yo*.

17 Three goddesses in Taoism who govern directions, also adopted in *in* and *yo*.

庚 are lucky.

In the third lunar month, the directions of Kinoto 乙, Hinoe 丙 and Hinoto 丁 are lucky.

In the fourth lunar month, the directions of Hinoto 丁, Mizunoe 壬 and Ken 乾 are lucky.

In the fifth lunar month, the directions of Kinoe 甲 Hinoe 丙 and Kanoe 庚 are lucky.

In the sixth lunar month, the directions of Kinoe 甲, Kinoto 乙 and Hinoto 丁 are lucky.

In the seventh lunar month, the directions of Kon 坤, Son 巽 and Gon 艮 are lucky.

In the eighth lunar month, the directions of Mizunoe 壬, Ken 乾 and Son 巽 are lucky.

In the ninth lunar month, the directions of Kanoto 辛, Mizunoe 壬 and Mizunoto 癸 are lucky.

In the tenth lunar month, the directions of Kon 坤, Gon 艮 and Son 巽 are lucky.

In the eleventh lunar month, the directions of Mizunoe 壬, Kon 坤 and Gon 艮 are lucky.

In the twelfth lunar month, the directions of Kanoe 庚, Kanoto 辛 and Mizunoto 癸 are lucky.

The above three lucky goddesses and their directions can be represented as the sun, moon and the stars but also as heaven, earth and man, and are lucky for everything.

With these above seven[18] ways, you can know a [lucky] direction and you can also refer to the above writings.

According to one theory, the direction of Gyokujo [as described above] for any specific day is the ninth direction counting [clockwise] from the animal given for that day. For example, if it is a day of Rat, counting nine places on a sexagenary calendar will take you to the direction of Monkey and is the lucky direction of Gyokujo for that day.

[Unnamed article]

When you choose an auspicious day for a battle, you should decide the date and the time for the battle with due consideration to which direction is lucky for you and whether you will win or lose if you make an advance. Generally, when

---

18 The text states 'eight'.

Figure 30.
[Unnamed article]

going to war or setting out on a sea voyage or other kind of journey, you should consider very carefully the direction, the date and the time. This is especially true for a departure on a ship, as there are a number of unlucky days.

Understanding the relationship between elements[19]

Wood destroys Earth.

Those who are of an Earth character should completely avoid those people of a Wood nature.

---

19 A common idea in Chinese thought is the Five Elements and the way they interact. One direction of interaction is creative while the opposite is destructive.

Those of Wood should not avoid those of Earth. However, the opposite way is beneficial and works for the rest of these examples.

Water destroys Fire.
Those of Fire should completely avoid those of Water.
Those of Water should not avoid those of Fire.

Fire destroys Metal.[20]
Those of Fire should not avoid those of Metal.
Those of Metal should avoid those of Fire.

Earth destroys Water.
Those of Earth should not avoid those of Water.
Those of Water should avoid those of Earth.

Metal destroys Wood.
Those of Wood should carefully avoid those of Metal.
Those of Metal should not avoid those of Wood.

The theory of creating and being created

Wood creates Fire. Even if a person who is of Wood likes someone of Fire they should not use[21] Fire. It is good for Fire to use Wood.

Fire creates Earth and may like Earth; however, they should *not* use Earth. However, it is good for Earth to use Fire.

Earth creates Metal and may like it, but should not use it. However, it is good for Metal to use Earth.

Metal creates Water and may like it, but should not use it. However, it is good for Water to use Metal.

Water creates Wood and may like it, but should not use it. However, it is good for Wood to use Water.

---

20 For an unknown reason Fujibayashi changes the format here from positive first and negative second to negative first and positive second.

21 The text does not specify 'a person'; however, the context is about human interaction. Therefore, the word 'use' in this list is based on the understanding that the reference is to interaction between humans.

The two ways as above should be considered carefully. If the enemy's element *creates*[22] the element of your side [as shown above] it is lucky, while it is unlucky if your side's element creates the enemy's element. If your side destroys the enemy it is very lucky, while if the enemy destroys your side it is very unlucky. If the enemy and your side are equal, then either could be destructive and there is no advantage in this situation.

The flourishing phases of the seasons

In spring:
> Wood flourishes, Fire helps, Earth dies, Metal is captured and Water hibernates.[23]
> In the *doyo* period[24] Earth flourishes, Metal helps, Water dies, Wood is captured and Fire hibernates.

In summer:
> Fire flourishes, Earth helps, Metal dies, Water is captured and Wood hibernates.

In autumn:
> Metal flourishes, Water helps, Wood dies, Fire is captured and Earth hibernates.

In winter:
> Water flourishes, Wood helps, Fire dies, Earth is captured and Metal hibernates.

You should not confront the enemy when you face them [if they are positioned in] a direction that is flourishing.[25] If the nature of your lord is flourishing, it is lucky while if the nature of the enemy lord is flourishing, it is equally unlucky. In general, when divining the luck of an army [you should be aware that] the luck or bad luck of the lord decides the luck or bad luck of the army.

---

22 The Creation Cycle means that each of the elements helps create another in a specific format. This is the Cycle of Creation. Therefore, if the base element for an enemy is the element that creates the element allotted your own lord, then it is a positive position.

23 The text says 'becomes old' but this section is taken from Chinese literature and the connotation is 'rests'.

24 *Doyo* is the eighteen-day period before the first day of each new season according to the lunar calendar. Here it seems to refer to the *doyo* period before the first day of summer.

25 The Five Elements also correspond to cardinal directions.

Knowing the directions of Ko 孤 and Kyo 虚
[to aid in positioning your army]

For ten days from a day of Kinoe and Rat:
Ko 孤 is in the direction of the Dog and the Boar.
Kyo 虚 is in the direction of the Dragon and the Snake.

For ten days from a day of Kinoe and Dog:
Ko 孤 is in the direction of the Monkey and the Cockerel.
Kyo 虚 is in the direction of the Tiger and the Hare.

For ten days from a day of Kinoe and Monkey:
Ko 孤 is in the direction of the Horse and the Ram.
Kyo 虚 is in the direction of the Rat and the Ox.

For ten days from a day of Kinoe and Tiger:
Ko 孤 is in the direction of the Rat and the Ox.
Kyo 虚 is in the direction of the Horse and the Ram.

In any of the above examples, you should take up a position with the direction of Ko 孤 behind you and the enemy in the direction of Kyo 虚. Do this and you will win without doubt.

Calculating an auspicious day for departure depending on
the nature of the lord

If the lord is of Wood:
In spring or winter, depart on a day of Kinoe or Kinoto.
In summer, it is unlucky, however, to depart on a day of Mizunoe or
    Mizunoto.
In autumn, it is unlucky, however, to depart on a day of Kinoe or Kinoto.

If the lord is of Fire:
In summer, depart on a day of Hinoe or Hinoto.
In spring, autumn or winter, depart on a day of Kinoe or Kinoto.

If the lord is of Earth:
Any *doyo* eighteen-day period before the start of a new season is lucky for
    departure.
In spring, it is unlucky, however, to depart on a day of Hinoe or Hinoto.
In summer, Tsuchinoe or Tsuchinoto are lucky days for this.

In autumn, depart on a day of Hinoe or Hinoto.

In winter, it is unlucky, however, to depart on a day of Tsuchinoe or Tsuchinoto.

If the lord is of Metal:

In autumn or winter, depart on a day of Kanoe or Kanoto.

In summer, depart on a day of Mizunoe or Mizunoto.

In spring, depart on a day of Tsuchinoe or Tsuchinoto.

If the lord is of Water:

In autumn, winter or spring, depart on a day of Mizunoe or Mizunoto.

In summer, the situation is unlucky – therefore, you should use Mizunoe or Mizunoto.

In a *doyo* eighteen-day period before a new season this combination [of a Water lord and *doyo*, which is an Earth element] is extremely bad luck. Therefore, in this case you should use Mizunoe or Mizunoto [because they are of Water].

As seen in the above, those days or months that are of the same element as the lord and those elements that generate the lord's own element [in the Creation Cycle] are considered to be lucky. Those months that destroy the element of the lord are to be considered unlucky, but if you are in urgent need there are things you should be aware of. Below are a few examples of these issues.

The three months of summer are of the element of Fire, and if the lord is of Wood, then, the element of the month [summer] has priority over the element of the lord [Wood], so [as Fire destroys Wood] it is unlucky. Therefore, adopting a day of Mizunoe or Mizunoto, which are of the element of Water, will weaken the element [Fire] for the period in question and will create a Wood element, which in this example is the element of the lord [and is a positive thing].

As autumn is of Metal, and if the lord is of the Wood element, then Metal destroys Wood, so it is unlucky in this situation. By adopting a day of Kinoe or Kinoto, which are days of Wood, this will reduce the effects of the Destruction Cycle and increase the element of the lord, which again in this case is Wood. In this way, you can increase [the power] of the element you need and reduce the [power] of the Destruction Cycle. You can use this principle in any of the above information.

Also consider this in terms of the way you see the enemy in relation to your side. If it is winter and on a day of Mizunoe or Mizunoto, which are days associated with the Water element, and the enemy lord is of the Water element and is in the north, while your lord is of the Fire element and your army is in the south, then you are in the Destruction Cycle, which, when seen in relation to the enemy, makes this situation an example of extreme bad luck. In such a case, make someone of the Earth element a temporary commander-in-chief and also choose the time of the Dragon or of the Ram out of the four times of Ram, Monkey,[26] Dragon and Snake as these four are of the Earth element. Alternatively, you take a day of Hinoe or Hinoto as they are of the Fire element or even use a *kishuku* lucky day, and thus make a rapid move [against the enemy]; this way [you will have gained all the positive aspects] and you will destroy your enemy. You should judge all situations in this way.

The concept of *shinsho* and *shinpu*, that is the art of knowing if an advancing army[27] will win or lose

- The white circles are *shinsho*, which means it is advantageous, and the black circles are *shinpu*, which means it is disadvantageous. If it is spring or summer then use this chart in an anticlockwise way and if it is autumn or winter use it in a clockwise way.
- [The days of the month are represented on the illustration by the small dots on the outside of the main circle] and the first day of the month is at the point where each month is written[28] [on the inside of the circle]. For the final day of a thirty-day month, the dot for the twenty-eighth[29] day should be applied. The twelve zodiac signs are to be used to know the direction.[30]
- If both the date and time are in *shinsho* [which is winning], then you should attack as soon as possible, no matter which direction it is from. If both are in *shinpu* [which is defeat], then you should wait for the enemy to come to you.

---

26 Monkey is of Metal. This presumably is a transcription error for Dog.

27 This chart (figure 31) is used to find a lucky or unlucky day to advance an army. Each circle represents a day and depending on what the season is you count clockwise or anti-clockwise, one circle for each day of a lunar month.

28 The twelve Japanese ideograms on the inside of the circle represent the months of the year. The first month on this image is at the 'eight o'clock' position and moves in a clockwise manner.

29 This appears to be incorrect, as there are actually thirty days represented, so finding the thirtieth is no problem to the reader. It is possible that later transcriptions put these two extra dots in place.

30 Zodiac signs have a set direction and can be seen on the chart.

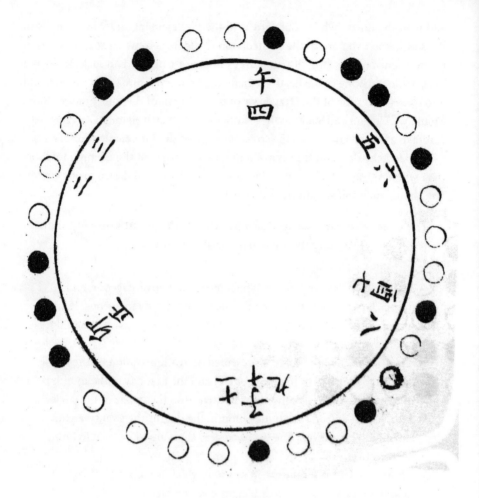

Figure 31. *Shinsho* and *shinpu*

If the date is *shinsho* but the time is *shinpu* both [armies] will[31] attack each other, while if the time is *shinsho* and the date is *shinpu*, both armies will retreat. If you start the attack you should choose the direction of *shinsho* [winning], but details are to be orally transmitted.

31 The word 'will' does not appear in the original text, but has been added for clarity.

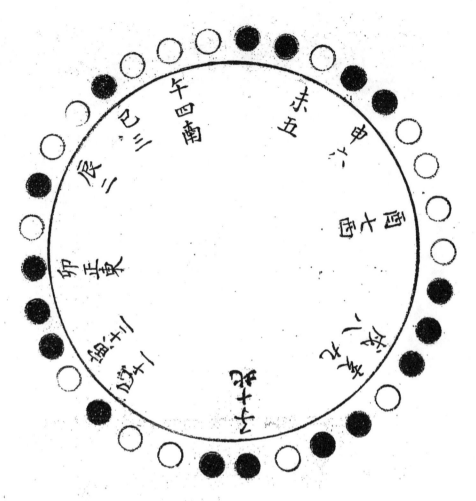

Figure 32. Wen-wang's way of divining dates

Divining a date by Wen-wang of the Zhou Dynasty

To count on this above image [*figure 32*], go clockwise if the date you are in is of *to* (negative) and anticlockwise if the date is of *e* (positive). You should start counting where the name of each month is on the illustration.

This is the secret way of divining auspicious dates by which Wen-wang won his victory.

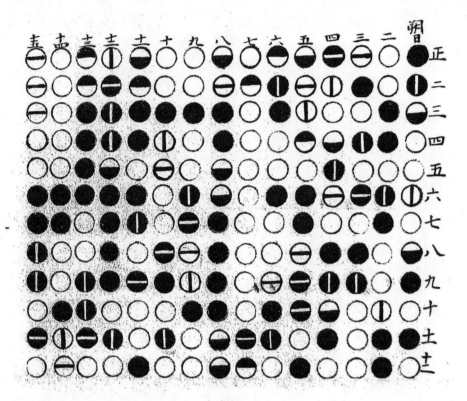

Figure 33. Yoshitsune's way of divining dates

Yoshitsune's handy system for the divination of dates[32]

○ Where this mark appears then it will be *shinsho* all day.

● Where this mark appears then it will be *shinpu* all day.

⊖ Where this mark appears then it will be *shinsho* at midday [and after[33]].

⊖ Where this mark appears then it will be *shinpu* at midday [and after].

⊖ Where this mark appears then it will be *shinsho* until midday.

⊖ Where this mark appears then it will be *shinpu* until midday.

---

32 Literally, 'The Manual at the Right Hand of Yoshitsune'.
33 The text uses the word hiru 晝, meaning 'daytime' or 'midday'.

Where this mark appears then both armies should attack.

 Where this mark appears then both armies should retreat.

In applying this, if the final day of a thirty-day month is *e*, then you should apply the dot used for the second day of the previous month.[34] If it is a *to* day, then apply the dot for the fifth day from the previous month. There is nothing greater than this deep and secret way for divining lucky and unlucky days in warfare.

Divination for a day to defeat the enemy (a system used by the founder of the Han Dynasty [in China])

Days 9, 12, 20, 21 and 22 of the first lunar month are days to defeat the enemy.

Days 7, 10, 18 and 19 of the second lunar month are days to defeat the enemy.

Days 5, 8, 16, 17 and 18 of the third lunar month are days to defeat the enemy.

Days 3, 6, 14, 15 and 16 of the fourth lunar month are days to defeat the enemy.

Days 1, 3, 4, 12, 13 and 14 of the fifth lunar month are days to defeat the enemy.

Days 2, 10, 11, 13 and 26 of the sixth lunar month are days to defeat the enemy.

Days 8, 9, 23 and 26 of the seventh lunar month are days to defeat the enemy.

Days 4, 5, 6, 20 and 23 of the eighth lunar month are days to defeat the enemy.

Days 2, 3, 4, 18, 21, 29 and 30 of the ninth lunar month are days to defeat the enemy.

Days 1, 2, 16, 19, 27 and 28 of the tenth lunar month are days to defeat the enemy.

Days 13, 16, 24, 25 and 26 of the eleventh lunar month are days to defeat the enemy.

Days 11, 14, 20 and 23 of the twelfth lunar month are days to defeat the enemy.

The above days are great and lucky days, so much so that even the three kinds of unlucky day, which are *tenmo shicho*, *jushi* and *hyakushi*, are turned from unlucky

---

34 The image used is a layout of the days of a traditional month. The first vertical line (from the right) is the first day of the month, the second is the second etc. The image only has fifteen days and therefore is either half of the month or you have to move backwards as you get to the end of each month. This is based on the Celestial Stems.

when they fall on these above dates. They are lucky for everything, including departing for war and making decisions in meetings concerning *budo*.[35]

The lucky directions of Kyuten 九天 and Kyuchi 九地[36]

In spring, the direction of the Tiger is Kyuten and the direction of the Monkey is Kyuchi.

In summer, the direction of the Horse is Kyuten and the direction of the Rat is Kyuchi.

In autumn, the direction of the Monkey is Kyuten and the direction of the Tiger is Kyuchi.

In winter, the direction of the Rat is Kyuten and the direction of the Horse is Kyuchi.

Great and lucky times to initiate battle

On a day of Kinoe or Tsuchinoto, at the hour of the Tiger or Hare
On a day of Kinoto or Kanoe, at the hour of the Dog or Boar
On a day of Hinoe or Kanoto, at the hour of the Monkey or the Cockerel
On a day of Hinoto or Mizunoe, at the hour of the Horse or Ram
On a day of Tsuchinoe or Mizunoto, at the hour of the Dragon or Snake

Great and lucky times for departure

On a day of the Rat, Ox, Dragon or Dog, at the hour of the Cockerel
On a day of the Tiger, Hare or Monkey, at the hour of the Horse
On a day of the Hare, Horse or Cockerel, at the hour of the Ram
On a day of the Snake or Boar, at the hour of the Tiger
On a day of the Ram, at the hour of the Hare

Days to celebrate the war gods

In the first lunar month, it is on the days of Kinoe and of the Tiger.
In the second lunar month, it is on the days of Kinoe and of the Dog or Horse.
In the third lunar month, it is on the days of Kinoe and of the Dog.
In the fourth lunar month, it is on the days of Hinoto and of the Hare.
[Text for the fifth lunar month is missing from the original.]
In the sixth lunar month, it is on the days of Hinoto and of the Snake.

---

35 In this context *budo* means 'military arts' and is not to be confused with the concept of *budo* as 'martial arts'. This section is concerned with preparations for war.

36 Kyuten literally means 'nine' and 'heaven' and Kyuchi is 'nine' and 'earth'. Their meaning is not known, but presumably it can be said they are 'lucky' directions.

In the seventh lunar month, it is on the days of Kanoe and of the Tiger.
In the eighth lunar month, it is on the days of Kanoe and of the Rat.
In the ninth lunar month, it is on the days of Kanoe and of the Dragon.
In the tenth lunar month, it is on the days of Mizunoto and of the Boar.
In the eleventh lunar month, it is on the days of Hinoto and of the Ram.
In the twelfth lunar month, it is on the days of Mizunoto and of the Snake.

[Version two[37]]

In the first lunar month, it is on the day of the Tiger.
In the second lunar month, it is on the day of the Hare.
In the third lunar month, it is on the day of the Snake.
In the fourth lunar month, it is on the day of the Ram.
In the fifth lunar month, it is on the day of the Cockerel.
In the sixth lunar month, it is on the day the Boar.
In the seventh lunar month, it is on the day of the Hare.
In the eighth lunar month, it is on the day of the Snake.
In the ninth lunar month, it is on the day of the Ram.
In the tenth lunar month, it is on the day of the Cockerel.
In the eleventh lunar month, it is on the day of the Boar.
In the twelfth lunar month, it is on the day of the Hare.
Use these days [in the above lists] in accordance with the elements.

Lucky days for night raids

Between the first lunar month and up to and including the sixth lunar
    month, the lucky days are of Kanoe, Tsuchinoto, the Dragon and the
    Snake.
In the seventh lunar month the lucky days are the Horse and the Hare.
In the eighth lunar month the lucky days are Kinoto, the Ox and the
    Cockerel.
In the ninth lunar month the lucky days are Kanoe, the Rat and the Horse.
In the tenth lunar month the lucky days are Mizunoto and the Boar.
In the eleventh lunar month the lucky days are Kinoe, the Monkey and the
    Dog, and Kanoe and the Tiger.
In the twelfth lunar month the lucky days are Mizunoe, Mizunoto, the Tiger,
    the Cockerel, and Kinoe.

---

37 Fujibayashi gives no explanation for these days. Therefore, it is presumed to be a second
    version of the list of days for celebrating war gods.

Discerning the direction and *yugyo*[38] of Marishiten, the Buddhist goddess of war

On the days of the Rat, Horse, Hare and Cockerel, it is in the ninth direction.[39]

On the days of the Ox, Ram, Dragon and Dog, it is in the fifth direction.

On the days of the Tiger, Monkey, Snake and Boar, it is in the first direction.

When you obtain forces or weapons,[40] you should celebrate the gods of war and face the above directions, for they are great and lucky directions. Use the animal sign of that day and apply the number of moves to the direction that will be indicated by the calendar. However, you should not confront the enemy or shoot an arrow at the enemy at these directions.

The direction in which you should dispose of decapitated enemy heads

On a day of the Rat, then it is in the direction of the Horse.

On a day of the Ox, then it is in the direction of the Snake.

On a day of the Tiger, then it is in the direction of the Monkey.

On a day of the Hare, then it is in the direction of the Dragon.

On a day of the Dragon, then it is in the direction of the Snake.

On a day of the Snake, then it is in the direction of the Horse or Ram.

On a day of the Monkey, then it is in the direction of the Snake.

On a day of the Cockerel, then it is in the direction of the Ram.

On a day of the Dog, then it is in the direction of the Monkey.

On a day of the Boar, then it is in the direction of the Tiger.

You should throw the heads away in the above directions. However, be sure to avoid the direction of Hagun.[41]

---

38 In this context, it shows the position of the goddess of war is 'at rest', the direction she resides in for that period.

39 Again, this is based on the sexagenarian cycle of Chinese lunar dating and the direction means one space in a clockwise direction from the start point originated in the text.

40 This section could mean just 'weapons'.

41 The word Hagun 破軍 comes from the Chinese name of one of the stars of Ursa Major. The star is the seventh star of the constellation and is the end star of the 'handle' of the 'dipper' shape. Hagun 破軍, literally means 'destroying army'. In Onmyodo magic the direction that this star points was considered very unlucky and if you fight facing this direction you will be defeated and fail; therefore, throwing the heads in this direction would be considered very malign.

[The days of *shakko* and *shakuzetsu*]

Concerning the days of *shakko*[42]

In the first lunar month, they are days 4, 12, 20 and 28.

In the second lunar month, they are days 3, 11, 19 and 20.

In the third lunar month, they are days 2, 10, 18 and 26.

In the fourth lunar month, they are days 1, 9, 17 and 25.

In the fifth lunar month, they are days 8, 16 and 24.

In the sixth lunar month, they are days 7, 15 and 24.

In the seventh lunar month, they are days 6, 14, 22 and 30.

In the eighth lunar month, they are days 5, 13, 21 and 29.

In the ninth lunar month, they are days 4, 12, 20 and 28.

In the tenth lunar month, they are days 3, 11, 19 and 27.

In the eleventh lunar month, they are days 2, 10, 18 and 26.

In the twelfth lunar month, they are days 1, 9, 17 and 25.

Concerning the days of *shakuzetsu*[43]

In the first lunar month, they are days 3, 11, 19 and 27.

In the second lunar month, they are days 2, 10, 18 and 26.

In the third lunar month, they are days 1, 9, 17 and 25.

In the fourth lunar month, they are days 6, 14, 22 and 30.

In the fifth lunar month, they are days 5, 13, 21 and 29.

In the sixth lunar month, they are days 4, 12, 20 and 28.

In the seventh lunar month, they are days 3, 11, 19 and 27.

In the eighth lunar month, they are days 2, 10, 19 and 26.

In the ninth lunar month, they are days 1, 9, 17 and 25.

In the tenth lunar month, they are days 6, 14, 22 and 30.

In the eleventh lunar month, they are days 5, 13, 21 and 29.

In the twelfth lunar month, they are days 4, 12, 20 and 28.

The days of *shakko* or *shakuzetsu* as above are unlucky for activities involving deception, such as *shinobi* [missions], while they are not unlucky for lawsuits or disputes. However, this does mean that on these days any enemy deception will be revealed, as they are days when any deceit is corrected [by heaven]; therefore, they are not good for a false lawsuit.

---

42 One of the Japanese calendar's six types of inauspicious day. They are unlucky for all activities, with only the period around noon being auspicious.

43 In Onmyodo these are unlucky days governed by the Taoist *raksasha* demons, who have fiery red tongues.

Fujojunichi[44] or the days of no success

In the first and seventh lunar months, they are days 3, 11, 19 and 27.

In the second and eighth lunar months, they are days 2, 10, 18 and 26.

In the third and ninth lunar months, they are days 1, 9, 17 and 25.

In the fourth and tenth lunar months, they are days 4, 12, 20 and 28.

In the fifth and eleventh lunar months, they are days 5, 13, 21 and 29.

In the sixth and twelfth lunar months, they are days 6, 14, 22 and 30.

Be warned, the above days are unlucky for everything.

The directions of Sashigami[45]

An example of this system is if it is a day of the Rat, Sashigami is the direction of the Dragon.

On a day of the Rat, it is the fifth direction from that of the Rat.

On a day of the Ox, it is the ninth direction from that of the Ox.

On a day of the Tiger, it is the tenth direction from that of the Tiger.

On a day of the Hare or Dragon, it is the fifth direction from that of the Hare or Dragon.

On a day of the Snake, it is the sixth direction from that of the Snake.

On a day of the Horse, it is the eighth direction from that of the Horse.

On a day of the Ram, it is the sixth direction from that of the Ram.

On a day of the Monkey, it is the eighth direction from that of the Monkey.

On a day of the Cockerel, it is the tenth direction from that of the Cockerel.

On a day of the Dog, it is the fifth direction from that of the Dog.

On a day of the Boar, it is the seventh direction from that of the Boar.

The above are unlucky directions for everything and any suits or disputes will be cursed with bad luck.

How to understand the directions of Tomobiki[46]

The way of calculation for this is the same as for the direction of Sashigami, as shown above [and should be considered identical].

Some poems state the following on the issue of the direction of Tomobiki:

On a day of the Rat or Ox, it is the fourth direction.

On a day of the Tiger or Hare, it is the sixth direction.

On a day of the Dragon, it is the eighth direction.

---

44 Also found in the *Shoninki* manual.

45 The name of a god also known as Arichishin in the Onmyodo tradition.

46 One of the Japanese calendar's six types of day, as classified in terms of auspiciousness.

On a day of the Snake, it is the eighth direction.
On a day of the Horse, it is the fourth direction.
On a day of the Ram, it is the fourth direction.
On a day of the Monkey or Cockerel, it is the sixth direction.
On a day of the Dog, it is the eighth direction.
On a day of the Boar, it is the eighth direction.
These directions should be strictly avoided.

The above directions are where you should do something lucky for you and unlucky for the enemy, such as the gaining of the possession of treasures and the burying of enemy heads. However, be sure not to send any allies who are injured, [or who have been] killed or [who are] ill to these directions. Also *watamashi*[47] should be strictly avoided in these directions.

The directions of Hagun

In the first lunar month, it is in the fifth direction.
In the second lunar month, it is in the sixth direction.
In the third lunar month, it is in the seventh direction.
In the fourth lunar month, it is in the eighth direction.
In the fifth lunar month, it is in the ninth direction.
In the sixth lunar month, it is in the tenth direction.
In the seventh lunar month, it is in the eleventh direction.
In the eighth lunar month, it is in the twelfth direction.
In the ninth lunar month, it is in the first direction.
In the tenth lunar month, it is in the second direction.
In the eleventh lunar month, it is in the third direction.
In the twelfth lunar month, it is in the fourth direction.

For example, if it is the first lunar month and it is the hour of Rat, you should not go toward the fifth direction from that of the Rat, which in this case is the direction of Dragon [and the direction of Hagun]. For the rest of the above rules, follow this example and apply the method.[48]

The 'first direction' used in the ninth month means that if it is the hour of Rat, then the direction that you should arrive at should be that of the Rat. You should not fight or face in this direction. A more detailed way of knowing the direction of Hagun will be described later in the next chapter in this writing.

---

47 A ritual where Buddhist statues are moved, or also possibly when nobles move.
48 Fujibayashi is giving the correct direction here so that no mistakes are made with the rest.

Tenji II

Opportunities Bestowed by Heaven II

Astronomy and astrology

This volume[1] contains the following:
- Fifteen[2] points on forecasting for wind and rain
- Verses pertaining to wind and rain
- Three points on calculating moonrise and moonset
- Four points and illustrations on understanding the ebb and flow of the tides
- Two points on how to know the direction on a moonless night
- Two points on understanding the time

Fifteen points on forecasting the wind and rain

To know about wind and rain is essential in *ninjutsu* because it is best that *in-nin* stealthy infiltrations are performed on a night of wind and rain. Also, setting fires requires a close examination of the wind and rain, so you should never [commit arson] without careful consideration of these factors.

---

1 The verses on wind and rain are notes taken by Fujibayashi from the Bantenkyo volume of the Chinese *Bingjing* manual. Unfortunately, either Fujibayashi or the scribe made mistakes and the text deviates at some points from the manual. Here we have corrected these mistakes and used the original Chinese manual as a foundation.

2 The text says sixteen points; however, there are only fifteen. Either one point is missing or it is a transcription error.

I

When the stars are twinkling like blinking eyes it will be very windy within three days.

II

If at night black clouds hang over the mouth of the Big Dipper, or if black clouds spread over the Celestial River[3] and look like fish or any aquatic animals,[4] or a boar or a dragon, then it will be windy and rainy during the hour of Ram[5] of the next day. However, if there are only normal clouds crossing over the Celestial River, flowing one after another, then the wind will not last long.

III

If the sun has a halo, it will be rainy, while if the moon has a halo, then it will be windy. Also, in the direction the moon is waning, it will most likely be windy and rainy in that area.

IV

If the sunset is as red as deep crimson it will *not* be rainy, but it will be windy.

V

If it is windy early in the day and it is calmer in the evening, you should expect a large wind the next day.

If *chi* is piercing the sun like a black snake, it will be rainy.

If black clouds pierce sunrise or sunset, then there will be tempest within the three days.

If the sun is high and shining strongly and there is black *chi* that is shaped like a snake or dragon, it will be windy and rainy.

When the sun rises, if it has a cover [of clouds] arching over it, like the cover used to arch over a cart, then it will without fail be rainy.

If there is a pale and weak sun and it is dark in the day and it continues until the evening, then there will be a flood.

On the eleventh day of the first lunar month; the eighth day of the middle month; and the ninth day of the last month [of each of the four three-month seasons], the moon should have a halo, but if it does not, then it will be windy and rainy within three days.

If an eclipse occurs in the east, it will be terribly windy within that month.

---

3 The Milky Way.

4 Literally 'fish and soft-shelled turtles'. However, this is an idiom for all animals in the sea.

5 The ideogram used here means 'end' 末 instead of 'Ram' 未, which is a transcription error.

VI

Spring winds are quick to change and it can be a south wind blowing one day and a north wind the next. If it is windy early in the day, it will be calm in the evening without fail.

If the south wind blows and if it has a tail of north wind and a head of south wind[6] it will increase in ferocity as it is blowing, and then if a north wind rises it will be advantageous.[7]

VII

If a cloud is shaped like a gun carriage then it is a sign of a large wind.

VIII

If the clouds are spread out in a low position [in the sky] and are wide and broad in all directions, like smoke or mist, then this is called *fuka* – 'of turning into the wind' – and it is a sign of a wind rising.

If the clouds are shaped like fish scales, it will be windy but will not be rainy.

IX

If you can see the colour of indigo blue at the edge of water, it will be windy and rainy.

X

In autumn, if there are no clouds nor any wind, it will not be rainy.

XI

If storm petrels fly in large flocks, it is a sign of wind and rain.[8]

XII

If dolphins are playing in the water, then it is a sign of a large wind.

XIII

If a water snake coils[9] where reeds are high and green, it is a sign of a rise of the water level. If the snake turns its head downwards the rise will be immediate, while

---

6 The meaning is not clear here, as the two winds appear to go against each other.
7 This point has been simplified.
8 The storm petrel is known in other cultures to predict bad weather. This is because these birds are pelagic (they inhabit the open seas), which means they would be spotted by a land-based individual only at the time of a storm, as bad weather drives them inland. (Source: ornithologist Professor Tim Birkhead.)
9 Literally 'water snake', thought to be a freshwater snake, possibly *Homalopsinae*, which is not native to Japan. This highlights the fact that this information comes from a foreign manual.

if it turns its head upwards, it will be slow.

XIV

If there is no rain on the last day of any given lunar month, then you will have heavy rain without fail at the beginning of the next month.

XV

When the moon is in one of the following four lunar mansions,[10] then wind will rise.

1. The Basket 箕
2. The Wall 壁
3. The Wings 翼
4. The Chariot 軫

Take note that only the first three are mentioned in the *Bingjing* manual.

The moon travels through the sky each day and night moving by thirteen[11] degrees,[12] and it travels around the whole sky in a matter of twenty-eight days and on the thirtieth and the first of each month it is difficult to see the degrees shift.[13] When examining the periods of *chuki* 中気, which are the twelve *even-numbered* sections of allotted time in the system of the twenty-four solar terms,[14] the sun and the moon meet together in the same mansion and make *shusui* 首推.[15] The four quadrants of the sky have seven lunar mansions in each one; however, remember that they are not divided into equal sections.

The degrees [where the sun and the moon meet in the same lunar mansion are listed below and were] recorded by Li Quan.

[These meetings happen at the even-numbered solar terms:]

雨水 The time of rain water: the Encampment mansion (8°)

春分 The vernal equinox: the Stride mansion (14°)

穀雨 The grain rain: the Mane mansion (2°)

---

10 This is a famous quote from Sun Tzu and proliferates both Chinese and Japanese incendiary warfare and meteorological methods.

11 This number is not constant, it is variable and could be closer to 12.8° than 13° or just over.

12 The term 'degrees' has been used here. However, it is based on the Chinese system where a circle has 365° instead of 360°. Therefore, one 'Chinese' degree is equivalent to 0.98630137 standard degrees. To convert the Chinese degrees used in this manual into standard degrees, simply multiply the number written by this previous figure. For example, the Willowing Basket mansion has an arc of 11 Chinese degrees, which is 10.8493151° in standard terms.

13 Literal translation; the text is ambiguous here.

14 The twenty-four solar terms is an old system of measuring time through a year. Each solar term covers 15° along the ecliptic.

15 Unknown term.

小满 The time of full grain: the Three Stars mansion (4°)

夏至 The summer solstice: the Well mansion (25°)

大暑 The major heat: the Seven Stars mansion (4°)

处暑 The limit of the heat: the Wings mansion (9°)

秋分 The autumnal equinox: the Horn mansion (4°)

霜降 The descent of the frost: the Base mansion (14°)

小雪 The minor snow: the Basket mansion (2°)

冬至 The winter solstice: the Southern Dipper mansion (21°)

大寒 The major cold: the Emptiness mansion (5°)

Here is a list of the twenty-eight lunar mansions and the angle of degrees they take up in the sky.

[Each number represents the arc angle that each mansion occupies in the night sky.]

The east group of seven lunar mansions adds up to 75° in total:

1. The Horn has an arc of 12°
2. The Neck has an arc of 9°
3. The Base has an arc of 15°
4. The Chamber has an arc of 5°
5. The Heart has an arc of 5°
6. The Tail has an arc of 18°
7. The Basket has an arc of 11°

The north group of seven lunar mansions adds up to 98° in total:

1. The Southern Dipper has an arc of 26°
2. The Ox has an arc of 8°
3. The Maid has an arc of 12°
4. The Emptiness has an arc of 10°
5. The Rooftop has an arc of 17°
6. The Encampment has an arc of 16°
7. The Wall has an arc of 9°

The west group of seven lunar mansions adds up to 80° in total:

1. The Stride has an arc of 16°
2. The Bond has an arc of 12°
3. The Stomach has an arc of 14°
4. The Mane has an arc of 11°
5. The Net has an arc of 16°
6. The Turtle Beak has an arc of 2°

7. The Three Stars has an arc of 9°

The south group of seven lunar mansions adds up to 112° in total[16]:
1. The Well has an arc of 33°
2. The Ghost has an arc of 4°
3. The Willow has an arc of 15°
4. The Seven Stars has an arc of 7°
5. The Extended Net has an arc of 18°
6. The Wings has an arc of 18°
7. The Chariot has an arc of 17°

For example, in the time of rain water in the first lunar month,[17] if the moon is 8° into the Encampment mansion at midnight on the first day of [the time of rain water], then its position will move 13° or more by midnight on the second day, which means it will reach 5° into the territory of the Wall mansion. Furthermore, at midnight on the third day it will reach 9° into the lunar mansion named Stride.

Verses pertaining to wind and rain

The heavens stretch above and consist of the sun, the moon and the stars, while the earth stays below, with the gods of wind, rain and thunder reigning above it. You can forecast[18] [the weather] by the brightness of the Big Dipper and the colour of the moon.

If black clouds are covering the four stars forming the ladle of the Big Dipper and are over the opening in a ridge shape, then there will be rain on that night.

If there is yellow *chi*[19] in front of the seventh star of the Big Dipper, you should know that plenty of rain will come.

If the Big Dipper is fully covered with clouds, it will be rainy within three days.

If the Big Dipper is partially covered [with thin clouds], then it will be rainy for five days.[20]

---

16 The original has a transcription error and states '120'.

17 This is in or around February on a solar calendar.

18 The text says 'divine'; however, this word has been substituted by 'forecast' in all cases.

19 *Chi* or *ki* in Japanese is a difficult concept to grasp. When it comes to *chi* in the sky there are two possible conclusions: either it is the presence of invisible *chi*, which only a select few can see; or the *chi* is the energy that shapes and colours the clouds, which is visible to all.

20 The text says 'half a day', but the Chinese original text says 'half of a *jun*'. A *jun* is a period of ten days. Also Fujibayashi's footnote says it will be rainy for 'three times five days', which does not make sense and should be regarded as a transcription error.

On a day of Dog,[21] Snake or the Six[22] Dragon (which are the days Tsuchinoe-Dragon[23] and Tsuchinoto-Snake), you can determine the weather by the sun at dawn [just after the sunrise or in the early morning], in the evening [just before the sunset] or by the Big Dipper at night. If there are clouds that are blue and moist and appear in a 'fish scales' pattern, it will rain heavily on that day or night and without fail.

Look to the Big Dipper: if there are clouds of five colours and that move into the shape of a turtle or a dragon, then it will be rainy.

Red *chi* is a sign of burning fire and yellow *chi* a sign of a sandstorm or dusty wind. When you observe the Big Dipper and there is red *chi*, it is a sign of a drought and sultry weather, while if there is yellow *chi*, which is not spreading but is thick, it indicates a lot of dusty wind [will come]. In addition to this, if [the *chi*] has an element of the blue Dragon[24] or Boar, Rat, Mizunoe or Mizunoto [all of which have connotations of water], then it is a sign of rain.

If there is white *chi* in front of the fifth and sixth stars of the Big Dipper [which make up the handle], then there will be a heavy wind and rain to come.

If you see mist dyed crimson, then it will rain before the end of the solar term that you are in and thus wind and rain will come and in due course the farmers will benefit greatly.

If there are no clouds on any of the six versions[25] of days of Kinoe, it will be sunny for the next ten days.

According to the clouds you can see, the following can be predicted in connection with the Five Elements:[26]

By observing from which the direction the clouds or *chi* rise, you can know if there will be rain. For example, the days of Kinoe or Kinoto [both of which are of the Wood element] are associated with the east [which is also of the Wood element].

The rest of the elements and variations are shown below and you should apply this method to them.

---

21 The original Chinese Bantenkyo 盤天経 manual, from which all these points are taken, says Tsuchinoe (which is the name of a specific day) instead of Dog and also Rat instead of Snake. The ideogram for Dog 戌 and Tsuchinoe 戊 are very similar and could be a transcription error while the issue of Snake and Rat is clearly a substitution.

22 There appears to be no explanation for the numerical in the text.

23 The original Bantenkyo 盤天経 Chinese document writes this as Rat.

24 This has connotations of an easterly direction.

25 As the cycles of the Twelve Earthly Branches and the Ten Celestial Stems rotate, six different versions of Kinoe appear.

26 Each direction including the centre has an element attached to it, so do the names for the days. Therefore, Fujibayashi is saying that if the two intersect in the manner he describes then you can predict the weather.

If there are blue clouds [in the east, then it will be rainy on a day of] Kinoe or Kinoto.

If there are red clouds [in the south, then it will be rainy on a day of] Hinoe or Hinoto.

If there are yellow clouds [in the centre of the sky, it will be rainy on a day of] Tsuchinoe or Tsuchinoto.

If there are white clouds [in the west, then it will be rainy on a day of] Kanoe or Kanoto.

If there are black clouds [in the north, then it will be rainy on a day of] Mizunoe or Mizunoto.

[As can be seen] the five colours are connected to the five directions [which also include the centre].

On the five days of the Hare,[27] as the Hare is of the Wood element, this means you can predict the upcoming atmospheric conditions. On the five days of the Hare together with the six days of Kinoe [which is also of the Wood element], rain can be predicted. If the sun and/or the Big Dipper are not covered with clouds, then the weather will remain the same for the next ten days.

By observing the sky at sunrise or sunset, including the changing conditions and phenomena, you can predict the weather for the next ten-day cycle of the Ten Celestial Stems [as each one has a specific element attached to it]. For example, to predict at sunrise, you should observe in which direction black clouds are to be seen. If they are in the east, you will know that it will be rainy on a day of Kinoe or Kinoto because they are connected with the direction of east.

If the sun looks purplish and the moon whitish, there will be a long spell of rainy weather; this means that the celestial *chi* has descended and the earthly *chi* has not risen, and it means that there will be a long spell of rain.

If the sun is whitish and the moon reddish, then the earthly *chi* has risen but the celestial *chi* has not fallen and there will be a drought.

If the sun is bluish and the moon greenish, then it means that the celestial *chi* has descended but the earthly *chi* has not risen, but in this case the two forms of *chi* have not mixed, which means it will be very cold.

If the sun is dark and blackish and the moon is blue, the celestial *chi* and the earthly *chi* have mixed but not very densely and therefore it will look like it is about to rain at any time. However, understand that there will be no rain and a rainbow will appear.[28]

---

27 In the Japanese calendar cycle of sixty days, each animal is associated with five days.

28 Two issues arise from this point: firstly, what is truly meant by 'black sun'; and secondly, as the original Chinese text talks of mist, it is possible that this is a method of predicting mist.

If you forecast on a day of the Hare, and if the clouds are gathering together in the centre [of the sky] and a strong and cold wind is raging, tearing the ground and breaking the trees, and heavy rain continues to fall and pour everywhere, then this is a sign of a terrible disaster. It means that warfare or an escalating situation will take place within five days.[29]

There are five notes in the Chinese pentatonic musical scale and they are: *gong* 宮, *shang* 商, *jiao* 角, *zhi* 徵 and *yu* 羽.
The days of the Rat and the Horse are connected to the note *gong*.
The days of the Hare and the Cockerel are connected to the note *yu*.
The days of the Dragon and the Dog are connected to the note *shang*.
The days of the Snake and the Boar are connected to the note *jiao*.
The days of the Ox, Ram, Tiger and Monkey are connected to the note *zhi*.

The element Earth is connected to the note *gong*.
The element Water is connected to the note *yu*.
The element Wood is connected to the note *jiao*.
The element Fire is connected to the note *zhi*.
The element Metal is connected to the note *shang*.

If on a day[30] of *zhi* there is a wind of *zhi* and an element[31] of Ox, Ram, Tiger or Monkey is added, then a fire will break out.
If on a day of *jiao* there is a wind of *jiao* and an element of either Snake or Boar is added, then an epidemic will break out.
If on a day of *shang* there is a wind of *shang* and an element of either Dragon or Dog is added, then a war will break out.
If on a day of *yu* there is a wind of *yu* and an element of either Hare or Cockerel is added, a heavy rain will fall.

The art of judging the six emotions[32] in connection to the weather

On a day of the Tiger or of the Horse – which are connected with judiciousness and fidelity – if a wind comes from the south, an auspicious or pleasurable event will take place.

---

29 This appears to go beyond using the environment to predict the weather and enter the realm of using the weather to predict future human events.
30 Each note is attached to an animal and these animals represent specific days; thus, if it is a day of the Ox then it is also a day of zhi.
31 Each note is attached to an animal, and these animals represent specific directions, times etc. For example, the Hare is east, which means that any element that is connected to the Hare in the above situation becomes 'mixed' into the equation, and then the stated result will happen.
32 The *Shoninki ninja* manual states seven.

On a day of the Snake or the Cockerel – which are connected with generosity – if a wind comes from the west, then take it as a sign of booze or sex to come.

On a day of the Ox or the Dog – which are connected with fairness – if a wind comes from the southwest, it is a sign for mutual virtue and harmony.

On a day of the Monkey or the Rat – which are connected with greed and cruelty, like that of a wolf – if a wind comes from the north, it is a sign that invasion, robbery of property or money or a war will take place.

On a day of the Boar[33] or the Hare – which are connected with *in* or negative nature – if a wind comes from the east, raiders will invade across the border and pillage a fortress within seven days.

On a day of the Dragon or the Ram – which are connected with viciousness – if a wind comes from the northeast, then an astonishing, unusual and evil event will take place within seven days.

Also, if the wind is fresh and not cold, it is considered proper, while if it is a dark and gloomy wind, breaking houses or trees, it is a sure sign of [further] bad luck.

For the six days from the day of Mizunoe-Rat to the day of Hinoto-Snake, if it is rainy and dark for three days, it will be the same for the rest of that [six-day] period. Also, if there are no clouds for the three days from the day of Tsuchinoe-Horse to Tsuchinoto-Ram and Kanoe-Monkey,[34] it will be sunny for the following three days. This method can be applied to other days in the same way.

For the six days from Hinoe-Rat to Kanoto-Snake, if the clouds are low and thick [on the first day] then it will be rainy in various provinces [for the rest of that period]. If there is a cloud shaped like a snake over the Celestial River, mist will gather to become clouds; if boar-like clouds cross over the Celestial River, then the wind will subside and it be rainy.

In the case where there are no clouds to hide the sunlight and yet the trees or grasses do not grow for the ten days [because of a lack of rain], then look for black moist clouds that cross over the Celestial River, as this means it will be rainy and the rice fields will become soaked.

If there is a black cloud at midnight on a day of Mizunoto-Ox, and it is shaped like a dragon and is in the east, then it will be rainy on a day of the Dragon.

If there is a cloud shaped like a horse early on a day of the Horse and it is also in the south, then it will be rainy on a day of the Horse.

At the beginning of a lunar month, if the sun and the moon are blue-black, moist and bright, there will be plenty of rain in that month. If they are yellow-red, then it will be dry and sunny.

---

33 The original text states Tiger. However, Tiger has already been used and Boar is missing; therefore, it is considered a mistake.

34 Three individual days in the sixty-day cycle.

If there is a belt of clouds across the centre of the sun at sunrise and if the clouds are not dispersed until the sun is at the height of three *jo* [from your point of view], then this means that soon there will be plenty of rain.

When you look east in the morning, if there is a cloud shaped like a pile of soil, it will be rainy.

When you look west in the evening and if there are clouds in the shape of a pile of soil close to the sun, then it will be rainy.

When you look north in the early morning, if there are lots of yellowish-black clouds, it will be rainy.

When you look south at dawn, if there is *chi* that moves toward the south,[35] it will be rainy.

If there is a black cloud shaped like a boar at sunrise, it will also be rainy on a day of Rat [or within seven days].

If heavy clouds are blown by a south[east] wind to the northwest, then it will be rainy within eight days.

If there are clouds stretching between the direction[36] of the Tiger and the Hare, then it will be rainy on a day of Kinoe or Kinoto.

If the clouds stretch in the direction of the Dragon to the Snake, then it will be rainy on a day of Hinoe or Hinoto.

If the clouds stretch in the direction of the Horse to the Ram, then it will be rainy on a day of Tsuchinoe or Tsuchinoto.

If the clouds stretch in the direction of the Ram to the Monkey, then it will be rainy on a day of Kanoe or Kanoto.

If Mars reaches the Celestial River or goes into it and there are fewer stars seen, then it is a sign of drought.

If the stars in the Celestial River look 'thick' or 'dense' and the stars of Pegasus look bright and swaying, then there will be a lot of rain.

If the celestial powers become angry, then there will be hail and clouds will spread all over the sky. Also, if it is raining slightly and the wind is gentle, then it is a sign that a righteous lord will cherish his people and be respected. In addition, if a lord is righteous and the retainers are faithful, then the weather will be windy first and rainy later on. If the lord is arrogant and the vassals are not faithful, it will be rainy at the start and become windy in the end.

When Saturn enters the Celestial River from the reverse side, then the laws [of humans] will be in dilemma and it will result in a heavy rain.

If Mars gets within [twenty-one centimetres] of Jupiter[37] [when looking at

---

35 This description has been inserted from the original Chinese text.
36 Each animal represents a direction.
37 Fujibayashi writes this as Mercury in his annotation, but the original manual states Jupiter.

arm's length] then the governing principles [of man] will be overturned and there will be a serious drought.

If you have enough knowledge of the heavens, that is periods of *in* and *yo* and 'open' and 'closed', including an understanding of the 'movements' of the second and third stars [of the Big Dipper], then, when combined with [an understanding] of the four earthly branches of Rat, Horse, Hare and Cockerel, then the following will happen: if clouds are raised in the time of Hare, Horse, Cockerel or Rat, then it will rain without fail.

Also, in the year, month, day or hour of the above four branches, if Polaris moves to another Celestial Palace[38] and it is covered with clouds that are blue-black and moist, it will invariably be rainy.

On the six days of Mizunoe, then [the element of] the Dragon or Water will be summoned and therefore it will be rainy.

For the three months of spring, on the days of Hinoe and Hinoto

For the three months of summer, on the days of Tsuchinoe and Tsuchinoto

For the three months of autumn, on the days of Mizunoe and Mizunoto

For the three months of winter, on the days of Kinoe and Kinoto

For the periods of *doyo*, on the days of Kanoe and Kanoto

On each of the above days of the Ten [Celestial Stems] and in connection with the lunar mansions, no matter if there are clouds or *chi*, then there will be heavy rain or a long spell of rainy weather.

On the first day when Venus or Mercury appears, then it will be heavy wind and rain.

If the moon 'invades' the area of stars that are in the lunar mansion called the Net, then it will be rainy.

If copper sparrows[39] chirp then the harvest is ripe, and if they do not it is a sign of a year of drought. Also, if you see a spider-snake stretch its four wings, then a three-year drought will follow.

If stone sparrows fly around, rivers will be in flood and if the *shoyo* one-legged bird is hopping around vibrantly with its wings stretched, it is a sign of a flood.

If the virtue of the lord and if the five phases of weather are thrown out of balance, new things will prosper.[40] The wisdom of the lord is constructed from

---

38 宫 A nine-square grid used in ancient China in connection with astrology/astronomy.

39 Fujibayashi is referencing legendary Chinese animals in these sections. However, by his syntax it is clear he believes in them; therefore, these mythical names may be associated with real creatures, or alternatively, he may simply be carrying the 'belief' across from the Chinese text.

40 The Chinese is highly ambiguous here and this sentence is hypothetical.

the ten righteous perfect principles and is formed as a whole and because these ten are adhered to, then wisdom will manifest itself. Heaven should be respected; also, value the earth and have perfect principles. With a subtle and secret method [the lord] enhances sincerity, shows respect for spirits, worships the gods and thus acquires perfect function [in this life] and in this way he establishes his bloodline.

[This is the end of the verses on rain]

Examine these Chinese poems or sayings of wind and rain, each of which are of four lines and seven ideograms in length, and note that things concerning the twenty-four sections of heaven[41] will not deviate from these above verses. You should read the text thoroughly and think through it with much care, giving consideration to the generating and conflicting cycles of the Five Elements, and in this way there will be scarce a chance that any forecasting you do shall fail.

I have extracted and summarized some essential points from the *Bingheng*[42] and *Bingjing*[43] Chinese manuals and other texts and written them above. Apart from these quoted above, there are a multitude of other ways for divining both wind and rain. However, these are to be passed on orally.

To know how heavy a rain will be, you should be aware of the following:

If it is a period of *chishigo*[44] and [if you expect rain], then a medium-sized shower will actually turn out to be a larger cascade. On the other hand, if it is not a period of *chishigo* then the rain may be medium in level even [if it is expected to be] a large squall.

[A method to establish which one of the Five Elements represents your character][45]

• [In *figure 34*] the ideograms marked at the top of the connecting line say 'wind' and 'rain'.

---

41 Possibly the twenty-four points of the Loupan Compass of feng shui.

42 An unknown manual.

43 The Soldier Mirror of Wuzi 兵鏡, a Chinese military manual written about 1620.

44 A period where people are considered more likely to die. Such times are predicted in connection with tides.

45 In the original text, this is a list of ideograms next to the image of the hand. The *Bansenshukai* does not explain their presence, but it is in fact a Chinese-based method to establish which of the Five Elements represents a person. The top line of ideograms corresponds to the upper joint on the inside of each of the fingers; the next line represents the middle joint; and the bottom line represents the lowest joint, which is the joint between the finger and the palm of the hand. Armed with the animal-zodiac of a person, anyone skilled in this method can determine which of the Five Elements a person is connected to, which fits in with the skills described in this volume, many of which require you to know a person's element.

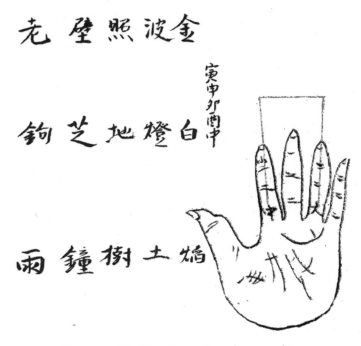

Figure 34. The Five Elements and personality

- [When you use this method[46] of weather prediction] you should start counting from the Rat.
- The ideogram at the top of the index finger is 'small', the one at the base of the index finger is 'medium' and the ideogram at the base of the ring finger is 'large'.

[This list of ideograms[47] starts at the thumb and goes across each upper finger joint until they reach the little finger:]

Gold – Wave – Illuminate – Wall – Old

The animals connected with this upper tier are the Rat, Horse, Ox and Ram.

[This list of ideograms starts at the thumb and goes across each middle finger joint until they reach the little finger:]

White – Light – Earth – Grass – Hook

---

46 Fujibayashi does not clarify these labels on the image. However, they appear to be connected to the above issue of large, medium and lesser rainfall and are most likely a method of prediction.

47 The original Chinese text differs slightly from Fujibayashi.

The animals connected with this middle tier are the Tiger, Monkey, Hare and Cockerel.

[This list of ideograms starts at the thumb and goes across each lower finger joint until they reach the little finger:]

Flame – Soil – Tree – Bell – Rain

The animals connected with this lower tier are the Dog, Boar, Dragon and Snake.

Three points on calculating the time of the moonrise and moonset

There is a set method for doing this:

Split a Japanese hour into ten parts. These are called the 'ten sub-hours' [each of twelve minutes], making ten of them add up to one Japanese hour [120 minutes].

On any day in a lunar month, multiply the number of the day[48] by four, and add it to the [start of the] hour of the Dragon [7am]; the answer you arrive at will be the time of the moonrise for that day. However, remember the moon sets six Japanese hours after it rises [twelve standard hours].

An example of the above formula:

If it is the *eighth* day of the lunar month, multiply *eight* by *four*, this equals *thirty-two*. Now you know the time [of moonrise] will be: *three* Japanese hours plus *two* sub-hours [twenty-four minutes] after the hour of the Dragon [7am].[49] In this case the time [of moonrise] would be during the first third of the hour of the Ram [between 1pm and 1.40pm].

[An example using a two-digit day number:]

If it is the *twenty-fourth* day of the lunar month, multiply *two* by *four*, this equals *eight* Japanese hours, and next multiply [the second part of the day number] *four* also by *four*, which equals *sixteen*. [Sixteen is made up of one and six, which correspond to one Japanese hour and six sub-hours of twelve minutes each,] thus, add the *eight* hours and *one* hour, then the *six* sub-hours. When added you get *nine* Japanese hours and *six* sub-hours [nineteen hours twelve minutes in standard hours]. In this case, you now know the time will be in the second third of the hour of the Ox [between 1.40am and 2.20am[50]]. Remember, six Japanese hours later the moon will set in the second third of the hour of the Ram on the 'next' day.

---

48 That is, the first, second or third day of the lunar month, etc.

49 Three Japanese hours, plus two sub-units equals six hours twenty-four minutes. Adding this to 7am gives the time 1.24pm. The hour of the Ram falls between 1pm and 3pm.

50 The actual time would be 2.12am.

For the rest of the days, the same method should be applied. You should now become familiar with this system and you should fully understand [and memorize] how to calculate the time of moonrise for the fifteenth and twentieth day of the lunar month [as a guideline].

The three ways of beating the drum for the hour

In the first ten days of a month:

You should beat Hare 'on the head' – that is, as the hour changes to the hour of the Hare. Do this so that people know it is the hour of Hare, this means that people will know the time until you beat the drum for the next hour, which is the hour of Dragon.

In the middle ten days of a month:

You should beat the Hare 'on the hip' – that is, in the middle of the hour of Hare.

In the last ten days of the month:

You should hit the Hare 'on the tail' – that is, at the last section of the hour of Hare. This means that the drumming will finish at the start of the hour of Dragon.

Four points on how to know the ebb and flow of the tides

I

Spring tides equal ten days and neap tides equal five. Although the drawing is included here (see *Figure 35*), there is also a secret that goes with it.[51]

II

You can have an approximate idea of the time of the tides by using the way of *chishigo.*[52]

[The month is divided into three sections of ten days, making the first, second and third parts of a month.[53]]

On the first, second, ninth and tenth days in each of the three ten-day sections

---

51 The white circle in the centre of the chart rotates. However, the oral tradition is the missing element of this puzzle and therefore its full explanation cannot be given.

52 In the Chinese skill of Onmyodo, it is said you can know the period or time of a person's death by the tides or the Chinese zodiac sign of the person's birth date.

53 The manual does not include this section as these thirds are discussed earlier and would equate to a 360-day year. As with all lunar calendars the points would change, as the solar year does not correspond exactly to the lunar year.

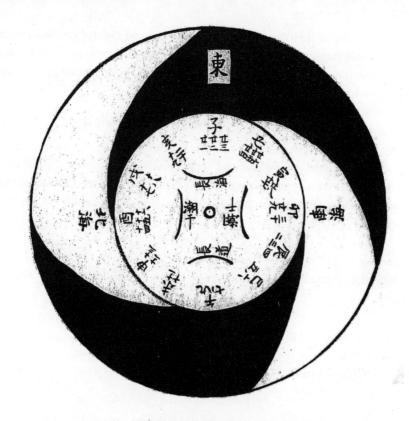

Figure 35. A tidal time chart
You should set the date [which can be found on the inner rim of the white circle
in *figure 35*] to the character of east 東 [which is the ideogram in the white square
set inside the black section at the top of the chart].

of a month, it will be low tide[54] in the hours of the Rat, Horse, Hare and Cockerel.

On the sixth, seventh and eighth days in each of the three ten-day sections of
a month, it will be low tide in the hours of the Tiger, Monkey, Snake and Boar.

On the third, fourth and fifth days in each of the three ten-day sections of a
month, it will be low tide in the hours of the Ox, Ram, Dragon and Dog.

The following information is taken from poems for spring, mid-range and
neap tides.

Spring tides are from the fourteenth to the eighteenth days of a lunar month
and from the twenty-ninth day to the third day [of the next] lunar month.

Mid-range tides are from the fourth to the eighth and from the twenty-fifth to
the twenty-eighth days of a lunar month.

---

54 The manual states 'time of the tide'. However, this appears to imply 'low tide', as *chishigo* is
based on the low tide.

Neap tides are from the ninth to the thirteenth and from the nineteenth to the twenty-fourth days of a lunar month.

III

The time of the moonrise always parallels the time of the high tide. Therefore, you can know the tidal times by calculating the time of moonrise or moonset. The second tidal system should occur in the seventh Japanese hour[55] after the rise of the moon. There are more oral traditions here.

In the above information on tides, the tidal time may sometimes gradually shift over time, but with the method [of observing moonrise and moonset] you will always be correct.

IV

Here is Ota Dokan's poem about tides:

遠クナル近ク鳴海ノ濱千鳥声ニソ潮ノ満干ヲバシル

By listening to the call of plover birds[56] and checking if it is near or distant, you can know if it is low or high tide.

Two points on identifying the direction

I

You can know east, west and south by observing the Big Dipper. Generally, you should always have a celestial map on the wall so that you can learn what the twenty-eight lunar mansions and the stars look like; also, you should watch the sky to get used to their position in the heavens. The *Bingjing* manual says that the sky is as obscure as a spacious plain [on the ground] and if you have no clue to the direction you wish to head in, then you should observe the Big Dipper and the 'middle stars'[57] 候中星 every night, so that you easily know how to find your way.

---

55 Tides work on a twelve-hourly basis; therefore, the term 'seventh' here could be a transcription error meaning 'sixth', or it could be owing to the fact that Fujibayashi would have started counting on his initial hour. Modern readers start counting from the hour after the start point, whereas the Medieval Japanese started counting from their actual starting position.

56 Plovers forage along the shoreline as the tides come in and out. Therefore, if the bird's call is far away, then so is the shoreline and vice versa. (Source: ornithologist Professor Tim Birkhead.)

57 This is a complex Chinese system which changes and moves from lunar mansion to lunar mansion as time progresses.

[The stars will be in the following lunar mansions and positions:]

The first month – they are in Mane at the time of twilight and in Heart at sunrise.

The second month – they are in Well at the time of twilight and in Willowing Basket at sunrise.

The third month – they are in Willow at the time of twilight and in South Dipper at sunrise.

The fourth month – they are in Base at the time of twilight and near the star of Altair at sunrise.

The fifth month – they are in Horn at twilight and in Rooftop at sunrise.

The sixth month – they are in the South Dipper at twilight and in Wall at sunrise.

The seventh month – they are in Tail at twilight and in Bond at sunrise.

The eighth month – they are in Emptiness at twilight and in Net at sunrise.

The ninth month – they are in Ox at twilight and in Well at sunrise.

The tenth month – they are in Emptiness at twilight and in Encampment at sunrise.

The eleventh month – they are in Encampment at twilight and in Chariot at sunrise.

The twelth month – they are in Stride at twilight and in Neck at sunrise.

II

If you carry a compass with you, you can identify east or west, even on a rainy night.

The *Bingjing* manual says that if the sky is clouded or gloomy or even pitch black at night and you cannot identify the direction you need, then you should let an old horse walk in front of you, as he will know the way.

An alternative to the above method is to use the compass known as the 'south-pointing fish' to identify the position of the cardinal points. To make one of these 'fish-compasses' you should do the following: cut a fish shape out of thin iron leaf to the measurement of two *sun* in length and five *bu* in width and with a pointed head and tail. Then heat this iron-leaf fish in a charcoal fire until it becomes thoroughly red-hot, then take it out by the head with iron tongs and place it so that its tail is in the direction of north. In this position it should then be quenched in a basin of water, so that [only] its tail is submerged and up to several tenths of an inch. This 'fish' is then kept in a tightly closed box.

To use it, fill a small bowl with water and set it up in a sheltered area, then the fish is laid as flat as possible upon the water's surface,[58] so that it floats, whereupon its head will point to the direction of south.

Two points on knowing the time

I

By observing the four stars [that make up the 'pan'] of the Big Dipper you can know the time. These stars travel one *shi* (30°) for each Japanese hour (approximately 120 minutes). You can calculate the time by counting anticlockwise by four places on a zodiac calendar. [Remember these four sections are represented by animals in the Chinese system,] also, do not forget you need to apply the number of the month.

Here is an example of this method: if it is any day in the first lunar month of a year and if the end of the 'handle' of the Big Dipper points to the direction of the Tiger, then count four spaces anticlockwise, i.e. Ox, Rat, Boar, Dog – therefore, the time will be the hour of the Dog when the handle of the Big Dipper is in the direction of the Tiger (approximately northeast). Another illustration would be: in the hour of the Cockerel the 'handle' of the Big Dipper will point to the direction of the Ox [because they are four sections away from each other]. Another example: if the 'handle' of the Big Dipper points in the direction of the Hare (east), then counting anticlockwise you can calculate the time is the hour of the Boar. As you can see, the Hare is three places down from [and including] Ox, as the Boar is three from [and including] the Cockerel.[59] The same method should be applied for every one of the twelve zodiac signs and for every month.

The Big Dipper

In the Big Dipper, stars one, two, three and four make up the 'pan' and stars five, six and seven make up the 'handle'. The seventh star or 'Flickering Light' 揺光 is the star of Hagun [as described in volume sixteen].

I I

On a rainy and starless night, you should use a sand clock, a weight or the following poem *The Cat's Eyes*:

At the hour of six [6am and 6pm] the eyes of a cat are round.

---

58 The text does not talk of a leaf or any supporting sheet, meaning that this was either obvious or that the sheet it is made of is thin enough to float.

59 This last sentence has been inserted by Fujibayashi to highlight that the system is the same as it moves around the Chinese calendar. When this method is applied to the modern illustration given in the introduction, the system immediately becomes apparent.

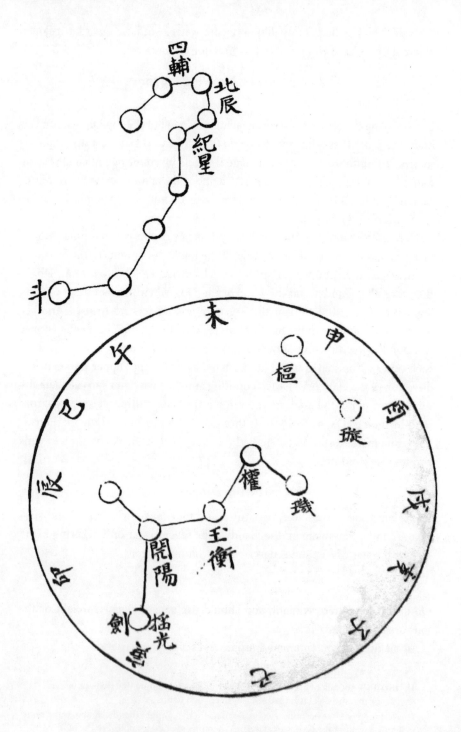

Figure 36. The Big Dipper and unnamed image

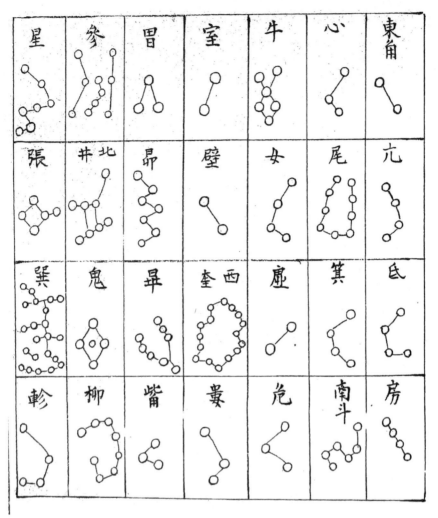

Figure 37. The twenty-eight lunar mansions

At the hour of five [8am and 8pm] and eight [2am and 2pm] the eyes of a cat are egg-shaped.

At the hour of four [10am and 10pm] and seven [4am and 4pm] the eyes of a cat are like persimmon seeds.

At the hour of nine [midday] the eyes of a cat are like needles.

The lunar mansions

There are twenty-eight lunar mansions, which are arranged in four groups of seven and are allotted to each of the four cardinal points. The two stars called Keisei 経星 and Bosei 昴星 of the star cluster Pleiades are found in a lunar mansion of the western side of the sky. Also, to find the western lunar mansion called the Triad, find the stars Karasukiboshi 唐鋤星 [which are well known[60]].

In order to learn the above subject of the divination of the wind and rain, the diagrams and instructions on how to know the tidal times, the rising and setting of the moon, the Big Dipper and the twenty-eight lunar mansions as mentioned above have been included. You should always observe astronomical phenomena and study [the night sky] very closely, so that after much practice you will know these things instantly.

---

60 Fujibayashi gives this paragraph to highlight how to use well-known stars of the time to find the lunar mansions in question.

Ninki I

Ninja Tools I

Climbing tools

Not only climbing tools but the whole range of *Ninki ninja* tools can be said to be similar to the mesh of a net. Even if the net has millions of interwoven links, it may catch a bird with only a small area. It is exactly the same with the way of *ninja* tools. You do not need to use all of the tools in your arsenal every time you 'steal in' but you should have a well thought out plan beforehand and consider the status of the enemy, taking only those tools that suit the requirements. Do not carry too many tools and remember that those who can achieve multiple tasks with a single tool can be called good *shinobi*.

The tied ladder

There are two types of this ladder: the *proper* 真 and the *temporary* 草. The proper version is what you are usually prepared with in advance and is pre-constructed. The temporary version is made on the location with two bamboo posts you have carried with you; this is done to avoid suspicion when en route to your target.

Split bamboo into thin bamboo sticks and form them as you would form an *uchie*[1] spear handle. You can make it as long as you like, but not so long that its length makes it bend. The rungs should be bamboo and tied up with thin rope. There is a secret way of tying them. People in ancient times made the width between the two vertical posts eight or six *sun*, and varied the length between the rungs according to the place. I say that the length between the rungs should

---

1   An *uchie* is a lightweight and cost-effective type of spear handle. It is formed with split bamboo put around a shaft of wood then glued and bound with strings.

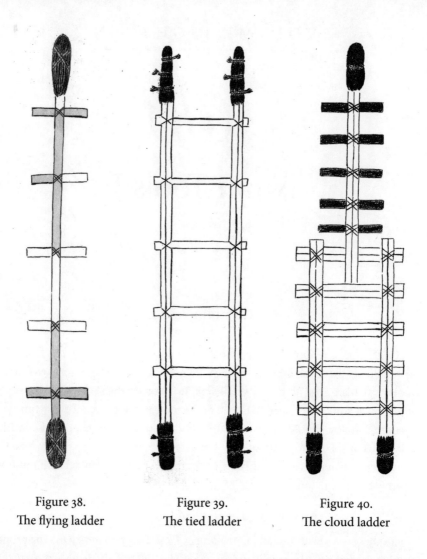

Figure 38.
The flying ladder

Figure 39.
The tied ladder

Figure 40.
The cloud ladder

be changed as one likes and as suits the individual. Both ends of the posts should be wrapped with straw matting at a length of two or three *shaku*, so that they will make no noise. If not straw matting, then use anything soft and available at that time; rather than following exactly this above example, you should always be flexible.

The flying ladder

This should be made in the same way as the tied ladder above by splitting thicker bamboo into thinner strips and attaching it to a central pole. The ends of the shaft should be wrapped with straw matting in the same way as the tied ladder.

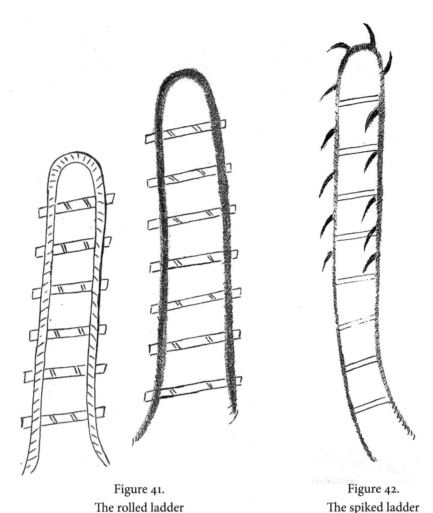

Figure 41.
The rolled ladder

Figure 42.
The spiked ladder

The cloud ladder

This is not a ladder in its own right. For a place you cannot reach with a tied ladder or a flying ladder, secure a flying ladder onto a tied ladder as in the drawing and use it to climb. This is called the cloud ladder. There are further things to be orally transmitted here.

The rolled ladder

This should be made of hemp rope and its length should be the height from the floor to a man's wrist when he stands and holds his hand [directly above him] in the air. More to be orally transmitted. The rungs should be made of bamboo.

The spiked ladder

The length of this should be two *jo* and five *shaku*[2] and the width should be six *sun*. The rope should be of hemp or bracken and the hooks should be attached as illustrated above. The rungs can be bamboo or rope; more things to be orally transmitted here. This should be used on a steep rocky cliff with trees on top.

The high ladder or tool-transportation wire

Tie [two ropes] onto an iron ring as in the drawing [so that the ring can be pulled between two agents] and have it [travel] along one fixed rope, which goes through the ring. This high ladder is a tool to transport other *ninja* tools.

The *kunai* digging tool

The length should be one *shaku* two *sun* or one *shaku* six *sun*. It should be made of iron and constructed using the same method as for the *hera kunai*, which is the flared digging tool.

The *saguritetu* (also called the *tsukihake*) probing iron

This should be made of iron. The length should be one *shaku* five *sun* or one *shaku* two or three *sun* with a handle of six *sun*. There are oral traditions with this tool.[3]

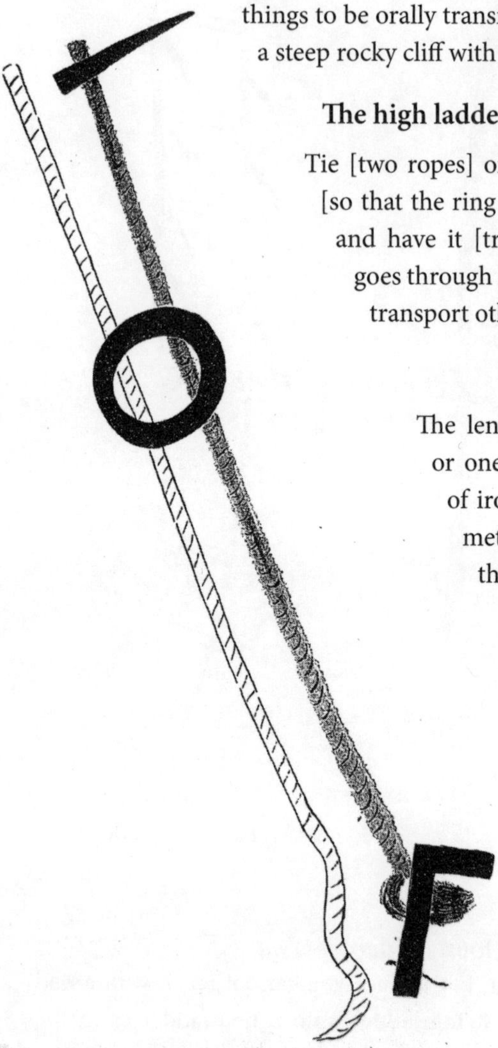

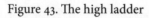

Figure 43. The high ladder

---

2   This is longer than expected and measures seven and a half metres.

3   The *kuden* or oral traditions referred to here are discussed in the Shinobi Hiden manual of 1560, where it says that the probing iron should be used with a lubricant to dampen any sound.

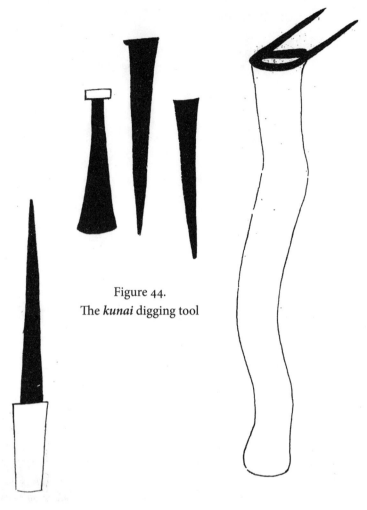

Figure 44.
The *kunai* digging tool

Figure 45.
The *saguritetu* probing iron

Figure 46.
The *nagabukuro* long bag

The *nagabukuro* long bag

The bag should be made of cotton, with a length of two or three *jo*. Sew two pieces of cloth together and have a semi-circular bar sewn into the mouth at the top; also attach iron nails [as in the illustration]. There is a way of putting an iron ball at the bottom of the bag; however, I do not believe in this method.

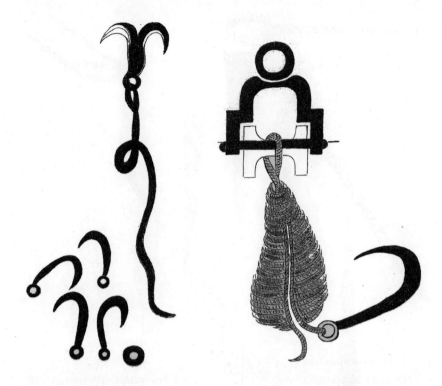

Figure 47. *Uchikagi* grappling hooks   Figure 48. The spider ladder

Uchikagi grappling hooks

Uchikagi comprise four separate hooks made of tempered iron. Use the small iron ring [in the drawing] to combine them all into one grappling hook. The rope should be one *jo* five *shaku*[4] long and made of hemp. I say that the rope should be varied according to the opportunity.

The spider ladder

Rope goes through the ring at the top, and there is a secret about the spacing of one *shaku*; oral tradition only.

The outer roller on this tool is made of wood.[5]

There is a hole at the side of the tool, which allows the central axle to pass

---

4   This is quite short for a grappling hook and measures four and a half metres, which shows that it was mainly for climbing over low walls and such. However, as Fujibayashi states, the situation will dictate the length.

5   This is the white section in the image and is a greased roller on an iron axle – the original says metal with an internal wooden roller, but this appears to be a transcription error and should be reversed.

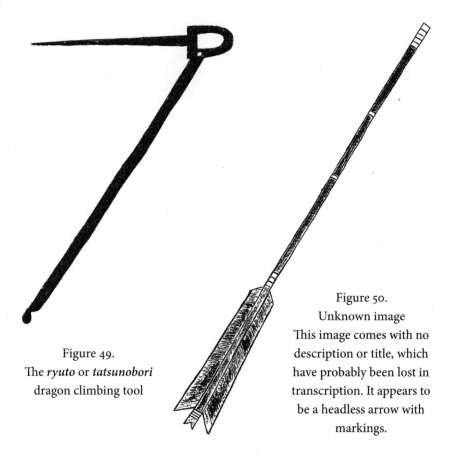

Figure 49.
The *ryuto* or *tatsunobori*
dragon climbing tool

Figure 50.
Unknown image
This image comes with no
description or title, which
have probably been lost in
transcription. It appears to
be a headless arrow with
markings.

through the wooden roller. The axle should be wrapped[6] in cloth and covered in lacquer.

The rope should be braided like *shirashime,*[7] and at two-*shaku* intervals and should be constructed in a fret-like manner like a stringed [instrument].[8]

The *ryuto* or *tatsunobori* dragon climbing tool

It is four and a half *bu* thick and has a square cross-section[9] on the spike.

It is six *bu* thick and has a square cross-section on the main and longer arm.

The length of the spike is four *sun* and five *bu*.

---

6 The text says wrap cloth of four or five tan around the axle. However, one tan is extremely large and it is believed to be a transcription error and that it simply means wrap the axle in cloth four or five times.

7 Unknown term.

8 While ambiguous, this would most likely be a knot to place the feet on or hold onto – the text implies that you place this 'knot' in position while the rope is being made.

9 These two statements are referring to the descriptions on the right of the image, which point to the central hub.

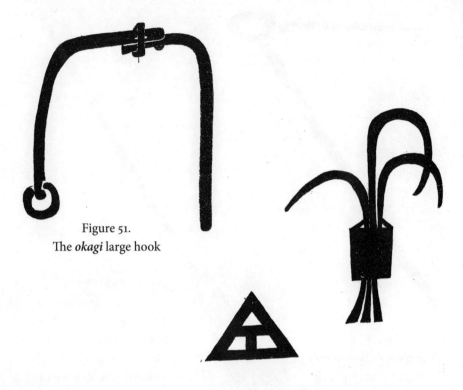

Figure 51.
The *okagi* large hook

Figure 52.
The *mitsukagi* three-pronged hook

The main lower bar is nine *sun* four *bu* long, two *bu* wide and one *bu* thick.
Put a thin thread on the bottom ring; the length of the thread should be
   forty *ken*.

The *okagi* large hook[10]

The bar on the right is six *sun* long.
The top bar is eight *sun* long when unfolded.
The tool opens out around the central connecting joint.
Lock the tool in place with a locking ring.
The bar on the left and side is five *sun* long.

---

10 This is a fold-out hook. When collapsed it would most likely fold in half, forming an L-shape,
   and when a *shinobi* needed to make a fastening onto a wider wall or point, he could use this
   fold-out hook to hold fast a rope for others to follow.

The *mitsukagi* three-pronged hook

Attach the rope to the bottom of the hooks.

When the triangular socket is pulled down the hook folds away, and when it
is pushed up the three prongs will spread [forming the grapple].

The image on the left [*figure 52*] is the view of the socket from above.

[Using weapons as climbing aids]

Climbing with your tachi long sword[11]

Use this method for a wall up to seven or eight *shaku* high.

Using a spear as a temporary climbing aid

This is used for climbing a wall up to one *jo* one *shaku* in height.

Climbing with a spear designed for climbing

With a spear [handle] of two *ken* in length, you can climb up a wall two *ken* high.
For a two and a half *ken* and also a two *ken* and four *shaku* wall, there is a secret
aspect found around the butt of the spear, but this is to be orally transmitted.

Also, there are tools [for] the spider ladder and various useful methods of
using a rope that are to be orally transmitted.

---

11 This method is described earlier and appears in various manuals; it is the skill of using your
sword hilt as a foothold.

Ninki II

Ninja Tools II

Water tools

There are tools to help you cross over water; however, if you find yourself in an emergency situation, you may not always have them to hand. In such a case, you should make a makeshift raft of anything available – for example, bamboo, wood, bamboo grass, reeds, cattails, tubs, jars, wooden mallets and mortars etc. To illustrate how to create these makeshift tools there are drawings and guidelines within this chapter.

In ancient times there were many examples where a massive army had to tear down houses to supply themselves with building materials for these forms of craft, done so in order to cross a river.

The *mizugumo* water spider [floating seat], the *hasami-bako bune* war boat and other tools of our school are the best tools that you can use to cross over a river, moat or so on and are vitally important in *shinobi no jutsu*. They are handy and allow you to cross water in complete safety. Being of a quality rare in the world, they should be kept in strict secret. However, these have no benefit for a large army and should be considered as secret tools that only benefit *ninjutsu*.

The floating bridge

The length of the bridge will depend on the situation at the time, but there are things to be orally transmitted here. The width should be one *shaku* and two *sun* and the rope should have an extra two *shaku* or more at the end to secure the iron *hoguse* digging tools[1] that go at each end of the bridge. You use split bamboo for the rungs as in the illustration, there is more to be orally transmitted here.

---

1 Normally a small wooden or bamboo digging tool.

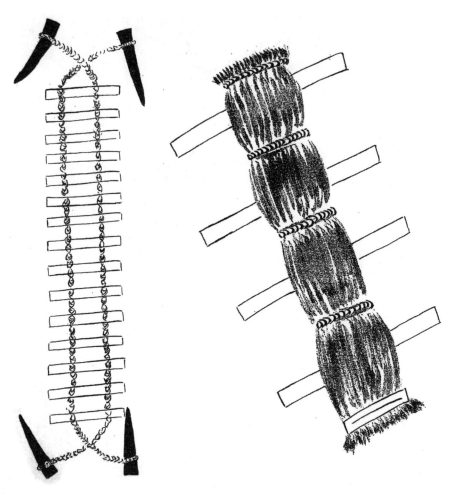

Figure 53. The floating bridge   Figure 54. The cattail raft

The cattail raft

Cattail rafts should be made with sections of wood and bundles of cattails. Place a bundle of cattails onto the top of the wooden shafts as in the illustration. In some cases you can put the wooden shafts through the stack of cattails.

The jar raft

Jar rafts should be made as in the illustration. Pans, buckets, wooden mallets and mortars and such can be used.
How to use this jar raft is an oral tradition.

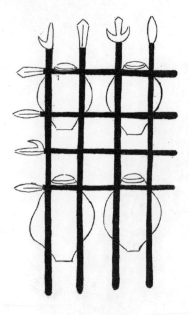

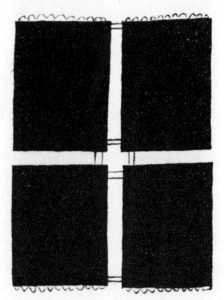

Figure 55. The jar raft   Figure 56. The wicker-basket raft

The wicker-basket raft

For the wicker-basket raft, you should take leather-lined wicker baskets and hinged sockets[2] with you, and when you need to cross over an expanse of water, put the four basket bottoms and the lids together and connect them with the hinge sockets so that you can get on the raft. Those who are engaged in this way should consider using leather-lined wicker baskets.[3]

The four squares are the leather wicker baskets.

You can see the hinged sockets connecting them.

The water spider[4] floating seat

- The full diameter of the water spider is two *shaku* and one *sun* eight *bu* and the internal diameter is one *shaku* and one *sun* eight *bu* when you have cut

---

2   Hijitsubo.

3   This sentence implies you should keep this type of basket with you.

4   One of the major misconceptions within *ninjutsu*, and possibly the second most damaging, is the belief that the 'water spider' is a form of floating shoe and that *ninja* would use two of them to 'walk on water'. The water spider is in fact a single tool (not a pair) and is, in essence, a floating seat. A shinobi would sit on the central leather seat and paddle or swim to the opposite side of a waterway. Cross-referencing this tool in other manuals (such as the Rodanshu) shows variations that, again, are singular and are described in the exact same way as within this manual – as floatation devices, akin to the modern life jacket.

out the centre, which leaves a wooden ring with a width of five *sun*.

- The board used should be two *bu* and five *rin* thick.[5]
- The hinges[6] should be two *rin* in thickness and two *sun* and two *bu* in length and then eight *bu* in width. These should be fixed with five nails at each end of the hinge.
- The type of *kakegane* latches you should use are *hakakegane* or 'winged latches'.[7]
- The *hirogekane* collapsing joints: the outer collapsing joints measure three *sun* and five *bu*, while the internal joints measure three *sun*.[8] The rivet [that fits into and fixes together the collapsing joints] should be thicker at the top and thinner at the base.[9] This is to be orally transmitted.
- The seat suspended in the centre is made of leather and can be of cowhide and be eight *sun* in length and four *sun* and five *bu* in width. Put a leather ring on each of the four corners, which are attached in turn to a ring, to which a braided cord should be connected [as in figure 57].[10]

However, generally the leather should be horse leather as this leather is thin and is desirable. Apply bitumen or asphalt[11] onto the leather; there are things to be orally transmitted here.

Figure 57 shows the upper side of the water spider when folded out and prepared for use.

The four thin gaps or pathways [at each cardinal point] should be narrower in

---

5 This is seven and a half millimetres.
6 These are the four 'strips' in the image, two on each side. They are used to fold away the tool when not in use and are redundant when the tool is set up, as the entire tool is held together by the other joints mentioned above this point in the text.
7 These appear to be the thin metal bars that are hooked through the four holes at the top of the image and the four holes at the bottom. The 'winged' description refers to the angled metal, over which the second half is slotted and held in place with a rivet.
8 While not clear in the drawing, Fujibayashi says that the four thin 'gaps or pathways' in the circumference of the 'wheel shape' are wider on the outer rim and narrower on the inner rim.
9 This is the same rivet that can be seen in the images of the collapsing joint, below. It appears to be the rivet that holds the two joints together. The original says nail; however, rivets and nails are similar and the substitution is possibly a transcription error – 釘 'nail' and 鋲 'rivet'.
10 Notice the lack of 'sandal straps', which are often incorrectly depicted on this section in modern images.
11 In *ninjutsu* manuals this is generally done to form a watertight seal for inflation. However, there is no mention of inflation here, but that could be the *kuden* or secret aspect of the text that has been lost. Alternatively, it may be possible that the entire ring is covered in leather and waterproofed to stop water penetrating the wood. The latter is most likely as there are holes going through the wood, which would stop any inflation but which could be sealed on their inner rim.

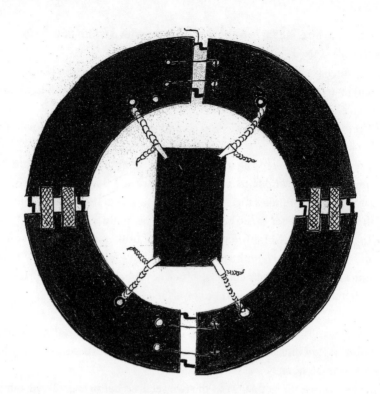

Figure 57. The water spider floating seat

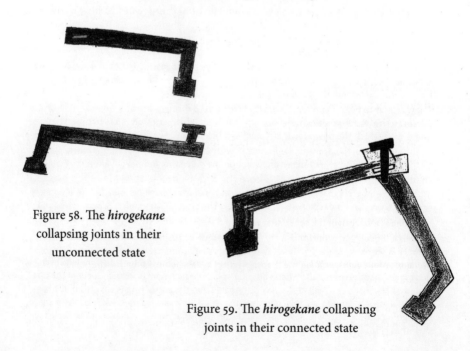

Figure 58. The *hirogekane*
collapsing joints in their
unconnected state

Figure 59. The *hirogekane* collapsing
joints in their connected state

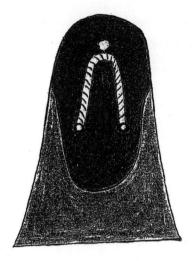

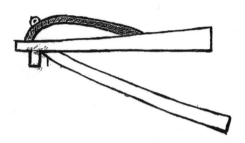

Figure 60. *Mizukaki* flippers
(from above)

Figure 61. *Mizukaki* flippers
(from the side)

the centre and wider at the edge. All eight[12] [collapsing joints] are constructed in the same way. More to be passed on orally.

The head of the rivet [that holds the two sections above together] rotates and thus locks the two together. Each of the eight collapsing joints should be made the same.

Mizukaki flippers[13] [to be used when in the water spider]

Mizukaki flippers should be made like the wooden sandals of *katahama*.[14] They should have a revolving spool[15] on the bottom and a thong on the top so you can put them on as you would put on sandals.

This is the view from above:

The mechanism can be found on the bottom of the flipper. Here is the secret.[16]

This is the view from the side:

You can see the mechanism [where the flipper meets the sole of the sandal].

---

12 You can see in the illustration of the two sections of the collapsing joint (figures 58 and 59) that one is longer than the other.

13 This is a flipper that propels an agent forwards when he is sitting upright. The fact that the flipper is set between the two floating seats hints to its connected usage; however, in some versions of the *Bansenshukai* the flippers section comes before both floating seats.

14 Unknown term.

15 The text says 'rokuro', which means 'to turn' or 'a turning action'. In view of the nature of this particular tool, it is translated here as 'spool'.

16 This annotation presumably refers to the device on the bottom of the flipper.

A water spider from another school

Take thin round sticks of hard bamboo or whalebone by shaving them and construct a series of rings. Connect the rings together in a line with thread at three or four places, so that it is similar to the internal frame of a paper lantern. Cover the ends with round board-caps made of the *Paulownia* tree and which are four *sun* in thickness, and cover the frame with horse or deer leather using glue and lacquer. However, you may also rivet the leather on. Cut a hole into one of the end board-caps and attach a screw seal to it; you then use this to inflate[17] the tool. There are more points to be orally transmitted here. One theory says that you can use *jumonji* paper and the juice of persimmons applied to it as a covering. When you use this version of the water spider, blow air into it, screw on the cap seal and wear it below your navel. More to be passed on by word of mouth.

[In *figure 62*] the drawing on the right shows the internal framework of the water spider and the drawing on the left shows the completed water spider with the leather stretched around it.

The *hasamibako-bune* collapsible boat

[Text found directly on the drawing:]

- All of the boat's bottom boards should be hinged together[18] [so that they can fold into a portable size].
- Some of the bottom boards should have the same dimensions; each should have a width of one *shaku* three *bu* and five *rin*. However, the central bottom board should have a length of two *shaku* nine *bu*, while the outer bottom boards should have a length of two *shaku* two *bu*.[19]
- All of the bottom boards should be three *bu* five *rin* in thickness.
- The port and starboard bulkheads are identical in size.
- [The bulkheads fold up into one portable piece,] alternate hinges are on the inside and the outside of the wall [so that it can fold in a concertina fashion].
- Each bulkhead has five main sections of the same dimensions; each

---

17 The concept of the water spider as a 'floating shoe' is fully at odds with this section of the *Bansenshukai*. Fujibayashi himself shows that the water spider is a form of medieval life jacket and his comparison to versions from other (unknown) schools, totally eliminates the myth of the ninja walking on water. This myth and incorrect interpretation can be traced back to early twentieth-century published works by Fujita Seiko.

18 The pairs of white dotted rectangles on the bottom boards represent the hinges that are on the top side. The line or section next to these double hinges has a hinge on the underside. This means that when folded, it folds like a concertina and into a single folded rectangle.

19 This means that when the boat is erected, the sides where these bottom boards gently slope inward, toward the bow and the stern, give it a more hydrodynamic signature.

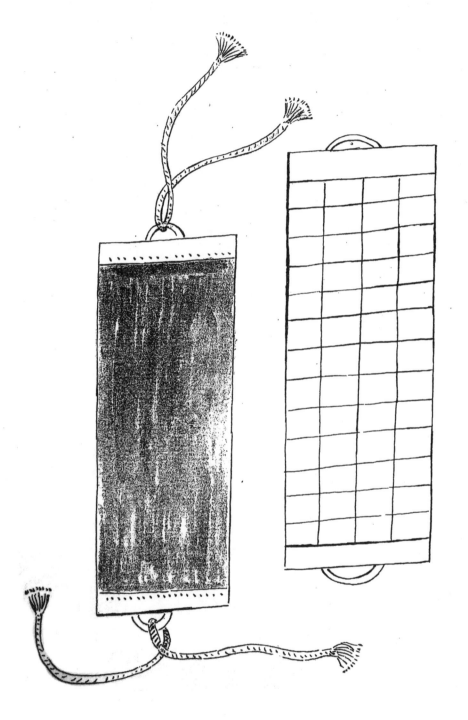

Figure 62. A water spider from another school

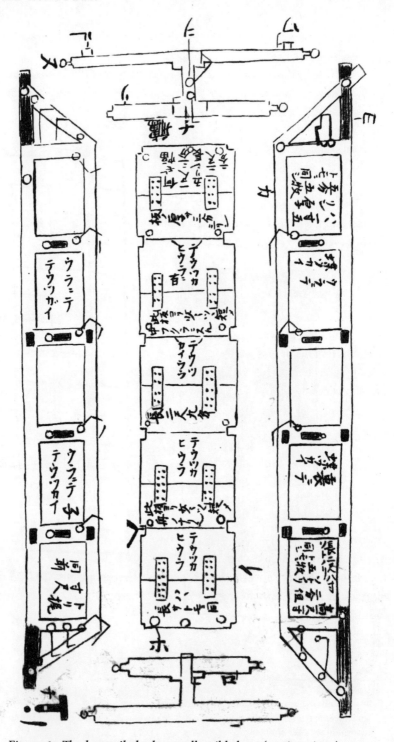

Figure 63. The *hasamibako-bune* collapsible boat (section views)

section measures one *shaku* and one *sun* in height and two *shaku* and eight *sun* in length.
- The bulkhead structure is made of beams that measure one *sun* and five *rin* in width and five *bu* in thickness. They are all the same in all five parts of the bulkhead.

[Text accompanying the drawing:]

イ [20]

Concerning the hinges: plane the boards so that the metal hinges and the boards are flush with each other.[21]

ロ

Each half of the lower bar on the stem post is one *shaku* two *sun* and four *bu* in length [and attaches to the stem post]. The position of the thwarts in this boat make the bulkheads flare outward. Therefore, you need to angle the joints at the end of this section so that they fit correctly. This bar is eight *sun* in width and six *bu* in thickness.

ハ [22]

The length of the *tsuku* stem post between the connecting joint and lower horizontal bar on the transom is six *sun* eight *bu*.

二

The upper bar of the transom is two *shaku* one *sun* and five *bu*, not including the connecting joints at each end. The width is one *sun* and five *rin* and it is six *bu* thick. It is joined [in an angular fashion] where the *tsuku* stem post comes together.

---

20 These symbols represent the equivalent of A, B and C in Japanese and match the text to the image. Some are missing from the original image.

21 The hinges in question here are the white rectangular bands which are dotted and in pairs and would also be found on the reverse.

22 This identifying mark does not appear in the drawing.

ホ

Plane the bottom boards so that all the metal fittings are flush with the wood and are the same level as the board. There are markings for all the fittings for the bulkheads and all of these fittings should be the same.[23]

へ

The width of the rectangular cutouts on the sides of the bottom boards is two *sun* five *bu* and five *rin*.[24] The dimensions of the thwart-hole are six *bu* by four *bu*, four *rin*.

ト

On the joints of the bulkheads at the area where the thwart sits, you will find a ring where the hook that is attached to the thwart is positioned.

チ

Insert the peg at the bottom of the picture into the holes on all four corners – this fits the main shape of the boat together. This symbol チ at the top of the picture[25] shows a hook, which should hook into a hole on the forward thwart.

リ

Here the cross-beam is one *shaku* nine *sun* and four *bu* in length, and also one *sun* in width and seven *bu* in thickness. This is made of hard wood.

ヌ

This joint has a metal attachment on the top; when you place this in the socket you need to open the metal link so that it will be self-trapping and fit in place.[26]

---

23 All of the circles on the bottom boards are metal rings for the side latches. All of the small 'U' shapes with rings that are found on the bottom beam of the bulkheads are *kakegane* or metal hooks that go into the rings on the bottom boards, to give the boat its shape.

24 The text does not specify if this is the line parallel to the fore and aft line or if it is the line that is perpendicular.

25 The word here is *tomo* or *hesaki*; this lends confusion, as it can mean both 'bow' and 'stern', depending on the context. However, the top of the image is considered the bow.

26 This appears to be of Fujibayashi's own invention and is a locking mechanism which can be opened and closed and in all likelihood is placed within the small white square on the picture of the wooden peg in the bottom right corner. The technology is believed to be a

ル

These two squares are rowlocks for attaching the oars.

ヲ

Join [the two halves of the bow] at the centre here.

ワ

The upper beam at this point should be two *shaku* one *sun* in length, one *sun* two *bu* in width and eight *bu* five *rin* in thickness and should be made of oak.[27]

カ

As the gunwale flares outwards, the edges of the bottom boards should be shaved at an angle, so that the bulkheads fit perfectly.

ヨ

The width of this supporting metal band [seen in black in *figure 63*] is the same width as the section it is on. The length of the small protrusion at the end is two *sun* five *bu*. There are two of these metal plates on each corner [one on each side]. The metal fittings on all four corners are the same. When dismantled these metal fittings should be folded over onto the bulkheads.

[The thwarts]

The drawing at the top [see *figure 64*]
The degree of the opening of the boat can be adjusted with the angle at which this thwart is made.

The second drawing
The hook latch seen on both sides of the thwart, should be hooked into the eye

---

form of lock internal. It would seem that the small needle next to the peg on the bottom left of the image is the tool with which to operate this self-locking joint.

27 This diagram is a view of the boat from above. Due to the limitations of medieval art in the East, there is no perception of depth. However, the lengths and the diagram and the syntax all lean toward a 'V'-shaped bow when this section is upright.

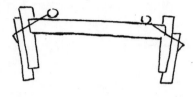

on the bulkheads[28] [as seen on the full plan] to help fix it in place. The horizontal wood for the thwart in these images should connect to the leg sections with a dovetail joint.

The third drawing
[No text]

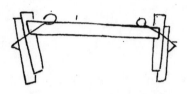

The fourth drawing
The wood *between* the outer 'leg' and the horizontal thwart is one *sun* two *su* in width.

The width of the outer 'leg' is seven *bu* five *rin*.

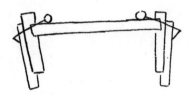

The distance between the bottom boards and the thwart is six *sun* seven *bu*.

The thwart is two *shaku* long, one *sun* and five *bu* wide and five *bu* thick.

The last drawing
This thwart is at the end.

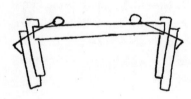

The ring in this drawing that is attached to the underside of the thwart connects to the latch that is marked in the middle of the stem post at the end of the boat.

[The leather skin of the hull]

When attaching the strings to the leather skin, a round leather washer of one *sun* in diameter should be put on one side of the leather skin and fully sealed. The leather should be stitched with *furoshiki-nui* stitches.[29]

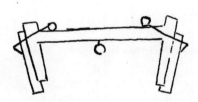

Figure 64. The thwarts

---

28 The hole or ring that the hook goes into can be seen in figure 64 just above the black rectangles on each vertical beam. This hole or ring will be above the thwart when in place.

29 The main point here is that the instructions before this are for the frame of the boat, whereas this image is of the skin of the hull, which is wrapped around the frame to create the outer hull. The idea is to use the string and tie the leather to the framework and to fully seal the area where the string comes through the leather.

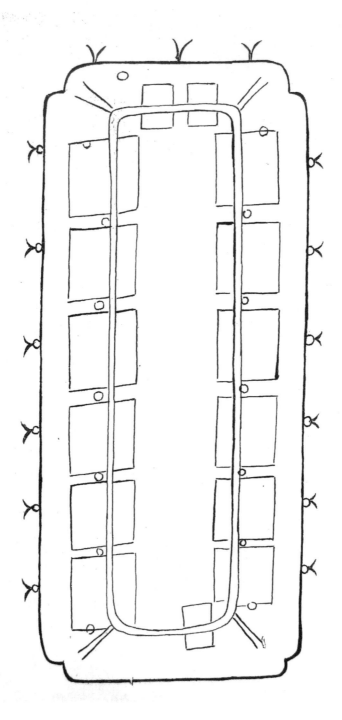

Figure 65. The leather skin of the hull (view from underneath)

Treating the leather for the skin of the hull

The recipe for the treatment:

- one *sho* of pure perilla oil
- three *go* of raw wheat
- thirty leaves of the Japanese star anise tree (*Illicium anisatum*)

Place the above in a kettle and decoct it. To check if it is appropriately decocted, place straw vertically in the mixture. If it is correct then the straw will stand unaided.

Applying the mixture to the leather

As oil does not dry well, add one *go* of lead tetroxide to speed up the process. Then, thinly and evenly apply it to the leather with the type of brush used by lacquerware craftsmen. Next use the lacquerman's bamboo spatula to spread the excess and create a thin and even finish. Strain lacquer from Yoshino[30] through a cloth and mix one hundred *me* of the lacquer to twenty *me* of water. Apply two layers of this mixture onto the above leather. The next step is to apply a good-quality lacquer onto it for two or three more layers – this should also be filtered through a cloth as in the method above. Apply one layer of lacquer to the inside of the skin.[31] Pitch can be used instead of lacquer. To see if the pitch is appropriately decocted, put a straw in the kettle; again, if the straw stands up on its own then it is suitably done.

The oar for the boat

Fasten the two sections with U-clamps in two places, as in the illustration, right.

- You can see the rope for the oar attached to the handle.
- The handle of this oar is made from the handle of a *hasamibako* luggage box.
- The handle goes into the blade of the oar by inserting it into a groove.
- Put a wooden peg through both the handle and the blade.
- Add a small protruding and extra joint.
- The blade length should fit diagonally inside of a *hasamibako* luggage box.

---

30 A place famous for lacquer.

31 This is just an interpretation – the text is ambiguous and could mean 'on the internal skin' or to do it externally.

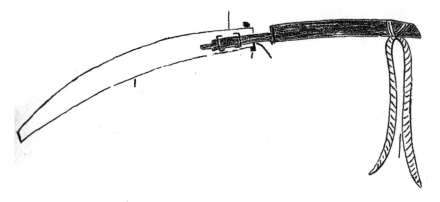

Figure 66. The oar for the boat

Ninki III

Ninja Tools III

Opening tools

Opening tools are designed to help you open the doors of the enemy house with ease. Therefore, of all the arts, this is the one conducted when you are closest to the enemy. This means that any tool that is bulky should be avoided; and, secondly, that the number of tools you carry should be limited; and, thirdly, that any tool that does not work smoothly or makes relatively loud noises should be avoided.

Having seen those tools that have been in existence since ancient times, I have found them inconvenient, due to their bulky nature and a need to carry many of them, and have deplored that there is no one tool that is versatile and can be used for various purposes. Because of this, after quite a number of years of effort spent, I have invented the tools described below by modifying the old versions and manufacturing new variations of these tools.[1]

When extended, [my new inventions] have the benefits of long tools, while when shortened and folded they form a short tool, or also while rolled up they all become six *sun* in size. These tools are adaptable and fit many requirements, such as the need to be long, short, large, small, high, low, wide or narrow, and just one tool can now serve for multiple functions. Also, they are so handy that they can be carried within the sleeve or at your chest.

---

1 Many of the tools are 'modern' variations on ancient tools and some are brand new. As Fujibayashi states earlier, the updates were necessitated by changes in castle technology and warfare techniques.

Those who learn at our school must devote their ingenuity to making them even better so that they will be made more lightweight, compact and flexible. However, it is not acceptable if they are weak or soft so easily bent or broken. You should take due care and attention and make all things appropriate to their function. The iron to be used should be well tempered. If it only consists of steel, it is easily broken while if only of pig iron, it will bend easily. Thus, it is strongly recommended to mix steel and pig iron and temper it very well.

The *toihazushi* probing tool

The angled protrusion on the end of the *toihazushi* probe should be one *sun* and two or three *bu* in length and with a hole at two or three *bu* from the edge. The main bar should be six *sun* long and very thin. The square base section should be one *sun* and two or three *bu* long and five or six *bu* wide and as thin as possible. It should have a blade on top of the square section, as in the illustration.

- There is a hole in the centre of the top spike
- The whole length is six *sun* in total
- The small white section above the main square base is a blade for cutting
- The square 'box' at the bottom is the main base

This *toihazushi* probing tool has five major advantages:

With the angled end, you can examine and feel where the *shirizashi* locking bars or *kakegane* latches are or where they are not. Secondly, you can knock off *shirizashi* locking bars with the end of the tool. Thirdly, you can hook or catch the *sen* wooden pegs that are forced into *wakakegane* ringed latches and remove them. If the peg will not come off, put a nail onto the hole at the end of this tool and remove it with the help of the nail. Fourthly, if the *sen* peg cannot be removed with the said nail, use the square base on the opposite end and knock it out by hitting the *sen* peg from below. Fifthly, if the *sen* peg cannot be removed by the nail or the plate section, use the blade on the outside of the base to cut into the head of the peg and remove it. More to be orally transmitted.

Figure 67.
The *toihazushi*
probing tool

The *hamagari* angled saw

The *hamagari* angled saw should be made as thin and as narrow as a *kogatana*[2] knife and should consist of four sections that are six *sun* long and jointed with hinges. The front two segments have blade edges on the inside and are serrated on the back. The first segment has a hole for a nail at two or three *bu* from the tip. When this tool is folded, it is only six *sun* long, and when extended it can reach two *shaku* four *sun*. The hole on the corner of the second segment should be a little rectangular[3] and is where you can fix a nail to the tool. There is more to be orally transmitted on how to attach the nail to the end.

The round holes are for the rivets of the hinging mechanism.

- The rear two sections have no blades or saw edges.
- The rectangular holes on three of the sides house *sen* wooden pegs.
- Every one of the four parts is six *sun* long.

Figure 68. The *hamagari* angled saw

---

2 Also called *kozuka*, a knife inserted alongside a sword sheath.
3 This can be seen on the top left of figure 68.

- The *hamagari* angled saw can change its shape in various ways; it is sometimes long but also, when folded, it is short, or it can be square or it can be triangular. Thus in this drawing it appears this way, this is so you can have a full understanding of its abilities.
- It seems that there are many nail holes; however, note only four.[4]
- The internal side of the two end segments should be bladed.
- The rear of the saw is serrated for these two sections.

The *hamagari* angled saw has five benefits:

I

It can be used as a *hakagi* latch key when you find a *kuroro*[5] latch with a keyhole. You put this tool through the keyhole and use it as the key. It can be used according to the length, regardless of whether it is six *sun* or one *shaku* two *sun*.

II

If there is no keyhole[6] and this tool cannot be used as a *hakagi* key to open a latch, use it through a door as a *kugikagi* or 'nail key' [which means you should use the spike].

III

If a door with a *kakegane* latch has a vertical support [and there is no gap in the wall to put a tool in], then shape the angled saw as in the right-hand drawing and insert it between the vertical pillar [and the door] and remove the lock by force.

Figure 69. How to use the angled saw

---

4 Translated in the simplest of forms and given here in Japanese: 釘穴ハイクツモ有ヨウナ
   レドモ釘ハ四ツナラテハサス所ナシ.

5 In this context, a *kuroro* is a latch on the inside of a door. It is opened and locked via a small hole that goes through the door. A person locking the door would close it, with the person on the outside, and use a *kurorokagi* (here it says *hakagi*), which is a U-shaped iron bar. This bar fits through the hole and catches the latch, allowing a person to lock and unlock the door. *Ninja* before Fujibayashi's time would identify the size of key needed and take a set with them. Fujibayashi's point here is that you can angle this tool to the size you need and thus make the carrying of sets of keys redundant.

6 Described in the footnote above.

IV

For the *sen* locking peg of a *wakakegane* or ringed latch, angle the saw as in the above drawing – the image on the left – and pull the *sen* peg out or remove it by force with the three-pronged tip or the saw blade.

V

When out of use, this tool can be of any length you like – six *sun*, one *shaku* two *sun*, one *shaku* eight *sun* or two *shaku* four *sun*. It can be used for many purposes; it can be long or short, large or small, reach high or low, wide or narrow. Also, it can be straight if you need it to be straight – this is a great advantage.

The *nobekagi* extendable key[7]

The *nobekagi* extendable key consists of nine[8] pieces hinged together, each of which should be of well-tempered iron and have a measurement of eight *rin* in thickness, one *bu* three *rin* in width and six *sun* in length. The end piece [at the top of the main bar in the image] has a square hole and a hole that is used to insert the connecting rod for the attachments.[9]

Also make a very thin plate of iron [which is the head attachment in the image] that is one *sun* seven or eight *bu* in length and one *sun* in width, and put a connecting rod of seven or eight *bu* in length onto it and put it into the hole of the previously mentioned piece, which is at the end of the main tool. Alongside this, there should be another attachment [as seen here in the drawing] and it should measure one *sun* and four or five *bu*. Make it with two holes on the surface and note that this attachment also goes into the socket hole at the end. You should be prepared with two attachments, both of which should have a connecting rod [so that they are interchangeable and have holes so they can be secured with a peg].

The two pieces that make up the handle should have the ability to change and be set at various angles, as is the case with the *hamagari* angled saw.

It is essential for a *nobekagi* extendable key to be lightweight while not being easily broken or bent. Remember, each of the iron pieces is six *sun* long and is hinged with each other. The pieces on the main arm of this tool have two

---

7 This tool has complex instructions and they have been translated here in the text. However, in short, this tool is a nine-section extendable bar of around five feet in length, which has changeable heads. Each section folds out and the bottom L-shape section can be angled in the centre to change the angle of usage for the tool.

8 In the illustration, groups of white circles and rectangles can be seen; these are the hinges for the nine small sections. The shape and size of this key can be manipulated.

9 This hole is on the very flat of the tool and cannot be seen on the image. All that can be seen is the connecting rod of the attachment where this hole is located.

holes each and hinges and they are an oral tradition.

Notes for the diamond section on the top right
- These two holes on the diamond attachment are to manipulate the *kakegane* latch and the hook.[10]
- You should attach to the main body by means of a rivet.

Notes on the left of the drawing
- There is a hole on the end of the main body; this is so you can remove the attachments and fixing rivet when they are not in use.

Notes at the bottom
- At the hole in the centre of the handle, near the square protrusion, the tool can be right angled – if needed.

The *nobekagi* extendable key has five advantages:
- It enables you to open a door from the outside at the top, bottom, left or from the right – this adds up to four advantages.
- The fifth advantage is that it can be as long as five *shaku* four *sun* or it can be shortened to two times by six *sun;*[11] therefore, it can be both extended and retracted to the required length.

Figure 70.
The *nobekagi*
extendable key

The connecting rod on the tip is also to take out the *sen* wooden pegs that are securing latches [and have a string attached], while the plate attachment is to

---

10 Most likely for a bolt and not a latch.
11 The text here literally states 'two, six *sun*' and possibly means that, when folded down, the *nobekagi* becomes an L-shaped tool of six *sun*.

hit the *sen* peg from beneath so that you can remove it, that is if the *sen* peg has no string and you cannot push it by manipulating the cord. Also, fasten a nail onto the plate attachment – do this to remove the *sen* peg or to take out the *wakakegane* ringed latch by force. You can also open a *kakegane* latch on a door with a strengthening board with this *nobekagi* key.

In all of the above cases you need a practised hand to perform these skills freely. More secrets are to be transmitted.

Figure 71. The *irekokagi*
retractable key

The *irekokagi* retractable key[12]

The L-shaped handle section is eight *sun* in length from the inner corner of the handle and should be forged and extended by hammering. The inside hollow section is two *shaku* long. Between the hollow section and the handle, the tool is solid for five *bu*[13] and also extended and forged by hammer. The handle should be made of brass. The cross-section of the handle should be two *bu* five *rin* square and the mouth for the extendable rod should also be square and one *bu* five *rin* and should be perfectly straight, so that the bar, when inserted, will run smoothly.

The *ireko* or extendable and retractable rod section [that comes out of the housing] should be one *shaku* nine *sun* five *bu* long and one *bu* square and should be constructed of a square bar of tempered iron [so that it fits into the mouth perfectly]. This bar should have a V-shaped notch at the tip [as in the drawing] just like *kirine* [joints in construction]. You should have detachable and interchangeable plates and also nail-like attachments that fit onto the end to suit any given purpose, just as the *nobekagi* extendable key does, so you can

---

12 This is literally a 'nesting key', but is best understood as a socket handle with an extendable and retractable square rod that has changeable tips to suit certain and specific tasks. Looking at the dimensions, this tool is a very lightweight and extremely thin tool, making the illustration misleading.

13 The hollow section in the drawing stops before it reaches the handle; this length is five *bu*, or alternatively from the hollow to the edge of the tool is five *bu*.

use either of the attachments according to the need. There should be a hole on the outer housing and also a hole on the retractable key itself, [this is so you can lock it in place when they line up] but there is more to be orally transmitted.

- At the top of the tool at the V-section is a hole on both sides. This is for a fixing rivet to secure the attachments.
- The detachable head at the top of the tool has four holes, one on each side.
- The separate attachment on the left of the tool is one *sun* three *bu* wide and one *sun* seven *bu* long [not including the nodule].
- The hollow in the handle section is two *shaku* long and the solid part before the handle is five *bu* long.
- From the inner corner to the end of the handle is eight *sun*.
- The white circle on the internal rod section is a hole for a rivet.
- The length from the bottom of the hollow to the handle is five *bu*.

The *hasami* snippers

The length of these is six *sun* and they are made of well-tempered *nanbantetsu*[14] so that they can cut iron.

These snippers have four advantages:
- To cut thin iron.
- To cut bamboo or wood that cannot be cut with a knife or sickle.
- To take out a *shirizashi* locking stick from behind a door. This is in the case where you cannot remove it with the *hazushigane* tool.[15] You do this by thrusting with these snippers.
- If you need to force something into a door, insert this into the gap with vigour.

The *nomi* chisel

This consists of two iron pieces of six *sun* that are joined with a hinge [so that it can fold down to half size]. The thickness is about one *bu* and the width is two *bu* five *rin*. The tip should be hammered and made of well-tempered steel so that it can cut into iron. It

Figure 72.
The *hasami* snippers

---

14 Refined iron imported by early European traders.
15 Unknown. Presumably toihazushi probing tool.

has a hole near the hinge which you can put a nail into, but this is to be orally transmitted.

This chisel has four advantages:
- To shave iron.
- If the socket of a door hinge is stuck and if there is a padlock attached to it and the door cannot be opened, put this tool into any gap and force it into position around the socket and then remove it by pushing.[16]
- When you open a *kuroro* bolt, use this to take it out with force.[17]
- Use this tool to remove the supporting struts that hold a door together [so that you can get through the door]; this is a good use of the chisel. More secrets to tell.

Drills

Drills should be six *sun* long and of three types. Produce them as in the drawings.

Small screw drill
- The width between the blades is seven *bu*. The whole length is six *sun*. That is one *sun* five *bu* for the iron part and four *sun* five *bu* for the handle.

Large screw drill
- The width between the blades is two *sun* six or seven *bu*, or just three *sun* if required.
- The whole length is six *sun*; that is, two *sun* for the iron part and four *sun* for the handle.
- The handle should be made of oak.

Spear drill
The iron part is two *sun* six or seven *bu* long and the handle is three *sun* three or four *bu* long.

These three types of drills have two[18] advantages:
- In cases where there is no gap between the door and the frame and there are wooden boards on both sides, so that you cannot use any opening tool, you can use the small screw drill to make a hole so you can put an opening tool through it.

---

16 Here it could mean push through or use as a lever. However, the main point of the text is to take the pin out of the socket of traditional hinges and thus 'take the door off its hinges', which allows you to enter.

17 The idea here is to smash the bolt off its fittings from the outside, thus releasing the door.

18 This is a transcription error, as there are in fact three.

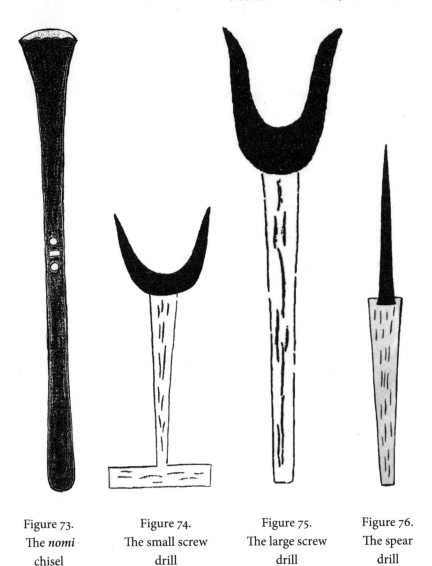

Figure 73.
The *nomi*
chisel

Figure 74.
The small screw
drill

Figure 75.
The large screw
drill

Figure 76.
The spear
drill

- Secondly, the large screw drill can be used when a padlock is on the inside of a door or in other cases where you get stuck when using an opening tool. Use this drill to make a hole and use a *tekagi* hook [to get to the lock]. Also, this drill has superior advantages over all the opening tools that are outlined here. Use well-tempered iron for the blade.
- Thirdly, the spear drill can be used for *deba shirizashi* and *san shirizashi* locking bars and so on. There are more usages other than these, but not all can be listed.

The *shikoro* saw

The length of this saw is *six* sun; that is, two *sun* for the handle and four *sun* for the iron blade. The width is three to four *bu* or even up to five *bu* depending on your choice. The blade should be double-edged – one side for cutting bamboo and the other for normal cutting.[19]

The *shikoro* saw has two advantages:
First, it can break *shinobi-gaeshi* or spiked defences against the *ninja*. It can also break through bamboo fences such as the basic *hari* style or the *yarai* diagonal-crisscrossed fences and so on; these you cannot easily break with a sickle. How to break through these defences is described in the earlier *In-nin* chapter.

Secondly, when you break in by cutting out a wooden panel from a door or such things, you should make a hole with a drill and put this *shikoro* saw into the hole and cut out around the board. More to be orally transmitted here.

The *kama* folding sickle

In older times the sickle was four *sun* long with a handle of five *sun* and the blade was fixed in place. In these modern days the blade and the handle should each be six *sun* and the handle should be hinged [so that the handle and the blade fold together] and you should keep a nail to fix the blade in place when you use the sickle. When you carry this *kama* in your kimono, the handle and the blade lie side by side.[20] The blade should be double-edged but a single-edged version should also be prepared. Details to be orally transmitted.

- The handle is six *sun* long.
- It is hinged.
- The iron blade should be six *sun* long and double-edged.

This folding sickle has three advantages:
- First, it allows you to cut like a normal sickle.
- Secondly, with the edge on the upper ridge [as it is double-edged] you can cut with a pushing motion.
- Thirdly, it is handy and can be carried secretly within your kimono or sleeves without difficulty.

---

19 On closer inspection this difference can be seen in the image.
20 As a modern flick knife would fold away.

Figure 77.
The *shikoro* saw

Figure 78.
The *kama* folding sickle

Figure 79.
The *kuginuki* nail
remover

The *kuginuki* nail remover

There is no secret to producing nail removers [as they are common]. The length is six *sun*, the thickness should be preferably a little less than for normal versions.

This nail remover has two advantages:
- First, you can remove iron fittings such as sockets by twisting them out of place.
- Secondly, it has the ability to remove things constructed by bamboo and wood which will not come off easily; do this by twisting.

 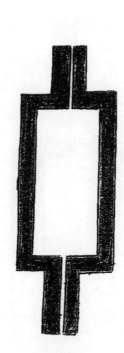 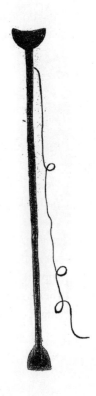

Figure 80.	Figure 81.	Figure 82.
Joshinuki lock-picking shims	The *sejoshinuki* back-padlock pick	The *tsukibiraki joshinuki* pick for 'thrust and open' padlocks

Joshinuki lock-picking shims[21]

The length should be six *sun*, the thickness should be as thin as thick paper, and the width should be five *rin*. They should be made of iron and it is essential they be made so that they are applicable to any size of padlock. There is a tremendous amount to be transmitted orally here.

These lock-picking shims have five advantages:

You can open any of the *tsukidashi* padlocks,[22] twist padlocks, back padlocks or drawer padlocks because these tools bend [to each variation]. These above are four advantages. All of these depend on how skilled you are. The fifth advantage

---

21 These are iron slivers that are used to manipulate lock internals, much like modern-day lock picks.

22 Any padlock with a 'thrust and open' mechanism.

is that if a door with a *kakegane* latch has a gap [around it], you can spring the latch with these tools.

The *sejoshinuki* back-padlock pick[23]
- The middle straight section is one *sun* long.
- The vertical straight section at the top is four *bu* long.
- The vertical length at the bottom is five *bu* long.
- The gap at the bottom has deep secrets to be transmitted orally.

The *tsukibiraki joshinuki* pick for 'thrust and open' padlocks
- There is an attached thread to aid in pulling.
- The end has a movable scissor action [for gripping].
- There is a long 'V'-shaped cut out down the length of the tool.
- The length of this tool is six *sun* and it is thinner than the central pole of a spindle wheel.

A number of these tools should be prepared in a variety of sizes.

The *hikidashi joshinuki* pick for guided padlocks[24]
- The length of this tool is six *sun*.

The above three lock picks can serve for only a single usage so they have less advantage. There are more oral secrets here. It is most advisable that you should practise and become very skilled with the first set of lock-picking shims outlined above [as they can be reused].

Figure 83.
The *hikidashi joshinuki* pick for guided padlocks

---

23 To pick this form of padlock you need a tool that can go around the internal mechanism. Therefore, these tools are 'U'-shaped and are inserted and manipulated until the lock is sprung.

24 Fujibayashi does not in fact give any instruction on this tool.

Silent sandals

These should be made of *kiri* wood. Their length is one *shaku* two sun, the width is eight *sun* and the corners should be rounded like the wooden sandals of Hamachigi. Put cloth on the bottom with a thin layer of flossy material between the shoe and the cloth. This cloth should be fixed to the shoes by sewing[25] and the thongs should be attached as in the drawing. More details to be orally transmitted.

The wooden sandals are used if the floor makes noises when you sneak into the enemy's house. Sometimes they are hinged so you can fold them away and carry them in your kimono. More in oral tradition.

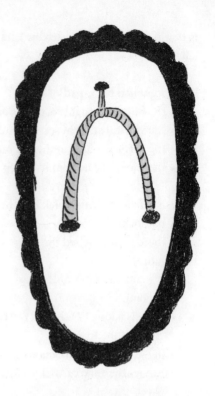

Figure 84. Silent sandals

---

25 The method here is to gather up and stitch the material so that when it has been completely stitched together it will not slip off the shoe.

Ninki IV

Ninja Tools IV

Fire tools I

The use of fire tools is universally considered one of the most basic principles underlying *ninjutsu* and is of utmost importance within the art. The primary principle of this skill is that, no matter how strongly a castle or a position is fortified, the technique of setting it on fire and reducing it to ashes will be effective. Secondly, be it by day or by night, you need to send signals to your allies. Thirdly, those torches or fires that cannot be extinguished by the wind or rain will aid you and your allies in the most difficult situations.

Therefore, those who study this way should train and prepare themselves so that they are useful when needs arise. Seemingly, in this day and age, those who are called *shinobi no mono* are said to have mastered *shinobi no jutsu* with the fifty-three[1] fire tool recipes. However, as they do not know the fundamental essence but learn and use only the leafy details, it is a matter of great regret that this art is wrongly understood.

The deep doctrine of our school enables you to master the deepest truth of the principles of both the *in* and *yo* arts, which allow you to infiltrate an enemy castle with ease so that you can annihilate the enemy within an instant.

Sun Tzu says:

Attack by fire is an inferior tactic. However, if it cannot be helped it should be used.

For this reason above, these volumes are attached at the end of this manuscript.

---

1   There are in fact only forty-nine skills included in the first list and much more when all lists are put together. According to Yunoki Shunichiro, there is a total of 213 different items and 279 individual recipes.

イ [2]

卯花月夜方

A spring moonlit night [3]

• Pine wood containing a high quantity of resin – 20 *momme*
• Powdered green tea – 2 *momme*
• Mouse droppings – 6 [*momme*]
• Saltpetre – 100 [*momme*]
• Sulphur – 40 [*momme*]
• Camphor – 9 *momme* 5 *bu*
• Moxa – 12 *momme*
• Hemp ash – 10 *momme*
• Pine resin – 6 *momme*

Make a powder [4] of the above and mix it with hempseed oil and put the mixture into a bamboo cylinder. Shave the outside of the cylinder very thin and wrap with [paper] and 'tea glue' and ignite with tinder.

ロ

秋月方

The autumn moon

• Saltpetre – 20 *momme*
• Sulphur – 14 *momme* 5 *bu*
• Camphor – 18 *momme*
• Hemp ash – 1 *momme* 5 *bu*
• Pine wood containing a high quantity of resin – 1 *momme* 7 [*bu*]
• Mouse droppings – 1 *momme* 5 [*bu*]
• Cattle dung – 2 *momme*

Make a powder of the above, mix it with the hempseed oil and put it in a bamboo cylinder. Use the same method as for the tool above.

---

2   At the top of each of the first forty-nine recipes, there is an identifying mark such as the one here. These are taken from the old alphabet, known as the *iroha*, and together form a Japanese pangram. They also may act as a quick reference table for the *ninja*.

3   Literally, 'Month of the deutzia flower', or the 'fourth lunar month'.

4   The word 'powder' appears throughout the recipes – the original ideogram is 茉 and is considered to mean 'grind down' or 'powder'. Questions arise with some of the ingredients, such as wood, as Fujibayashi sometimes states 'sawdust of', which implies powder of wood, yet in other cases he does not. Therefore, while the recipes say 'powder' this is best thought of as the smallest unit or size possible for that specific ingredient.

八
花ノ曙方

Cherry blossoms at dawn

- Saltpetre – 20 *momme*
- Sulphur – 12 *momme*
- Pine resin – 1 *momme*
- Hemp ash – 2 *momme*
- Moxa – 6 *momme*
- Used [powdered] charcoal – 300 [*momme*]
- White lead – 4 *momme*
- Camphor – 12 *momme*

Make a powder of the above, mix it with hempseed oil, wrap it in cloth and put it in a bamboo cylinder.

二
天火照火者之方

The one who brings heaven's fire

- Saltpetre – 80 *momme*
- Arsenic (Arsenious anhydride) – 5 *momme*
- Lacquer – 20 *momme*
- Camphor – 50 *momme*
- Japan wax (sumac wax) – 10 *momme* 5 [*bu*]
- Sulphur – 30 *momme*
- Blue vitriol (chalcanthite) – 10 *momme*
- Beef tallow – 20 *momme*
- Hemp ash – 50 *momme*
- Japanese tiger beetle – 8 *momme*
- Chinese wax – 8 *momme*
- Alum – 8 *momme*
- Powdered tea – 11 *momme*
- Pine resin – 30 *momme*
- Moxa – 150 *momme*
- Iron filings[5] – 20 *momme*

---

5 The ideogram is literally 'iron sand', which has a few small differences from iron filings. However, iron filings is a more likely ingredient in explosives. Also, 'iron sand' in the modern sense has a different name in Japanese from the one listed in the *Bansenshukai*.

- Mouse droppings – 3 *momme*
- Red chilli pepper – 120 *momme*
- Fine sand[6] – 20 *momme*
- Cattle dung – 8 *momme*
- Pine sawdust – 50 *momme*
- Red bayberry bark (*Myrica rubra*) – 100 *momme*
- Privet (*Ligustrum obtusifolium*) – 20 *momme*
- Japanese nutmeg-yew (*Torreya nucifera*) – 15 *momme*[7]
- Charcoal – 80 *momme*
- Japanese nutmeg-yew (*Torreya nucifera*) sawdust – 28 *momme*
- *Raigan* (a form of *Polyporaceae*) – 8 *momme* 5 [*bu*]

Make a powder of the above, knead it with oil until it is sticky and wrap it in cloth. Light the end using *hokuchi* tinder and throw it into the enemy hut or where people are holed up in defence.

ホ
梅花月方

The plum blossom moon

- Alum – 5 *momme*
- Pine resin – 12 *momme*
- Powder of *Polygonum longisetum* – 8 *momme*
- Saltpetre – 8 *momme*
- Pine sawdust – 28 *momme*
- Cattle dung – 10 *momme*
- Powdered green tea – 3 *momme*
- Moxa – 50 *momme*
- Camphor – 6 *momme*
- Japan wax – 5 *momme*
- Mouse droppings – 3 *momme* 5 [*bu*]
- Sulphur – 9 *momme*

---

6 Literally, 'small sand'.
7 Taken from an unrecorded section of the tree.

へ

千里新々関口流炬火

The one thousand *ri* torch from the Shin Shin Sekiguchi school

- Sulphur – 3 *momme* 5 [*bu*]
- Saltpetre – 1 *momme* 2 [*bu*]
- Camphor – 13 *momme*
- Pine sawdust – 3 *momme*
- Moxa – 5 *momme* 8 [*bu*]
- Pine resin – 2 *momme*
- Mouse droppings – 2 *momme*
- Gunpowder[8] – 2 *momme*
- Hemp ash – 1 *momme* 7 [*bu*]
- A small helping of cattle dung
- A small helping of white lead

Make a powder of the above and pack it firmly by doing the same as above.[9]

ト

衣炬火方

The cloth torch

Wrap cotton cloth around five or six reeds. Mix pine resin and camphor with oil until it is sticky. Apply the mixture onto the cloth-wrapped torch a couple of times and dry it so that it is ready for use. This torch will not fail in wind or rain. It is also called the *komyo kohi* or 'bright torch'.

チ

五里炬火方

The five *ri* torch

Split sawtooth oak (*Quercus acutissima*) into thin pieces, apply oil, and tie firmly at intervals of one *sun*. The circumference of the torch should be eight *sun*, with a length of three *shaku*. Details for this are to be orally transmitted.

---

8 Literally, 'musket powder'.

9 This is a problematic issue, as the preceding tool has no construction instructions, which leads us to suspect that there is a transcription error in the preceding tool or that it could be a reference to the generic method of packing and wrapping the bamboo as used in most fire tools.

リ

雨炬火

The rainproof torch

- Saltpetre – 2 *momme*
- Sulphur – 1 *momme* 5 [*bu*]
- Pine tree knot[10] – 3 *momme*
- Camphor – 2 *momme*
- Moxa – 3 *momme*
- Pine resin – 2 *momme*
- Mouse droppings – 3 [*momme*]

Make a powder of the above, put the mixture into a bamboo cylinder, scrape the exterior of the bamboo until it has thin walls and burn paper [covered with a layer of] powder on top of the cylinder. Use and light it with tinder.

An alternative recipe for the above tool

- Saltpetre – 80 *momme*
- Sulphur – 7 *momme* 5 [*bu*]
- Camphor – 7 *momme*
- Ash – 7 *momme*
- Pine wood containing a high quantity of resin – 7 *momme*
- Moxa – 10 *momme*
- Flax stalks – 2 *momme* 5 [*bu*]
- Mouse droppings – 4 *bu*

Make a powder of the above and put it into a cylinder as always and apply oil to the top.[11]

---

10 The gnarled or knotted area of wood.
11 This could be either the 'top' or the 'outer surface'.

ル
第等明松

The *yawara*[12] 'soft' torch

- Saltpetre – 2 *momme*
- Sulphur – 3 *momme*
- Camphor – 3 *momme*
- Borneol – 1 *momme*
- Privet (*Lingustrum obtusifolium*) – 3 *momme*

Mix the above with hempseed oil and put the mixture into a bamboo cylinder as in the previous examples.

ヲ
風雨炬火

The wind- and rainproof torch

- Flax stalks – 100 *momme*
- Saltpetre – 5 *momme*
- Moxa (crumpled until it becomes white and soaked in water overnight) – 100 *momme*
- Sulphur – 10 *momme*
- Camphor – 50 *momme*
- Japanese nutmeg-yew (*Torreya nucifera*) – 15 *momme*
- Sesame – 8 *momme*
- Pine resin – 20 *momme*
- Privet (*Ligustrum obtusifolium*) – 5 *momme*
- Borneol – 3 *momme*
- Pine sawdust – 25 *momme*
- Powdered green tea – 8 *momme*

ワ

An alternative recipe for the above tool

I experimented with this version of the torch in the year of Ram and it burned quickly.

- Saltpetre – 80 *momme*

---

12 The phonetic sound here implies 'softness' and the latter ideogram of the name is most probably a phonetic suffix.

- Camphor – 7 *momme*
- Pine wood containing a high quantity of resin – 7 *momme*
- Sulphur – 7 *momme* 5 [*bu*]
- Ash – 7 *momme*
- Moxa – 10 *momme*
- Mouse droppings – 4 *bu*

Its construction is the same as the above examples.

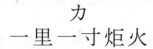

One *ri* for one *sun* torch

This torch will not fail in the rain.

- Walnut tree bark (finely chopped) – 120 *momme*
- Camphor – 40 *momme*

The above two items should be dried.

- *Shochu* spirits (boiled) – 2 *go*
- Borneol – 5 *bu*
- Japanese nutmeg-yew (*Torreya nucifera*) – 5 *momme*
- Pine resin – 2 *momme*
- Mouse droppings – 5 *bu*
- Cattle dung – 1 *momme*
- Whetstone[13] – 8 *momme*
- Moxa – 50 *momme*
- Saltpetre – 3 *momme*

ヨ

生滅ノ方

The torch of appearance and disappearance[14]

- Saltpetre – 120 *momme*
- Sulphur – 50 *momme*
- Borneol – 9 *momme*
- Japanese nutmeg-yew (*Torreya nucifera*) – 30 *momme*
- Camphor – 80 *momme*

---

13 The sharpening block.

14 An unknown tool, possibly a fierce-burning weapon. Its title has Buddhist connotations of birth and death.

- Iron filings – 53 *momme*
- Fine sand – 30 *momme*
- Hemp ash – 200 *momme*
- Privet (*Ligustrum obtusifolium*) – 50 *momme*
- Pine sawdust – 80 *momme*
- Charcoal – 150 *momme* Privet (*Ligustrum obtusifolium*) sawdust – 85 *momme*
- Hair – 60 *momme*
- *Peucedanum japonicum* – 250 *momme*
- Chilli pepper – 200 *momme*
- Flax stalks – 300 *momme*
- Moxa – 150 *momme*
- Red bayberry (*Myrica rubra*) bark – 200 *momme*
- White limestone[15] – 15 *momme*
- *Rokanseki* stone[16] – 18 *momme* 5 [*bu*]
- Lime powder – 120 *momme*
- Fine sugar – 1 *sho* 5 *go*
- Alum – 32 *momme* 5 [*bu*]
- Mouse droppings – 15 *momme*
- Cattle dung – 12 *momme*
- White lead – 12 *momme*
- Blue vitriol (chalcanthite) – 150 *momme*

Make a powder of the above.

The recipe continued:

- Pine resin – 85 *momme*
- Japan wax – 150 *momme*
- *Raigan* (a form of *Polyporaceae*) – 100 *momme*
- Lacquer – 35 *momme*
- Manteiga (boar's fat) – 28 *momme*
- Beef tallow – 25 *momme*
- Glue[17] – 100 *momme*

Decoct the above seven[18] ingredients in one *sho* of oil, then include the previous twenty-seven items, and mix well. You should add more oil if the mixture is

---

15 *Kansuiseki* 寒水石.
16 Unknown stone.
17 This has connotations of glue taken from an animal.
18 The original says eight; however, this is a mistake.

too stiff. When it is appropriately done, wrap the ingredients in cloth and light with tinder. It is a torch to be thrown in where people are defending or into an enemy hut.

タ
南蛮山方

Nanbanyama – the European mountain[19]

Make this in the same method as the above tool.

- Camphor – 70 *momme*
- Ash – 3 *momme*
- Privet (*Ligustrum obtusifolium*) – 3 *momme*
- Mouse droppings – 1 *bu*
- Saltpetre – 5 *momme*
- Sulphur – 5 *momme*

三タイ [20] 方

An alternative recipe for the above tool

- Camphor – 50 *momme*
- Mouse droppings – 2 *bu*
- Privet (*Ligustrum obtusifolium*) – 3 *momme*
- Sulphur – 3 *momme*
- Ash – 3 *momme*

レ
水ノ松明

Waterproof torch (also known as the palm torch 手内松明)

- Alum – 5 *momme*
- Mouse droppings – 1 *momme*
- Pine resin – 5 *bu*
- Ash – 1 *momme*
- Moxa – 1 *momme*
- Camphor – 5 *momme*
- Saltpetre – 5 *bu*
- Blue vitriol (chalcanthite) – 5 *bu*

---

19 This implies that the tool was imported from Europe.

20 The ideogram here could mean that the following recipe is an alternative one. However, the first word, meaning 'three', is followed by phonetic markers whose meaning has been lost.

Put the above contents into a bamboo cylinder of five or six *sun* and ram and compact it with force. Light it with an ignition fuse or a split cedar splint with sulphur upon it. This tool is used for observing inside [a room] through a window or knothole.

ソ
同方

An alternative recipe for the above tool

- Saltpetre – 20 *momme*
- Camphor – 15 *momme*
- Sulphur – 10 *momme*
- Hemp ash – 30 *momme*
- Pine resin – 10 *momme*
- Cattle dung – 8 *momme*
- Alum – 3 *momme*
- Borneol – 1 *momme*
- Pine sawdust – 8 *momme*
- Moxa – 20 *momme*

Make powder of the above and mix it as is done in all cases.

ツ
秘傳雨松明

The secret tradition of making a rainproof torch

- Camphor – 20 *momme*
- Sulphur – 10 *momme*
- Pine resin – 5 *momme*
- Moxa – 50 *momme*
- Cloth made from the fibre of the Japanese banana tree – 20 *momme*
- Japan wax – 10 *momme*
- Saltpetre – 3 *momme*
- Privet (*Ligustrum obtusifolium*) – 5 *bu*
- Mouse droppings – 5 *bu*
- Cattle dung – 8 *momme*
- Powdered deer antler – 5 *bu*
- Japanese nutmeg – 1 *momme*
- Pine sawdust – 25 *momme*
- Powdered green tea – 10 *momme*
- Oil – 3 *go*

子 ²¹

義経水炬火

The Yoshitsune waterproof torch

- Camphor – 5 *bu*
- Sulphur – 25 *momme* 5 *bu*
- Ash – 2 *momme* 5 *bu*
- Saltpetre – 25 *momme*
- Moxa – 5 *bu*
- Pine sawdust – 3 *momme* 5 *bu*

The method of construction is the same as with most torches.

ナ

上々水炬火　極秘ノ方

A secret recipe for the finest waterproof torch

- Saltpetre – 7 *momme*
- Sulphur – 7 *momme*
- Ash of a Japanese pussy willow (*Salix chaenomeloides*) – 5 *bu*

Make a bag of thick paper, put the above mixture into it and prod it down with force, then wrap it with a flat braided cord and wrap thick paper around it with glue and apply a covering of wax to it.

ラ

打松明

The attack torch

- Saltpetre – 5 *momme*
- Ash – 2 *momme*
- Pine sawdust – 7 *momme*
- Mouse droppings [unknown amount]
- Moxa – 1 *momme*

Put the above into a bamboo cylinder, scrape the bamboo until it is thin and wrap it in paper with glue.

---

21 As the tools are listed following the Japanese alphabet, Fujibayashi strays from the norm here by using an ideogram 子 instead of the *kana* or phonetic mark of ネ. The ideogram 子 is often used instead of the kana ネ.

ム
振リ松明

The swing and hurl torch

Soak bamboo grass (*Arundinaria simonii*) in water for about fifteen days, then dry it thoroughly, and add powdered sulphur. Bundle fifteen shoots and [ignite and] swing the bundle toward the enemy. The desired length should be about one *shaku*.

ウ
第等松明方

The *yawara* 'soft' torch

When I have used this torch, the fire goes out if you swing it but it reignites if you blow onto it. Also, if you cut off the tip with a *kogatana* knife, the torch will burn again.

- Saltpetre – 15 *momme*
- Camphor – 15 *momme*
- Ash – 2 *momme*
- Sulphur – 8 *momme*
- Horse dung – 2 *momme*
- Hemp cloth – 5 *momme*

To construct this torch so that it will not[22] go out when blown upon, add five *bu* of camphor and ten *momme* of pine sawdust.

An alternative recipe for the above tool

- Saltpetre – 15 *momme*
- Sulphur – 11 *momme*
- Camphor – 10 *momme*
- Horse dung – 2 *momme*
- Hemp cloth – 6 *momme*

If you make it with ten *momme* each of saltpetre and sulphur it will go out if you blow upon it.

---

22 It should be noted here that in this version of the tool it states that it will not go out, while the following torch will. Looking at the ingredients it is possible that the transcriber mixed these two entries and they should in fact be reversed.

卉 [23]

削火之方

The scraping match[24]

- Kumano[25] tinder – 3 *momme*
- Saltpetre – 1 *momme* 2 *bu*
- Borneol – 1 *momme* 2 *bu*
- Sulphur – 1 *momme* 2 *bu*
- Japanese royal fern (*Osmunda japonica*) – 1 *bu*
- Crystal – 5 *bu*
- Ash – 1 *momme* 5 *bu*
- Camphor – 1 *momme* 5 *bu*
- Pine sawdust – 3 *bu*
- Pine resin – 3 *bu*

Make a powder of the above and decoct the thin inner bark of a pine tree, and then mix the powder into the liquid. Dry to a completely solid form and cut it with a knife and light it.

ノ

袖火方

The sleeve fire

- Saltpetre – 10 *momme*
- Sulphur – 5 *momme*
- Ash – 2 *momme*

Mix the above thoroughly. Take a bamboo cylinder of six or seven *sun* and drill a hole in the bamboo joint and fill the bamboo with the mixture. Wrap the cylinder with [missing text] light it from within your sleeve.

---

23 Again, this phonetic marker is changed and does not follow the normal pattern.
24 Presumably used as an ignition aid.
25 An area in Wakayama province.

オ
ツケ火ノ方

The illuminating arrow

- Saltpetre – 20 *momme*
- Sulphur – 5 *momme*
- Ash – 5 *momme*
- Camphor – 3 *bu*
- Mouse droppings – 3 *bu*

Make a powder of the above, put the mixture into a cylinder and scrape the outer surface of the cylinder and wrap it with paper and glue. Attach it to an arrow that is one *shaku* five *sun* long and that has an arrowhead. When you need to see inside [a fortress], shoot the arrow through an arrow or gun port so you can see within.

ク
敵討薬

Enemy-attacking powder

- Saltpetre – 10 *momme*
- Sulphur – 5 *momme*
- Ash – 2 *momme*
- Chilli pepper – 3 *momme*

Make a powder of the above and put the mixture into a cylinder of four *sun* or so. Sprinkle it over the enemy.

ヤ
夜討テンモン火方

The night-attack sky arrow

- Saltpetre – 10 *momme*
- Borneol – 1 *momme* 1 *bu* 3 *rin*
- Well-aged sake – 20 *momme*
- A decoction of mugwort (*Artemisia indica var. maximowiczii*) – 20 *momme*

Make a fine powder of the above and put the mixture into a bag and attach it to an arrow. Light the mixture before you shoot the arrow.

マ
義経火

The Yoshitsune fire (also known as the long-lasting torch 不滅松明)

Scrape ox horn until the walls are very thin and place five cormorant feather spines at the bottom. Next place mercury into the spines of the feathers and cover with a lid.

ケ
胴ノ火極秘ノ方

The secret recipe of the *donohi* body warmer

Cut very old hemp cloth into pieces and mix the soot from a kettle into glue thoroughly and cover the pieces of cloth with it. Knead the entire mixture thoroughly and put the whole mixture firmly into a bamboo cylinder, cover it with a layer of soil on top and then smother it in bran [and create a fire above it to char the internals of the cylinder].

Oral tradition says that you should wash out thin pieces of cloth and expose them to the sun thoroughly. According to one theory, covering a bamboo cylinder with clay and then charring it will also do.

フ

An alternative recipe for the above tool

Knead powdered green tea with rice broth, ram it firmly into a [bamboo] cylinder and bury and roast it in bran. The bamboo should be shaved down. Drying it in the sun instead of smothering and roasting it in bran will also suffice.

コ
北地方

Tinder

• Charred *Peucedanum japonicum* – 5 *momme*
• Camphor – 1 *momme*

Make this into a powder [and use as tinder].

An alternative recipe for tinder

- Leaves of pokeweed (*Phytolacca esculenta*) – 10 *momme*
- Camphor – 2 *momme*
- Saltpetre – 5 *momme*
- Sulphur – 1 *momme*

Make this into a powder.

工

An alternative recipe for tinder

Take mushrooms that sprout on chestnut trees and dry them in the shade, but take care not to let them get wet with rain or dew. Char them and add a little saltpetre.

テ

An alternative recipe for tinder

Fully crumple moxa leaves, soak them in water for two nights and dry. Mix a little water to ten *momme* of dried moxa and add two *momme* of saltpetre. Decoct all and dry completely. This recipe is better than the previous ones.

ア

火筒拵様

How to prepare a *hizutsu* fire container

Mix alum and rice paste at the ratio of one to three. Apply the mixture onto[26] a cylinder several times and add a layer of powdered green tea.

サ

ナラズ薬

Silent gunpowder

- Saltpetre – 100 *momme* (roasted down to about 70 *momme*)
- Sulphur – 11 *momme* (cover large chunks of sulphur with rice paste, expose to rain or dew for 100 days and nights)
- Ash – 8 *momme*
- *Uchi* (bird droppings) – 3 *momme* 5 *bu*

---

26 The grammar here suggests that this is applied to the outside of the cylinder.

- Charred tiger fur – 3 *momme*
- Charred droppings of the cormorant bird – 1 *momme*
- Grilled bones of a sea bream

This recipe and the following one are both for gunpowder.

White powder

- Saltpetre – 8 *momme*
- Cinnabar – 1 *momme*
- Grilled bones of a sea bream – 3 *momme*
- Leaves from the *Gleichenia japonica* (dried in the shade) – 3 *momme*

Sleeping medicine

Cut the head off a brown dog at night, take the blood and dry it[27] out of the sun. Another recipe is to extract the liver of a live brown dog and dry it in the shade.

The waterproof watch fire

- Chestnut wood (dried in the shade and pan-fried in hempseed oil) – 50 *momme*
- Camphor – 20 *momme*
- Alcoholic spirits (*shochu*) – 2 *go*

Mix the first two with the alcoholic spirits and knead it. Roast the mixture over a fire and harden it, this will now burn when you are in and around water[28] – and will burn surprisingly well.

Also, when you dive under water, it is said that it is beneficial if you apply the 'Oil of Toad[29]' ointment to the nine holes of the body and put a green leaf of the

---

27 Other schools talk about using blood on paper and burning it in a guardhouse to induce sleep.
28 Literally 'in water'.
29 This is also found in the Shinobi Hiden manual – with the same usage – and is made from a mixture of toad secretions mixed with pork grease.

Rose of Sharon tree (*Hibiscus syriacus*) in your mouth. I have not tried this yet.[30]

Water musket shot

Put two *momme* of gunpowder into a barrel of a gun that is designed to take three *momme* and five *bu* [of gunpowder]. Add two *momme* of powdered green tea and ram it *thoroughly*. Put one *go* of water into the barrel and shoot. When you shoot someone they will faint.

The waterproof fuse

- Saltpetre – 70 *momme*
- Water – 2 tea cups' worth

Put a section of *hinawa* fuse in the above mixture and decoct it. Next, mix seventy *momme* of camphor and fifty *momme* of pine resin with camellia oil until it is sticky. Apply this to the *hinawa* fuse and cover in wax several times.

エ

An alternative recipe for the above tool

Mix powdered alum with thin glue. Add camphor to the mixture and apply it to the *hinawa* fuse several times.

ヒ
一寸火縄

The three-centimetre *hinawa* match

- Pine resin – 2 *momme*
- Camphor – 1 *bu*

Mix the above with rapeseed oil and apply it to a *hinawa* fuse several times and dry it.

---

30 Presumably he means he has not tried diving during a *shinobi* activity or diving with this leaf in his mouth. The reference is ambiguous but it is certain he has tried the actual torch.

モ
濡火縄

The shiny *hinawa* fuse

Soak a piece of *hinawa* fuse in water overnight and dry it in the sun for one day. Repeat this process for three days and nights – three times in total. Next, put the *hinawa* fuse in water in which buckwheat has been boiled, leave it overnight and then dry it in the sun in the daytime. Repeat this three times.

Then soak it in *kanemizu*[31] liquid made of an acetic acid with iron dissolved in the solution. Repeat this several times so that the fuse becomes impregnated with the liquid completely. Then put Chinese sumac (*Rhus javanica var. roxburghii*) in the liquid and soak the *hinawa* for one more night. Again, dry it completely and bury it in the ground for two or three days, then take it out and dry it. It will now be ready for use. I think you should do this before the *hinawa* fuse is braided.[32]

セ
暗薬

Blinding powder

Load gunpowder into a rifle and add powdered *hihatsu* long pepper (*Piper longum*) [into the barrel]. Apply the appropriate amount of *kuchigusuri* fine gunpowder and shoot the weapon. This is used when those defending a building are within. This will totally blind the occupants who are inside. One manual says it should be *hihatsu* as above or use the seed of *Pittosporum glabrum*.

ス
明松方

The torch

- Saltpetre – 25 *momme*
- Sulphur – 12 *momme*
- Charcoal – 2 *momme*
- Pine wood saturated with resin – 7 *bu*
- Pine resin – 1 *momme* 2 *bu*
- Powdered green tea – 2 *bu*
- Mouse droppings [unknown amount]

---

31 A liquid used in Japan for dying teeth.
32 Before the rope fuse is formed.

- Moxa – 3 *momme*
- Camphor – 5 *bu*

Mix the above with sake of high quality and firmly ram it into a bamboo cylinder.

1 [33]

An alternative recipe for the above tool

- Saltpetre – 40 *momme*
- Sulphur – 9 *momme* 9 *bu*
- Charcoal – 4 *momme* 4 *bu*
- Camphor – 4 *momme* 2 *bu*
- Salt – 3 *momme*
- Mouse droppings – 5 *bu*
- Wax – 1 *momme*

Mix the above with oil and put it in a cylinder as usual.

2

キサミ火

Chopped fire

- Horse dung (old dung is better) – 2 *momme*
- Charred floss of the Japanese royal fern (*Osmunda japonica*) – 1 *momme*
- Ash – 5 *bu*
- Sulphur – 5 *bu*
- Saltpetre – 5 *bu*
- Coarse crystal – 1 *momme* 5 *bu*

Mix the above with *kanemizu* tooth-dying liquid and then knead and harden the mixture. [Powder it] and sprinkle the mixture onto saltpetre paper and cut it into thin pieces.

---

33 The text now continues with numerical markers.

3

胴火方

The *donohi* body warmer

- Charred[34] old cloth – 1 *momme*
- Powdered moxa – 3 *bu* 3 *rin*
- Charred Japanese royal fern (*Osmunda japonica*) – 5 *bu*
- Old rope covered in birdlime – 2 *bu* 5 *rin*
- Old tea – 5 *bu*
- Charred *Polygonum longisetum* – 1 *momme*
- Saltpetre – 2 *bu* 5 *rin*
- Charred *sugihara* paper – 5 *bu*

Mix the above with *kanemizu* tooth-dying liquid and solidify it. Mix with the dust of crushed stone and mix it into rice glue.

4

狼煙方

The *noroshi* signal flare[35]

- Saltpetre – 13 *momme*
- Sulphur – 1 *momme*
- Ash – 2 *momme*

Mix the above in the same way as gunpowder, put it into a bamboo cylinder, ram the mixture firmly and put a flare-bullet[36] down the cylinder. Make sure this is rammed down again, after the flare-bullet. If there is any gap at all, the bamboo will shatter.

---

34 This is *kuroyaki*, or 'black burnt'. Dry roast the material in a closed pot without oil until black.

35 There are variations on the *noroshi*; some are flares and some are smoke and fire signals.

36 This is a bamboo cylinder packed with the explosive powder described here. The ball is a form of 'bullet' that can be found in fireworks manufacture. When fired from the tube, it will create a flare-like signal that shoots into the air. The ball or bullet's construction is discussed in volume twenty-two.

5

不眠薬

Keeping sleep at bay powder

Take only the white part of the droppings of hawks. Put it into your navel and stick paper over it; with this you will not fall asleep.

6

アハウ薬

Fool's brew

Dry hemp leaves, powder them and use as you would the equivalent of three cups of tea. This will make people feel fuzzy and become foolish. You should reap the leaves of hemp in the seventh lunar month.

7

中蝋燭

The 'in the air' candle

Put mercury into the centre of a normal wax candle, ignite it and press the ignited end onto the [underside of a] branch of a tree or something similar. Release the [candle] with care so it will remain in place and burn.[37]

8

角蝋燭

The horn candle

Place a deer horn into horse dung for two or three days until it is soft. Then straighten it as much as possible, scrape the surface [thin] and deep-fry it in rapeseed oil. Next, deep-fry it again in perilla oil, cover it with paper and light it. It is said that a length of seven *sun* will hold out for seven nights.

---

37 Grammatically, it appears that the ignited end attaches to the tree, which would seem impossible. It is not entirely clear how this tool works.

9

不滅明盉

The immortal torch

Take the centre spines of twenty or thirty feathers of the Japanese crested ibis (*Nipponia nippon*) and cut them to the length of one *sun*. Empty the inside of each, then fill them with a thimble full of mercury. Seal the ends and tie them together with a thread. Place gold leaf in an incense box and place the tied feathers on top of the gold leaf and fix them so that they are secure. Warning: the feathers should be of a *mature* Japanese crested ibis or the torch will not glow. However, the centre spines of the feathers of the black kite (*Milvus migrans*)[38] will suffice. According to one script, you can use the pinions or flight feathers of black kites with mercury in them to reflect the light of the neighbouring house. You should put this tool on your *tachi mitsu*[39] and swing it, or alternatively using a mirror to reflect the light [to illuminate your area] will work well.

10

義経明盉

Yoshitsune's torch

Hollow [or shave] the horn of a water buffalo until it is very thin, so you can see through to the inside. Empty the spines of feathers of a Japanese crested ibis (*Nipponia nippon*) and put them into the above horn; cement the gaps [between the feathers and the horn] with lacquer so that they are watertight. Next, put a small cup full of mercury into the horn. According to one theory, hollowing the horn of a brown cow to this thinness would be best. This torch will light up as bright as a moonlit night, especially if the horn is of a brown ox.

---

38 The ideogram for this means 'owl'; however, the phonetic markers change the meaning to 'black kite'.

39 Unknown tool or area; however, it is possibly the blade of a sword.

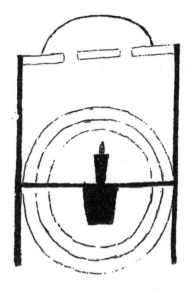

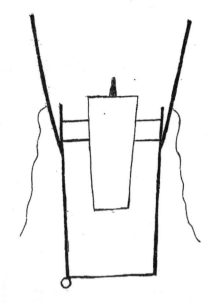

Figure 85. The handheld gimbal lantern Vent holes can be found at the top of this image.

Figure 86. The *ireko-hi* adjustable lantern

11

剛盗挑灯製作圖説

The handheld gimbal (gando) lantern with illustration (similar in form to a portable censer)

Use a circular tube[40] aas large as a small bucket, and attach an iron handle to the bottom. Include a three-ringed iron gimbal system as can be seen in the drawing.[41] The outer ring is fixed to the cylinder and is stationary; the two inner rings should be free to rotate and should be positioned exactly in the middle and hung with iron needles at certain points.[42] The candle should be hung and oil should be put in it, and then you should light it. Vent holes should be put near the handle.

---

40 A cylinder that has been steamed into shape.

41 This is the same set-up as that used on a ship's compass. The idea is that the gimbal rings keep the candle or illumination source upright.

42 The text says three points, however, this must be a transcription error as if that was the case the system would not rotate.

12

入子火圖説

The *ireko-hi*[43] adjustable lantern with illustration

Beat copper into a thin cylinder so that it has a diameter of two *sun* and a length of three *sun*. Suspend a candle on the inside [as in the drawing] and attach a second 'flared cylinder' or funnel of the same length and with a slightly larger diameter [to where it connects]. This latter funnel has no bottom and can be detached [at will].

The torch has an air hole on the bottom. The 'flared copper cylinder' should have cords so that it can be secured to the base section of the torch and so that it will not fall off.

- The candle is in the middle.
- The flared cylinder is at the top.
- The cords are at the side [and used to secure the funnel].
- The air hole is at the bottom.

13

狼煙薬方

Noroshi smoke-signal powder

- Wolf droppings
- Moxa
- Saltpetre
- Ash

The powder of the above should be used [for smoke signals].

It is written[44] that the following is also a recipe for the above tool:

- Wolf droppings – one third
- Pine needles – one quarter
- A large amount of straw

The 'one third' means that if there are three bundles of straw, put wolf droppings of the amount of one third of the total straw. If one quarter the amount of gunpowder is added to the mixture, the smoke will reach even higher. This way was invented by Kusunoki Masashige.

---

43 The Japanese name given here as 'ireko-hi' is used many times throughout the text.
44 This appears to be taken from the Gunpo Jiyoshu manual.

Oral tradition says:

Dig a hole and pound the ground firmly. Put the above mixture in the hole and leave a *hinawa* match on top so that it will catch fire spontaneously. Cover with an upturned bucket, pan or so on that has a square hole of one *sun* across in the bottom. Seal the bucket at the edges with soil so that the smoke will not leak from the underside.

An alternative way: after burning the pine needles to a quantity of half the full volume, surround them with brushwood and stand a green bamboo stick in the centre. Then surround the stick with straw mats so that the smoke will rise upwards. The straw mats should be as an inverted cone. Adding gunpowder is without doubt a benefit.

14

An alternative recipe for *noroshi*

- Wolf droppings – 10 *ryo*
- Moxa – 3 *ryo*
- Iron filings – 5 *ryo*
- Cattle dung – 3 *ryo*
- Pine needles – 10 *ryo*
- Ash – 15 *ryo*

Powder the above and make balls of seven or eight *sun* in circumference. Light with *hokuchi* tinder.

15

An alternative recipe for *noroshi*

- Straw – 3 bundles
- Wolf droppings – one third the amount of straw
- Pine needles – one quarter the amount of straw

Mix the above; adding iron filings of one third the amount of straw will work well.

16

風雨炬火

The wind- and rainproof torch

- Camphor – 50 *momme*
- Saltpetre – 20 *momme*
- Sulphur – 30 *momme*
- Ash – 20 *momme*
- Pine resin – 20 *momme*

Make a powder of the above and mix it with oil and birdlime. Knead and solidify appropriately and then dry in the sun.

If you intend to make a 'palm torch' 手ノ内ノ火炬, produce a ball that is as large as a fifty-*momme* weight bullet, light it from a handheld position and throw it into the dark. When it is used as a torch, the above mixture should be applied onto cloth, then straw should be wrapped around the cloth and it should be tied with a rope. As a torch, a bamboo stick should be inserted into the straw [as a handle].

17

生滅火炬

The appearance and disappearance torch[45]

- Saltpetre – 25 *momme*
- Sulphur – 12 *momme* 5 *bu*
- Ash – 2 *momme* 5 *bu*
- Pine sawdust – 7 *momme*
- Pine resin – 1 *momme* 5 *bu*
- Moxa – 3 *momme*

Upon experimentation, this tool went out when it was swung around. However, it ignited again when blown upon; also, if you cut the tip off it will light again.

---

45 This is a reference to the Buddhist concept of birth and death and may or may not mean to appear and disappear in a physical sense.

18

An alternative recipe for the above torch

This should be made in the same way as above.

- Saltpetre – 20 *momme*
- Sulphur – 15 *momme*
- Camphor – 8 *momme*
- *Kunroku*[46] – 1 *momme* 5 *bu*
- Ash – 5 *bu*
- Mouse droppings – 1 *momme*
- Pine resin – 1 *momme*
- Old cloth – 1 *momme* 5 [*bu*]
- Moxa – 1 *momme*
- Cattle dung – 1 *momme*

For both of the above two recipes, ram the ingredients firmly into a bamboo cylinder.

19

一寸三里火炬

The three-centimetres to three-*ri* torch

This should be created in the usual way.

- Saltpetre – 15 *momme*
- Sulphur – 15 *momme*
- Ash – 1 *momme*
- Camphor – 3 *momme* 5 *bu*

Powder the above and mix it with hempseed oil.

---

46 Fossilized material of pine or cedar resin, used as medicine or perfumes; it is similar to amber.

20

篝火炬　梅田流

The basket torch of the Umeda[47] school

- Borneol – 1 *bu*
- Camphor [unknown amount]
- Scouring rush (*Equisetum hyemale*) – 2 *rin*
- Sandstone – 2 *rin*
- Saltpetre – 1 *bu*
- Sulphur – 2 *rin* ·
- Pine resin – 8 *rin*
- Seeds of Japanese honey locust (*Gleditsia japonica*) – 1 *rin* 5 *mo*
- Orpiment – 1 *rin*

Powder the above and mix it with rice brandy. If rice brandy is unavailable, use *shochu.*[48]

21

切火口ノ方　同人方

Sliced tinder from the same school

- Saltpetre – 3 *momme*
- Camphor – 10 *momme*
- Sulphur – 1 *bu* 5 *rin*
- Ash – 1 *bu* 5 *rin*
- Sandstone – 3 *bu*
- Bamboo sawdust – 3 *rin*
- Japanese royal fern (*Osmunda japonica*) – 7 *rin*
- Pine resin – 5 *momme*
- Moxa – 5 *momme*
- Borneol – 2 *bu*
- Pine sawdust – 5 *momme*
- *Kumano*[49] tinder – 1 *bu* 5 *rin*

---

47 An unknown school, possibly connected to the Umeda family of Iga.
48 Spirit distilled from sweet potatoes, rice, etc.
49 An area in Wakayama.

Powder the above and decoct the bark of pine trees, and mix the above powder with the decoction and solidify it. [Some text omitted]

2 2

篝火炬

The basket torch

- Borneol – 1 *ryo*
- Camphor – 20 *momme*
- Sulphur – 30 *momme*
- Saltpetre – 20 *momme*
- Litharge or lead monoxide – 1 *ryo*

Powder the above and mix it with rice brandy. If rice brandy is unavailable, mix with glue and knead it. There are oral traditions on how this should be done. Apply beaten egg to the surface of the mixture. Put it in an iron basket and hang it from a jointed rod and light it. If you use one hundred *momme* of orpiment, it will illuminate a square of six *cho* or will last through the distance of three *ri*.

2 3

同方　柘植氏流

An alternative recipe for the basket torch from the school of the Tsuge[50] clan
Remember a strong fire will not last long.
- Saltpetre – 100 *momme*
- Sulphur – 50 *momme*
- Ash – 3 *momme*
- Camphor – 30 *momme*
- Moxa – 15 *momme*
- Borneol – 2 *momme* 5 *bu*
- Pine resin – 12 *momme*
- Pine sawdust – 7 *momme*

Solidify this by kneading with liquid [rice brandy] as mentioned in the previous recipe.

---

50 A family of Iga.

24

取火方

The capturing fire

- Saltpetre – 10 *momme*
- Sulphur – 5 *momme* 5 *bu*
- Ash – 2 *momme* 5 *bu*
- Iron filings (of pig iron made into a fine powder) – 2 *momme*
- Mouse droppings – 1 *momme*

Figure 87.
The capturing fire

Powder the above as fine as *domyoji* powder[51] and mix together as one. Make a cylinder of copper with a length of six or seven *sun* and a circumference of five or six *sun*. The cylinder is open at one end and has a hole of about one *bu* at the other end [which is at the top of the illustration]. Put the powder in the cylinder and ram it down firmly and put a twisted paper string with *kuchigusuri* finer gunpowder within it. Also make a handle as in the drawing.

This tool is used when you capture someone or when fighting. No matter how strong the person is, he cannot fight against this fire. [Figure 87]

The powder should be rammed down firmly in the central chamber.

Peg and fix the handle in place with the central bar that goes through the tool; without this the handle will come off.

The handle should be made so you can grip it with ease.

---

51 Powder made of dried rice.

25

夢想火

The dream or illusion fire

- Saltpetre – 12 *momme*
- Sulphur – 10 *momme*
- Orpiment – 4 *bu*
- Camphor – 5 *bu*

Powder the above and put it into a bamboo cylinder that is eight *sun* in length and four *sun* or more in circumference with a bamboo joint on one end. Roll the cylinder with thin rope and ram the powder down firmly. Cover the top with paper, take away the rope, scrape the bamboo until it is very thin and paste paper around it.

26

胴ノ火

The *donohi* body warmer

Cut waterproof *hinawa* fuses into lengths of five *sun*, mix alum with glue and apply the mixture onto the *hinawa*. Also apply alum on new paper, light it and then wrap it [in something non-flammable so that it does not burn you but keeps you warm].

27

打火炬

The attack torch[52]

- Saltpetre – 10 *momme*
- Sulphur – 2 *momme*
- Ash – 2 *momme*
- Camphor – 5 *bu*
- Pine resin – 1 *momme* 5 *bu*
- Pine sawdust – 7 *momme*
- Mouse droppings – 2 *momme*

---

52 Used to throw into an enemy camp *en masse* as you carry out a night raid or possibly to set fire to thatch roofs and the like.

Put the above mixture into a bamboo cylinder that is two *sun* nine *bu* in circumference and five *sun* in length with a bamboo joint on one end. Attach a torch hilt on the end [that has the bamboo joint; this handle should be] four *sun* in length, octagonal and tapered to a point, like a bird's tongue[53] and should preferably be of steel.

Powder the above mixture and ram the powder into the cylinder very firmly. Scrape off the surface of the bamboo and paste paper around it.

28

飛火炬

The flying rocket (also known as the *okuni* fire arrow 大國火矢)

- Saltpetre – 22 *momme*
- Sulphur – 5 *momme*
- Ash – 6 *momme*
- Mouse droppings – 4 *bu*
- Camphor – 3 *bu*
- Iron filings – 2 *momme*

Powder the above as fine as *domyoji*[54] powder. The arrow should be four *shaku* two *sun* in length and the nock part is nine *sun* long.[55] The fletchings should be six *sun* in length. Firmly ram the powder into a bamboo cylinder of six *sun* in length and put a twisted paper string with ignition powder within it, and light it at this point.

The arrowhead should preferably be the shape of a bird's tongue[56] and be two *sun* and four or five *bu*.

The arrow itself should be four *shaku* two *sun* in

Figure 88. The flying rocket

---

53 This term comes from a form of arrowhead that is tapered and considered octagonal.
54 Coarse rice powder.
55 Presumably an internal strengthening rod. However, this has not been confirmed.
56 Tapering to a point.

length and the fletchings should be six *sun* and should be made from the feather of a crane or other large bird.[57]

The bamboo cylinder is six *sun* in length and the inside diameter should be six *bu*.[58]

The fuse should consist of ignition powder inside a twisted paper string and inserted into the bottom of the cylinder.

The nock [strengthening] shaft ends one *shaku* from the butt end of the arrow and the feathers are about eight *sun* long.[59]

Put a support plate[60] at the arrowhead, where the thin vines bind the arrowhead on. This is done so that you can fit the bamboo cylinder up to the edge of the arrow.

29

猿火ノ事

Monkey fire

Apply ample 'white alum' and saltpetre to a thin rope. Tie a stone wrapped in cloth on one end of the rope [as a weight]. Next tie a copper ring [further up] the rope and insert a torch in the ring. This can be freely lifted up and down so that you can inspect the bottom of a moat or the area beneath a *yagura* turret area. That is why it is called 'monkey fire'.

30

付竹ノ方

The match

- Saltpetre – 50 *momme*
- Sulphur – 30 *momme*
- Camphor – 20 *momme*
- Pine resin – 5 *momme*
- A dash of *shochu* spirits

---

57 This is possibly a reference to eagles, as in *Otori jinja*, or the 'eagle shrine'.
58 Transcription error; the original text says 'sun'.
59 This point is a transcription error, as the original says 'nine *sun*'.
60 This appears to be a fixed plate just below the arrowhead that stops the bamboo cylinder from coming off the shaft.

Powder the above, knead it with thin glue and apply it to *hoshogami* fine-quality paper. Cut it into thin pieces for use.

3 1

當圖ノ方

[Unknown torch][61]

Split pine wood that is saturated with resin into thin sections and apply a heavy dose of [missing text]; do this two or three times. Next, split thin bamboo into thinner pieces and boil them in water and allow them to dry completely. Bind the bamboo onto the outside of the split pine at intervals of one *sun*. The next step is to wrap paper around the torch with a layer of glue. After that, wrap equal amounts of saltpetre, sulphur, camphor, wax and resin[62] in cloth around the torch and apply oil to it and then roast it over a fire. Finally, wrap the torch in *shibugami*[63] paper and, to finish, wrap about five *sun* of the torch – at its base – with the plant-sheath that grows at the bottom of a bamboo plant [and use this section as a handle]. The length of this torch should be two *shaku* five *sun*. The details are kept oral. The circumference is seven or eight *sun*. It can sustain fire for six *ri* or for six hours.

3 2

南氣明枩方

The 'chi of the south' torch[64]

Split bamboo into thin pieces and bind them with pine wood in the same way as the torch above. This torch should be about three *shaku* long, and in addition, you put a nail of five or six *sun* on the bottom.[65] It is thrown into the enemy hut or where they are defending.

---

61 The ideogram simply says 'this illustration'.
62 Possibly animal fat.
63 Japanese paper strengthened with the juice of astringent persimmons.
64 This is similar to the 'thrown attack torch' described in the Gunpo Jiyoshu manual.
65 An image of this can be seen in the translation of the Gunpo Jiyoshu manual.

3 3

竹本明杏

The basic bamboo torch

Split the *Pleioblastus simonii* form of bamboo into thin pieces, soak the sections in clear water for about ten days,[66] and then dry them completely. How to bind them is to be orally transmitted.

3 4

風雨夜火炬方

The torch for a windy and rainy night

- Sesame – 8 *momme*
- Pine [?][67] – 20 *momme*
- *Lingustrum obtusifolium* – 5 *momme*
- Borneol – 3 *momme*
- Pine sawdust – 25 *momme*
- Hemp or flax stalks (soaked in water) – 100 *momme*
- Saltpetre – 5 *momme*
- Moxa (crumpled very well) – 120 *momme*
- Sulphur – 10 *momme*
- Camphor – 50 *momme*
- Japanese nutmeg – 15 *momme*
- Powdered green tea – 8 *momme*
- Alum – 12 *momme*
- Ash of *kiri* wood – 120 *momme*
- Japan wax – 50 *momme*
- Oil of the *raigan*[68] – 15 *momme*
- Camellia seed – 20 *momme*
- Manteiga – 5 *momme* 5 *bu*
- Coconut oil or a similar type of oil – 8 *momme*
- Powdered deer horn – 6 *momme*
- Perilla – 30 *momme*

---

66 This is done to remove all sap.

67 The meaning of the word 松関 is actually unknown – the first ideogram is for 'pine' and the second means 'to close' or 'relation'.

68 A form of fungus that grows to around one or two centimetres at the bottom of bamboo plants.

Powder the above, knead it with oil, and dry it very well. Then firmly ram it into a bamboo cylinder.

35

風雨火炬方

The wind- and rainproof torch

Strip thick sections of the bark of the rosebud cherry tree (*Prunus pendula var. ascendens*). Mix *shochu* spirits and camphor and apply to the bark two or three times. Dry it very well and bind together at intervals of one *sun* and make it three *shaku* in length and with a circumference of eight *sun*. The rope has a secret oral tradition.

36

玉中火炬方

The thrown fire ball

- Saltpetre – 10 *momme*
- Sulphur – 5 *momme*
- Ash – 3 *momme*
- Pig iron – 4 *momme*

Mix the above appropriately and throw it into the enemy. Further details are an oral tradition.

37

雷火炬方

The thunder [attack] torch

- Saltpetre – 100 *momme*
- Sulphur – 80 *momme*
- Ash – 25 *momme*
- Iron filings – 25 *momme*

Make a powder of this mixture and do the same as above.

38

An alternative recipe for the above tool

- Saltpetre – 30 *momme*
- Sulphur – 20 *momme*
- Camphor – 50 *momme*
- Pine resin – 20 *momme*
- Ash – 20 *momme*

Powder the above and knead with the same oil used for making birdlime. Apply it to a piece of cloth that is one *shaku* five *sun* in width and three *shaku* and five or six *sun* in length. Put about twenty hemp stalks together and bind them with vines. Bind three whole [and small] pieces of bamboo around [the bundle], so that it can be held.

39

玉コカシ火ノ方

The burning ball fire

- Lead – 200 *momme*

Make a ball of lead and split it into two. Put gunpowder into the centre and make a hole through the casing so that you can feed a *mizu-hinawa* or waterproof fuse into the grenade; this is used to ignite it. This weapon should be taken on board one of your ships and thrown onto [an enemy's] vessel. Oral tradition.

40

筒サキ薬

Musket gunpowder

- Saltpetre – 20 *momme*
- Sulphur – 6 *momme*
- Ash – 9 *momme* 5 *bu* (of which 5 *momme* is of beehive and 4 *momme* 5 *bu* is of snake skin)

41

キリ薬

An alternative gunpowder

- Saltpetre – 40 *momme*
- Sulphur – 20 *momme*
- Ash – 20 *momme*

42

イヌキ薬

Strong gunpowder

- Saltpetre – 40 *momme*
- Sulphur – 2 *momme*
- Ash – 3 *momme*

43

ツケ火方

Fire-starting powder

- Saltpetre – 10 *momme*
- Sulphur – 5 *momme*
- Pine sawdust – 2 *momme*

Powder the above and put it into a bamboo cylinder so that you can carry it. This is to be orally transmitted.

44

天宮火方

The 'heaven's palace' torch

- Saltpetre – 23 *momme*
- Sulphur – 5 *momme*
- Ash – 5 *momme*
- Camphor – 3 *bu*
- Mouse droppings – 3 *bu*

Put the above into a bamboo cylinder of three *sun* and scrape the surface thin and wrap paper around it. Take an arrow that measures one *shaku* five *sun* and remove the head and attach this torch to it. When you need to look inside [a compound], fire the torch in through an arrow or gun port so that you can see inside. There is more to be orally transmitted.

45

鉄炮二ツナリノ事

The double-shot musket

Put gunpowder and a bullet as normal into a musket. Next place wet paper [down the barrel] on top of the first bullet and then place a second charge of gunpowder down the barrel. Then, insert a bullet that is slightly smaller [than the latter one] and cut a *hinawa* fuse down to one *sun* in length; light this fuse and put it in. When the *hinawa* ignites the gunpowder, the outer bullet fires and then you may shoot the normal bullet as usual [giving you a second shot].[69]

46

篭火ノ圖説

The basket fire and illustration

Use this when you deal with those who are defending a building. This is a basket of woven iron and is of one and a half or two *bu* in thickness. It should be made appropriately so that a [hard-burning] candle can be put inside. This works very well in the case of dealing with those who are defending a building. Remember,[70] inattentive people may have a light source taken by a prisoner and even those who are very attentive can be careless at times and they cannot fight very well in darkness or may even fight among themselves in such a case. You should use this light to observe the status of the inside of a building. This light has the benefit of not allowing a criminal to capture it and also it has the benefit of not being easily extinguished.

---

69 This skill was possibly used in the assassination attempt on Oda Nobunaga.
70 This is taken directly from the Gunpo Jiyoshu manual of c.1612.

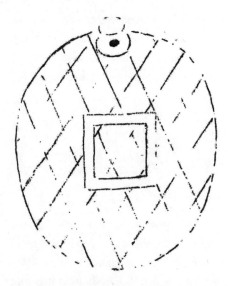

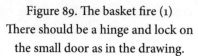

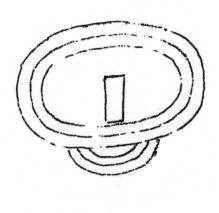

Figure 89. The basket fire (1)
There should be a hinge and lock on
the small door as in the drawing.

Figure 90. The basket fire (2)
The inside should be like [the gyro
system] of the *gando* lantern [as
mentioned in tool number eleven].

47

楯火炬ノ圖説

The shield torch and illustration[71]

This should be used for dealing with
those who barricade themselves in or for
carrying out a night attack. The shield
should be preferably of willow wood. It
is more or less two *sun* in thickness and
six *sun* in width. If it is too large, then it
is not so convenient.

The chain-mail skirt should be one
shaku and nine *sun* in length, but it
should depend on the size of the wielder.
The chain mail should be made of iron in
the same manner as a gauntlet.[72]

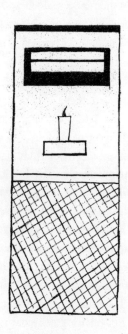

---

71 This is taken directly from the Gunpo Jiyoshu
manual of c.1612.

72 Compared to Western chain mail this is quite
thin and lightweight.

Figure 91.
The shield torch

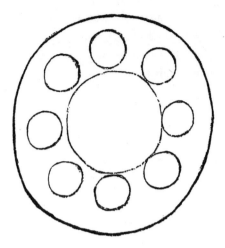

Figure 92. The hand grenade (1)   Figure 93. The hand grenade (2)

A handle should be put at six *sun* below the *monomi* viewing window and there is a cross piece at one *shaku* below the window on the outside of the shield. This is so you can put a [hard-burning] candle there.

48

拋火矢ノ圖説

The hand grenade with illustration[73]

During a night raid this should be thrown into where the enemy is gathering in order to create panic so that you can take the advantage and defeat them.

Use a twisted paper ignition powder fuse.

This should be made of clay in the shape as in the drawing. Fill it with musket gunpowder and iron filings, put the halves together and throw it where the enemy is gathering. Also it is good in the case that you need to flee very quickly from a *shinobi* mission. Further information is to be orally transmitted.

The number of holes can be changed as you wish.

Put burning charcoal into the chambers around the centre and then insert a

---

73 This is taken directly from the Gunpo Jiyoshu manual of c1612.

twisted paper fuse with ignition powder through the central hole,[74] then load it with shot and *tsuyogusuri* gunpowder and then cover the whole thing with paper. Throw it in the place where people are gathering. Further information is to be orally transmitted.

49

埋火圖説

The landmine or buried fire with illustration[75]

The size should vary according to the place and situation. The boards used for the box should be as thin as possible.

First, split bamboo in half and place it with the inside face down and place an [unlit] *hinawa* fuse under each bamboo section [with the ends coming out of one side and tied together].

Second, put a mixture of gunpowder and pebbles into the box [and close it].

Third, put one end of the *hinawa* [into the box] and make sure that the flame can pass through [the ground after you have buried the box[76]].

Fourth, put an old straw mat on the box and spread soil thinly on the top [to camouflage it].

This weapon should be positioned upon the enemy's path and should be made so that it will ignite when someone steps upon it.[77] More to be orally transmitted.[78]

---

74 Alternatively, this could simply mean 'fill the centre with ignition powder'.

75 This has been taken from the *Gunpo Jiyoshu* manual. However, in this edition the translation has been expanded upon. The original text is quite ambiguous and is meant to be supported by an oral tradition. Therefore, this more accessible translation has been cross-referenced with 'explosives manuals' from different schools to offer a better understanding to the reader.

76 Alternative manuals show that a separate section of bamboo normally comes out of the side of the box, which marries all the fuses together. This would then be covered over and camouflaged after being lit.

77 The general idea among other manuals that have been investigated is that when a person stands on the mine, their weight cracks the bamboo with the lit fuses and also the thin lid of the box. This empties the embers and burning sections of fuse into the box, which ignites the gunpowder and launches the stones upwards into the groin and soft underside of the human who triggered it.

78 It is believed that this image is inverted and incorrectly displayed as it is known that this is taken from the *Gunpo Jiyoshu* manual, which is of Hattori lineage. It is possible that the author of the *Gunpo Jiyoshu*, the samurai Ogasawara misinterpreted Hattori and drew the box upside-down, which was then also miscopied by Fujibayashi. This would account for the differences between the image and the text and also the differences highlighted by cross-referencing with other schools. It would appear that Fujibayashi was not aware of the correct procedure for this weapon and was simply recording this tool as a separate tool from another clan.

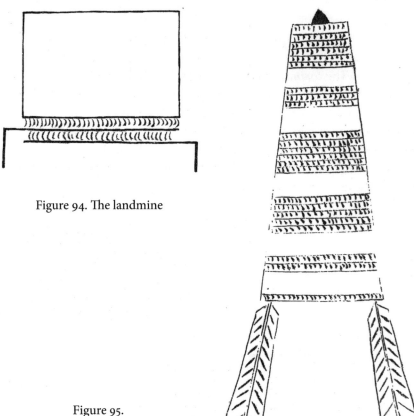

Figure 94. The landmine

Figure 95.
The rolled burning arrow

50

巻火矢圖説

The rolled burning arrow with illustration

- Cut out a hardwood seal and place it in the centre and at the back of this arrow.
- Wind a thin rope onto a bamboo cylinder.
- Apply ignition powder around the tip and in the bamboo joint.

For the flight of the arrow, the bark of the cherry tree is recommended. The size can be varied as you wish.

51

鳥ノ子ノ事并圖

The *torinoko* night-attack tool with illustration

Take the ears off straw and pound them in a mortar well and then dry them in the sun. Make a four-*sun* long bundles of straw and tie it at both ends. [To make it secure] weave straw around the tool at intervals [as can be seen in the drawing] and put the [pounded] ears inside it. You can carry this tool.

How to construct and use the night-attack *torinoko* and the *shinobi torinoko* has more to be orally transmitted.

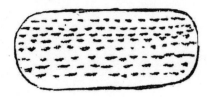

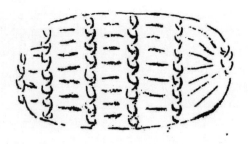

Figure 96. The *torinoko* night-attack tool

The top image is a *torinoko*.
The bottom image is a *torinoko* that has been wrapped in straw.

An alternative recipe for the above tool

Take the ears of straw and pound them in a mortar, then soak and fry them in oil and then dry them out. Next, wrap in straw in the same way as above. Also, applying a solution of sulphur is recommended.

52

車火炬ノ事

The cart torch

Make a cart with the dimensions of six or seven *shaku*[79] square. Stand a wind- and rainproof torch that has a bright flare on the cart and attach a thin rope to the vehicle. If you are defending a mountain castle or any other situation, you should have this cart lowered down to the bottom of the valley by extending the rope; do this if there is something suspicious. There is more to be orally transmitted on the making of this tool.

53

胴火七方并圖

The seven recipes of the *donohi* body warmer with illustration

I

To make a body warmer that stays alight for a whole day and night, you should braid a hard rope with very old and bleached cloth and make it so that it is six *sun* in length and six *sun* in circumference. Lay it in a *hitsubo* charring jar and put a layer of ash to a depth of two or three *sun* on the section of rope, and then burn a fire on top of the ash. After roasting it in the jar [in this manner], take it out and put it into a sealed container so that the fire will go out. Wrap the rope in a thin layer of straw and tie it up with thread at eight or nine places and do this tightly. It can be carried in your kimono or on your waist, thus it is called the *donohi* body fire or the *koshi-donohi*, which is the waist body fire. The drawing right shows the version to be carried in your kimono. It can also be carried in a bamboo cylinder.

Figure 97. The *donohi*
body warmer

---

79 The original manual says '*sun*' – however, this would make the cart tiny in size and therefore it is most likely meant to be '*shaku*'.

II

To make a body warmer that will stay alight for two or three nights, cut old [hemp] cloth or cotton into very thin pieces, mix them with an appropriate amount of kettle soot and harden the mixture with glue. Ram it tightly into a bamboo cylinder that is six *sun* in circumference and cut it into six-*sun* lengths. Roast it with a covering of bran and in the same way as the above one. Then take it out, shave off the burnt surface, wrap it with the natural sheath found at the bottom of a bamboo plant and tie it up tightly at six or seven places.

III

Roast old hemp or cotton cloth in a closed jar and cut it into very fine pieces [or even powder it] then knead and solidify it with rice broth or persimmon tannin, after which you ram it into a bamboo cylinder and dry it completely. Then take away the bamboo cylinder and wrap it with bamboo sheath or simply keep it in the bamboo cylinder so you can carry it in your kimono. This is called *takedonohi* 竹胴火 or the bamboo body fire. When using charred aubergine stems you should use the same method as above.

IV

Soak *sugihara* paper in salted water for one night and dry it completely and then tear it into thin pieces. Pack it into a bamboo cylinder very tightly and char this paper. Glaze[80] some more paper and lightly grill it. Then wrap the first charred paper with this latter glazed paper [so you can keep it on you], or alternatively you can glaze thin tanned leather, make a small bag of this leather and put the [ignited] paper in it, so you can carry it in your kimono.

V

Mix charred *sugihara* paper and *funori* glue,[81] knead and solidify it. Light it and put it between boards, so that you can carry it.

VI

Break down charcoal of chestnut oak from Ikeda into very fine pieces and then thoroughly crumple *sugihara* paper and tear it into thin pieces. Mix both of them with glue and knead until sticky. Ram this paste into a bamboo cylinder very tightly and dry it in the sun; shave the outside of the bamboo and wrap it with bamboo sheath, tying it firmly.

---

80 Mix alum and glue and paste it onto the paper.
81 Glue made of *Gloiopeltis* (seaweed).

VII

Chew a piece of *sugihara* paper for two days until it does not have any taste at all. Dry it in the sun and ignite it. If you wish to extinguish this then you should wrap it in thicker *sugihara* paper.

懐中火ノ事

The pocket fire

Char thin pieces of *henon* bamboo (*Phyllostachys nigra var. henonis*) and solidify with glue, cover in powdered green tea and dry in the sun. Light the tool and then wrap it in glazed[82] paper so you can carry it.

小電

Small lightning[83]

- Saltpetre – 40 *momme*
- Sulphur – 11 *momme*
- Ash – 6 *momme*

無二

Uniqueness[84]

- Moon – 30 *momme*
- Sun – 60 *momme* 5 *bu*
- Star – 7 *momme* 5 *bu*

There is an oral tradition for each point.

水火縄ノ事

A waterproof fuse

Boil a normal *hinawa* fuse in *fushi*[85] liquid, stretch it out and dry it completely. Then scrub [the surface].

---

82 As in the previous example of glazed paper.

83 An unknown tool. However, this would form a type of black powder. It can be hypothesized from its name that this is a form of flash powder or bomb.

84 An unknown tool whose ingredients are given in code. According to Yunoki Shunichiro, the ingredients are saltpetre (sun), sulphur (moon) and ash (star). His theory is based on cross-referencing the amounts used here with other tools containing three elements. However, the issue is still open to investigation.

85 A black liquid made of an acetic acid with dissolved iron and gallnut and tannin powder.

Another recipe is to boil a *hinawa* fuse in water with the leaves of the *henon* bamboo (*Phyllostachys nigra var. henonis*). It has the advantage of having no smell.

As for a *kusa-hinawa*[86] fuse, soak the bark of Rose of Sharon (*Hibiscus syriacus*) in water and use it as a *hinawa* fuse. There is another version called the ambush *hinawa* 伏火縄, where washed-out cloth is used, as it has no smell.

洗玉ノ事

Musket-cleaning balls

Sew together a cloth bag of two *sun* in length. Put a mixture of equal amounts of fine sand and alum in it. Load it into a musket and shoot; this will clean out the barrel.

ホウロク火箭ノ事

The incineration[87] weapon

There are several methods, but they are all the same. You do not have to use a lot to burn down the enemy.

The stone dragon method [of the incineration weapon]

• Saltpetre – 200 *momme*
• Camphor – 10 *momme*
• Sulphur – 60 *momme*
• Pine wood/resin – 60 *momme*
• Ash – 40 *momme*

The iron dragon method [of the incineration weapon]

• Saltpetre – 100 *momme*
• Sulphur – 30 *momme*
• Ash – 25 *momme*

---

86 The text states '*kusa hinawa*', which could be a reference to the fuse being made of *kusa* ('grass') or it could be a reference to *kusa* troops who would wait in ambush in the grass. It is probably the latter, as this fuse is notable for being odourless and so would be particularly suitable for use in an ambush. Interestingly, the Gunpo Gokuhi states that you should send *shinobi* to smell for hinawa fuses.

87 On the surface this appears to mean 'pottery'. In a modern context, however, the etymology suggests that it was a form of Chinese execution by burning. This 'incineration' is probably one of two weapons. It is either a 'Chinese fire lance', which is a flamethrower on a pole, or it is a form of hand grenade.

• Camphor – 15 *momme*
• Pine wood/resin – 10 *momme*

胴火

The *donohi* body warmer

Mix equal amounts of washed-out cloth and Japanese royal fern (*Osmunda japonica*) and add a small amount of camphor. Knead them with glue. The ears of foxtail millet should be used as well.

An alternative method is to cut washed-out cloth into one-*shaku* circles, char them and cut them like moxa and wrap in bamboo sheath. A tool of five *sun* in length can last for twenty-four hours.

檜火炬

The Japanese cypress torch

Split *hinoki* Japanese cypress into thin pieces, apply sulphur onto them and bind them together.

Mixing wolf droppings and moxa is desirable.[88]

---

88 This last sentence is written on its own with no indication as to whether it is connected to the last tool. It sounds as if it belongs to a smoke-signal recipe.

VOLUME TWENTY-TWO

Ninki V

Ninja Tools V

Fire tools II

1

筒ノ火

The fire-carrying cylinder

Soak bleached cloth in the shallows of a river for about thirty days and then braid it to a segment that is three *sun* in circumference and five *sun* in length. Next, take a bamboo cylinder of the same measurements and split it in two and place the 'cloth rope segment' inside and reform the two bamboo halves back into one. Tie the cylinder up with rope and put *akatsuchi* red clay around it and char the whole thing until the clay cracks. Break off the clay and wrap it with rice straw and tie the whole tool up with oiled rope.[1] To extinguish the flame of this tool [when you need to], bury it in rice.

2

An alternative recipe for the fire-carrying cylinder

- Charred aubergine stems
- Moxa tinder – 10 *momme*
- Saltpetre – 10 *momme*
- Paper for tinder – 10 sheets

'Powder' the above and mix it together.

---

1 Literally, 'oil rope'.

3

A further alternative recipe for the fire-carrying cylinder

Cut *sugihara* paper into small pieces, soak them in water for about five days, take them out and dry them in the sun and then char them. Next, cut bamboo into small pieces and mix them into the charred mixture and place the whole concoction into a bamboo cylinder.

4

Alternatively, soak the *sugihara* paper in water for five days, then cut it up so finely that it resembles powder and put it into a bamboo cylinder.

5

A further alternative recipe for the fire-carrying cylinder

• Charred aubergine stem
• Japanese cypress sawdust
Mix in equal amounts with *sake* and solidify it.

6

A further alternative recipe for the fire-carrying cylinder

Cut *mizu-hinawa* waterproof fuses into five-*sun* sections and carry them in your kimono.

7

鳥ノ子

Torinoko[2]

Strip the ears off rice straw in the opposite direction,[3] pound them in a mortar and wrap a small amount of the powdered ears in a [tied] straw bundle.

---

2 This is a small – sometimes egg-shaped – bundle used for illumination or fire starting.
3 This appears to be a reference to the direction in which you strip the section of the plant you require.

8

檜火炬

The *hinoki* Japanese cypress torch

Scrape *hinoki* wood into sections eight *sun* in length and three *sun* in circumference. Tie them together with left-laid rope at three places with a left-sided knot. This is because the left is *yo*, which is joyous, and this method should be used in the construction of all torches. At the bottom of this torch put a four-*sun*-long nail so that the torch will serve well as a *shuriken* throwing blade.[4] This [spike] should have a square cross-section so that you can hold it, and also you should add *yakigusuri* powder secured at the centre of the torch for an easy ignition. There is more to be transmitted orally.

9

An alternative form of *hinoki* Japanese cypress torch

Bind and tie up three lengths of wood that measure one *shaku* two *sun* long and secure them at one *sun* from the bottom. [Missing text] should be put at the bottom of this torch. Secure a bar of tempered iron that is about five *sun* long and that has a [spiked] shape like a bird's tongue.

10

A further alternative *hinoki* Japanese cypress torch

Scrape the red heartwood of the *hinoki* Japanese cypress and shape it into triangular lengths of one *shaku* two *sun*. You should tie these together at three places, up to three *sun* from the bottom and with a *sukiyamusubi* knot. The top should be made in the shape of a bamboo tea whisk and it should have a hilt at the bottom.

11

火炬

A torch recipe

- White [saltpetre] – 10 *momme*
- Pine sawdust – 7 *momme*

---

4 The Gunpo Jiyoshu manual points out that this is not for throwing at people, but to be thrown into a compound.

- Black [charcoal] – 2 *momme*
- Moxa[5] – 1 *momme*
- Mouse droppings – 2 *momme*
- Sulphur – 2 *momme*

This can also be used as an attack torch 打火炬.

1 2

An alternative torch recipe

- White [saltpetre] – 10 *momme*
- Camphor – 5 *momme*
- Sulphur – 2 *momme*
- Black [charcoal] – 5 *momme*
- Borneol – 2 *momme* 5 *bu*
- Pine resin – 1 *momme* 5 *bu*
- Powdered moxa – 1 *momme*
- Pine sawdust – 7 *momme*
- Mouse droppings – 2 *momme*

Powder the above and firmly ram it into a bamboo cylinder. Then scrape off the surface of the bamboo skin and paste paper around it. It is the same as in the previous recipes.

1 3

An alternative torch recipe

- White [saltpetre] – 5 *momme*
- Sulphur – 2 *momme*
- Pine resin – 1 *momme* 5 *bu*
- Black [charcoal] – 2 *momme*
- Camphor – 2 *momme* 5 *bu*
- Pine sawdust – 7 *momme*
- Mouse droppings – 2 *momme*
- Moxa – [unknown amount]

Construct it as the above torch and when used as a [thrown] attack torch 打火炬, put lead in the bottom [for weight].

---

5   The ideogram used here does not exist. It has been assumed that Fujibayashi meant 'moxa'.

1 4

An alternative torch recipe

- White [saltpetre] – 5 *momme* 1 *bu*
- Sulphur – 2 *momme* 6 *rin*
- Camphor – 5 *momme* 1 *bu*
- Ash – 1 *momme* 5 *bu*
- *Hinoki* sawdust – 4 *momme*

Powder the above, knead it with sesame oil [*dama no abura*] and solidify it in a three-*sun* long bar.

1 5

An alternative torch recipe

- White [saltpetre] – 5 *momme*
- Black [charcoal] – 2 *momme*
- Pine sawdust – 7 *momme*
- Mouse droppings – 2 *momme*
- Moxa – 1 *momme*

Construct it using the method above. This can also be used as an attack torch 打火炬.

1 6

大火炬

The greater torch

- White [saltpetre] – 100 *momme*
- Sulphur – 20 *momme*
- Black [charcoal] – 3 *momme*
- Camphor – 50 *momme*
- Borneol – 2 *momme* 5 *bu*
- Moxa – 5 *momme* 5 *bu*
- Pine sawdust – 7 *momme*

Solidify the above for use.

17

クヌ木火炬

The *kunugi* Japanese chestnut oak torch

You require one *shaku* of this to sustain you for the distance of one *ri*, and also this torch will work very well in windy or rainy weather. Cut *kunugi* wood (*Quercus acutissima*) into three-*shaku* lengths, then beat it so that you do not cut through the fibre but so that it softens. Next, powder one hundred *momme* of saltpetre and mix it into three *sho* of water. Then soak the *kunugi* sections into this solution for seven or eight days and dry them in the sun. Apply powdered sulphur of the amount of fifty *momme* into the torch and bind it all together with a circumference of approximately one *shaku*. Soak straw in salted water, dry it in the sun, beat the straw to soften it and then wrap the above torch with it.

18

十里火炬

The ten-*ri* torch

Cut sections of *kunugi* Japanese chestnut oak into lengths of three *shaku* and beat it with stone into small pieces and crush it fully. Powder saltpetre and dissolve it in water and apply the solution onto the *kunugi* wood. Dry it for twenty-four or twenty-five days to harden it. Powder the above-mentioned amount of saltpetre and camphor, sprinkle the powder onto the *kunugi* wood, and wrap it with straw.

19

クヌキ火炬

An alternative *kunugi* Japanese chestnut oak torch

Pound *kunugi* wood into very small pieces, extract the fibres and bind them together neatly. Put camphor, saltpetre and nutgalls in *kanemizu*[6] and soak the *kunugi* wood in the solution for a whole day and night, take it out, put it in a pan together with the liquid and boil it through. Then wrap the mixture in paper and bury it in the ground for one day.

---

6   Tooth-blacking solution.

20

手火炬

The hand torch

Cut *kunugi* Japanese chestnut oak into lengths of three *shaku* and pound it into small pieces. Powder one hundred *momme* of White [saltpetre] and put it into three *sho* of water. Then soak the *kunugi* wood in this liquid for seven or eight days and dry it in the sun. Then, powder fifty *momme* of sulphur, sprinkle it onto the *kunugi* wood, and bind it into a torch with a circumference of approximately six *sun*. Next glue paper around it and apply lacquer. Finally, at the open end of the torch and at around the length of two[7] *sun*, tie [a packet] of attack-torch ignition powder.

21

[Powder for the above torch]

- White [saltpetre] – 25 *momme*
- Yellow [sulphur] – 2 *momme* 5 *bu*
- Blue [camphor] – 5 *bu*
- Black [charcoal] – 2 *momme* 5 *bu*
- Red [moxa] – 3 *momme* 5 *bu*
- Pine resin – 1 *momme* 5 *bu*
- Mouse droppings – 3 grains
- Powdered green tea – a pinch

22

手木薬

Tegi[8] powder

- White [saltpetre] – 10 *momme*
- Yellow [sulphur] – 9 *momme*

---

7 While ambiguous, it appears that you strap down this packet of powder two sun into the mouth of the torch.

8 A *tegi* is an alternative name for a *jitte*, which is a form of metal truncheon used in Japan. Here the *ninja* has attached a normal sword guard as a hilt to the weapon and has attached the bamboo cylinder to the bar of the truncheon, with the hole facing the enemy. This way, when he lights it he can attack the enemy with a spray of fire and protect his hand. However, it does appear to say 'through the guard', as though the lower end of the bamboo comes through and below the hard guard.

- Black [charcoal] – 2 *momme*
- Chilli pepper – 3 *momme*

Put the above powder into a bamboo cylinder four *sun* in length. Also, attach a flat plated hand guard (*tsuba*) to a short metal truncheon (*jitte*) and then tie the bamboo cylinder through the hand guard [with the end facing the opponent]. The method of manufacturing this and the measurements of the short metal truncheon are oral secrets.

23

Adding five *bu* of pepper and three *bu* of borneol to the above mixture will also work well.

24

[An alternative to the above]

- White [saltpetre] – 70 *momme*
- Yellow [sulphur] – 10 *momme*
- Black [charcoal] – 10 *momme*
- Pepper – 10 *momme*
- Chilli pepper – 15 *momme*
- Camphor – 10 *momme*
- Iron filings – 10 *momme*

Coarsely powder the above and firmly ram it into a bamboo cylinder, apply moxa at the top with glue, light it and allow the fire to spray over the enemy. There are more oral secrets here.

25

懐中火

The pocket fire

Powder white alum, mix it with glue and apply it to thick paper. Next insert the mixture into a bamboo cylinder two *sun* in circumference and ram the contents down firmly. Dry it in the sun and put it in your pocket between folded paper.

It is good to split the bamboo and use this to light the *toribi* fire tool [Tool number 30].

26

十二火炬

The 'twelve' torch

Scrape Japanese cypress to sections of six to eight *sun* in length and three *sun* in circumference and then tie it with left-braided rope at three places [from the bottom of the torch working your way to the top and also do this] with left-handed knots – this is done to symbolize *yo* (*yang*). Put a square nail of tempered iron of four *sun* in length on the end so that it can be also used to throw like a *shuriken*. When [a collection of] the above pocket fire tools is wrapped around this torch at a height of one *sun* five *bu*, it will ignite and you can throw it toward a position to ignite [the area]. Also, though it is called 十二火炬 'twelve torches', it is also known as 'two wisdom' or 'three wisdom'.[9] Details are to be orally transmitted.

27

打火炬

The attack torch

- White [saltpetre] – 25 *momme*
- Yellow [sulphur] – 22 *momme* 5 *bu*
- Black [charcoal] – 2 *momme* 5 *bu*
- Blue [camphor] – 5 *bu*
- Red [moxa] – 10 *momme* 5 *bu*
- Pine resin – 1 *momme* 5 *bu*
- Mouse droppings – 3 grains
- Powdered green tea – a pinch

Powder the above and place it in a bamboo cylinder five *sun* in length. Scrape off the outer skin of the bamboo and wrap it in paper [and glue]. Drill a hole and put a paper ignition fuse into it and ignite it with the fire cylinder. Light it just before you are about to attack the enemy. Use a hilt as normal – the way to attach the hilt to the base is to be orally transmitted.

---

9 Possibly a Buddhist reference.

2 8

An alternative recipe

- White [saltpetre] – 10 *momme*
- Black [charcoal] – 8 *momme*
- Sulphur – 2 *momme*
- Camphor – 8 *momme*
- Pine resin – 1 *momme* 5 *bu*
- Pine sawdust – 7 *momme*
- Mouse droppings – 2 *momme*

Powder the above and put it into a bamboo cylinder five *sun* in length and two *sun* nine *bu* in circumference with a bamboo joint at one end of the bamboo shaft.[10] On the bottom end attach a nail of tempered iron which is four *sun* in length and is of octagonal shape, like that of a bird's tongue (spiked). Construct it as above.

2 9

筒 火

The cylinder fire[11]

Also known as the 'fire within the sleeve' 袖火.
- White [saltpetre] – 10 *momme*
- Yellow [sulphur] – 5 *momme*
- Ash – 2 *momme*

Mix the above appropriately and ram it firmly into a bamboo cylinder six *sun* in length and with a joint at one end. Crumple paper and put it on the open end and then drill a hole at the bottom end [which is sealed by the natural joint] and insert a *kuchigusuri* ignition powder paper fuse. Carry this tool in the sleeve and light it as you take it out.

---

10 Bamboo forms natural joints, which act as internal divisions, creating compartments. In this case the upper compartment will be used for the combustibles and the lower one will be to hold the hilt.

11 A compact and hidden flame thrower, not to be confused with the fire cylinder; the above tool is a weapon, while the fire cylinder is an ember-carrying article.

30

取火

Fire for capturing people

- White [saltpetre] – 20 *momme*
- Yellow [sulphur] – 9 *momme* 5 *bu*, or 5 *momme* 6 *bu* [if refined]
- Black [charcoal] – 7 *momme* 5 *bu*, or 2 *momme* 4 *bu* [if refined]
- Iron filings – 4 *momme*
- Mouse droppings – 1 *momme*

Coarsely powder the above, mix it and put it into a bamboo cylinder six *sun* in length and four *sun* two *bu* in circumference and with a joint on one end. Ram the mixture into the cylinder firmly and fasten a lid of wood so that it is firm and will not come off. Drill a hole in the closed end and insert a paper rolled string with *kuchigusuri* ignition powder inside it. Light this tool when held in your hand.

31

人取火

Fire for capturing people

- Camphor
- White [saltpetre]
- Pine resin

Mix the above into equal amounts, [light it] and throw it into the face of the enemy.

32

生捕火

Fire that renders people redundant for capture

- Iron [filings] – 4 *momme*
- White [saltpetre] – 10 *momme*
- Yellow [sulphur] – 5 *momme*
- Black [charcoal] – 4 *momme*
- Chilli pepper – 3 *momme* 5 *bu*
- Black pepper – 3 *momme*

Make a powder of the above. How to bind it is to be orally transmitted.

33

鉄砲打薬

Musket powder [and ball for capturing people]

This is normal gunpowder and is used to make a bullet.

- White [saltpetre] – 9 *momme*
- Yellow [sulphur] – 4 *momme* 8 *bu*
- Black [charcoal] – 2 *momme*

Wrap the above powder in silk floss and wrap it with thread[12] [in the shape of a bullet].

34

袖火付入

Fire from the sleeve when rushing [the enemy holdout]

- White [saltpetre] – 10 *momme*
- Yellow [sulphur] – 5 *momme*
- Black [charcoal] – 2 *momme*
- Iron filings – 4 *momme*

Powder the above and fry it in oil.

35

付入取火

Fire to capture when rushing [the enemy holdout]

- White [saltpetre] – 10 *momme*
- Sulphur – 5 *momme*
- Black [charcoal] – 2 *momme*

Measure the above and grate it coarsely. Bind it in the same way as above.[13]

---

12 This is a bullet made of compressed and wrapped gunpowder. It is for firing at those you do not wish to kill but those you wish to capture.

13 Fujibayashi does not specify which tool it is bound like.

36

Here is an important point about bullets; you should remember this when using a musket. Make a [thin] leather bag of five *sun* and ram fine sand into it. Load it into a musket so that you should shoot it when you feel it is the best time to capture the target. You should capture the person with haste [after shooting it].

37

天狗火

Tengu goblin fire arrow

- White [saltpetre] – 23 *momme*
- Yellow [sulphur] – 5 *momme*
- Ash – 10 *momme*
- Mouse droppings – 3 *bu*
- Camphor – 3 *bu*

Powder the above mixture and insert it into a cylinder three *sun* in length. Scrape off the surface of the bamboo and wrap it in paper. The arrow should be one *shaku* five *sun* in length and its preparation is to be orally transmitted. When it is difficult for you to get into a castle but you need to investigate inside from your position on the outside, fire it in through a shooting port.

38

鉄砲生捕火

Fire to render the enemy redundant for capture

Always have your musket loaded with gunpowder. For the bullet [used in this skill], make it of round cotton that is the same size as a normal bullet, by rolling it with thin thread and soaking it in water then covering it with powdered chilli pepper. Shoot it when needed.

39

忍火炬

The *shinobi* torch

Saltpetre – 22 *momme* 5 *bu*
- Sulphur – 18 *momme*
- Old cattle dung – 1 *momme*
- Pine resin – 1 *momme*
- Ash – 2 *momme* 5 *bu*
- Moxa – 2 *momme* 5 *bu*
- Mouse droppings – 1 *momme* 5 *bu*
- Old cloth – 5 *bu*

Mix the above and put it into a cylinder.

40

忍焼薬

Shinobi burning powder[14]

- Ash – 10 *momme*
- Saltpetre – 100 *momme*
- Sulphur – 30 *momme*
- Pine resin – 2 *momme*
- Mouse droppings – 1 *momme*
- Bear's gall bladder – 3 *bu*

The following is a recipe for *kuchigusuri* ignition powder to ignite the above.
- Saltpetre – 9 *momme*
- Sulphur – 3 *momme*
- Ash – 2 *momme*

Put the above in a cylinder and use it.

---

14 The manual does not describe the purpose of this tool; also it divides the ingredients into two sections. Most likely this is a form of arson powder to be used by *shinobi* when infiltrating; however, other options cannot be ruled out.

41

忍火炬

The *shinobi* torch

- Saltpetre – 3 *momme* 3 *bu*
- Sulphur – 12 *momme*
- Ash – 5 *momme* 5 *bu*
- Moxa – 2 *momme* 5 *bu*
- Old cattle dung – 1 *bu*
- Pine resin – 1 *bu*
- Mouse droppings – 1 *momme* 5 *bu*
- Old cloth (either hemp or cotton can be used) – 5 *bu*

Mix the above and put it into a cylinder and use it.

42

An alternative recipe for the above

- Saltpetre – 1 *momme*
- Ash – 8 *bu*
- Camphor – 35 *momme*
- Borneol – 1 *momme* 2 *bu* 5 *rin*
- Pine resin – 1 *momme* 1 *bu* 5 *rin*
- Mouse droppings – 5 *bu* 5 *rin*

Mix the above and construct as the tool above.

43

A further alternative recipe for the above tool[15]

- Ash – 10 *momme*
- Saltpetre – 100 *momme*
- Sulphur – 50 *momme*
- Pine resin – 2 *momme*
- Mouse droppings – 1 *momme*
- Bear's gall bladder – 3 *bu*

---

15 This is most likely an alternative for shinobi burning powder.

The following is a recipe for *kuchigusuri* ignition powder to ignite the above.
- White [saltpetre] – 9 *bu*
- Ash – 2 *bu*
- Sulphur – 3 *bu*

Put the above into a cylinder and use it.

44

A further alternative recipe for the above tool

- White [saltpetre] – 25 *momme*
- Yellow [sulphur] – 22 *momme* 5 *bu*
- Black [charcoal] – 2 *momme* 5 *bu*
- Pine resin – 1 *momme*
- Hemp cloth – 5 *momme*

Mix the above and put it into a bamboo cylinder.

45

忍 焼 薬

Shinobi burning powder

- White [saltpetre] – 100 *momme*
- Black [charcoal] – 10 *momme*
- Yellow [sulphur] – 50 *momme* or 20 *momme* [if refined]
- Pine resin – 2 *bu*
- Mouse droppings – 1 *momme*
- Bear's gall bladder – 3 *bu*

The following is a recipe for *kuchigusuri* ignition powder to ignite the above.
- White [saltpetre] – 9 *momme*
- Yellow [sulphur] – 2 *momme*
- Black [charcoal] – 2 *momme*

Powder the above and put it into a bamboo cylinder.

46

忍隼火

Shinobi falcon fire

- White [saltpetre] – 23 *momme*
- Yellow [sulphur] – 5 *momme*
- Black [charcoal] – 3 *bu*
- Mouse droppings – 3 *bu*

Powder the above and put it into a bamboo cylinder five *sun* in length and six *bu*[16] in diameter. Scrape off the surface of the bamboo and wrap with paper and then attach [arrow] fletchings one *shaku* five *sun* in length. Attach the cylinder to an arrow; when you shoot it, it will [skit around and] attack the enemy, but how to make and attach the [arrow and] fletchings is to be orally transmitted.[17]

47

手ノ内火

The fire inside the hand

- Saltpetre – 2 *momme*
- Sulphur – 3 *momme*
- Ash – 2 *momme*
- Camphor – 5 *momme*
- Pine resin – 2 *momme*

Powder the above, mix it with thin glue and liquor, solidify [into a ball] and dry it completely. Hold this in your hand and light it just before you throw it. It will continue to burn no matter how far you throw it.

This is also named – the 'fire [thrown] into a ship' 舩中火.

---

16 The text says '*sun*'; however, this appears to be a transcription error. If true, the bamboo would be too wide to fire correctly.

17 The text is not clear here – most likely, this is a 'fire rat', a cylinder with compressed ignition powder inserted, which when ignited sends the cylinder spinning and skitting around an area. Therefore, the secret of attaching is probably how to tie the arrow so it detaches when it hits the ground, allowing the weapon to jump around the floor.

48

Unnamed tool

Insert mercury, cinnabar and one *bu* five *rin* of [powdered] tiger tooth into the hollow of the spines of the feathers of the Japanese crested ibis or cormorant bird. Tie three of these with white thread at two places and carry it in the hand.

49

夢相火 [18]

Illusion fire

- Saltpetre – 12 *momme*
- Sulphur – 7–10 *momme*
- Borneol – 4 *bu*
- Camphor – 5 *bu*
- Ash – 1 *momme*

Mix the above, and ram it tightly into a bamboo cylinder wrapped with thin rope. It should be eight *sun* in length and four *sun* in circumference with a solid bamboo joint at one end. Remove the rope from the cylinder [after firmly pounding the mixture] and scrape off the surface of the bamboo, paste paper around it, and light it at the top opening.

50

An alternative recipe for the above

- White [saltpetre] – 12 *momme*
- Yellow [sulphur] – 3 *momme*
- Borneol – 4 *bu*
- Camphor – 5 *bu*
- Ash – 1 *momme*
- Chilli pepper – 4 *bu*

The construction is as above.

---

18 Presumed to be identical to 夢想火, which has the same sound.

51

A further alternative recipe

- Saltpetre – 10 *momme*
- Sulphur – 10 *momme*
- Borneol – 4 *bu*
- Camphor – 5 *bu*
- Ash – 1 *momme*

Again, construct it as above.

52

無明火

The fire of spiritual darkness

- Saltpetre – 9 *momme* 5 *bu*
- Sulphur – 5 *momme*
- Soil – 4 *momme*

Mix the above together; also, it is good to use as 'heaven fire'.[19]

53

水火縄

The waterproof fuse

Soften a normal *hinawa* fuse until it is weak, soak it in *kanemizu* black liquid with the addition of Chinese sumac for a whole day and night, dry it in the sun, wrap it with paper and bury it in the ground for a whole day and night. Then take it out and dry it in the sun.

---

19 While only a theory, it is possible that this is a burning mixture poured onto enemy soldiers as they scale castle walls, allowing the burning soil to infiltrate their armour and cause 'irritation'.

54

水火炬

The waterproof torch

- Saltpetre – 27 *momme*
- Sulphur – 20 *momme*
- Ash – 1 *momme*
- Pine resin – 2 *momme*
- Pine sawdust – 2 *momme*
- Moxa – 2 *momme*

Mix the above and do the same things as above.

55

水中燃火

Waterproof burning fire

- Saltpetre – 10 *momme*
- Sulphur – 10 *momme*
- Camphor – 10 *momme*

Powder the above and put it onto a torch so it will burn in the rain.

56

水火炬

The waterproof torch

- Saltpetre – 5 *bu*
- Camphor – 5 *bu*
- Ash – 7 *bu*

Knead the above with sesame oil so it can be used in the rain as with the above torch.

57

水火

Water fire

- White [saltpetre] – 25 *momme*
- Black [charcoal] – 4 *momme* 5 *bu*
- Yellow [sulphur] – 12 *momme* 5 *bu*
- Blue [camphor] – 1 *momme*
- Red [moxa] – 3 *momme*
- Pine resin – 3 *momme*
- Mouse droppings – 3 *bu*
- Powdered green tea – 5 *bu*

How to bind the above is a secret passed on by mouth only.

58

水火炬

Waterproof torch

- Saltpetre – 27 *momme*
- Sulphur – 10 *momme*
- Ash – 5 *momme* 5 *bu*
- Camphor – 5 *bu*
- Pine resin – 1 *momme*
- Pine sawdust – 2 *momme*
- Powdered moxa – 2 *momme*

Ram the above into a bamboo cylinder and do the same as is always done with these tools. If you need the fire to burn less fiercely then omit the saltpetre.

59

義経水火炬

Yoshitsune's waterproof torch

- Saltpetre – 25 *momme*
- Sulphur – 25 *momme* 5 *bu*
- Ash – 9 *momme* 5 *bu*

- Camphor – 1 *momme* 5 *bu*
- Moxa – 3 *momme* 5 *bu*
- Pine resin – 1 *momme* 5 *bu*
- Mouse droppings – 3 pieces
- A pinch of tea

6 0

An alternative recipe for the above tool

- White [saltpetre] – 14 *momme* 5 *bu*
- Yellow [sulphur] – 4 momme 6 *bu*
- Black [charcoal] – 1 *momme* 5 *bu*
- Horse dung – 1 *momme* 7 *bu*
- Blue [camphor] – 19 *momme*
- Pine resin – 3 *momme* 4 *bu*
- Mouse droppings – 1 *momme* 7 *bu*
- Red [moxa] – 1 *momme* 7 *bu*
- Cloth – 1 *momme* 4 *bu*
- Powdered green tea – 5 *bu*
- Pine sawdust – 5 *bu*
- Tinder – 4 *bu*

Powder the above and knead it with sesame oil. Adding the same amount of liquor will also suffice.

6 1

陣中雨火炬

The battle-camp rainproof torch

- White [saltpetre] – 20 *momme*
- Yellow [sulphur] – 30 *momme*
- Black [charcoal] – 20 *momme*
- Pine resin – 20 *momme*
- Blue [camphor] – 50 *momme*

Powder the above, knead it with the oil used for birdlime paper until it is smooth, apply it to a piece of hemp or cotton cloth one *shaku* in width and three *shaku* in length. Put twenty pieces of flax stalk on the cloth and roll it [into a cylinder] and then bind it with rattan vine. Surround the torch with three pieces of round bamboo [to add support].

6 2

風 雨 火 炬

Wind- and rainproof torch

- Camphor – 50 *momme*
- Saltpetre – 20 *momme*
- Yellow [sulphur] – 30 *momme*

Powder the above, knead it with hempseed oil and apply it to cotton cloth one *shaku* in length. Place flax stalks within it and [roll into a cylinder], bind it with vine, then roll it up inside a bamboo, bind and secure it.

6 3

義 経 陣 中 雨 火 炬

Yoshitsune's battle-camp rainproof torch

- Saltpetre – 25 *momme*
- Yellow [sulphur] – 12 *momme* 5 *bu*
- Ash – 2 *momme* 5 *bu*
- Camphor – 5 [*momme*]
- Moxa – 3 *momme* 5 *bu*
- Pine sawdust – 3 *momme* 5 *bu*

Construct as with the above tool.

6 4

陣 中 風 雨 大 火 炬

The greater battle-camp wind- and rainproof torch

Soak thin bamboo in a river for one hundred days, beat it until it is soft and bind it so that it has a three-*shaku* circumference and is two *shaku* five *sun* in length.

65

一本火炬

One-piece torch

Beat the joints of a pliant bamboo or *madake* bamboo (*Phyllostachys bambusoides*). Dry it for seven days and then soak it in water for seven days, then dry it again for seven days. This takes twenty-one days in all. Be careful not to expose it to rain or dew during the period. The fire will sustain itself for one and a half *ri*.

66

削リ火

The 'scraped' fire

- Tinder from Kumano – 3 *momme*
- Saltpetre – 1 *momme* 2 *bu*
- Diorite from Kurama – 5 *momme* 4 *bu*
- Floss of the Japanese royal fern – a small amount
- Ash – 1 *momme* 5 *bu*
- Pine resin – 20 *momme*
- Pine sawdust – 20 [*momme*]

67

An alternative recipe

- Tinder from Kurama[20] – 3 *momme* 2 *bu*
- Diorite – 5 *momme* 4 *bu*
- Saltpetre – 1 *momme* 5 *bu*
- Charred Japanese royal fern – 20 *momme*
- Tinder made from *sugihara* paper – 20 [*bu*]
- Sulphur – 1 *momme* 2 *bu*
- Borneol – 1 *momme* 2 *bu*
- Ash – 5 *bu*
- Pine sawdust – 1 *momme* 2 *bu*
- Pine resin – 1 *momme* 2 *bu*

---

20 Most likely he means *kumano*.

Powder the above. Decoct the internal bark of Japanese white pine (*Pinus parviflora*) with a sufficient amount of water to just cover it, and then simmer it until the water level drops by half. Knead glue so it is neither too thick nor too thin and it is almost in the same condition as the decoction, then mix the decoction with the glue. The construction is the same as 'scraped fire'.[21]

68

一寸三里風雨火

The one-*sun* to three-*ri* wind- and rainproof torch

- White [saltpetre] – 15 *momme*
- Yellow [sulphur] – 15 *momme*
- Black [charcoal] – 1 *momme*
- Horse dung – 2 *momme*
- Pine resin – 3 *momme*
- Pine sawdust – 3 *momme*
- Blue [camphor] – 10 *momme*
- Mouse droppings – 2 *momme*
- Moxa – 1 *momme* 7 *bu*
- Hemp cloth – 1 *momme* 5 *bu*

Powder the above, knead it with hempseed oil and ram it into a bamboo cylinder. After a while break off the bamboo cylinder [to reveal the hardened form of the mixture], then wrap it with paper and glue and put it into a larger cylinder.

69

一寸三里火

The one-*sun* to three-*ri* fire

- Saltpetre – 15 *momme*
- Sulphur – 15 *momme*
- Ash – 1 *momme*
- Mouse droppings – 2 *momme*
- Pine resin – 3 *momme* 5 *bu*
- Moxa – 11 *momme* 7 *bu*

---

21 Fujibayashi does not explain its construction.

• Pine sawdust – 3 *momme*

Powder the above and knead it with oil. Put it into a bamboo cylinder and then remove it as above, following the same process as the tool above.

70

一寸三里火

The one-*sun* to three-*ri* fire

• White [saltpetre] – 15 *momme*
• Sulphur – 15 *momme*
• Camphor – 3 *momme* 5 *bu*
• Hemp cloth – 1 *momme* 5 *bu*
• Moxa – 1 *momme* 7 *bu*
• Pine sawdust – 3 *momme*

Make it using the same method as above.

71

三寸火

The three-*sun* fire

Scrape away the inside white of *henon* bamboo (*Phyllostachys nigra var. henonis*) and char it. Then powder it down, solidify it with thin glue and put it into a bamboo cylinder. Scrape off the surface until it is thin, and dry it in the sun for five days and then put it into a larger cylinder. It will hold [a flame] from morning until night.

72

五寸火

The five-*sun* fire

Burn Japanese cypress to get ash and perform the same as outlined above for the three-*sun* fire. Next firmly ram the above powder [which is named in the above three-*sun* fire] into a bamboo cylinder three *sun* in length. Next, wrap and sew a lead ball in leather and attach it to the bottom [on the outside] – this way the fire will not go out. Also, a cylinder of eight *sun* in length can be used. Tie [the same kind of ball] in the same way as described above.

73

矢倉落火

The turret-collapsing fire

- White [saltpetre] – 14 *momme*
- Yellow [sulphur] – 8 *momme*
- Iron filings – 3 *momme*
- Black [charcoal] – 4 *momme*
- Borneol – 3 *bu*

Put the above into a bamboo cylinder three *sun* in circumference.

74

魔王火

The devil's fire

- Sulphur – 1 *momme* 2 *bu*
- *Hokuchi* tinder made from decayed wood – 10 *momme*
- Borneol – 1 *momme* 2 *bu*
- Perilla oil

Mix the above with old sake and use it.

75

熊坂火

The fire of Kumasaka

- Powdered yellow [sulphur] – 2 *momme*

Apply to hemp stalks and bind fifty pieces of it together.

76

An alternative recipe for the above

- White [saltpetre] – 15 *momme*
- Powdered green tea – 1 *momme* 2 *bu*
- Floss of the Japanese royal fern – 1 *momme*
- Black [charcoal] – 1 *momme* 1 *bu*
- Hemp cloth – 1 *momme* 9 *bu*
- Horse dung – 1 *momme* 9 *bu*
- Pine resin – 1 *momme* 5 *bu*
- Paper tinder – 1 *momme*
- Cattle dung – 1 *momme* 5 *bu*

Add oil and liquor to the above. How to bind it together is a secret.

77

付火

The fire-setting tool

- Saltpetre – 10 *momme*
- Sulphur – 5 *momme*
- Pine sawdust – 2 *momme*

Put the above in a bamboo cylinder and make holes on all four sides.[22]

78

An alternative recipe for the above

- White [saltpetre] – 10 *momme*
- Yellow [sulphur] – 5 *momme*
- Pine sawdust – 2 *momme*
- Pine resin – 2 *momme*

Construct as above.

---

22 A powder-packed cylinder with four holes in it, so that when it is lit and thrown into the enemy, fire will spray in many directions.

79

A further alternative recipe for the above

- Saltpetre – 10 *momme*
- Sulphur – 5 *momme*
- Ash – 3 *momme*
- Soil – 3 *bu*
- Pine sawdust – 3 *momme*

Construct as above.

80

第等火炬

The *yawara* or soft-burning torch

There are three variations. As they are same as described in the previous volume, they are omitted here.

81

火炬

Torch

- Saltpetre – 5 *momme*
- Sulphur – 2 *momme*
- Pine sawdust – 7 *momme*
- Mouse droppings – 2 *momme*
- Moxa – 1 *momme*

Powder the above and firmly ram it into a bamboo cylinder. Construct as above. If you want to make an attack torch 打火炬, then simply put lead at the bottom.

82

ホウロク火

The incineration fire [lead hand grenade]

The ball container should be made of lead, which should be thinly extended out so that it can contain about three *sho* of materials. Split it in half and place inside it a layer of gunpowder and then a layer of stones. Be careful that it does not become too heavy and lose its shape. Wrap this ball [with paper] and make three holes for fuses; here you can insert waterproof *hinawa* fuses into the [internals of the tool]. When you attack a castle, light the tool and throw it through an arrow or gun port. Also, it is desirable to put it in the enemy's path, or to throw it onto [the deck] of a ship so that it will destroy the whole vessel. When the enemy is besieging your castle, you should throw it out through the arrow and gun ports. Throwing it in the path of the enemy when they are following you or into the enemy's camp are also preferred methods.

83

敵大勢ノ向フトキ鎗ニ付ル火

Fire to be put on the end of a spear when fighting with a large number of enemy soldiers

- White [saltpetre] – 7 *momme* 5 *bu*
- Yellow [sulphur] – 5 *momme* 5 *bu*
- Black [charcoal] – 11 *momme* 5 *bu*
- Iron [filings] – 10 *momme* (5 *momme* of which should be fried in oil)
- Dried ginger – 4 *momme*
- Black pepper – 4 *momme*

As always, mix the above and thinly scrape the outside of the bamboo.

84

振火炬

The swing torch (to be used at the same time as the above tool)

Soak bamboo (*Arundinaria simonji*) in a river for seven days. Then add powdered sulphur into the bamboo and bind fourteen or fifteen pieces together each measuring two *shaku* five *sun* in length. Swing this toward the enemy when fighting them. As ignition powder, boil one *shaku* of cloth in water with fifteen *momme* of saltpetre. Then tear it up into strips and put it onto the openings of the above tool and use it as an ignition point.

85

夜討天文火

The night-attack celestial fire arrow

- White [saltpetre] – 10 *momme*
- Yellow [sulphur] – 2 *momme* 2 *bu* 5 *rin*
- Borneol – 9 *momme* 7 *rin*
- Old sake spirits – 20 *momme*
- A decoction of moxa – 20 *momme*

Powder the above [and add it to the liquid], put a small amount in a bag and attach it to an arrow that you will fire. There is more to be transmitted orally here.

86

An alternative recipe

- Yellow [sulphur] – 2 *momme* 2 *bu* 5 *rin*
- Saltpetre – 10 *momme*
- Camphor – 1 *momme* 8 *bu* 6 *rin*
- Borneol – 1 *momme* 7 *bu*
- Old sake spirits – 20 momme

Dry the above completely, place a small amount in a bag and then attach it to an arrow. Light it and shoot the arrow.

87

玉火

The ball fire[23]

Char *sugihara* paper and solidify it with rice broth for use.

---

23 Small flammable balls thrown into the enemy position or roof; used to start fires.

88

忍下天狗火

The *shinobi* lesser-*tengu* fire

- Saltpetre – 23 *momme*
- Yellow [sulphur] – 5 *momme*
- Ash – 5 *momme*
- Camphor – 2 *bu*
- Mouse droppings – 3 *bu*

Put the above into a cylinder three *sun* in length. Wrap it with paper and attach it to an arrow one *shaku* five *sun* in length and which has had the arrowhead removed. When you need to look inside [a fortress], fire this through an arrow or gun port so you can see the inside.

89

敵討薬

Enemy-attack powder

As this is the same as previously mentioned, it is omitted here. Turn the opening [of the tool] toward the enemy and spray it at them.[24]

90

狐火

Fox fire[25]

- White [saltpetre] – 20 *momme*
- Black [charcoal] – 2 *momme* 3 *bu*
- Blue [camphor] – 16 *momme*
- Horse dung – 2 *momme*
- Yellow [sulphur] – 9 *momme* 2 *bu*
- Hemp cloth – 5 *momme* 4 *bu*
- Floss of the Japanese royal fern – 5 *bu*
- Pine sawdust – 8 *bu*

---

24 A form of spraying fire from a cylinder.
25 In Japan the fox has magical or supernatural connotations.

- Mouse droppings – a small amount
- Powdered green tea – a small amount

Powder the above and mix oil with it.

9 1

蛍火

The firefly fire

- Hemp cloth – 5 *momme*
- Yellow [sulphur] – 8 *momme*
- Borneol – 10 *momme* or 3 *momme*[26]
- White [saltpetre] – 8 *momme*
- Horse dung – 2 *momme*

How to bind this is to be transmitted orally. This recipe[27] makes me think that this may burn in water.

9 2

有明火

The dawn fire

- White [saltpetre] – 15 *momme*
- Black [charcoal] – 2 *momme*
- Yellow [sulphur] – 11 *momme*
- Cloth – 14 *momme*
- Camphor – 10 *momme*
- Horse dung – 1 *momme* 8 *bu*

How to bind this tool is to be transmitted orally, but you should mix it with old spirits.

---

26 In most of the other cases where dual measurements are given, the ingredient is sulphur or charcoal and the distinction is probably between coarse and refined. The reason for the dual measurement in this case is probably the same.

27 The literal translation of the text is 'in water'; however, it could also mean 'in heavy rain'. The syntax here suggests that Fujibayashi has not tried this tool.

93

楠名火

Kusunoki's renowned fire

- White [saltpetre] – 14 *momme*
- Yellow [sulphur] – 15 *momme*
- Blue [camphor] – 9 *momme* 2 *bu*
- Hemp cloth – 5 *momme* 2 *bu*
- Black [charcoal] – 1 *momme* 8 *bu*
- Powdered green tea – 8 *bu*
- Horse dung – 1 *momme* 8 *bu*
- Red [moxa] – 1 *momme*

Powder the above; however, the binding process is to be transmitted orally.

94

The recipe for *jiyaki* ground-burning powder[28] 地焼 and 埋火 the buried fire[29]

This is also called the double powder 二重薬.
- White [saltpetre] – 10 *momme*
- Yellow [sulphur] – 5 *momme*

It is said that no liquid is required to solidify this, but I recommend you use *kanemizu* tooth-staining liquid with Chinese sumac or alcoholic spirits. Spread it out on the ground ready for burning.

95

火炬

Torch

- White [saltpetre] – 100 *momme*
- Yellow [sulphur] – 20 *momme* or 5 *momme* [if refined]
- Black [charcoal] – 3 *momme*
- Blue [camphor] – 30 *momme* or 10 *momme* less [if refined]

---

28 Powder used to start grass fires upwind from an enemy to burn troops.

29 Normally buried fire refers to a landmine; however, it has also been used for other tools and seems to mean burning powder here.

- Red [moxa] – 15 *momme*
- Borneol – 2 *momme* 5 *bu*
- Pine resin – 12 *momme*
- Pine sawdust – 7 *momme*

How to solidify this is to be transmitted orally. I tried this in the year of Ram and it worked well.

9 6

飛火炬

The fire rocket[30]

[Basic recipe]
- Saltpetre – 15 *momme*
- Yellow [sulphur] – 4 *momme* 1 *bu*
- Ash – 7 *momme*
- Iron filings – 4 *bu*
- Camphor – 3 *bu*

This is a recipe for the distance of one *cho*.

[The following is a selection of recipes for rockets that can fly various distances.]
For a distance of three *cho*[31]
- Saltpetre – 23 *momme*
- Sulphur – 5 *momme*
- Ash – 6 *momme*
- Iron filings – 4 *momme*
- Camphor – 3 *momme*

For a distance of four *cho*
- Saltpetre – 56 *momme*
- Sulphur – 15 *momme* 3 *bu*
- Ash – 17 *momme* 3 *bu*

---

30 Literally, 'flying torch' – it could be a fire rocket or a signal rocket, making its use change between attacking and signalling. Here it has been translated as a fire rocket, because the word for 'distance' has been used. If it had been intended as a signal rocket, its function would more likely have been described in terms of height rather than distance.

31 For quick reference: one *cho* is equal to 109 metres.

- Iron filings – 6 *bu*
- Camphor – 5 *bu*

For a distance of five *cho*

- Saltpetre – 180 *momme*
- Sulphur – 45 *momme*
- Ash – 55 *momme*
- Iron filings – 7 *bu*
- Camphor – 6 *bu*

For a distance of five *cho* and five *tan*[32]

- Saltpetre – 90 *momme*
- Sulphur – 53 *momme* 5 *bu*
- Ash – 27 *momme* 5 *bu*
- Iron filings – 4 *bu*
- Camphor – 3 *bu*

For a distance of six *cho*

- Saltpetre – 40 *momme*
- Sulphur – 31 *momme*
- Ash – 35 *momme*
- Iron filings – 5 *bu*
- Camphor – 4 *bu*

For a distance of seven *cho*

- White [saltpetre] – 32 *momme*
- Sulphur – 21 *momme*
- Ash – 26 *momme*
- Camphor – 1 *momme*
- Iron filings – 1 *momme* 5 *bu*

For a distance of eight *cho*

- White [saltpetre] – 23 *momme*
- Sulphur – 20 *momme*
- Ash – 5 *momme*
- Mouse droppings – 4 *bu*
- Camphor – 3 *bu*
- Iron filings – 5 *bu*

---

32 A *tan* is one tenth of one *cho*.

For the distances there are further details to be transmitted orally and also, you only need to grate the ingredients in a coarse way. The cylinders of all the above signals should roughly be six *sun* in length and six *bu* in diameter. Use a square spiked gimlet to create three holes at the bottom to allow for a fuse and insert a paper twisted string with ignition powder contained within it.

97

飛火炬

The flying torch

- Saltpetre – 13 *momme*
- Sulphur – 5 *momme*
- Ash – 6 *momme*
- Mouse droppings – 4 *bu*
- Camphor – 3 *bu*
- Iron filings – 2 *momme*

Coarsely grate the above. The arrow to be used should be four *shaku* and two *sun* in length, and the nocking support[33] should be five *sun* long; also, the fletchings should be six *sun*. The cylinder used [to propel the rocket] should be six *sun* in length and six *bu* in diameter.

An alternative measurement: the arrow should be four *shaku* two *sun*; the fletchings eight *sun*; the nock support six *sun*; and the cylinder six *sun* in length and six *bu* in diameter. For the fuse, make three holes with a square spiked gimlet.

The powder to be used in fuses for the above tool.[34]

- White [saltpetre] – 20 or 30 *momme*
- Black [charcoal] – 7 *momme* 5 *bu* or 4 *momme* 1 *bu* [if refined]
- Yellow [sulphur] – 5 *momme*
- Blue [camphor] – 3 *bu*
- Mouse droppings – 3 *bu*

---

33 This appears to be a small dowel of wood inserted into the rear of the arrow to strengthen the nock.

34 The ideogram used here is 道薬, the first one literally means 'path' or 'to lead' and the second one 'powder'. Possibly powder used in a fuse.

9 8

火 口

Tinder

- Moxa – 10 *momme*
- White [saltpetre] – 10 *momme*
- *Sugihara* paper tinder – 10 *sheets*

Grate the above finely.

9 9

焼 薬

Burning powder

- White [saltpetre] – 40 *momme*
- Yellow [sulphur] – 50 or 20 *momme* [if refined]
- Blue [camphor] – 20 *momme*
- Pine sawdust – 4 *momme*
- Black [charcoal] – 4 *momme*
- Pine resin – 3 *momme*
- Mouse droppings – 2 *momme*

How to bind the above is secret.

1 0 0

矢倉ノ事

The turret tool[35]

- Up to one *cho* five *tan* [away], the *turret tool* should be two *sun* long.
- For two *cho*, it should be two *shaku* three *sun* in length.
- For a *masuyagura* [that is a bigger version of this tool, add] two *sun*.
- For three *cho*, it should be two *shaku* six *sun* in length.
- For four *cho*, it should be three *shaku* one *sun* in length.
- For each five *tan* that is added to the distance, add three *sun* to the measurement.

---

35 The tool is not described, however it appears to be a projectile launcher that increases in length as the required distance for the projectiles to travel increases. Most likely it is a fire rocket used against castle turrets.

101

狼煙火

Noroshi – the signal rocket

White [saltpetre] – 23 *momme*
Black [charcoal] – 8 *momme* 6 *bu*
Yellow [sulphur] – 10 *momme* 5 *bu*
Mouse droppings – 4 *bu*
Blue [camphor] – 3 *bu*

Powder and mix the above, ram it into a bamboo cylinder, scrape off the surface and wrap it with paper and attach it to an arrow. Details to be transmitted orally.

大村雨

The large squall

This also is a *noroshi* signal fire.

- White [saltpetre] – 20 *momme*
- Yellow [sulphur] – 3 *momme*
- Blue [camphor] – 12 *momme*
- Black [charcoal] – 1 *momme* 5 *bu*
- Mouse droppings – 1 *momme*
- Red [moxa] – 2 *momme*
- Pine sawdust – 4 *momme*
- Hemp cloth – 2 *momme*

Grate the above finely and construct as with the above tool [that is, use a bamboo cylinder]. The cylinder should be eight *sun* in length and eight *bu* in diameter. Scrape off the surface and wrap it in one layer of paper and then roll it with hemp cloth [or rope] and then wrap it with paper a second time.

Glue a section of leather over the bottom of the rocket where you have inserted ignition powder and make a hole for the ignition fuse. The hole should penetrate through the leather and to a depth of two *sun* five *bu* – make the hole with a square spiked gimlet. Next insert a paper twisted string with ignition powder within it into the hole as a fuse.

For the tip of the cylinder, take Japanese cypress wood and shape it as a [spear] butt and attach it. The arrow should be four *shaku* three *sun* in length, the fletchings should be six *sun* and two *bu*, and the completed cylinder should be attached to it.

The ignition powder used for the above tool:

- White [saltpetre] – 11 *momme*
- Yellow [sulphur] – 2 *momme* 5 *bu*
- Black [charcoal] – 9 *momme* or 4 *momme* [if refined]
- Mouse droppings – 2 *bu*
- Blue [camphor] – 2 *bu*
- Iron filings (fried in oil) – 4 *bu*

103

[The signal flare recipe in three parts][36]

[Part I]

玉狼煙

The signal flare gunpowder

- Saltpetre – 14 *momme* 4 *bu*
- Sulphur – 7 *momme* 4 *bu* or 3 *momme* 4 *bu* [if refined]
- Black [charcoal] – 7 *momme* or 4 *momme* [if refined]
- Mouse droppings – 2 *bu*
- Blue [camphor] – 2 *bu*

This can be used as a signal.

[Part II]

The balls use to produce dropping fire trails

- White [saltpetre] – 3 *momme* 8 *bu*
- Yellow [sulphur] – 8 *bu* 5 *rin*
- Black [charcoal] – 1 *momme*
- Mouse droppings – 6 *bu*
- Blue [camphor] – 6 *rin*
- Copper filings (fried in oil) – 1 *bu*

Coarsely powder the above ingredients to be put it into a cylinder [later]. Make balls with the above powder and wrap them with cotton material and put these

---

36 One of the forms of the *noroshi* fire signal, this is a tube with a layer of gunpowder (part I), which then has small ammunition balls placed on top (part II), and finally a layer of ignition powder (part III) covers the balls. When lit, they fire into the air as a signal flare while dropping and leaving a trailing flare.

on top [of the layer of signal flare gunpowder as described above]. You can use two or three of these at one time if you wish.

104

[Part III]

The powder used to fill the gaps between the balls of ammunition
- White [saltpetre] – 10 *momme*
- Black [charcoal] – 1 *momme* 8 *bu*
- Yellow [sulphur] – 1 *momme* 9 *bu*

Powder the above finely and make it into small pips the size of mustard seeds, then pour this into the cylinder on top of the cotton balls described above. Normal gunpowder will also suffice if you need to use it.

There is a way to construct this so that it will fly three *cho* and fall with a trail of one *cho*.

There is also a way to construct this so that it will fly four *cho* and fall with a trail of one *cho*.

[This is the end of the signal flare recipe.]

105

大國火矢

The *okuni* fire arrow

[Recipes for various distances.]

For the distance of one *cho*
- Saltpetre – 15 *momme*
- Iron filings – 4 *bu*
- Sulphur – 3 *momme* 5 *bu*
- Ash – 4 *momme* 3 *bu*
- Camphor – 3 *bu*

For the distance of two *cho*
- Saltpetre – 13 *momme*
- Blue [camphor] – 3 *bu*
- Iron filings – 4 *bu*
- Yellow [sulphur] – 3 *momme* 5 *bu*
- Ash – 7 *momme* 5 *bu* (or 2 *bu* will also work)

For the distance of three *cho*
- Saltpetre – 23 *momme*
- Blue [camphor] – 3 *bu*
- Iron filings – 4 *bu*
- Sulphur – 5 *momme*
- Ash – 6 *momme*

For the distance of four *cho*
- Saltpetre – 26 *momme*
- Blue [camphor] – 3 *bu*
- Iron filings – 4 *bu*
- Ash – 11 *momme* 2 *bu*
- Sulphur – 9 *momme*

For the distance of four *cho* **and five** *tan*
- Saltpetre – 90 *momme*
- Blue [camphor] – 5 *bu*
- Iron filings – 4 *bu*
- Sulphur – 45 *momme*
- Ash – 85 *momme*

For the distance of five *cho and* **five** *tan*
- Saltpetre – 90 *momme*
- Blue [camphor] – 5 *bu*
- Iron filings – 4 *bu*
- Sulphur – 23 *momme* 5 *bu*
- Ash – 27 *momme*

For the distance of five *cho*
- Saltpetre – 180 *momme*
- Blue [camphor] – 6 *bu*
- Iron filings – 7 *bu*
- Sulphur – 45 *momme*
- Ash – 85 *momme*

For the distance of six *cho*
- Saltpetre – 200 *momme*
- Blue [camphor] – 4 *bu*
- Sulphur – 31 *momme*

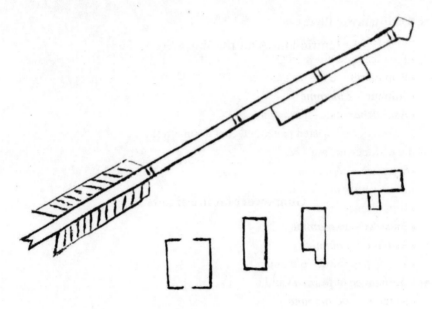

Figure 98. The *okuni* fire arrow

- Ash – 35 *momme*
- Iron filings – 5 *bu*

For the distance of seven *cho*
- Saltpetre – 72 *momme*
- Iron filings – 1 *momme* 1 *bu*
- Blue [camphor] – 1 *momme*
- Sulphur – 21 *momme*
- Ash – 51 *momme*

Coarsely grate the above. In all cases the cylinder should be six *sun* in length and six *bu* in diameter on the inside. For the fuse, pierce three holes with a square spiked gimlet and insert an ignition fuse.

[Attach the bamboo cylinder] three *sun* from the end, not including the length of the arrowhead.[37]

The arrow should be four *shaku* long for a trajectory that spans eight *cho*.

The length should be changed according to the distance.

---

37 Three sun from the end of the shaft.

106

Ignition fuses for the above fire arrows

- White [saltpetre] – 10 *momme*
- Sulphur – 7 *momme*
- Black [charcoal] – 1 *momme* 5 *bu*

Apply the above to twisted paper and coat in pine resin.

107

Gunpowder for fire arrows

- Saltpetre – 10 *momme*
- Ash – 10 *momme*
- Yellow [sulphur] – 6 *momme*

An alternative recipe.

- Saltpetre – 60 *momme*
- Yellow [sulphur] – 40 *momme*
- Ash – 4 *momme*
- Camphor – 30 *momme*

Mix the above so it will not extinguish, even if it is shot into water.

108

松浦火薬

The gunpowder used by the Matsura clan[38]

- Saltpetre – 5 *momme*
- Camphor – 2 *momme*
- Sulphur – 5 *momme*
- Iron filings – 1 *momme*
- Ash – 1 *momme*
- Pine resin – 1 *momme*

Mix the above six ingredients.

---

38 Thought to be the same Matsura clan that was renowned for its seamanship.

109

筒火矢道薬

Powder used in fuses – for the cylinder of a fire arrow
- Saltpetre – 20 *momme*
- Sulphur – 20 *momme*
- Ash – 5 *momme*

110

焼薬

Ignition powder for the cylinder fire arrow

- Saltpetre – 10 *momme*
- Sulphur – 9 *momme*
- Ash – 1 *momme* 5 *bu*

Details are to be transmitted orally for the way to prepare the above.

For the nock of the arrow, insert a wooden dowel support one third of the way down the bamboo shaft, and remember the fletchings should preferably be wet [when you fire the arrow].

111

[Unnamed tool]

- Sulphur – 5 *momme* 5 *bu*
- Ash – 11 *momme*
- Dried ginger – 4 *momme*
- Saltpetre – 7 *momme* 5 *bu*
- Iron filing – 10 *momme*
- Pepper – 4 *momme*

Out of the ten *momme* of iron filings, five *momme* should be used as in standard firework manufacture, while the remaining five *momme* should be fried in normal oil before they are inserted. Powder the above and mix in the iron filings. Then scrape down the outside of the cylinder thinly and wrap it with paper and glue. This tool should be lit when you fight against the enemy in a large number.

112

付木火

Quick-light match

- Camphor – 3 *bu*
- Sulphur – 4 *momme*
- Saltpetre – 1 *momme* 5 *bu*

Knead the above with thin glue and apply it to paper. Put two sheets of this paper together and cut into appropriate-sized pieces [and strike sparks over them when needed].

113

紙燭火

Shisokubi – the paper candle

- Saltpetre – 20 *momme* or 10 *momme*
- Sulphur – 7 *momme* 5 *bu* or 7 *momme* 3 *bu*
- Cinnabar – 5 *momme*
- Camphor – 9 *momme* or 8 *momme* 9 *bu* [if refined]

Knead the above with thin glue, apply it to paper, wrap the paper around thin bamboo as a paper candle and take away the bamboo and dry it in the sun; then you can light it.

114

雨大火炬

The greater rainproof torch

Mix and knead camphor and sesame seeds in sesame oil, and apply to a torch so it will light in the rain.

115

[An alternative for the *noroshi* signal rocket]

The following signal rocket can go up as high as four or five *cho*, as when I tried this in the year of Snake. This experiment was achieved by mixing only a small amount of each of those ingredients that will make it rise as high as possible.

- White [saltpetre] – 14 *momme* 4 *bu*
- Yellow [sulphur] – 3 *momme* 4 *bu*
- Black [charcoal] – 4 *momme*
- Mouse droppings – 2 *bu*
- Blue [camphor] – 3 *bu*

Prepare the above so it is coarser than gunpowder. The saltpetre and sulphur should feel smooth enough that you can sprinkle it with your fingers. The cylinder should be eight *sun* in length and eight *bu* in diameter; however, when I experimented, I tried this with a cylinder six *sun* in length and seven *bu* in diameter and with a bamboo wall-joint at one end.

Next, I put two spoonfuls of the powder in, little by little; then, I inserted a hardwood rod (which was five *bu* in diameter) into the opening of the seven-*bu* wide bamboo cylinder and beat [the powder] as many as forty times with this hardwood pounder and an iron hammer until the amount was about half of the depth of the cylinder. Then I removed the rope [which was holding it together], and scraped down the surface of the cylinder. Note: only scrape off the surface of the bamboo from the top of the cylinder to two *sun* five *bu* down from the end bamboo wall joint [at the top of the rocket], then gradually you should make the cylinder thinner as you work toward the bottom end of the rocket – at the bottom of the cylinder the bamboo walls should be as thin as paper. After this, I put leather over the end joint but this leather end is a secret to be transmitted orally, so I should not write it down here.[39] Next double wrap the tool with paper from Mino and dry it in the sun. Then, firmly [attach it to the arrow by] wrapping it with a string made of the *ramie* plant and glue and wrap it again with paper three times in

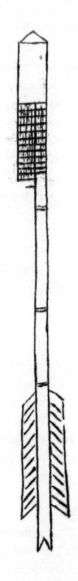

Figure 99.
An alternative for the *noroshi* signal rocket

---

39 This seems like a strange statement, earlier in the work Fujibayashi writes that this end of leather is to seal it. Therefore, either it is a different mechanism or it is evidence of the possibility that Fujibayashi wrote only twenty-one chapters and that this volume is an extra and later addition, which may explain its repetitiveness.

a neat manner without any strain. [Unintelligible text]

Hand-drill holes for the fuse to a depth of two *sun* and six *bu* and then carefully insert paper twisted strings containing ignition powder. The holes should be straight and without any form of bend in them.

- Wrap with *ramie* string and paper to a length of two *sun* [to attach it to the arrow].
- The balance point of the arrow should be just below the cylinder.
- The length of the arrow should be three *shaku* seven *sun* and five *bu*, while the fletchings should be six *sun* and the internal nock support should be six *sun*.
- The fletchings should be thin.
- The cylinder should be six *sun* in length and seven *bu* [in diameter] and about twenty *momme* of powder will suffice.

116

飛火炬

The flying torch

- White [saltpetre] – 30 *momme*
- Black [charcoal] – 4 *momme* 1 *bu*
- Yellow [sulphur] – 5 *momme*
- Blue [camphor] – 3 *bu*
- Mouse droppings – 3 *bu*

Mix the above but make sure that it is a little coarser than the previous signal rocket mentioned. The cylinder should be six *sun* in length and six *bu* in diameter. Put the powder in the cylinder in the same manner as for the signal rocket above; scrape the surface off the bamboo by taking only the skin off at the top joint end and then gradually thin it out as you get to the bottom of the rocket cylinder. Double wrap it with paper and glue. Next bind it with flat *ramie* rope and then double wrap it with paper again and fix it to an arrow.

- Drill a hole of about three *sun* in depth and put an ignition fuse into it.

Figure 100.
The flying torch

• It should balance just below the cylinder.
• Insert the ignition fuse delicately – without forcing it too much.

For a *yagura* or turret rocket of three *shaku* two *sun* that will fly for two and a half *cho* and will embed itself in the ground to a depth of three *sun*, put seventeen *momme* and three *bu* of powder into a cylinder of three *sun* in length and six *bu* in diameter.

When you use this as a *noroshi* signal rocket or flying fire, *hikigusuri* powder or *yakigusuri* ignition powder should be added at the end of the cylinder [for better ignition].

117

A general guideline for the ingredients used in these fire tools[40]

• The more white [saltpetre] that is included, the more intense the fire will be.
• The more yellow [sulphur] included, the more bluish the flame will be.
• The more camphor included, the weaker the fire will be.
• The more ash included, the softer and weaker the fire will be.
• The more horse manure included, the longer the fire will hold out.
• The more pine resin or sawdust included, the better it will burn.
• The more cloth, cattle droppings or moxa included, the more the fire will be suppressed, and the weaker it will be.
• The more mouse droppings included, the weaker the fire will be. Mouse droppings should preferably be added to a fuse to slow it down.

With the above principles you can discover any appropriate method of construction for your purpose, as any kind of torch can be created.

[A general torch]
To make a torch, split bamboo in two, wrap the bamboo with rope and put the powder inside and ram it down very firmly. Then remove the rope and the bamboo and wrap three layers of paper around the solidified powder. In the case of the waterproof torch or the capturing fire, there is no need to scrape or wrap the cylinder. Details are to be transmitted, but this method is from Nagai Matabei of Iga province.

---

40 The manual simply states here 'a guideline for torches'.

118

A tradition from Ogawa Shinbei

- Saltpetre – 60 *momme*
- Sulphur – 11 *momme* 2 *bu*
- Ash – 13 *momme* 8 *bu*

Mix the above and make a powder of it. If you powder the ingredients separately, they will not mix very well later on, so be sure to powder them together from the start. If ash rises into the air when you are pounding them, apply a little water with a bamboo whisk. The powder should be as fine as possible. When you grate the powder, you should do it very hard and without any rest because if you do not work hard enough, the powder will be weaker and its potency will become dull. This powder is called *tomioka* one-*bu* powder and is named so because you require only one tenth of the normal amount of powder.

119

雨火炬

The hanging rainproof torch

This is also called the five-*ri* torch 五里火炬.
- Sulphur – 13 *momme* (3 *momme* should be smashed as small as rice grains and 10 *momme* should be powdered down.)
- Saltpetre – 21 *momme* (1 *momme* should be smashed as small as rice grains and 20 *momme* should be powdered down.)
- Camphor – 9 *momme* (powdered)
- Pine sawdust – 2 *momme* (Use wood that has lots of resin, and make sawdust from it by sawing downwards. Dry the sawdust in the sun; if it is not dry enough, the fire will not hold out for long.)
- Ash – 7 *bu* (powdered)
- Pine resin – 2 *momme* (Ideally, use Japanese red pine – put the wood in boiling water to extract the resin, then dry the resin in the sun and grind it in a mortar into a very fine powder.)
- Moxa – 1 *momme* 5 *bu* (This should be crumpled very well then rolled into a hard bar and cut into small pieces.)

The above seven ingredients are used in the following way: the bamboo to be used should be *Arundinaria simonii*, which should be large enough for your needs; however, if you intend to make a larger torch then *henon* bamboo (*Phyllostachys nigra var. henonis*) will be best. Scrape the surface of the bamboo down, split it in two and remove all the internal joints – that is, all but the end one [while leaving a small overhang as in the drawing]. Then, put the halves together and paste them with astringent juice or the glue made from *Gloiopeltis*. Put holes the thickness of a brush here and there – these holes are called 'drain holes'. Again wrap more paper around the bamboo and apply lacquer to it once.

- Put the joint at the top [near the strings].
- Use the holes for strings.
- The fire is open at the bottom; therefore, you should paste, wrap and cover it.

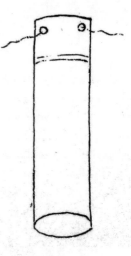

Figure 101.
The hanging
rainproof torch

How to ram the powder into the cylinder is to be transmitted orally. Next you need to wrap this cylinder with thin rope and put the above powder in it, little by little with a spoon. Ram the powder down very firmly with [a rod and] a hammer and repeat this, remembering to ram it down firmly. You should turn the cylinder so that the open end is facing downwards, then let the access powder drop out, collect the powder and ram it down again and make sure to do this firmly. If the size of this tool is one *shaku* five *sun* in length and five *sun* in circumference, it will last for five *ri*. This is why it is called the five-*ri* torch. How to ignite this torch is a secret.

120

傳火

Trail fire

Saltpetre – 10 *momme*
Sulphur – 2 *momme*
Ash – 1 *momme* 5 *bu*
Camphor – 5 *bu*

Mix the above and grind it all in a mortar into a very fine powder. This is called trail fire because fire trails along exactly where this powder has been laid, and that is amazing.[41]

---

41 The idea here is that once a *shinobi* has infiltrated the enemy castle or camp, he puts a trail of this powder to the gunpowder stores or to something flammable and lights it.

PART TWO

The *Bansenshukai Gunyo-hiki*

Secrets on Essential Military Principles

by

Sasayama Kagenao of the Ohara Clan

On the position of watch fires

This task should be assigned to [the *samurai*] commander of the foot soldiers and all brushwood should be prepared beforehand. The fires should be tended by *ashigaru* foot soldiers, who should take turns every two hours or even take half of a night, and should be stationed on the outside of the earthwork of the main gate of your castle or position. If the earthwork stretches out east and west, it is preferable to make the fires when the wind comes from the north or the south because if the wind blows from east or west, then it is difficult to maintain the fire; in such a case as the latter, stand doors or *tatami* mats on the windward[1] side of the fire. The earthwork wall near where the watch fires are to be built should be made about three metres high. If there is not enough firewood, you have to burn brushwood or straw, and it is not desirable to make a fire in a pot; instead it is best to have an ironworker cast a four-*shaku* square [of iron for burning firewood on[2]]. Even if you are taking up positions for only one night while confronting the enemy, it is desirable to build earthworks, even if they are not very high, and you should burn watch fires. Remember to set your fires at an adequate distance from your main position; they will light up the inside of your own defences if they are too close.

---

1 The original, which says 'leeward', probably contains a transcription error.
2 This is probably so that the light of the fire extends outward and is not directed up by the sides of the pot.

Unattended watch fires

These should be built when the route that the enemy is approaching by has been confirmed. Build earthworks between you and the enemy and make a fire on the other side of the wall [so that the fire is on the side closer to the enemy]; this is done so that the enemy can see the flare of the fire but you cannot. Also, build a number of fires at intervals, so that when the enemy is coming, you can ignite one and retreat, leaving the fire unattended. Then burn another [along the path] and retreat, again leaving it. That is why it is called *sute kagari* or the unattended watch fire. You should be aware of the true meaning of this.

In addition, cut cherry bark into strips of one *sun* in width, dry them very well and tie them to a torch [as arrow fletchings]. To use this torch, you should throw it outwards so you can obtain a good view [as it illuminates the area]. If the torch is three *shaku* long, you should put two rods of wood [stuck through] the torch in a criss-cross manner; do this at one *shaku* from the bottom, then throw the torch. With the two criss-crossed [rods] going through it, when it lands it will not fall over.[3]

On the position of *rangui* trip wires[4]

These traps should be built in the sea, in a river or in a moat. In an inlet, the stakes should be planted so that they are hidden underwater by at least one *shaku* at high tide. Also, the stakes should be put at an interval of one and a half to two *ken*. If the interval is too small, it will be disadvantageous for your allies; however, this is dependent on the situation. Stretch rope at the top and bottom [of the stakes] and secure them at both ends. Be sure to mark a way so that your allies can pass through the complex [of traps]. Also, you should build them a little way from the shore, where it is always covered with water, [so that they are still hidden] when the tide is out.

In the case of a river, if the stream is curved, plant stakes around the shallows [where the enemy may cross] so that they cannot see them coming out of the water's surface, tie a thick rope onto them and let the rope flow without securing the other end. Two or three ropes should be made flow like this.[5] Remember, if you plant another stake downstream and you secure the other end of the rope [to it], then [the rope] is likely to be cut. If the riverbed is stony and it is hard to

---

3   At one foot from the bottom, you should thrust a rod directly through it, then turn it ninety degrees and do it again. These long rods will form a cross '+' that goes through the torch. When the torch is thrown, as long as it lands handle first the rods will form a stand and keep the torch at an angle that will allow the fire to burn upwards.

4   These are stakes placed at irregular intervals with rope tied between them.

5   The idea here is that the thick rope is secured to a hidden strong point and that its own weight and the heavy flow will make it rigid and a stumbling point for the enemy.

plant a stake, use a long *jakago* bamboo basket with pebbles and attach the above rope – and, again, let it flow.

For a moat, plant stakes in the shape of a triangle one or even two *shaku* under the water surface so that they will not be seen. The rope should be doubled up on these. Planting stakes in the shape of a pentagon will also suffice.

How to build a river bridge 川梯

Use this if the river is not very wide, but is too deep for footed warriors to cross over easily. Heap stones in the shallows of your side, cut and gather wood or bamboo, or break down any houses nearby and take their wood. Lay three beams across the river and on top of the stone foundation, one in the middle and two on either side, and then tie many rungs at intervals to make it secure. When the bridge is long enough [for you to walk out to the centre of the river], you should tie three *jakago* long baskets to lengths of rope, then float these baskets on the upstream side of the bridge and manoeuvre them into position on the opposite bank; do this by using the downward flow of the river. Next put stones in the baskets so they form a foundation for the opposite end of the bridge. If the river is too wide for a single bridge, then make two bridges and have them connect by creating a mound or foundation in the centre of the river – also, you will need to attach buoys along the structure of the bridge to help it float. This bridge is for foot soldiers to cross over.[6]

Of thorny shrubs 荊朶

Mogari is written as 'thorny shrubs' in our ideogram-based language. In old times thorny shrubs were used to defend against the enemy. Later on, bushes with many branches were used and were positioned high, so that they reached horses' chests or bellies and so that the base of the shrub was pointed toward your own side. However, this hinders you when you are departing on horseback.

If thick and long bamboo is available, cut off the branches and attach two[7] pieces of [shrub or thorny] wood to the horizontal bamboo. Plant stakes where needed and tie this barrier onto them – make it so that it opens [like a door] and you can draw it back when your people are going or coming, but so that it is a hindrance for the enemy. Also, use shrubs in a river.

---

6 This point has been expanded on to allow it to be understood more clearly in English.

7 The idea here is most likely that you get two branches which have their natural direction, so when put together they fan out covering more space.

The quick rope 早綱

This is called *mogari* or *koraku* – the 'tiger fall' –
which is used in foreign[8] counties as a method for
capturing a tiger. On a path along which the enemy
is expected to come for a night raid, plant bamboo
stakes of the length of a Japanese *obi* belt. Rope
should then be stretched double horizontally at
two points, one high and one low so that the enemy
cannot walk through or pass over it. This should

Figure 102.
The quick rope

have pathways through in the form illustrated below, so that your allies can pass
by freely. Though this is a shallow skill, it still has a great benefit.

The horizontal stake 横杙

If the enemy is close and it is difficult to build the quick rope and you want to
build something lightweight and at speed, this method should be used.

Make forked tripods of bamboo and stand them at various points. Then put
bamboo or wood across from stand to stand and collect as much bamboo or
wood as possible and tie it onto the horizontal beams [creating a temporary
wall].

The bamboo-bundle shield 竹抱

If the bundle is too large, it will be too heavy and cannot be used freely. Principally,
it should be two *shaku* in circumference, bound at five places, and seven *shaku* in
length. In the case of thin bamboo, use the whole bamboo [without splitting it]
while if it is large bamboo, mixing split pieces will suffice.

If you are close to the enemy castle, you should have longer versions, and to
make it stronger, bind and entwine [rope] internally in at least three[9] places and
then tie it at five points on the outside.

[How to build the shield bundle stands]

Make tripods of wood and stand them up in line, without burying them in the
ground[10] and put horizontal beams onto the tripods, fastening them together
with rope if necessary, then stand the bamboo shield bundles against them [to
make a fence]. Remember, they should be put on the outside of the bar so you
can move freely on the inside. When it is raining you may create temporary

---

8   As there is no plural in the Japanese language, this may refer to one or many foreign
    countries (probably China).

9   This means internally bind it and also bind it on the outside.

10 That is to say, freestanding.

roofs, which will allow you to shoot muskets from under the roof. Sometimes it is good to have the [sheeting] of the roof overhanging and resting on the outside of the 'wall' but this depends on the location. Alternatively, there is another type of bamboo shield bundle that has two legs [which enable it to stand on its own].

In all cases, putting sandbags at the front to a depth of one layer – or even two or three layers – will help.[11] In addition, you can have a wooden stand, like a saddle stand, and place bamboo bundles against it and tie them onto it; then, with a few people, lift the stand [and temporary wall] up into position. Depending where you are, you should construct a fence of wood with horizontal and vertical posts; make this sturdy and then secure bamboo bundles onto this fence. If you are facing a mountain or an earthwork, make sure to build it high enough to cope with the enemy. There are various ways to do this and you should choose the most appropriate one for your situation.

Figure 103.
Types of bamboo-
bundle shield

As well as the above methods, you should discuss and gain advice from experienced people so you can always choose the best way, as there is no definite principle to be followed. The bamboo bundles do not have to have gun ports as you can shoot over them. If need be, you can use a cylinder of thick bamboo [which acts as a shooting port in the bundle] to put a musket through, then cover above and below the cylinder with bamboo or plaster and use this to shoot through. There are various ways to build [these defences of bamboo] – it all depends how the *koguchi* gateway of the castle or camp is constructed.

Defences for the besieging army 仕寄

Defences when you are conducting a siege are usually constructed at night in order to avoid being attacked by arrows or muskets, which would be expected during the daytime. Also, use white rope on a moonless night [to construct your

---

11 The original talks ambiguously about one, two and three collections of sandbags.

defences[12]]. And, if you dig a trench[13] in a straight fashion, it can be easily shot into with arrows; therefore, dig it diagonally [in relation to their forces]. This is called the *hiraki* siege position. These trenches should be about four *shaku* in width and you should also dig out spaces for people to pass each other at various places. Depending on the distance [to the enemy] and the topography, you can make the width of these trenches up to five *shaku*. Dig the trench three *shaku* deep and make an embankment of soil on the front, which should rise up about two *shaku*, so that the total will be five *shaku* and it will cover the height of people.[14] The closer it is to the castle, the deeper the trench should be.[15]

The retractable bridge 引橋

Build a bridge as normal, but make it so that the floor boarding in the centre can be retracted backwards and [should go into] the flooring below your side. Attach three ropes on the [moving] floor that is to be retracted and operate it in the following manner.

When you need to retract the flooring, you should pull the two ropes on the outer sides so the flooring will be retracted and the way [for the enemy] is cut off. Then, when you pull the rope in the middle, the flooring will go back across the bridge so that you can cross it freely.

Walls external to your camp[16] 附塀

A [wood or bamboo] fence with paper can be used to make one of these walls, and so can a wall that looks like a normal lattice fence. This wall should be positioned in front of the sprung catapults and these catapults should have a frame on the embankment and have stones within the frame. As shown in the illustration [missing], secure the bent trees and attach them to posts that have been drilled into the ground, with spikes that you can remove. When these spikes are removed, the trees will spring back. Take note, to identify if there is a fake wall on a position you wish to attack, observe the embankment as this will let you see if one is present.[17]

---

12 There appears to be part of the text that is not displayed here and may be lost. Therefore, it is put forward in its most basic form.

13 The text is literally 'moat'. However, what is being described here is trench warfare.

14 This is a great reminder of the diminutive stature of Japanese men of the period, as this measurement is only five feet in total.

15 Presumably, to protect against arrow attacks.

16 The connotation here is of a wall that is outside the main camp defences but that is still close by, and in this case is used to hide artillery.

17 This and the next point are highly problematic. The original text describes images that are not present in the original transcription. Therefore, the text has been simplified and rearranged. The first point contains a reference to rocks and a trap, which has been removed from this translation as without the original illustration it confuses the paragraph.

The spring wall 刎塀

Instead of putting a stone in a catapult as normal, you should construct a lattice cage woven out of thick bamboo. Next tie horizontal bars onto both sides of it and attach rope onto these four ends. Pull and fasten the rope as in the drawing [missing] so that it forms a wedge, then pull and fasten the other two ropes in place.[18] When the enemy is climbing up, you should cut the ropes and let the fence go, then attack with the catapult – remember that the bamboo you use needs to be strong enough.

The fake suspended wall section[19] 釣塀

At [every] one-*ken* section of a wall, you should have two posts stood side by side [around the area you wish to build this wall]. Viewed from outside, the trick should not be seen and the wall should be seen as one, as though it is one continuous surface. The foundation of the wall is also false. The supporting posts should be made as in the drawings [missing]. The fake section should be secured only temporarily with wedges and when the enemy soldiers are advancing over the wall, remove the wedges so it will fall down [and crush them].

The items you should carry in your portable box

A comb, scissors, tweezers, one[20] or a half roll of white cloth, a razor, a whetstone, white powdered makeup, a mirror, a magnet, threads of five colours and needles, the root of a *kudzu* (*Pueraria lobata*) plant,[21] glue, dried bonito, a long thin strip of dried abalone,[22] [strong paper] strings, a torch, *domyoji* rice powder and *kudzu* plant starch.

The items you should carry in a portable pouch [and on your person]

Including: a panacea multi-purpose medicine, a telescope for looking to the distance[23] and several tags with your title and name written upon them.[24]

While in an army, if you are asked by someone to be a witness [to their deeds]

---

18 Without the illustration, this is very unclear. One possibility is that it refers to a basket used to throw rocks at an enemy from a catapult when a fake wall has come down. However, the text remains unclear.
19 A fake section of wall that collapses on the enemy.
20 One roll is enough to make a kimono.
21 A medicinal plant used to treat fever.
22 Possibly a symbol of luck.
23 While telescopes did exist in Japan at the time, it is unknown to what extent they were available.
24 Used to prove your deeds or leave with people as tokens of proof or even to be placed in the mouths of important decapitated heads.

then agree but only as long as you survive. You should state: 'It is my honour that you would like me to stand as witness for you and I would be happy to testify exactly what I see you achieve – if I remain alive that is. However, if I am killed, please take evidence of [my deeds]. I have prepared this tag in my own handwriting for such a case as I have just mentioned.' At this point give him one of the tags with your name and title.

How to ask someone to be a witness

You should state to the intended person: 'As you [my witness] have many things to remember, it may be the case that you may not remember [my achievements at a later point]. As I happen to see you here at this time, here and now, I would appreciate it if you give me anything of yours to show you [when we meet again] to remind you of this time after the battle.' To do this, you should ask him to cut out a piece of the inside of his helmet and give it to you. When he gives you this, you should say: 'If I am killed, so be it, but if you later talk about this battle, please accept this [name tag and repeat my deeds].' As you say this, give him a name tag [from your pouch].

The loincloth

You should first don a simple loincloth and then an outer loincloth after that. When you are killed in battle, it is often the case that the loincloth is what people may take off the body,[25] so it would be to your dishonour if they find you are wearing a poor loincloth. This is one of the necessary ways of the *samurai*.

As you can see, the loincloth is split as shown in the drawing – this is so you can tie it at the back once then wrap it around your waist and then tie it at both sides.

Warning: when you come back after you have achieved something great, you should be careful to avoid a route where lots of people are gathered, as it is often the case you may get into trouble.[26] However, if there is no bypass it cannot be helped, but be sure to talk in a modest way with your achievements.

Figure 104.
The loincloth

---

25 Most likely to check for hidden items.
26 Most likely this means that others will try to take decapitated heads from you.

The reversible jacket

Battle jackets or any other such garments should be white on the inside and black on the outside with a crest adorning them as in the rules of each clan. They should be black so they will not stand out at the time of night attacks and such. The crest can be hidden by cutting out black paper and putting it over the crest [when needed]. The reason that the jacket should be white inside is because of its multiple advantages.[27] You should be prepared with such jackets and garments of your own and so should your men be dressed in the manner described above.

How to tether a horse using the 'connecting grass skill'[28]

There are various ways to do this. However, here I say pull and fasten the *kokake*[29] on the front so it will not move. Next, back comb the 'dragon's hair' of the horse's legs and twist it and tie it firmly with strings, so the horse will not move [because of the pain].

How to wear a spear [on horseback]

There are various ways to do this. However, it is good to place a three-foot *tenugui* cloth between your sash [and your side] and tie this cloth around the spear so that it can be held vertically or horizontally as you need. Alternatively, holding it with the use of a hinge is also common.

How to wear a [horse] lead at your waist

Coil the tether of the horse and secure it, then wrap it around your waist from the left side, then around your back and then drape it over the lead and put a hitch in it.

Saddle flaps or saddle skirt

For these, tanned leather will suffice. Also, it is desirable to attach a bag onto the underside of the saddle flap so that you can store your rations, etc. Also you can equip the horse with buoyancy aids, for a time of need.

---

27 The text does not state the advantages.

28 Literally, 'horse-grass connecting' or 'rope'. This text is ambiguous and talks simplistically and with 'jargon'. It appears that you should twist and tie the hair from sensitive areas of the horse's underside and legs together. In this manner, when the horse tries to move the pain will prevent it from doing so.

29 カウ掛 Unknown horse equipment – normally horses' legs are tethered together in various ways to stop them running.

The manner in which you should use a helmet-bearer – while on the march

It is desirable to have your helmet worn by your groom. It is said that you can have your standard or anything else of less importance carried by the lower men. However, be careful of their poor abilities, as it is likely that if you take someone on for that job he will drop behind and fail to be available in an emergency. For these reasons I say it is best to have it worn by your groom.

The manner of how you should wear your bow, musket and spear on horseback

Hold your musket between the gap[30] in the right stirrup leather, with the butt of your musket pointing backwards and the muzzle pointing forwards, over and across the saddlebow. Your spear should be held vertically while you are on the march. It should stand on the stirrup and lean against your shoulder. The bow should be put at the left side and under your bottom.[31]

Of horse buoyancy

If you do not have buoyancy prepared beforehand and if the need arises, you should roll up the saddle flap toward the inside and keep it held down with the stirrup [leathers] while you are in the water. Alternatively, you should make buoyancy 'floats' with tanned leather and put them at the front and rear sides. There are things to be orally transmitted on how to place them. It is best to have two long 'floats'.

How to cook rice with sea water

Put any bowl of pottery on the bottom of a pan with its bottom upwards and place rice on top of the pot [and cover it with water] and when you cook it the salt will be reduced and will be drawn beneath the inverted bowl.

How to cook rice without a pan

There are various ways to do this but one method is to wrap rice in a straw mat or straw bundle, soak it in water, dig a small hole and then bury it. Burn a fire on the ground over it and in time it will be cooked. Remember, rice should be washed and soaked in water very well. Another way is to wash rice and put it in a bucket and add hot rocks into the bucket so it will cook.

---

30 Japanese stirrup leathers are doubled up creating two straps that go side by side.

31 The text appears to mean that you should sit on your bow where it probably rests under any fur or padding that is used.

How to make fresh water out of sea water

When you are on board a ship and have no water, you have to use sea water. To make it safe to drink, apply unmixed red clay[32] on the bottom of the boat and put sea water into it. After a while the clay will attract salt [and the water is better to drink].

How to use water from a marsh

Dig a small hole and put paper around the rim. This way you can take the water [that filters] through the middle [of the paper].

Frostbite ointment

Take oil from the Japanese anise tree (*Illicium anisatum*) and apply it to the whole body, including the hands and legs. Also applying sake can prevent this.

How to [safely] feed a person who is suffering with starvation

Boil red clay in water and make the person drink this mixture. After this you can give them food. Alternatively, decoct the bark of a Japanese white-barked magnolia (*Magnolia hypoleuca*) and give a rice bowl full of this decoction to the person before you give them food, little by little.

A recipe for thirst pills
- Beat pickled plum until it is soft – 1 *ryo*
- Sugar crystals – 2 *momme*
- Dwarf lily-turf (*Ophiopogon japonicus*) – 1 *momme*

Chop the above three ingredients and make pills of them. This works amazingly well if you take them when you are thirsty.

A recipe for hunger pills
- Asiatic ginseng (*Panax ginseng*) – 10 *ryo*
- Buckwheat flour – 20 *ryo*
- Flour – 20 *ryo*
- Japanese yam (*Dioscorea japonica*) – 20 *ryo*
- Liquorice (*Glycyrrhiza glabra var. glandulifera*) – 1 *ryo*
- Coix seed – 10 *ryo*
- Rice powder – 20 *ryo*

Powder the above and soak it in three *sho* of sake for three years until it is all dry.

---

32 A reddish clay which has a high iron content.

Then make balls the size of a peach stone. [To sustain yourself, take three of these a day.] This will help you when you have no alternative way to feed yourself. If you take three of them, you will not be mentally or physically drained.

How to attach a decapitated head to your horse

On one end of a cord measuring two *shaku* five *Sun*, you should put a hook which is as sharp as a needle for making *tatami* straw mats. Pierce the head[33] with the hook and attach it onto the rear *shiode* saddle horn or ring. Another way to attach a head is called *oitsuke* or 'adding another head' and is attached onto the rear left[34] saddle horn or ring. When you are feeling ambitious and want to fight more, you should cut off the nose of the head before you attach it to the horse. Remember, lower-level people often steal heads if they are not so obedient. You should be aware of this and save the evidence of your achievements.

The principles of military rules and formations

- Of formations of lower soldiers
- Of *bugyo* commanders and their logistics
- Of *monomi* scouting

Unless there is an urgent need, you should not march long distances. It is a principle to march for three old Japanese hours (six standard hours) a day. However, this depends on the situation. Marching before dawn or late at night should be strictly avoided.

Of drums

There are two types of drum. One is the *oshidaiko* marching drum and is one *shaku* eight *sun* in diameter and is also used when you are in the battle camp. The other is the *kakedaiko* attacking drum, which is one *shaku* two *sun* in diameter.

These should be carried by two people at normal times and on a mountain path one person should carry one on his back. The job of drumming is the task of a *domyo*.[35] The number of beats should be three and four then four and then three. When used for marching, it makes the troops walk in step and settle down mentally. When the beat finishes, marching should be stopped. Alternatively, you should choose a good person of *samurai* status as a drummer of the *kakedaiko* attacking drum. It is said drums quicken the spirits of soldiers and that they can

---

33 Alternative writings talk about piercing between the cheek and the lower jaw.
34 Some manuals differ on this point.
35 Unknown position.

fight vigorously with them; thus you will gain a high advantage when advancing. The beat [for attack] should be quick while the beat for retreat should be slow.

Of horns and bells

Horns are conch shells. They are called 'horns' because the mouthpiece is made of horn. They should be blown by a mounted warrior. Basically they are used three times at three points of the day: in the morning, at midday and in the evening.

In the morning you should blow the horn in three [double sections of five[36]] while facing the rising sun in the east. With the first [double set of five] blows, the army should wake; with the second set, they should prepare; and with the third set, they should assemble [in formation]. However, this all depends on the decision of the general. For example, it can be arranged so that the vanguard or the second, third, fourth or even fifth companies of force will assemble in formation, all of which is done by signals from the conch shell.

On the midday call, you should blow the horn facing south because of the word consisting of 'harmony' and 'south' 和南 ['show reverence to the elders']. In the evening, you should face east again as west and north are made up of *in* negativity and should be avoided. In any case it should be blown five times, twice. Make the first set of five shorter and then the second five should be prolonged notes. Each note should be distinct 明音 – non-distinct 表音 sounds should be avoided.

There are three types of bells: gongs, bells and small bells 釩. In Japan[37] gongs are in use – your gong should be made of brass[38] and beaten into shape. The striking part of the gong, where it is beaten flat, should be a three-*sun* square and higher than the edges of the gong. The drums should be used for attacking while the gongs should be used to retreat. Bells should be used to rally defeated and retreating soldiers or used for night attacks. The number of strikes to be used should be arranged by prior agreement. When in an urgent situation, the bells should be rung quickly [and continuously].

For all drums, gongs or horns, the above are only general rules.

---

36 It appears that this signal is given three times a day. One set consists of two groups of blows, one group consists of five lesser blasts and the other consists of five prolonged blasts – however, the original states lighter/stronger blows and therefore could refer to the strength of the blow. This would make a total of thirty individual blows on the horn – ten in the morning, ten at midday and ten at sunset.
37 This is most likely a transcription error and should say China.
38 Literally – 'yellow'.

[Taking up position]

When you are going to take up a military position, you should send scouts stealthily (*monomi-shinobi*) to check ahead and start to set up positions beforehand. You should choose land that is higher at the centre and lower in every direction around, like a tortoise shell. Be sure not to choose land where firewood, grass or water is not available.

Places inappropriate to take up formation

Such places as near a big river, beneath a high mountain, in a village, around a forest, having a steep place to the rear, are not good. However, having a steep place to the front is not a problem.

[Types of formation]

Essentially, formations should not have strict and set forms and the formation should be appropriate to the enemy and the topography. However, if there are no set principles, you cannot fight a battle, thus the following guidelines are mentioned here.

Formations are originally based on the number five – that is, the formation should represent and reflect principles of east, west, north, south and the centre and also reflect the Five Elements. From the *one* comes *in* and *yo*, and then moves to the Five Elements. The Five Elements generate everything and everything can be reduced to the Five Elements, which can end in the two variants of the *chi* of the moon and the *chi* of the sun [*in* and *yo*], and thus the two *chi* become the *one* again.[39] Also, the eight dispositions created by Zhuge Liang[40] , though there are various theories, seem to be based on the number five.

[A unit] consists of five people and the centre person is the group leader [as seen in the left drawing].

This unit of five can be ordered to

Figure 105.
The squad of five

---

39 This is a retelling of the story found earlier in the *Bansenshukai* which concerns itself with the creation of matter from the principal energy of the universe. See the chapter *Seishin* Part II.

40 The famous Chinese strategist (181–234).

gather together to make a troop of twenty-five people. Even a force of millions[41] of people starts with this basic [component of five]. Two groups of twenty-five make fifty mounted warriors – this is called a *sonae* formation. This basic formation should also have the following men:

- One *samurai daisho* or formation commander
- Two spear captains (*bugyo*)
- Two banner organisers (*bugyo*)
- One *samurai* captain (*musha bugyo*)
- Two logistics officers (*bugyo*)

This adds up to a total of fifty-eight mounted warriors [because one formation is equal to fifty men plus the above eight]. This is the way that a formation is formed. Sometimes, a formation of fifty mounted warriors has a *samurai daisho* who serves as a *musha bugyo* too, meaning that the total will add up to fifty-seven warriors instead.

For a formation of fifty mounted warriors, if lower soldiers are included in the count but those people for logistics are not, the number adds up to more than three hundred people. If even the lowest people[42] are included, the total number for an army of about sixty mounted warriors adds up to around 420 people. If this army is marching in one line, the length will be eight *cho*, and if in two lines then it will be four *cho*. With this in mind, you can estimate the numbers by the width of the army.

A formation with more than fifty mounted warriors should always have two *musha bugyo samurai* captains, as it is risky to advance or retreat or manoeuvre an army with only the formation commander (*daisho*) present.

The formation of the crane wings

- The two front 'wings' are *ashigaru* foot soldiers
- The first line are the spearmen
- The second line are mounted warriors
- The fourth line is the commander
- The last line are mounted warriors

In a wide and open space, the front should flare out [as seen in figure 106] and be formed of archers and musketeers.

---

41 Not literally millions – the term here means 'many' or 'an immense number'.
42 Probably non-combatants such as labourers and servants.

Figure 106.

The formation of the crane wings

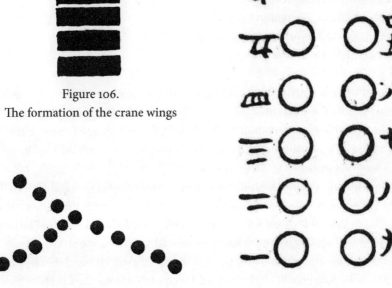

Figure 107.

The formation of the shape 入

Figure 108.

The great circle

The formation of the shape 入

When you go into the wilderness, such as a field of Japanese plume grass, where you are not sure from which direction the enemy may attack you and thus you have to pay attention to every direction, you should have your *ashigaru* in the 入 Formation as in the drawing.

The great circle[43]

As you can see in the above image, the dots are numbered, starting with the top right: one, three, four and five [on the same marker], six, seven, eight and then

---

43 This is a highly confusing section and Fujibayashi himself says that it can never be understood without direct teachings. However, it appears to be a selection of troops who are stationed in opposition to the enemy and who continually attack and retreat in a revolving order to cause confusion with the opponent and to hopefully wear down their defences and

finally on the bottom right, the number nine. Then, moving across to the bottom left, you can see that the numbers start with one, two, three, four, five, six and seven [on the same marker] and eight and nine together at the top left.

An example of this formation when attacking a castle and fighting the enemy or when night-attacking an enemy position is as follows: you should have one force attack from the rear while others are attacking from the front and they should also attack in combination. However, without direct teachings this skill and the following information can never be clear.

Concerning the drawing above, you can see that it starts with the numbers one and three and ends at nine and also on the left-hand side you can see it starts with one and two yet also it ends with nine. This is because nine is a *yo* number[44] and is auspicious. Therefore, this revolving formation should always start at one and end at nine. The principle is that the formation attacks from the front and rear continuously revolving [from troop to troop], just as there are no ends to an ancient Chinese jade disk.[45] This is called the formation of the great circle[46] because it teaches everything about the previously mentioned formations. The great circle is a concept in which you revolve in your mind all the various possible outcomes [of the enemy attack]. There is nothing that is not taken into consideration in this concept. This includes all things: the world and the nation, the mountains and the forests, the rivers and the seas, the easy and the difficult. There are deep secrets to be passed on by word of mouth here. In essence it is ever changing, like the relationship between a wheel and the terrain it moves along. Also, remember this: victory is like a wheel going down a mountain, when you are in an advantageous phase your army continues to win [and gain a winning spirit from it], but if in a disadvantageous phase it is then like a wheel going uphill and your army will struggle to fight well. Therefore, attack as swiftly as the wind and be immovable like a mountain.

[Unnamed formation]

[An explanation of the illustration on the next page]
- The black circle at the top left represents the side troops named 'three and four in battle'.

---

find a gap to lead to victory. The numbers appear to relate to different troops and have in parts been manipulated to fit in with Japanese numerology and to gain the benefit of the magical number nine.

44 In the way of *in* and *yo*, even digits are *in* while odd digits are *yo*. Thus, nine is the biggest *yo* digit and is thought to be the strongest of all.

45 Round disks found in China with no clear function or form. They may be ritual objects.

46 The Japanese word *dairin* or 'great circle' comes from Buddhism and means the Palace of the Five Wisdom Buddha.

- The next lower black circle represents the side troops named 'two and one'.
- The distance between these troops should be fifty *tsue*.[47]
- The distance between the second and third black circles is also fifty *tsue*.
- The distance between the third and fourth, the fourth and fifth, and the fifth and sixth black circles and the lower right black circle is thirty *tsue*.
- One commander is placed ahead of the two lower black circles in the zigzag section of the formation.
- The two lower black circles (in the zigzag area at the top) represent the auxiliary forces, which have horses between them. Also, the distance between them and the flag which is below them on the image is eighty *tsue*.
- In the middle of the formation, behind the two lower auxiliary troops – as described above – are the standards and flags.
- Behind the flags and standards comes the logistics division which is eighty *tsue* in length. Also note, if there are too many horses in this division then you should keep the horses at a distance.
- At the rear is another commander and more standards and horses.

A battle commander and the 'evidence officer' should be attached to the flag commander and they should control the drums and conch shells. The *yokome-tsukai* observer[48] should

Figure 109.
Unnamed formation

---

47 One *tsue* is equal to 2.2 metres.

48 This appears to be a form of messenger scout, the make-up of his name brings connotations of 'from the side'.

also be connected to this group. In addition, you should have an estimate of the measurements [for your own formation] by observing your own flags. The distance that you keep from the enemy will depend on their numbers and the topography. After the first clash you should be able to estimate how strong the enemy are and after both vanguards have connected you can decide who is the stronger and if the enemy will follow up. In reference to this situation, you have to consider whether troop 'two' will save troop 'one' or if troop 'four' will save troop 'three'.[49] Remember, the vanguard should have a strong leader and the second or third sets of troops should have a brave leader.

In battle there needs to be a powerful current[50] [in the army]. If the first section is defeated in a clash and the troops behind them do not hold, this negative current (*chi*) within the army will spread. Therefore, you need to understand the feeling of the enemy's second and third forces. If you find them wearied, then it is a good sign [because they will not hold]. If you rejoin troops that have been separated, then they will double their fighting spirit.

If you have your forces at the front but decide in the last to use a part of these forces from the rear, thinking that the enemy is few in number, your army will lose impetus. Basically, if you change your formations or replace the front with the rear before actually confronting the enemy and when you are at a relatively short distance, then this will undoubtedly lead you to failure. Lastly, if you are going to use a force that comes from the side, you need to consider the topography and the direction.

[Flags and colours]

- The top circle is red
- The next down and on the left is blue
- The one to the right and on the opposite side to the blue is white
- Then the circle below these two is yellow
- Then the circle below the yellow one is black[51]

As in figure 110, the formations should be set up with these five coloured flags and the drums and bell are used to inform those sections if they should advance or retreat, or if it be quickly or slowly done; all is dependent on the situation.

---

49 This is a reference to the above diagram, which shows troops 'one' to 'four' represented by the two upper black circles. The point Fujibayashi is making is that you have to consider whether the troops behind the ones who hit the enemy first will have the ability to save the forwardmost troops.

50 鋭力 'Strong power' or a psychological feeling of power and victory.

51 There is no information on the three circles at the bottom of the image (figure 110).

Figure 110.
Flags

This colour system is very useful – this way soldiers will not be left in confusion in the case where you are defeated and need to retreat.

How to initiate battle

In principle, you should keep as quiet as at normal times when initiating a battle, especially when you are advancing in an advantageous situation. If you advance quietly, the force will step in time and the power and momentum will not be lost. When the force actually attacks, be warned that the step will always increase in speed. At this point remember that if soldiers fall out of step and are straggling around, this is negative.

Humans will always be exhausted after they use up 'three bursts of energy'. In advancing, you use one burst. If the distance is large and you have to move quickly, then you use the second burst and in fighting you use the final burst. Once you use up these three bursts of energy, your men will be exhausted. Therefore, when advancing, their footsteps should be quiet so that only one burst will be used up, leaving you two final bursts. By doing this, the army will have spare energy to invest in intense combat. Therefore, you should understand these three surges of energy in relation to attack.

On war cries

Fundamentally, there are four types of war cry.

Before battle, a war cry should be a single person who cries out エイエイ '*Ei, Ei*[52] at which point everyone cries out a long ワ ウ '*Ou*' sound and in chorus.[53] It is considered bad form for a war cry not to be [in unison]; therefore, the cry

---

52 Pronounced as 'A-A'.
53 Even in modern Japan people cry out '*Ei Ei Ou*' at political rallies and sports events.

master[54] should raise a war cry at the most appropriate time because momentum is important for victory and defeat – unity is paramount.

After you win in combat, you should make a war cry when stepping into the position that the enemy used to occupy, in order to make it known that you have won the first battle of the day. There is a deep reason why a victory in the first assault is especially important.

When you capture a castle, the war cry should be cried out twice ('*Ei Ei Ou*', '*Ei Ei Ou*'), thus a troop commander or even a rank-and-file warrior[55] should cry out the full cry of '*Ei Ei Ou*' and then everyone should repeat in unison, '*Ei Ei Ou*'. If everyone does not cry, '*Ei Ei Ou*' this action should be repeated again.

At the time of inspection of the decapitated heads and when that inspection is finished, the lord should begin a war cry, at which point all those present should cry out together as one. The purpose of this war cry is to unite the power of the entire army and there is something to be orally transmitted for before and after this cry.

Advancing and retreating

Advancing and retreating are of critical importance in a battle. You should advance when you have the chance to win, while you should retreat when there is a benefit in retreating. However, a reckless lord tends to like to advance and does not favour withdrawing, which can bring ruin upon his army. A thoughtful lord has a long-term view of the full process of the battle and will not refuse to order a proper retreat if needed at that moment nor does he get too eager after a temporary victory.

It is critical to understand that you should retreat in the case where the enemy defends itself closely and in a very organized way or is positioned in an advantageous place and there is no chance of gaining a victory upon an attack. However, when you retreat, if the enemy follows you, you should defeat them by taking advantage of their confusion. This should be considered as a tactical retreat, which allows you to take advantage of their movement.

It is a principle to think of the element of retreat even while advancing and to think of advance while retreating. Advance and retreat are indivisible and they are like wind and tide. Advance is like wind as wind has no shape but hits hard. Retreat is like a tide. Even if it seems to be full, it all retreats naturally and in accord, thus you do not notice its gradual withdrawal. The way tide retreats

---

54 'Official *samurai*'.

55 To be clear, the cry before war is a single person who shouts '*Ei Ei*' and everyone else shouts '*Ou*', and after the battle a single person cries out '*Ei Ei Ou*' and then everyone in unison repeats '*Ei Ei Ou*'.

should be the way that you retreat – gradually. It should be done in an accord and without confusion and fluidly. If you retreat completely and smoothly and throughout the entire movement, the enemy cannot attack. That is, if you have no gap to take advantage of and they force an attack on you, it will end up with them ruining themselves [on your structured retreat].

Knowing if you should wait to attack

It is essential to have good judgement on whether to attack the enemy or to wait until the enemy moves, so that you can make the correct assault. Such measures as surprise attacks or feint tactics should be considered individually.

The following four aspects are fundamentals: the general, the topography, the distance, and combat with a smaller enemy.

The general – against slow and sluggish generals, you should make the first move and attack the enemy with added confidence. There is more to be orally transmitted here.

The topography – it is required that you understand whether the ground is beneficial for waiting or for attacking. There is more to be orally transmitted about this.

The distance – if there is five *cho* between you and the enemy, you should make the enemy advance four *cho* forward. When the distance reaches one *cho*, you should make your move; this is because the enemy is tired and disordered through moving the four *cho*. If you get within thirty *ken* of the enemy in an organized manner, it is advantageous to move straight on to attack. If this is done the enemy soldiers will be shaken as they are stationary and thus there will be a gap, as they have no momentum. Even with a distance of forty or fifty *ken*, attacking depends on how strong the enemy and your spirits are. [If you have the momentum,] it is like wind or even like rolling a round stone down [a high mountain]. When you are to move on to attack in this manner, you will be able to change your method of attack depending on the counter-order given by the enemy [in reaction to your charge]. This is done to outwit them; therefore, being in the rhythm is essential.

A smaller enemy – the general rule is that if you are on a flatland and of a large number, then you should move to attack an enemy of a lesser number. However, you should be aware that this is not always the case.

Whether to wait to attack or not attack will depend on tactics rather than the number of the army. Details are to be orally transmitted.

The manner in which to commit reinforcements to the front line

In the case where the enemy vanguard is large in number while your vanguard is relatively small, you should insert reinforcements from the auxiliaries together with a battle commander (*ikusa bugyo*) and they should be added to the second division [which is behind the vanguard]. The next step is to join the third and fourth divisions together as one, which now go behind the reinforced second division. Then join the fifth division with the *hatamoto* command group and together they should close up to the rear of the fourth division; however, the *hatamoto* command group [with the fifth division] and the pack-horse train should stay in position [if the formation moves].

How to deal with a strongly defended enemy

If the enemy is strongly defended, it is a primary tactic to send a squad of *ashigaru* foot soldiers to provide 'temptation' so that you can initiate the battle in accordance with how the enemy reacts or changes its status. However, starting a battle with this tactic is not very beneficial. The first strike by the first division is of most importance while sending a 'temptation' squad has the objective of discovering how strong the enemy is according to how it reacts.

Double the number of your vanguard and initiate the battle while having the second division reinforced so that it can prepare for the second strike action. This is so that if the first wave fails you will be able to gain a victory with the second division.

If the enemy is not so well organized, you should position the second and third divisions on both wings of your force. When your side is winning, you should pursue the enemy by using the above forces, which are stationed in the wings. When you are losing the battle and the enemy is following you over to your side, you should attack from both sides with those side forces. Then, when the side troops have attacked, those at the rear should make war cries and attack the enemy. If the enemy second or third divisions are defeated, the remnants of the enemy will not fight properly, and how to follow them or how to find them is to be orally transmitted.

If the enemy sends a 'temptation' squad against you, you should fathom their intentions and know they are

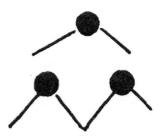

Figure 111.
The three-headed formation
Above is the three-headed
formation as led by three
commanders.

doing this to induce disorder in your army which they will take advantage of. If you are tempted by the squad and you follow up, the enemy will act as though they are defeated but in reality, it will end up that their vanguard will destroy you. Therefore, to counter this and so that you can maintain a defence after defeating this 'temptation' force, use the three-headed formation, which is led by three commanders as illustrated in the drawing on the previous page [*figure 111*]. Also, to deal with the enemy's 'temptation' tactics, you should figure out what their intention is and outwit them at any opportunity. For example, you could let them believe that you have fallen into their trap and then take advantage of their change [that you have predicted]. Further details are to be orally transmitted.

Withdrawing – step by step[56]

Even if the enemy is at a far distance, if you do not withdraw in lines properly it will be dangerous and you will become vulnerable. Therefore, when withdrawing from any of the above-mentioned formations, you should have your rear guard hold together very tightly with a line of spears held ready to attack, and when the signal is given by beating drums in the rear force the front forces should start to withdraw. In any formation, you should follow this practice [of keeping signals and such prepared] at all times. You have to be aware of exactly what the distances [of the divisions] are within each of the formations. The *hatamoto* command group should withdraw first, and then the vanguard and the second division should retreat. One should take an inside route, while the others should move on the outside, but this will depend on the topography. When they have arrived at the rear they should reform. Then, have the third division retreat, then, after them, the fourth and the fifth divisions will follow the same pattern and get into formation at the rear. Lastly, have the auxiliary forces on both wings retreat and get the entire army in formation as it was in the original position.

Withdrawing – immediately

This is a way to withdraw urgently when you are at a short distance from the enemy. The *hatamoto* command group should stay longer [and not withdraw early]. If the lord retreats first, the army will be in panic and its strength will be weakened, and if the enemy attacks, your forces will suffer defeat without any doubt.

You should start by having the vanguard and second forces retreat quickly and get in formation at the rear; then, at this point, the lord should withdraw.

---

56 Basically, this is the concept of holding a guarded position by which individual sections of your troops retreat to the rear, section by section, until they end up in their original positions, yet set back in a zone of 'safety'.

The rest of the forces should withdraw as described in the previous tactic, which is step by step. In such an emergency it is a rule that the *hatamoto* command group should not retreat at an early point. In all situations it is essential to reform the rear guard and for it to hold ground and keep the army [in control].

The formation of four in harmony

A brave lord will attack, while a stupid lord will not. When you are massive in number and the enemy is small in number, have the vanguard and the second division move forward in two wings [that is, on either side]. With them should be two *samurai* captains (*musha bugyo*), one leading each force; have them observe the enemy status. If the enemy is not starting an attack, you should have your auxiliary forces [divide into] two and move forward along both sides [behind the forces you sent forward] to attach themselves to the rear of these men. Then, the first two divisions in their wing formation should move around onto both sides of the enemy. The *bugyo* commander should [not advance with the men but] remain with the rear force. If the enemy is still not moving to attack, then the middle divisions should move forward into the space where the auxiliaries were, as they have now gone forward just behind the front divisions. Then the *hatamoto* should move forward a little, just onto the back of the middle force. Whether to adopt this formation and whether the *hatamoto* command group should move forward or not depends on the distance in each situation.

When the enemy is larger in number and your forces are smaller in number

It is a basic principle that the greater will win over the lesser. However, if you need to fight against a massive army with a smaller number, you should have tactics designed to allow a lesser number to gain victory over a greater number. The first principle is to attack the enemy when they do not expect it and are negligent. According to the fundamental principles of war, you should apply three criteria to find a gap within the enemy: the stupidity of the lord, trouble among people, and the benefit of the location. A massive army under the control of a stupid lord is seriously problematic. Trouble among people makes for a weak point, whereas the benefit of the location is the key for your smaller army against a massive enemy. In warfare, the benefit of the location is a great help for an army, and steep grounds are considered the best position and allow a small number to defeat a larger force. If you occupy a beneficial location and take advantage of a gap in the enemy and work out a plan by all possible measures, such as night raids and attacks at all times of the day, be it midday, in the evening or in the early morning, then you should not fear a massive army.

Your greater force against a lesser enemy

If an enemy of a smaller number is attacking your larger number, and they have discovered a prospect for possible victory, then you should not underestimate them. It is easy to manoeuvre a smaller number of people freely by orders and also to keep them tightly under control, while a larger number is difficult to keep united. On top of that, if the enemy is larger, they tend to count on this larger number and relax their attention. Also, it is often the case that they underestimate an enemy of a smaller number, which is beneficial for the opponent [of such a non-thinking force]. You should, therefore, keep this point in mind, as it is the key [to winning].

If you have double the number of the enemy and are in a wide open space, you should try to exhaust the enemy as much as possible; you should attack them harshly and deprive them of their courage. If the enemy of a smaller number attacks you with all the spirit they have, you should give them musket fire in succession, and then if the enemy is still moving forward, have archers shoot intensely and have mounted warriors positioned behind them. By doing this, the enemy will be dispersed, at which point you should retreat lightly and do the same thing with the second, third, fourth and fifth divisions. If this is repeated several times, no matter how strong the enemy soldiers are, they will be exhausted and you will win without fail.

The art of attacking an enemy that is taking an advantageous position (including the art of the battle on a mountain)

If you take a position on a height, there is benefit in having a full view of the enemy and its tactics; also, this height increases your fighting potential when fighting against an enemy that is in a lower position. The side attacking from the lower position will have trouble climbing up and can be struck by wood or rocks. Therefore, if you have the height, you should make the enemy climb up; while if you are in the lower position, you should draw the enemy from its height and down to your level. Thus there is no benefit in ascending or descending and an army does not move in such a manner. Therefore, a 'temptation' tactic should be undertaken in an attempt to force the enemy to move and you should take advantage of any gap that they show, with the intent of drawing them either upwards or downwards.

An important point: if the enemy does descend from the mountain, there will be a weakness in their force at the point when they are one *cho* away from the bottom of the mountain. Also, when the [enemy] is descending on horseback there [unknown word].[57] How to go up and find its position is to be orally transmitted.

When hard pushed by the enemy [as you retreat uphill], when you get to the base of the mountain you should take a side route and not go directly up the centre. Do this either to the left or to the right, because if you retreat up the middle [path] you will be shot by arrows.

If you are in a mountain area that has a number of peaks, it is beneficial that you should traverse a ridgeway and take positions on those peaks [and do not go directly up the straightest and most open route].

You should be aware of a few things when you take the detached position [that is, when your forces are at separate positions], and also when you are in a position behind a forest on a mountain; these are as follows. These two positions have the advantage of making the enemy misunderstand the true situation and they will not realize the actual size of your army – that is, if you are a small number – and their courage will be shaken. Warfare is the way of deception. There is always a skill to make the greater look like the lesser or the lesser look like the greater. One technique is to hide a large number in a thicket of trees and send out only a small detachment and then have [the hidden troops] emerge from the thicket and take up a formation. To counter deceptions like this last one and the above examples, you need to have a reliable estimation of the total number of the enemy and there are ways to do this, but they are to be orally transmitted. Unless you have *shinobi no mono* 忍者 to investigate the strength of the enemy before any action, you will be deceived by them and you yourself will have no way to deceive them in turn.

If an army counts on the advantage of a mountain or a forest, then you should know that it will have weak points that you should find. This is because they are negligent and less guarded – there are more oral secrets here. Remember, you should attack them and separate them from their advantages.

How to alter enemy formations dependent on the topography

When both sides have advanced as far as they will and are confronting each other, it is sometimes the case that the topography is beneficial to the enemy but not to your side. If you cannot avoid fighting when in a disadvantageous place, you should attempt to alter the enemy's formation with tactics, because the enemy will have to respond to your change. The vanguard should be kept in position, but you should move the second and third divisions toward the right or the left, dependent on the topography [of course] and this should not be done at

---

57 An unknown word, literally 'stand' and 'ship' – presumably a weakness in the enemy line.

the same time but one after the other and in formation. Then you should move the *hatamoto* command group and then the auxiliary forces, one by one – also move the packhorse troop. Lastly, the vanguard should be moved, at which point you will be in full formation. Doing it in this order should be the example used in all cases. If you move the vanguard first of all, the enemy will take advantage of the move and attack you. But if done as prescribed above, and you leave the vanguard in position and move the second and third divisions, then, if the enemy strikes, you can have the second and third divisions – which are moving to one side of your army – attack the enemy from their flank as they battle with your vanguard. It is unusual for a great commander to set up his formation in a disadvantageous way, but just in case such a thing happens, you should be sure to plan [your move] as described above. Also, as time passes the elements change and you may end up facing the sun, the moon or the wind – in which case, you should change position.

Things you should be aware of when the enemy gives battle

'Giving battle' means when both sides are getting close to each other to initiate a battle. If only the enemy tries to engage in combat, you should fathom their real intention. If the enemy is too eager and rash and attempts to initiate battle, be sure to grasp their situation [before you commit]. According to the topography, they might have sent forces to cut off your rear, to surround you, or have reinforcements at the back of your army. However, if it is not a trap, initiating battle may simply be an established custom in the enemy clan.[58] Be aware that they will not normally act rashly and attempt a fast engagement unless they have alternative tactics. It is a principle [of war] that you should not fight unless you know what the enemy tactics are and that you should have appropriate measures to deal with any changes they may make. If they withdraw, reinforce your front with double the number of archers and musketeers and prepare for the upcoming battle and wait for any confusion or gap in the enemy. If the enemy attacks you, you should destroy their spirit with archers and musketeers and then defeat them by taking advantage of their confusion.

How to alter your formation after winning in battle

You should not try to hold a battle in the same place you have previously won a battle. As you have been victorious at this spot, it now becomes a dangerous place. The enemy will be familiar with the area, so you should leave it and build your formations in another appropriate position. You should move with

---

58 Meaning that they may prefer direct and fast assaults in their clan.

the rear forces at the front and the forward troops at the rear; this is because it is beneficial for keeping the army invigorated as [those in the rear] will move vigorously while those in the front will be tired from the battle and thus will need to rest. This [move] has the advantage of changing both the army's position and its frame of mind.

In warfare, hidden within victory is defeat, but also within defeat is found victory. Victory contains defeat because you get conceited or negligent. Even if you lose in a battle, you should not give in to fear but motivate your soldiers and inspire their fighting spirits even more.

The method of using your standards when you have been defeated

As I mentioned earlier, you should display the *dairyu* big dragon [banner] because it is difficult to manoeuvre your army freely by orders alone. You need to display your orders by flags to their eyes and by bells and drums to their ears, so that they will advance or withdraw according to your intentions. Flags also should be used to build formations or to rally; therefore they are guides for your entire army. If you are taking a defeat, you should arrange for an agreement in advance, that is the agreement that everyone will rally on the *dairyu* big dragon. The *hata bugyo* or commander of flags should know the importance and the use of flags. The proper person for the task of the [*hata*] *bugyo* should be selected and he needs to conduct a preliminary survey of the topography. Therefore, use locals or *shinobi no mono* to have a good knowledge of the land ahead. When you are defeated, stand flags on a height or use a bell so that every soldier can rally to the banner. Sometimes your soldiers can be spirited and sometimes they can be intimidated, all dependent on the way of using flags. Therefore, you should choose a person with proper abilities for the job of *hata bugyo*.

When attacking a castle, if the flags are brought close to the castle, the army will be spirited; but when the flags are withdrawn, the soldiers will lose heart. It is a great achievement if you can get a flag into the castle by choosing the right moment. If a flag is taken by the enemy while you are in a flat field, it is a dishonour for the [*hata*] *bugyo*, but it is no dishonour if the flag is taken while you are attacking a castle. In urgent situations, the [*hata*] *bugyo* should be resourceful and sometimes he should have the flags furled and detached from their poles and tied to the waists of the flag bearers [this is done to avoid dishonour].

Regaining control of an unsettled army

An army under a great lord will not be disturbed easily. However, a disturbance can occur even under a great lord and often the *bugyo* or commanders try to control the situation by riding a horse around and giving out orders, but this will make the disturbance seem more serious than it actually is and make the people even more agitated. Therefore, all the leaders should be asked to dismount and they should tell the men that these commotions before a battle are not an ill omen. Do this in the case where the enemy are still not so close and also when a disturbance takes place for no reason.

Know that standing[59] up is *yo*, so it creates a disturbance, while being seated is *in*. Therefore, being seated makes the situation quiet – this principle covers all situations, even among footed soldiers.

On giving orders before close combat

There are lows and highs in people's spirits, so it is vital to know if your own army is spirited or not, rather than knowing about the enemy, as victory or defeat does not depend on the enemy but your allies. It is the rule that you need to fortify your army before you can fathom any enemy tactics. When your warriors are in a weak mood, it is orders that will spirit them, and details are to be orally transmitted on how to do this. The mind affects mood and mood affects appearance. On a battlefield, generals should never turn tailcoat, but always be confident, as soldiers are affected by the general's frame of mind. Remember, the soldier's state of mind all depends on what the general says.

Things you should be aware of if the enemy rearranges its battle lines to launch a counter-strike

If the enemy rearranges its formation with the survivors of a battle to counter-strike, know that it is meant to attract your attention in most cases. However, you should be fully aware of several of the following things.

You should not be too eager to arrange your formation in response to the enemy movements, as the first principle is to fathom their intention and have a broader point of view on the battle as a whole.

As a general rule, if it is not possible for you to know the enemy tactics, you should not fight but try to bring your army to perfection [as a form of defence]. Remember, their intention may be to attract your attention by the rearrangement of forces while actually manoeuvring other troops around you in secret. Another aim they may have in mind is to fathom the status of your army and to have a flanking force take you. If you are overly concerned, you may become intimidated by their change, leading you to retreat. The enemy may intend to divide you and make your army react, so that they can take advantage during

---

59 It is unknown if this is practical or metaphorical. It could mean sit the men down or keep them settled or even dismount the mounted riders – however, basically it means that when a commotion arises getting people seated/dismounted and calm is the best option.

this unsettled period; remember this.

You should consider what the topography and the formations are like to aid your understanding of what the enemy intention is. You may not win a battle that you should win by rights and you may lose a war that you should not lose because you do not have the proper understanding of such essential points.

When facing an enemy, if you are taking up the formation of *dairin*, that is the formation of the great circle, do the following. An example: if we think of the left wing of the army, you should have the auxiliary division move alongside the outside of the second division. Also, a *bugyo* commander should attend each of the five divisions [and should work together] to build the formation according to the distances required. The distances involved are mainly dictated by the topography. Also, you should not fight with a single division but with forces doubled and fortified and with a *bugyo* commander to lead them. Also, you should attach warriors who are great and famous to the vanguard; this is done so that the soldiers will be brimming with courage.

To battle in a mist

A mist [or fog] is identical to a situation at night, as it gives both sides no freedom, making the condition precarious. Therefore, it is the general rule that you should not fight in the mist. However, this depends on the situation, the time and the place. Mist is always cleared away to the leeward side; therefore, the only case where it is advantageous to face the wind in battle is during a battle in the mist. This is the same principle as when you use lights at night. In this situation, the enemy side will be revealed earlier than your forces and thus you can know their formation or set-up while you yourselves cannot be seen [as you are hidden] and in this way, you can take advantage of the enemy. This strategy is also useful for a lesser army to defeat a greater force.

If you are attacking a castle, you will have the benefit of being able to advance close to the castle and [if you stay in the mist] their muskets cannot be used effectively.

If you clearly know the [enemy] lord's intention, the [enemy] formation and the position, then you will not be disturbed or confused either in the mist or in the dark.

Turn your face away from the three blades of nature

You should not turn your face to the following three elements of nature: the sun, the moon and the wind – if you do, it will be disadvantageous. Remember to construct a plan so that the enemy will face them.

Precautions against night raiders

In warfare, be it day or night, it is always a key to victory to take advantage of the enemy's tactics to benefit your own agenda. Therefore, you should keep your plans a deep secret for this very reason. A great lord knows everything of the enemy tactics, such as where the enemy should lay a troop, when they should make a surprise attack, when they should engage in a night attack, and where in your castle they should strike to capture it. They know these things because they use *ninja* effectively. In old times when Iga and Koka were independent,[60] there were countless cases of armies who had *ninja* defeating the enemy by surprise instead of being defeated themselves by such a surprise attack.

Night attacks should be conducted with total surprise. If the information is leaked to the enemy, it is exactly as if you willingly put yourself into a trap of the enemy's design. You should always use *ninja* and you should also send them out for scouting; do this every night to know the status and movements of the enemy. Also, you should always have your forces prepared and if you are raided against during the night, it is essential that you should not be troubled by this fact too much but instead take measures to cut off the raiders' retreat or even follow them so that you can gain entrance into their castle.

Fighting across a river

When confronting [an enemy] across a river, it goes without saying that both sides have their own tactics. Therefore, you should estimate the chances of winning and also those of losing by any means and try to take advantage if you can. If the enemy moves all its forces down to the riverbank without having backup troops at the rear, then you have a good chance of victory – if you let them cross the river without disturbing their crossing, that is. You should prepare to attack them at an appropriate distance away from the river so that [you can strike them] after they have crossed over and are tired and confused from the effort required. Also, the distance at which you set up your attack position differs depending on whether it is summer or winter and on the depth and width of the river. The set-up of your forces should depend on the number of the army and on the topography of the area and there are teachings that should be passed down about these topics.

On the other hand, if the enemy divides its musket troop into upper, middle and lower sections, or they construct horse buoyancy units, have foot soldiers stand in the middle or at lower positions [of the river] and help others cross, or

---

60 The text has a subtext that is difficult to express within the sentence and alludes to when Iga and Koka were self-governing and the Iga and Koka *shinobi no mono* were taken on as retainers.

after crossing the river, if they do not follow you immediately but get back into a formation on the riverside, in this situation, you should not attack them.

How to ford a river by boat

The rules of warfare strongly warn against disarray in an army, as any slight confusion can lead to disorder in everything and it is best to keep your army in a completely organized fashion throughout its movement.

When crossing a river by boat, it is always the case that the lines [of the army] are interrupted and commotion results. Sometimes, if you board [the boat] recklessly, it will sink.

If you are close to the enemy, you should be careful as they may attack you in the middle of your crossing. Therefore, you should have pike-men positioned in lines, making a pathway to the boat; this is done to get others on board in a proper fashion. An officer should be appointed to control this crossing and everyone should listen to his orders. Also, *monomi* scouts should be ferried first of all and without fail; after this, the forward outpost groups[61] with muskets should come over to secure the other side for landing. The formation they should use depends on the topography of the area. On the next boat, the *musha bugyo* or *samurai* commander and his messenger-warriors[62] should board, and, for the rest, the standard order of procession [given later] should be applied. The above is for when the enemy closes; however, if the enemy is at a distance, then the officer should take responsibility for the orders given and all should be the same as in the normal procession.

How to signal from the vanguard to the command group

The vanguard is the front division of your army. In a massive army it may extend out so far that if urgent needs arise, you may have trouble communicating a message with speed back to the command group. Therefore, you should prepare flags in five colours and arrange an agreement among yourselves, including the troop commanders, on how to signal and what message is given by each coloured flag. Then, if a situation arises you should wave the appropriate flag and send a relay from flag to flag. Do this repeatedly until the command group gets the message. If the flagpole is not long enough, it should be tied onto a spear when you signal with it.

---

61 *Mononmi oshi.*
62 *Tsukaiban.*

The various ways of signalling

Whether in a castle or a battle camp, there are sometimes disturbances. [To deal with such situations] you should have an agreement on the methods of signalling and have them set up in advance, so that you can communicate with signal tools during night attacks, quarrels, fires or any other kinds of commotion that may occur. The arrangements should be made according to your intentions.

To gather troop commanders when a situation arises, a conch shell should be used, while a bell should be struck to inform people of the time. In the case of a night patrol, a small bell should be used instead – the ideogram for this bell is written as 鈴 in Chinese but as 令 in Japanese, which is only half of the original ideogram.

For vigilance within your own area and quarters, clappers should be used. The *ashigaru taisho* or the commander of the foot soldiers should take responsibility for this precaution and you should have an agreement among all the troops for the various ways of clapping. It is desirable to use false holly (*Osmanthus heterophyllus*) wood. Japanese evergreen oak (*Quercus acuta*) is also good for clappers as it makes a good sound. The clapper itself should be eight *sun* in length, one *sun* two *bu* in width and eight *bu* in thickness.

If you have arranged the signals with the instruments mentioned above, you will have no unnecessary commotion and everything will settle down with ease – if a commotion arises, of course. Also, whether in a castle or not, the way of a fire or smoke signal should always be arranged as a means of signalling.

On the march

Marching is a risky time for both sides. Fighting may take place suddenly and at any point during the march. No matter how organized the procession is, it is always possible to attack an army at a narrow path, where the defenders cannot save themselves. Or even on a flatland, it is possible that you can break the enemy's spirits and send their procession into disarray. When you are in another domain and you are not so familiar with the area, you should be cautious. Conversely, in your own domain you are familiar with the land and thus you can act freely, attack or withdraw, as on home ground you will be in full spirits and have a great advantage in [unintelligible text], even if you have not struck the enemy.

When the enemy is getting close to an encounter with you, they will try to keep their procession even more organized and their soldiers will brace their spirits and morale all the more and guard themselves strictly. Therefore, you should attack them in order to break their spirits.

When attacking an army on the march, it is said that a lesser army can defeat a greater army, if they catch them by surprise at night. Therefore, it is essential for you to make the arrangements to send *ninja* or long- and short-distance *monomi* scouts. Do this in order to defend your army against any surprise night attack that may have been prepared along your path. This is why *shinobi* or *monomi* are the true key to victory and the very basis of warfare.

[On decapitated heads]

The inspection of decapitated heads by the lord is the same in various writings, so I will not mention it here. Some lords only inspect another lord's head and not others. However, for the lord to pay a tribute of praise to his warriors' achievements, it is best to inspect all the heads no matter how many there are. Taiko[63] and Nobunaga were great lords, rare in history, and they inspected all the heads no matter how many there were. This is an issue you should be aware of.

The three things the lord should consider regarding his frame of mind

If the lord opens up his mind and displays his thoughts to others, the army will fight in a wise way. However, if done this way, this may cause some failures, thus it is best that it is avoided. If he closes his mind fully, the army will not make an error and the plan may be deeper. However, the army will not respond to a prompt and sudden change of situation; therefore, this also should be avoided. A dauntless and overbearing lord will always underestimate the enemy and become arrogant, so he too should be avoided. In short, you should be careful about your own way, while trying to perceive the enemy correctly and by following this way, you can construct your strategy. This is the basis of victory or defeat.

The manners of the lord's military fan and the batons

There are two directions [for the fan or the baton] – forwards and backwards.[64] When pointing toward the enemy, the tip of the baton should be used. However, when pointing to your own side, the handle should be used [as a pointer]. It is the same for a rod or fan. When beckoning the enemy [in symbolic challenge], do it with the point of the rod, keeping your palm up. However, when moving your army, gesture with your palm downwards. For the command of attack, to be observed by your army, raise the fan or baton up from the left side of the body [upwards to the right] and bring it down and around. For the command of retreat, lower the baton from high above to the left side and do it strongly. For the command to halt, raise it up high and hold it fast at that position.

---

63 This refers to Toyotomi Hideyoshi.
64 Also, correct and incorrect.

Strategies of control

There are two methods to discuss on this point, and they depend on whether the area is spacious or not. If the number of people is too many for the location they currently hold, it can be a weakness, while if there are too few people, it too can be negative. These both conflict with the strategy of control.

In a relatively narrow place, you should divide your army into a number of groups. If you choose a steep place to fight with such a massive army, you will not be able to fight very well, as you will count on the topography too much. If you are a massive army, you should try to utilize the positive elements of having such a large group [instead of relying on the topography]. However, for a lesser army, they should take advantage of steep and narrow places, as in such a place ten warriors could defend in place of one hundred men – topography can compensate for lack of forces. Further to this, if you are in a narrow and steep place do not overly rely on its natural advantages and become lax, as this will be no advantage to you. On the other hand, when not in these types of steep and narrow places and you are in normal terrain, you know that you cannot rely on topography to aid you. If you understand this, your frame of mind can benefit you in the same way that natural defences can.

These points above are the ways that you should use the topography of the land.

Victory and defeat bring forth the true strengths and weaknesses of lords.

- Overbearing and hot-blooded lords will be overconfident after victory.
- Ordinary lords will feel relieved after victory.
- Ignorant lords will be negligent after victory.
- Wise lords will be careful after victory.
- Vigorous and brave lords will be braver after a defeat.
- Tactical lords will be even more discreet with their tactics after defeat.
- Stupid or cowardly lords will not contemplate the next step after defeat.

Using the above, you should fathom the enemy and contemplate your own nature.

You should not only focus on how to win over the enemy but instead concentrate on your own faults and contemplate where you are not aware of your own gaps and also fortify your defences so that you will not be defeated. Then, you can look for a gap within the enemy and, without a distorted viewpoint, find the way of victory.

Those who do not overly strive to win but achieve victory with ease are considered good lords. Therefore, perfect your army and you will overcome the enemy.

Victory exists inside of the enemy's form and defeat exits within your own form. This is identical to how an expert *Go* player succeeds, as, with their defences fortified, they will take advantage of the weak points within the enemy.

People often lose wisdom when they are out of balance. For example, if they get too greedy, they will not dispense righteous rewards and punishments; while also, if they are too frightened, they may mistake a magpie for an enemy flag. If they indulge too far in joy, anger, sadness, easiness, depression, grief or any other state, they will not be able to follow on the righteous path but instead they will be surrounded by gloom. If you feel gloomy, you will not be very perceptive of the enemy tactics and alterations. But if you detach yourself from such emotions, then a new plan will voluntarily enter your mind, exactly like a clear mirror that leaves nothing that is not reflected in its surface.

In this way, you should be very prudent about your own state, and use yourself as a model to know the enemy and use the enemy to know yourself.

When defending a besieged castle, especially if you have an ally on the outside who is attacking the besieging enemy to aid you, then you should position four or five *ninja* within ten *cho* to twenty *cho*, or even one *ri* outside the castle. Before doing this, you should arrange the ways of signalling among yourselves very firmly. This set-up [of *ninja*] is beneficial in various ways. If your castle is surrounded by a massive army and it is hard to communicate with the general of the reinforcement troops who are at the rear of the besieging enemy force, you will be able to send signals from inside the castle to outside freely [by using this method and the *ninja*]. There are vast amounts of oral transmission for this.

For example, at the Battle of Nagashino,[65] Okudaira Kuhachiro was defending a castle, which was surrounded by a massive army under Takeda Katsuyori. The defending Okudaira could not communicate with Lord Nobunaga or Lord Ieyasu, who were the reinforcements on the outside and were attacking the besieging forces, and he could not tell them that the people inside the castle were in a perilous situation and were quickly running out of food. Then Torii Sune'emon, one of his retainers, escaped the castle without being noticed and went to Lord Nobunaga to ask him to attack from the rear and for aid with supplies. However, he was detected on his way back to the castle. This is an example where they had difficulty and also this warrior above was killed in the end because they did not take this method into consideration. In our school it is called 'one mind shared between the people' and you should keep this secret.

---

65 A famous battle which took place in 1575 in Mikawa province between Takeda Katsuyori and the allied forces of Tokugawa Ieyasu and Oda Nobunaga. Katsuyori surrounded Nagashino castle while Nobunaga and Ieyasu surrounded and totally defeated the attacking army.

[The six *bugyo* commanders]

At the top [and under the lord] you have two *musha bugyo* or *samurai* captains –
they always take responsibility for giving orders to the army. Respected warriors
should be assigned to this job. Therefore, accomplished and experienced warriors
are desirable.

After the above pair come the two *hata bugyo* or flag commanders – one is
for positioning the signalling flags and the rallying banner and the other is for
estimation of distance and of margins within your troops. For the task of positioning, the most accomplished warrior should be assigned as he will have a
solid judgement on the present status of battle and decide where flags should be
positioned properly. The task of the estimation officer is to estimate the proper
distances [between flags] and to position the seven to nine flags that represent
the whole army in the determined area, so that the retainers may form up after
this with their own standards. This [*hata*] *bugyo* should have knowledge of the
estimation of distances and therefore his task is called 'the estimator of margins'.

Next comes the two *yari bugyo* or spear commanders – the average army
normally holds *ashigaru* foot soldiers in the number of 1,200,[66] including eight
hundred muskets, three hundred bows and two hundred spears [and it is the job
of the *yari bugyo* to control them].

The above are called the six *bugyo* commanders and only those who are
capable should be recruited for these positions.

The next *bugyo* commanders to be selected are for the rear guard and for
logistics. The *bugyo* for this rear guard are not usually allotted beforehand but
need to be appointed when the correct time arises. For the *bugyo* commanders
of logistics, you should have those who are good so that they can continue the
task throughout the campaign.

The army marching order

The vanguard
The *monomi osae* or position-securing scouts
Reserves – footed clan retainers[67]
Pulling team[68]
The *dairyu* or big dragon standard
Reserves – footed clan retainers
The *hata bugyo* – positioning flag commander

---

66 This calculation is incorrect by one hundred men. However, it has been put here in its
original form with the mistake, as it is unknown which number is the incorrect one.
67 Most likely low-ranking samurai retained by the clan.
68 This is an unknown number of people pulling or carrying the main standard.

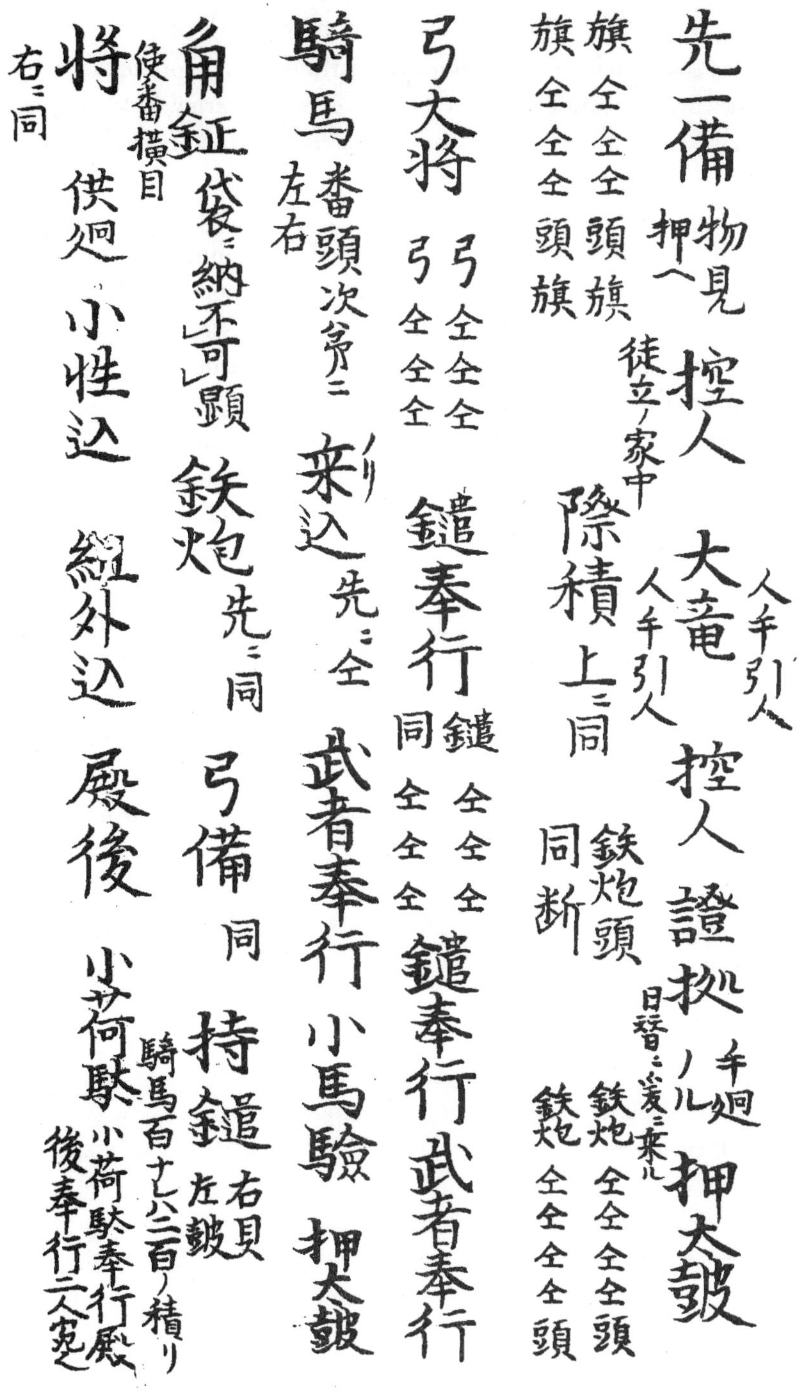

先一備 物見

旗全全全頭旗
旗全全全頭旗
旗全全全頭旗

控人 大竜 控人 證拠

徒立ノ家中

人手引人
人手引人
人手引人

際積上ニ同 押大皷

鉄炮頭

鉄炮 全全全頭
鉄炮 全全全頭

同断

日替ニ変ニ来ル

押ニル 千廻

弓大将 押ヘ

左右

番頭次第ニ

騎馬

左右

弓全全全
弓全全全

采込先ニ全

刕込先ニ

鑓奉行

同全全全
鑓全全全

角鉦

袋ニ納不可顕

使番横目

将

右ニ同

供廻 小性込 紅外込 殿後

武者奉行 小馬験 押大皷

弓備同

持鑓 右貝 左皷

鉄炮先ニ同

小ザ荷駄 小荷駄奉行殿後奉行二人宛

騎馬百九ニ二百ノ積り

Figure 112. The army marching order

Aides to the above

(the above aides are on a rotation system)

The marching drum

Flags – Flags

Flags – Flags

Flags – Flags

Flags – Flags

Two flag chiefs

Flags – Flags

The estimation commander

Aides to the above

Two musket troop captains

Musketeers – Musketeers

Musketeers – Musketeers

Musketeers – Musketeers

Musketeers – Musketeers

Two musket troop captains

The archery commander

Archers – Archers

Archers – Archers

Archers – Archers

Archers – Archers

The commander of the spears

Spearmen – Spearmen

Spearmen – Spearmen

Spearmen – Spearmen

Spearmen – Spearmen

The rear commander of the spears

Samurai captain or *musha bugyo*

The mounted warriors

> (they take turns on a daily basis to work as captains[69] who march at both sides)

Mounted warrior raiding parties[70]

> (they take turns on a daily basis to work as captains who march at both sides)

Samurai captain or *musha bugyo*

---

69 *Bangashira*, this has connotations of captains on a rota system.

70 *Norikomi*, a form of mounted shock troop.

Lesser standards

The attacking drum

The conch shells and gongs

(these instruments should be kept in bags and not be shown)

Musketeers

(as illustrated in the formation above[71])

Archers

(as illustrated in the formation above)

Spear-owning[72] troops

Drums – conch shells

Messengers and *yokome*[73] – the lord general – messengers and *yokome*

The lord's aides

The lord's esquires

The individualists[74]

The rear guard[75]

The packhorse train

(for every one hundred mounted warriors you require two hundred
   packhorses)

Two commanders each are required for logistics and the rear guard

O-monomi or pre-marching large scout groups

Before advancing into enemy territory, you should know if the route is safe or not by scouting out ahead. You should use *monomi-shinobi* or scouting *shinobi* to detect ambushes hidden in or around steep or dangerous areas of mountains and forests. For this scouting task choose two or three mounted warriors from one troop. The total number of troops can go up to twenty, as each mounted warrior should be followed by between three and five *ashigaru* foot soldiers, who will check ahead to a distance of up to three *ri* and discover if there is an ambush on either side of the route.

Alternatively, choose two or three mounted warriors from the lord's messengers, each of whom is followed by two footed soldiers. They should be good ones selected from the esquires, and take turns each day. In all cases, everyone in the scouting parties should have the same identifying marks and

---

71 Meaning that it is identical to the formation at the start of the listing.

72 Warriors who own their spears as opposed to the 'loaned-spear troops' at the front.

73 People who closely observe an army's own men and report to the lord on any matters.

74 *Gumigaikomi*, this term is made up of 'group', 'outside' and 'collection' – possibly people not required for battle, such as priests, monks, logicians, diviners etc.

75 *Shingari*, literally 'after the lord', but used to protect the very rear.

are forbidden to fight, as they may wish, even if they come across the enemy *en route*, and, furthermore, they should stay within the said distance and report the forward situation to the command squad. On flatland, mounted scouts are quicker, while in mountains, those on foot are faster; that is why you should use both of them.

When you are proceeding to another province for battle to establish a position, you should arrange your marching order with precaution against sudden attacks *en route*. From the instant you leave your door, you should act as if the enemy is directly in your sight, and in this way, if all the necessary precautions are taken before anything occurs, you can avoid misfortune and fend off disaster.

Index

saddle flaps/skirts 469
sageo sword cord 226–7
saguritetu probing iron 320–1
saisaku 20
sakamogi thorny branches 189
samurai xv, xxiv, 31, 88
san shirizashi locking sticks 233
sandals 356
Sankyo Gyokujo 276–8
sarusuberi sliding carts 155
Sasayama Kagenao 461–502
Sashigami directions 292
sataobito no jutsu 108–9
saws 237, 344–6, 352–3
schools of *shinobi* 27
scouts 59, 95–7, 250–1, 257–8, 501–2
'scraped' fire 431–2
scraping match 370
screw drills 350–1
sea crossings 186–7
sea water 471
seals 74–5, 103
seashores 143–4
seasons 195–6, 280
secrecy 66–7, 461–502
secret signs/marks 127–8
secret writing 67–70
security of *ninja* 76–7
seishin 32–54
sejoshinuki padlock pick 354–5
sen wooden pegs 240–1
senkakegane hooked latch 236
senses 50
seppuku (ritual suicide) 65
Seven Plans 3
shadow-like *ninjutsu* 106
shadows 198–9
shakko/shakuzetsu, day of 291
shank sweepers 227–8
shield torch 398–9
shields, bamboo 464–5
shihogami 101
Shiji manual 35, 49
shikoro saw 352–3
shikyu no jutsu 119–20
shims 354–5
Shin Shin Sekiguchi school 361
shinobi xv–xvi, xviii, xx, xxiii–xxiv, xxvi–xxvii, 21–7
　　blocking 29–30
　　ideograms 36–43, 53
　　ninpo treasure 55–6
　　origins of name 19, 21–2
　　principles 8, 32

　　see also ninja
shinobi burning powder 421, 423
shinobi falcon fire 424
shinobi-gaeshi spiked defences 183, 186, 189
Shinobi Hiden xvi
shinobi iroha 69
shinobi lesser-*tengu* fire 439
shinobi night attacks 250–67
shinobi no jutsu xv, xxvi–xxvii, 61, 63–7, 100, 181–2
　　see also ninjutsu
shinobi no mono xv, xxvii, 55–6, 59–60, 77–80
　　see also ninja
shinobi no ri 56–65
shinobi torches 211, 421–3
shinpu/shinsho concept 283–4
shinso-no-uho steps 198
shirizashi locking sticks 232, 233–4
shisokubi paper candle 453
shochi 55–99
shoji sliding doors 238
Shoninki xvi, xxiii
short-term infiltration 122–37
shouting 220–1
shrimp padlocks 241–4, 246, 248–9
shrubs 463
shugo governor 25
sickles 352–3
signal flares 378, 447–8
signal senders 224–5
signals 70–3, 75, 124–5, 158, 493–4
　　castle infiltration 169–70, 174
　　tools for 378, 382–3, 446–8, 453–5
signs
　　of identification 91–3
　　secret signs/marks 127–8
silent gunpowder 373–4
silent sandals 356
single-track doors 236, 238
Six Secret Teachings 19, 68
sleep 169, 195–7, 207–10, 226, 229–30, 379
sleeping medicine 374
'sleeve' fire 370, 419
sliced tinder 386–7
sliding carts 155
sliding doors 238
small castles 174–5
'small lightning' recipe 405
small screw drills 350–1
smoke signals 70, 72–3, 382–3
snipper tools 349
snoring 207–9
soil colour, rice fields 145